India and the World Economy

Published by Academic Foundation
in association with

Indian Council for Research on
International Economic Relations,
New Delhi

India and the Global Economy

Editors Rajiv Kumar
Abhijit Sen Gupta

ACADEMIC FOUNDATION
NEW DELHI

First published in 2008
by

ACADEMIC FOUNDATION
4772-73 / 23 Bharat Ram Road, (23 Ansari Road),
Darya Ganj, New Delhi - 110 002 (India).
Phones : 23245001 / 02 / 03 / 04.
Fax : +91-11-23245005.
E-mail : academic@vsnl.com
www. academicfoundation.com

in association with:

Indian Council for Research on International Economic Relations
(ICRIER), New Delhi.
www.icrier.org

Cataloging in Publication Data--DK
Courtesy: D.K. Agencies (P) Ltd. <docinfo@dkagencies.com>

India and the global economy / edited by Rajiv Kumar and Abhijit Sen Gupta.
p. cm. Contributed articles.
ISBN 13: 9788171886616
ISBN 10: 8171886612

1. Infrastructure (Economics)--India. 2. Agriculture and state--India. 3. Manufacturing industries--India. 4. Competition--India. 5. India--Economic policy--1991-
6. Globalization--Economic aspects--India. I. Kumar, Rajiv.

DDC 338.954 22

Typeset by Italics India, New Delhi.
Printed and bound in India.

CONTENTS

List of Tables, Figures, Boxes and Annexures

TABLES

FIGURES

BOXES

ANNEXURES

Editors/Contributors

Editors:

Rajiv Kumar is currently Director and Chief Executive of the Indian Council for Research on International Economic Relations (ICRIER). He is also on the board of several important government organisations including the National Security Advisory Board and Telecom Regulatory Authority of India (TRAI). Dr. Kumar has completed his D.Phil. in Economics in 1982 from Oxford University. In a distinguished career spanning over 25 years, Dr. Kumar has held several key positions in a wide range of institutions. He served as a Professor at the Indian Institute of Foreign Trade. He has also worked as Economic Adviser in the Ministry of Finance, Government of India and in the Bureau of Industrial Costs and Projects, Ministry of Industry. From 2004 to January 2006, he was Chief Economist with the Confederation of Indian Industry (CII). Prior to joining the CII, he had worked at the Asian Development Bank for nearly 10 years as a Principal Economist. He has several books and publications to his credit and contributes regularly to newspapers and journals.

Abhijit Sen Gupta is a Fellow at the Indian Council for Research on International Economic Relations (ICRIER). He holds a PhD in International Economics from the University of California, Santa Cruz. Dr. Sen Gupta has worked as a researcher in a number of international institutions including the World Bank and the International Monetary Fund. He has also taught for two years at the University of California, Santa Cruz. He has published several articles in India as well as abroad and is a regular contributor to the popular press.

Contributors:

Shankar Acharya	Honorary Professor, Indian Council for Research on International Economic Relations.
Jaimini Bhagwati	Joint Secretary, Ministry of External Affairs.
Avik Chakrabarti	Associate Professor, University of Wisconsin, Milwaukee.
Pankaj Chandra	Professor of Production and Operations Management and Director, Indian Institute of Management, Ahmedabad.
D. Chattanathan	Deputy General Manager and Head of Community Control and Management Group, ICICI Bank.
Bibek Debroy	Professor, International Management Institute.
Sumila Gulyani	Assistant Professor of Urban Planning, Columbia University.
S.S. Johl	Vice Chairman, Punjab State Planning Board.
Vijay Joshi	Fellow of Merton College, University of Oxford.
Rajiv Lall	Managing Director and CEO, Infrastructure Development Finance Company.
Nirmal Mohanty	Principal, Policy Group, Infrastructure Development Finance Company.
Nachiket Mor	President, ICICI Foundation for Inclusive Growth.
Pranab Mukherjee	Minister of External Affairs, Goverment of India.
Rajiv Panthary	Chief Manager, ICICI Bank.
Abhijit Sen Gupta	Fellow, Indian Council for Research on International Economic Relations.
Tushaar Shah	Principal Scientist, International Water Management Institute.
Manmohan Singh	Prime Minister of India, New Delhi.

Foreword

This volume brings together the papers presented at ICRIER's Silver Jubilee Conference on "India and the Global Economy" held on November 6-7, 2006. The Conference was inaugurated by Prime Minister, Dr. Manmohan Singh and the valedictory session was addressed by Foreign Minister, Mr. Pranab Mukherjee. During the Conference, a number of policy makers, business leaders, senior government officials and eminent economists deliberated on the key issues facing the Indian economy including infrastructure, agriculture, manufacturing, macroeconomy and the financial sector. The papers in this volume provide insights on some of the most important challenges facing the Indian economy.

I am happy to note that over the past two decades and a half, ICRIER has emerged as one of the leading policy think tanks in the country. By encouraging high quality research and its dissemination, ICRIER has engaged with policy makers, emphasised the importance of economic reforms and facilitated India's integration with the global economy. The papers compiled together in this volume further substantiate the role that ICRIER has played in the field.

I take this opportunity to convey my sincere thanks to all those who have contributed to this volume.

Isher Judge Ahluwalia
Chairperson, Board of Directors
ICRIER

Introduction

RAJIV KUMAR

This conference volume on "India and the Global Economy" includes a set of papers that were presented during ICRIER's Silver Jubilee Conference in New Delhi on November 6-7, 2006 that was inaugurated by the Hon'ble Prime Minister, Dr. Manmohan Singh. His thoughtful inaugural address is included in the volume. The objective of the two day Conference was to spell out the challenges and opportunities facing India as it engages with the global economy in an attempt to accelerate growth while at the same time furthering social development and achieving better standards of living for the people.

The Conference brought together some of the best minds working on India. The papers, specially commissioned for the Conference, provided new insights in a range of policy issues and helped formulate an agenda of forward looking measures that hopefully would serve as inputs into the government's policy process.

In their paper, Rajiv Lall and Nirmal Mohanty address the infrastructure deficit issue in India and suggest details of financing instrumentalities for the deficit as well as the challenges involved in using them. They also deliberate on the initiatives required by various stakeholders to ensure successful implementation of the suggested strategy. Lall and Mohanty point out that resource constraints to infrastructure financing can be overcome provided the financial system is substantially strengthened to ensure diversified and more effective intermediation of savings. They also observe that effective governance remains the main challenge in meeting the infrastructure deficit. Their recommendations, spelt out clearly in the paper, would enhance governance standards and help prioritisation of reform initiatives that will contribute to eliminating the infrastructure deficit.

Sumila Gulyani presents a case study of self generation of power adopted by Maruti Udyog Limited and some other firms, and analyses the reasons and process behind such a solution. In contrast to previous studies she finds that not only these firms are able to self-generate electricity at unit costs that are often lower than the price of public power, but the electricity produced is far superior in quality and reliability compared to that supplied by public utilities. The primary reason for the low cost and superior quality of power is a dramatic reduction in economies of scales in generation due to significant advancement in technology. Moreover, the innovative power sharing arrangement developed between Maruti, its ancillaries and State Electricity Board has proved to be beneficial for all the participants. Gulyani recommends the government to encourage similar "models" elsewhere and points out that it is an effective step towards improving the power problem and catalysing power reforms in India.

Evaluating the existing programmes of agriculture credit and risk management, Nachiket Mor, D. Chattanathan and Rajiv Panthary point out that these programmes have largely failed in meeting the desired objectives. They argue that newer approaches that are fundamentally different from the existing ones need to be considered to realise the potential of Indian agriculture. They suggest that several preconditions will have to be in place to put rural credit and risk management systems on a firm footing. These include the setting up of a comprehensive rural information system through the introduction of smart cards, establishing a credit bureau, creation of new rural financial institutions and the development of complementary infrastructure among others. The establishment of these mechanisms will go a long way in instituting a well developed rural financial system that will be able to deliver a range of financial products at affordable rates to the farmers.

S.S. Johl focuses on the issue of environmental degradation in the agriculture sector due to overwhelming reliance on intensive cultivation and chemicals based production system in several countries. Highlighting the case of Punjab, which contributes more than 50 per cent of India's wheat and rice but accounts only for 1.5 per cent of geographical area, Johl shows that Punjab has paid a heavy environmental cost for this achievement. These costs include depleting water resources, soil and water pollution, large emissions of greenhouse gases etc. However, Johl points out that in recent years several technological advances have been made to ameliorate these costs. These advances include rice cultivation under aerobic conditions, use of bio-fertilisers, bio-pesticides and organic farming. These alternatives need to be pursued actively by putting in place a robust incentive structure that will encourage the adoption of these environment friendly practices in the agriculture sector.

One of the major causes of stagnation of agriculture is thought to be slow down in public investment, especially irrigation development, in agriculture. In his paper Tushaar Shah argues that Indian irrigation economy is undergoing a massive transformation as smaller farmers have wrested the initiative for irrigation development from the government through the development of atomistic irrigation with use of small pumps. Shah contends that the pump irrigation revolution has been amongst the most powerful rural poverty alleviation phenomenon. This is largely because it has helped in extending irrigation access to an overwhelming majority, drought proofed the country's agriculture against at least one monsoon failure and allowed intensive diversification to high value products like fruits and vegetables, especially in dry areas. Thus, the primary role of government policy should be to implement a more effective strategy for rain water harvesting, which will replenish the underground reservoirs and aquifiers.

The Indian manufacturing sector has witnessed a strong resurgence in the last few years. In their paper Rajiv Kumar and Abhijit Sen Gupta undertake a broad evaluation of the Indian manufacturing sector. They conclude that the current phase of manufacturing growth is one of the longest periods of upswing since the 80s and this has contributed to the robust economic growth in recent years. During the last 35 years there have been significant changes in the share of various states in manufacturing output with the provinces providing better investment climate significantly increasing their share. Kumar and Sen Gupta also contend that the low value added per worker in the unorganised sector is largely due to the lack of access to capital and credit faced by this sector. On the other hand, sustained automation in the organised sector has prevented it from becoming a source of employment generation. Finally, the authors analyse India's potential as becoming a hub for mass manufacturing and conclude that the main impediments in doing so include low level of R&D, inadequate infrastructure, policy induced barriers to entry and exit and complex government procedures among others.

The paper by Bibek Debroy analyses the importance of the manufacturing sector in the Indian economy and concludes that raising the level of competitiveness in the manufacturing sector is crucial to India's high growth regime and to ensure adequate employment generation. Debroy points out that the low employment elasticity in the manufacturing sector in recent years is partly explained by restructuring of the sector in response to competition, sustaining which has resulted in job shedding, as well as labour market rigidities. Substantive reforms are needed to increase the employment elasticity in the manufacturing sector and reduce the dichotomy between the organised and unorganised sectors. However, despite these measures the share of manufacturing in the next decade or so can at best rise to around 25 per cent of the GDP and anything above that is quite improbable. Finally, the paper goes on to highlight the major generic constraints hampering the competitiveness of the Indian manufacturing sector, which include the current fiscal structure of duties, taxes and subsidies, availability of credit, infrastructural bottlenecks and archaic labour laws.

Pankaj Chandra, in his paper, focuses on the twin challenges facing the Indian manufacturing sector namely, developing production capabilities for mass manufacturing and low-volume high variety products, as well as ensuring development and implementation of new technology to enhance productivity. Citing several examples, Chandra points out that large volume operation has already taken roots in India but there is an urgent need for policymakers to focus on several issues to ensure its continued success. These include lead time, availability of adequate skills, networking among SMEs to deliver scale and efficient tools of production, among others. Policy attention needs to concentrate on increasing operational productivity, improving quality and quantity of technical manpower, supporting appropriate scale of operations, and attracting world class R&D and technical know-how.

In recent years, India's external sector regime has been host to several controversies, like the existing exchange rate arrangement, convertibility of the rupee etc. Vijay Joshi provides a detailed overview and analyses the performance of the external payments regime since the 1990s. Looking at the future, Joshi considers various combinations of exchange rate regimes and degrees of capital account convertibility and analyses the pros and cons of each system. It is observed that India's current external payment regime, characterised by an intermediate exchange rate regime with some capital controls will continue to best serve India's economic interests over of the next five to ten years. Such a system provides the freedom to operate an independent monetary and exchange rate policy, which is crucial at the current stage of India's development.

In his paper, Shankar Acharya analyses the fiscal situation in India during the past one and a half decades and argues that it is extremely important to strictly monitor the level of fiscal deficit. During the last fifteen years fiscal deficit has moved in a cyclical pattern and has been inversely correlated with the growth performance of the economy with the former driving the latter to an extent. Acharya also points out that despite recent attempts at fiscal consolidation, the current levels of fiscal deficit and public debt in India are one of the highest in the world and thus a source of grave concern. Finally, Acharya highlights some of the major economic factors that are going to impact the fiscal deficit in the near future.

The importance of the infrastructure sector for economic growth is the focus of the paper by Avik Chakrabarti. Chakrabarti highlights the pattern of investment and current state of the Indian infrastructure and points out that chronic underinvestment has resulted in significant deterioration in the service quality and is seriously undermining the suppliers' ability to respond to new demands. Using empirical methods, Chakrabarti goes on to show that during the past 40 years there is a strong association between infrastructure development and overall growth of the economy across a number of countries and this association is stronger in developing countries compared to industrialised countries and hence India is likely to reap significant benefits by raising infrastructure investment.

The paper by Jaimini Bhagwati highlights that progressive deregulation of the Indian financial sector has yielded impressive gains but still there are systemic shortcomings in the sector that need to be dealt with. There is an urgent need to provide incentives to attract greater percentage of domestic savings to the formal financial sector. Greater weight should be given to productivity of investments while allocating credit and higher private sector participation should be encouraged. Moreover, further progress has to be made on deregulation of interest rates and capital account convertibility. Apart from this, Bhagwati also stresses the need to expand the corporate debt market and encourage exchange traded interest rate derivatives. Both insurance and pension sector are relatively small in India and there exists a tremendous potential for growth in these markets. However, according to him, to realise this potential some of the existing laws regulating these markets need to be reviewed.

The valedictory session of the Conference was addressed by the honourable Foreign Minister, Mr. Pranab Mukherjee. He used the opportunity to share his vision of India's evolving foreign policy and how it is being increasingly dovetailed to the country's overarching objective of achieving sustained rapid and inclusive economic growth. His speech is reproduced in the volume.

The high quality of the commissioned papers and the active participation of academics, policymakers and senior industry representatives ensured a lively and insightful discussion in all the sessions. But for the space constraint, it would have been useful to include the proceedings of the Conference as well in the volume. It is my hope that the volume will prove useful to all those who have some interest in India's policy reforms that provide the basis for effective integration of the Indian economy with global flows and which will help to achieve the twin objectives of growth and equity.

1

Research Agenda for Economic Think Tanks

MANMOHAN SINGH

I would like to begin by paying my tribute to the memory of Shri K.B. Lall, ICRIER's founder and builder. Till his very end, he took a keen interest in ICRIER's work and even after he had ceased to be the Chairman of the Board of Governors, would often visit the library and participate in seminars.

Shri K.B. Lall was a fine representative of a generation of visionary civil servants that India was fortunate to have in the early years after our Independence. They worked with the political leadership to create and sustain great institutions. It is significant that ICRIER was conceived of in the early 1980s, when Smt. Indira Gandhi was the Prime Minister. There was already a realisation that we had to pay greater attention to our economic relations with the outside world. Many of you will recall that in the late 1970s the Government had constituted several committees of experts to re-examine many aspects of our industrial and trade policies. Some of the distinguished personalities who authored these reports are present and I mention in particular, the name of Dr. Vijay Kelkar. This was also the time when China had initiated its Four Modernisations campaign and was becoming more open to the outside world.

Shri K.B. Lall was convinced that India had to make the transition from being an excessively inward-oriented economy to becoming a more outward-oriented one. This required preparation and changes in domestic policy. This would require Indian firms to become more competitive. The founders of ICRIER chose to build this institution to study all these issues and guide policy. It was only appropriate that ICRIER was initially housed in the building of the India International Centre.

I do believe that ICRIER, under a succession of dedicated chairpersons and directors, has lived up to the expectations of its founders. In this context, I would like to record with deep appreciation the outstanding contributions made by Shri R.N. Malhotra, who was succeeded by Dr IG Patel as Chairman of the Board of Governors, and Dr. Isher Ahluwalia in her many capacities of association with ICRIER in the transformation of this think tank as a leading forward looking institution on international economic relations. ICRIER's research work has covered many issues pertaining to trade policy, industrial policy, exchange rate and balance of payments management, the international financial system, capital flows, migration and labour policies, and in all these areas, ICRIER has made a profound impact on contemporary thinking on these issues. I do think that ICRIER must continue with its focus and emerge as one of the foremost think tanks not only in India but in the world as a whole.

I have often said in recent months that I do believe that there are today no binding external constraints on India's economic growth. Most constraints we face are inherently internal. This does not mean that external developments or trends may not re-emerge as constraints on our growth processes. Nor does it mean that we have taken full advantage of all the opportunities that are available to us. What it means is that the global environment is more benign today for India's development than at any other time in recent history. However, we must remain prepared at all times to deal with any external challenges to our development process, develop the necessary analytical tools to forecast and anticipate global trends and their implications for us and design policy response systems which are rapid but flexible enough for our needs. This requires, among other things, a continuous study of the global economic scenario and a contextualisation of this for our policy design purposes. This should be in my view the focus of ICRIER's work.

At the present time there is a great deal of optimism about India not only in seminar halls but also in boardrooms across the world. This optimism needs to be sustained and converted to tangible decisions that benefit our economy. For this, there is much we need to do at home. While the focus of the Government's policies will remain on domestic economic issues, institutes like ICRIER must continue to scan global economic developments and explore new opportunities so that our development goals are effectively met. ICRIER must chart for itself a clear research agenda that enables it to become the first stop and the last word on India's relations with the evolving global economy.

In addition to developing expertise on multilateral negotiations, particularly in the context of WTO, ICRIER must also create internal expertise on our understanding of the regional economies, especially regions that matter to us. We need more expertise in India on what is happening in our own neighbourhood in South Asia. Considering the rise of China on the global economic scenario, there must be a sharper focus on development trends in China and their implications for our development. ICRIER should consider acquiring a deeper understanding of China which would be of immense value to our economic planners, diplomats and the polity at large. And in this context, I listened with interest and approval to the steps that ICRIER is taking to study developments in China.

We also need expertise on economic trends in East and South-East Asia, West and Central Asia, Africa, Latin America, Europe and North America. An issue that could come up in the near future is that of India's membership of the Asia Pacific Economic Cooperation. As APEC is set to invite new members, we need to study the costs and benefits of APEC membership. We need to look at the effects of a pan Asian Economic Community or a Pan-Asian Free Trade Area. We need to examine the effects of the large number of Free Trade Agreements we are entering or planning to enter into. We also need a better understanding of the geo-political dynamics which are giving rise to a new range of economic relationships. Their costs and benefits need to be compared to those of a simpler multilateral system. ICRIER can guide policy makers in government with informed analysis.

An area of trade which is relatively less researched and understood is trade in services, particularly financial services. Much of the literature and data on external economic relations remains largely focused on merchandise trade. In popular discourse, we often refer to India performing below its potential in merchandise trade. However, the situation is quite different in services trade, including trade in labour services. The study of services trade is still in its infancy and much more needs to be done, particularly in India, on this important area. In the last decade, services trade and inward remittances have not only outperformed merchandise trade but have kept our balance of payments in a comfortable zone. We cannot therefore under estimate the importance of this for our macroeconomic management.

We need to know the extent to which principles that drive liberalisation in goods trade apply to the services trade, particularly trade in financial services. We need to have a deeper knowledge of our relative strengths in many services such as entertainment, business services, retailing, finance and banking, construction, education and health. What should our policies be and what international regimes should we seek to promote in order to benefit our interests in the global service economy? We need to have a better understanding of this whole complex area, particularly in view of its employment potential and our inherent strengths in some areas of services.

As the Indian economy modernises and grows we should expect a reverse migration of talent, especially from within the diaspora. What I would call a 'reverse brain drain' is in the making. How can we encourage this? What domestic policy changes should we make to encourage this? What are the likely implications for various sectors and regions of such a 'reverse brain drain'? These and similar other questions must engage the attention of ICRIER's researchers.

An area which is of increasing importance is trade in natural resources, particularly energy. India is not well endowed with natural resources on a per capita basis. We have to be therefore a major trading nation to overcome this natural resource constraint. However, trade in natural resources and energy is not governed entirely on a pattern similar to industrial goods. It is more complex and is closely dependent on geo-political relationships. We need to study far more deeply the characteristics driving trade in natural resources particularly the energy resources; the impact of international economic relationships on this trade; the perceived drive by some countries for securing sources of energy and minerals in third countries and the implications of this for free markets in these goods; and, policy guidance for our own planners and diplomats to secure our own economic future in this vital area.

With the opening up of the economy to capital flows from abroad, new issues arise regarding the optimum course for macroeconomic policies, particularly of fiscal and monetary policies, for a viable internal and external balance. We need to have a better understanding of the safe limits for capital flows from abroad. With a more open capital account, the management of the exchange rate also raises several new issues. Overall, the behaviour of international financial markets merits in-depth analysis.

Analysis of competitiveness has been a traditional research area in ICRIER. As global economic interrelationships change rapidly, we need to improve our understanding of competitiveness in various sectors including the industrial organisation, the progress of technology and the structures that are needed for a more integrated world. At the same time, technology is rapidly changing past modes of production, marketing, financing and service delivery with enormous implications for the growth of Indian firms. This needs greater analysis too.

I also believe that a think tank must engage public opinion at home and abroad and shape thinking on issues of interest to our country. For example, I have not seen adequately informed discussion at home on the pros and cons of the recent restructuring of voting rights within the IMF. Nor on the Asian Monetary Union that is being discussed in some circles. Nor even more importantly, on India's place in the new evolving global order.

Think tanks like ICRIER must participate actively in the public debate on India's place in the world and the consequences of increased global interdependence. I am often disappointed by the lack of adequate appreciation in our country, including among our political leaders, of the changing nature of our relationship with the world, and indeed with the region around us. Very often, we adopt political postures that are based in the past, indeed in the distant past and are out of line with our current interests as an increasingly globalised and globally integrated economy. India, I sincerely believe, is destined to be more globally engaged. We are destined to be more integrated with our own region. Even today, our energy security is closely intertwined with our political relationship with a wide range of countries around the globe. Our food security, technological security, indeed our national security are closely linked to developments around the world.

However, one feels at times that there is inadequate recognition at home about the increasing interdependence between India and the world, and the consequences thereof for our domestic policies. Think tanks like ICRIER must therefore invest in informing and shaping public opinion and policy making in all these vital aspects.

2

Addressing Deficit in Infrastructure

RAJIV LALL and NIRMAL MOHANTY

Introduction

One is often reminded that India's infrastructure does not match its growing economic and political ambitions built on the optimism generated by the high economic growth of recent years. There is a growing realisation that although India has the potential of achieving a sustained annual growth rate of 8-9 per cent (as opposed to 5-6 per cent in the past decade), this potential cannot be realised without addressing deficiencies in infrastructure. Recognising the significance of the infrastructure deficit, the Government of India (GoI) has expressed its desire to raise infrastructure development to unprecedented levels. The Prime Minister, in a recent conference (October 2006), has outlined the huge capacities in various infrastructure sectors that need to be created in the medium term to sustain an average annual GDP growth rate of 8-9 per cent. The infrastructure investment required to achieve this has been estimated at US $ 320 billion.

It is well known that despite high priority accorded to infrastructure, overall investments in infrastructure have been persistently falling short of requirements, with the result that the investment backlog has been growing over the years. Significantly, the shortfall has varied widely across sectors. Against this backdrop, the question arises as to whether investment of the high magnitude envisaged for the medium term is feasible or mere wishful thinking,

---

We are grateful to ASSOCHAM for hosting a committee on whose work the paper draws partially. In particular, we are grateful to Pradip Roy (IDBI), Anil K. Motwani (ADB), Rajesh Samson (Ernst and Young), Ratiranjan Mandal (SREI), Inderbir S. Dhingra, Ashish,Khanna and Varsha Marathe (all from The World Bank).

especially in sectors that have traditionally failed to attract adequate investment. What would it take to make these investments feasible, efficient and sustainable? To answer these questions in a meaningful analytical framework, it would be useful to take into account the following observations relating to India's infrastructure development in the past one and a half decades:

- Broad macroeconomic reforms have not helped boost investment in infrastructure, while sector-specific reforms have.
- With improvement in policy and regulatory frameworks in some sectors, the private sector has been showing increasing interest in those sectors—but, lack of long-term finance has been a major constraint in attempts to scale up.
- Public investment has been sluggish and priorities in public investment have often been distorted.
- In any given sector, the efficiency of service delivery and the scale of private sector participation have tended to depend on the scope of competition.
- In certain areas such as roads and urban infrastructure, physical assets built at massive costs have been eroded because of under-maintenance and require further investment.
- Public-private partnerships have not unfolded to the desirable extent in the face of institutional and individual capacity constraints.

India's overall experience with infrastructure development and the observations stated above in particular indicate that while sector-specific policy and regulatory initiatives are being taken to create appropriate facilitating frameworks, investment has been inadequate and unsustainable in several sectors due to: (i) inadequate long-term finance, (ii) poor prioritisation of public investment, (iii) absence of appropriate incentives and institutions and (iii) shortage in capacity to implement the new frameworks. Broadly speaking, the observations point to deficiencies in the financing system and in sector governance. While these factors are generally well known, the contribution of the political economy in perpetuating these deficiencies, especially in sector governance, has not been adequately recognised.

Motivated by the recent resolve of the government to step up infrastructure investment, this paper suggests a financing strategy to achieve the government's medium term goal, while attempting to examine the ability of the existing financing system and sector governance to deliver. It then recommends some critical and yet pragmatic measures to overcome the infrastructure deficit within a reasonable time period. The recommendations are only indicative and by no means comprehensive. Section II suggests a financing strategy, outlines the constraints of the financing system and some measures to overcome them. Section III highlights the need for changes in sector governance that would make such a strategy successful, while identifying some of the key political economy constraints. Keeping in view these constraints, Section IV recommends some strategic initiatives to facilitate higher and more sustainable investment. Section V concludes.

Financing Challenges

Table 2.1 gives an indication of the shares of broad categories of: (i) spenders on infrastructure (central and state governments, their enterprises and private companies) and (ii) the instruments used to finance infrastructure, in 2005-06. Under some reasonable assumptions, projections have been made to the spender, and instrument profile for the year 2010-11, such that $ 320 billion could be spent on infrastructure during the period 2006-07 to 2010-11. It can be seen from Table 2.1 that this would entail an increase in overall spending on infrastructure from 4.5 per cent of GDP to 7.5 per cent.

Let us first examine the kind of efforts necessary to meet the 'overall' resource mobilisation challenge. Without any incremental access to foreign savings, it appears that the challenge can be met relatively easily—if the domestic savings rise by about 4 percentage points of GDP during the period (2005/06 to 2010/11), a reasonable assumption given the current trend in savings—for two reasons. First, the rise in infra spending would not necessarily have to be at the cost of other sectors. Second, given the high priority accorded to infrastructure, targeting the required three-quarters of incremental savings for infrastructure would not be politically unacceptable.

Table 2.1

A Possible Financing Scenario

	2005-06		2010-11	
	% of GDP	*USD Billion**	*% of GDP*	*USD Billion**
Central Govt	0.5	4.0	1.0	12.0
Central PSUs @	2.1	17.0	3.0	36.0
State Govts. & their Enterprises	1.0	8.0	1.0	12.0
Private Sector	0.9	7.0	2.5	30.0
Total	4.5	36.0	7.5	90.0
Govt. Bonds	1.7	14.0	2.0	24.0
Bank Credit	0.8	6.0	1.2	14.0
Non-Bank Credit	0.7	6.0	1.8	22.0
Equity Issued by Pvt. Sector	0.3	2.0	1.0	12.0
Internal Accruals	1.0	8.0	1.5	18.0
Memo Items				
Savings/GDP (%)	34.3	38.3		
Financial Savings/GDP (%)	21.8	25.8		
Infra Spend/Financial Savings (%)	20.6	29.1		

Notes: * At 2005-06 prices; assuming an exchange rate of Rs 45 to a USD and a compound annual real growth rate of 9 per cent.
@ Railways have been included in this category

Source: RBI (2006). *Handbook of Statistics on the Indian Economy*; Government of India (2006). *Union Budget*; IDFC staff estimates and projections.

A closer scrutiny however reveals that it would be more difficult to mobilise the required resources from incremental domestic savings alone than appears at first sight. Because, in addition to the assumed increase in domestic saving effort to mobilise overall resources for the economy, higher intermediation efforts would be necessary to raise the share of domestic financial savings flowing into infrastructure from 21 per cent in 2005-06 to close to 29 per cent in 2010-11.[1] The current financial system may pose a challenge in achieving this, even despite reforms. Past attempts to raise the share of long-term savings (that can be potentially used to fund infrastructure) in total savings have after all not met with much success (Box 2.1). Clearly, limited additional access by infrastructure sectors to foreign savings would reduce the intermediation efforts required. Here, priority needs to be given to

1. It has been assumed that physical savings would remain unchanged at their current level (12.5 per cent of GDP) in the next five years.

foreign equity capital (see below). In addition, targeted access to long-term debt finance from overseas would help.

Box 2.1

Intermediation of Household Financial Savings

An analysis of the composition of household financial saving sheds some light on the kind of intermediation that household financial savings lend themselves to and their suitability for infrastructure finance (Table). Two points clearly emerge. First, notwithstanding financial innovations, bank deposits continue to be an important saving instrument accounting for 30-35 per cent of financial savings. Second, the share of insurance funds and provident and pension funds (together described as contractual savings) in household financial savings has not been significant—but broadly stagnant. These savings are long-term in nature and can potentially be an important instrument in allocating funds towards infrastructure sectors, which require lumpy investment and long gestation lags. As disposable income rises and life expectancy continues to increase, concerns regarding old age security can be expected to result in a rise in the share of these contractual instruments.

Table

India: Shares of Instruments in Household Financial Saving

(Per cent; Average)

Item	*1991-92 to 1995-96*	*1996-97 to 2000-01*	*2001-02 to 2003-04*	*2004-05 (Prov.)*
Currency	13.2	9.5	11.9	8.5
Bank Deposits	31.3	35.6	28.8	37.0
Shares and Debentures	17.1	5.1	2.3	1.1
Net Claims on Government	7.7	13.2	22.7	24.4
Insurance Funds	10.5	12.8	16.5	16.0
Provident and Pension Funds	20.2	23.7	17.7	12.9
Household Saving in Financial Assets	100	100	100	100

Source: Central Statistical Organisation.

Who would bear the burden of the additional expenditure and how? Following is a discussion on the rationale for the suggested (relative) reliance on individual instruments, constraints in using them and the initiatives required to make the suggested scenario work.

Budgetary Support

Fiscal responsibility and budget management (FRBM) laws will be a major determinant of the extent of budgetary support for infrastructure. Keeping in view the constraints of the FRBM laws, the state government's budgetary support to infrastructure has been projected to rise only marginally from 0.7 per cent of GDP to 1 per cent. This can be achieved comfortably within the FRBM parameters, given the buoyancy that VAT has been demonstrating. The Central Government, on the other hand, would simply have to maintain its current level of support (1 per cent of GDP), albeit with some changes in spending composition: while raising its grants from 0.5 per cent of GDP in 2005-06 to 1 per cent in 2010-11 to fund its ambitious programmes to scale up rural infrastructure, the GoI would have to cut its budgetary support to central PSUs by an equal amount. The infrastructure focused central PSUs would have to make do with declining budgetary support (and none by 2010-11) and yet raise capital spending on infrastructure from 2.1 per cent of GDP to 3 per cent. While the central PSUs would come under increasing pressure to rely more on the market to raise resources, the challenge would not be insurmountable given that the central PSUs are currently highly under-leveraged (Table 2.2).

Some additional fiscal efforts—*albeit* minor—would however be necessary to boost the finances of urban local bodies (ULBs). It has been observed that most ULBs do not have fiscal autonomy, which is critical for efficient delivery of urban infrastructure services, due to lack of a buoyant source of own revenue. It would therefore be useful to introduce a new (own) tax for ULBs, while continuing with the ongoing property tax reforms. The new tax would be in the form of a Local Benefit Tax and would have the sales turnover (at the final stage) as its base. It would piggyback on VAT and would not require any new skills, manpower or rules on the part of urban local bodies.

Commercial Bank Credit

The commercial banks' case however is more complex. Currently, banks are a significant financier of the infrastructure sector (about 19 per cent of total infrastructure spending). Bank credit to infrastructure accounts for about a quarter of the banks' incremental credit to the industrial sector and 7 per cent of incremental non-food gross bank credit during 2005-06. In the last five years, bank credit to infrastructure has grown enormously (Figure 2.1)—as a result, the share of infrastructure in gross bank credit (outstanding) has risen from 3 per cent to 8 per cent. It may be noted that private banks (including foreign banks) have generally not shown much interest in infrastructure with the exception of just a few.

Table 2.2

Outlay by Infrastructure Focused Central PSUs

(% of GDP)

	*2005-06**	*2010-11 (Projected)*
Total Outlay	2.1	3.0
of which:		
Budgetary Support	0.5	0.0
Equity	0.4	0.0
Loans	0.1	0.0
I.E.B.R**	1.6	3.0
Internal Resources	0.9	0.9
Borrowing from Markets	0.7	2.1

Notes : *- Includes PSUs under Ministry/Dept. of Atomic Energy, Civil Aviation, Comm. and I.T, Non-Conventional Energy Sources, Power, Shipping, Road Transport and Highways, Urban Development. and Railways.

**- I.E.B.R = Internal and Extra Budgetary Resources.

Source: *Budget 2006-07*, Government of India and IDFC projections.

It is perhaps too optimistic to expect the bank lending to infrastructure to continue to grow at similar levels as in the past, since exposure limits of various kinds are likely to act as inhibiting factors. Besides, it may not be desirable for banks to have very high exposure to infrastructure sectors while continuing to rely excessively on short-term deposits, since the asset liability management (ALM) mismatches resulting from this would make banks vulnerable to interest rate risk. Furthermore, a rapid expansion of bank credit to infrastructure in the face of a deficit in appraisal skills (that the banks are currently suffering), could result in a deterioration in credit quality. In view of

Figure 2.1

Infrastructure Financing by Commercial Banks
(Rs. Crore, Outstanding at End-March)

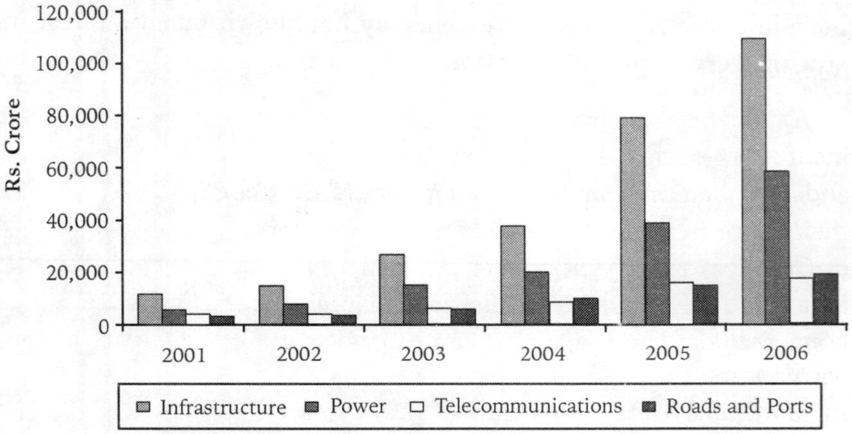

Source: RBI. *Handbook of Statistics on the Indian Economy 2005-06.*

these factors, the banks could be expected to raise their infrastructure funding from 0.8 per cent of GDP now to at most 1.2 per cent of GDP five years hence and in the process lower their share of infrastructure financing from 19 per cent at present to 16 per cent in 2010-11.

To ensure that banks remain important players in infrastructure financing, the following initiatives would be necessary.

- Mobilising resources through bonds (such as infrastructure bonds) can help banks reduce the risk of ALM mismatches. The regulations regarding issue of bonds by banks (such as restrictions on amount, maturity or purpose of use) needs to be liberalised to impart greater flexibility and make bond issues relatively more cost-effective.
- Banks would have to take greater recourse to take-out or mezzanine finance mechanisms to manage long tenor assets with short tenor liabilities.

- Banks could be allowed to categorise long-term non-SLR (Statutory Liquid Ratio) investments under Held-to-Maturity (HTM), which is currently not allowed by RBI.[2]
- Banks need to build and retain project financing skills in a much larger scale than they are doing at present.

Non-bank Credit

A moderate role by banks would mean that the long-term financing institutions such as insurance companies, pension and provident funds and Non Banking Financial Company (NBFCs) would have to raise their share in infrastructure financing significantly (from 0.7 per cent of GDP to 1.8 per cent). A critical component of this strategy would be a rapid development of the debt market, especially the corporate bond market. The Indian corporate bond market is under-developed with a size of 5 per cent of GDP (as compared to 38 per cent of GDP in Malayasia) and its issuance is dominated by banks, financial institutions and public sector undertakings, rather than non-financial private corporate sector.

A key impediment to the development of the corporate bond market is the absence of long-term debt—critical for infrastructure financing—resulting mainly from a shortage of investors in such tenor. Eligible investors such as insurance companies and pension and provident funds have little appetite for long-term papers issued by infrastructure companies, especially the less well-known and sub-investment grade ones. This is due partly to pre-occupation of these institutions with financing government debt and partly to restrictive investment guidelines. To ensure that non-bank debt accounts for a larger share of infrastructure finance, there is a need to implement the recommendations of the Patil Committee on debt capital markets expeditiously, especially those with respect to development of market for securitised assets. In particular, the authorities should:

2. As per RBI guidelines, non-SLR bonds and debentures held by banks/financial institutions are to be maintained only under Held-for-Trading (HFT) or Available-for-Sale (AFS) category where investors run the risk of making provisions due to possible Mark-to-Market (MTM) losses. This makes the banking sector averse to investing in bonds and thereby excludes a large chunk of potential investors.

- Allow insurance companies, PFs and India Infrastructure Finance Company Ltd. (IIFCL) to buy investment grade securities of long term infrastructure focused collateralised loan obligations (CLOs) and collateralised debt obligations (CDOs) as well as of investment grade infrastructure development companies and infrastructure projects.
- Allow FIIs to buy junior tranches of long term infrastructure focused CLOs and CDOs.

In the infrastructure space, NBFCs are a relatively new entrant, but their share is growing rapidly especially in the backdrop of a diminishing role of development financial institutions. In addition to providing loans—like banks—to large infrastructure companies, they often on-lend to a large number of small and medium players in transportation and construction. Their role is critical, since many large infrastructure projects are subcontracted to SME players, who do not enjoy easy access to bank loans. As compared to banks, NBFCs are more nimble and have more in-depth knowledge of customers. Since they are less likely to pose systemic risk and easier to be created and expanded under private sponsorship, they also have higher growth potential. A major constraint facing NBFCs, however, relates to funding. If infrastructure focused NBFCs are to play a significantly expanded role in future, the following two initiatives will be necessary:

- Allow these NBFCs automatic access to External Commercial Borrowings (ECBs).
- Allow insurance companies, PFs, and IIFCL to invest in long term investment grade bonds issued by these NBFCs.

Equity Finance

Mobilising equity finance is one of the key challenges of infrastructure project financing. In this context, the case for FDI has been made from time to time, as it would not only narrow the funding gap, but also usher in skills to implement and monitor projects in line with global best practices. Despite the position of the Government of India that "FDI will continue to be encouraged and actively sought in areas of infrastructure...", FDI inflows into infrastructure in India have remained low as compared to requirements. It is well known that higher FDI flows can be attracted through measures such as further liberalisation of sectoral caps on FDI, single-window clearance and reasonable convertibility on capital account together with efforts to make policies more stable, workforce more skilled and the legal system more efficient. While the need to do all these cannot be over-emphasised, it has to be recognised that most of these initiatives are either politically sensitive or can at best be medium to long-term objectives.

What interventions are then necessary in the short term to mitigate the dearth of equity finance in general and FDI in particular? For analytical clarity, it would be useful to categorise equity investors as strategic or financial, depending on the investment objectives.[3] To encourage overseas investors to bring in financial equity capital, the following initiatives are suggested:

- Allow insurance companies and provident funds to invest in funds and Special Purpose Vehicle (SPVs) owning infrastructure assets by classifying them explicitly as 'approved investments' in investment regulation.
- An additional facilitating measure would be to relax requirements of dividend payment history as a consideration for such investment.[4]

As regards strategic equity investment, there are many cases where investors with investible surpluses are available, but investment does not occur due to inappropriate project structuring or inadequate project returns. These problems can be addressed through capacity building (see below) and measures such as viability gap funding. In certain other cases, strategic investors with investibe surpluses are simply not available domestically. To encourage strategic equity

3. While equity investment in a project is purely for equity returns, strategic equity investment is incidental to a larger interest of the investor and not merely for equity returns. An example of strategic equity is the equity investment by a road contractor in a BOT road project, where the contractor brings in the required equity mainly to facilitate the execution of the construction contract, which is his primary interest in the project.

4. Many concession companies although stable in operations, may not be in a position to pay dividends in the initial years of operation.

investment by foreign contracting firms, especially in sectors where a large number of projects are bid out,[5] there is a need for active marketing of individual sectors to international players through showcasing of successful project experiences, as the international investors are not adequately aware of the attractiveness of BOT opportunities in India.

Governance Framework

Challenges for Governance

What challenges has infrastructure development been posing for governance in India lately? Would there be new challenges in the medium term? To answer these questions, it would be useful to examine the way the approach to investment in infrastructure has been evolving. The Eighth Plan (published in 1992) officially recognised for the first time a possible role for the private sector in providing infrastructure, but fell short of favouring it. Since then, however, there has been a shift towards a positive preference for private investment, primarily because of the government's resource constraint—a problem that has been accentuated in recent years by the fiscal responsibility laws.[6] As a result, more and more sectors are getting open for private sector participation. Recognising that pure private projects are not forthcoming to the extent desirable, the government has been in recent years attempting to promote public private partnerships. While infrastructure development can now take place through three routes: purely public, purely private and Public-Private Partnership (PPP), attempts are being made to channel progressively higher investment through the last two routes, particularly the last route.

Clearly, the two important components of the recent approach are: declining dependence on budgetary resources and increasing (relative)

5. In the National Highway sector for example the domestic contracting industry does not have the capacity to meet the full demand anticipated over the next few years. According to one estimate, the combined net worth of the large domestic players actively involved in BOT project implementation in India is only about two-thirds of the equity investment requirement of the highway sector.
6. Further, it is widely perceived that public sector providers are operationally inefficient and insensitive to consumer concerns and that private sector suppliers, operating within a competitive framework, can potentially reduce costs to the economy and be responsive to consumer demands.

reliance on private participation.[7] The medium term financing scenario suggested by us in Section II reflects essentially an acceleration of this approach. Challenges for governance to make the approach succeed emerge from the need to: (i) realise both these components, and (ii) create capacity to manage the new framework, as discussed below.

Challenges Due to Reduced Budgetary Support

Ultimately, there are only two ways in which infrastructure is funded: by consumers (*via* user charges) and by taxpayers (*via* subsidies).[8] Thus an expansionary strategy that relies progressively less on budgetary resources would have to necessarily increase focus on user charges. A user-charge financed strategy requires for its success a stronger and more stable governance framework not only to assure investors of adequate payment security (over a long period of time), but also to create greater willingness among users to pay their bills, by ensuring more competitive tariff and reliable service (through higher competition among suppliers).[9]

Challenges Due to Higher Private Participation

Higher private sector participation also gives rise to significant challenges for governance. Potential private investors need to be assured that they are on a level playing field with government sponsored operators and other private operators. Secondly, since the share of sunken investment in infrastructure is relatively high, viability of infrastructure investment depends relatively more on the consistency and predictability of the rules of the game as set out by the government and the government's commitment to adhere to them over a relatively long period of time. Thirdly, consultations with the public

---

7. Note that these are two independent characteristics and one does not necessarily imply the other.

8. Financiers can only change the time profile of taxes or user charges (that is, effectively smoothen the necessary tax and tariff increases) by providing financing. They would, however, not be forthcoming unless they feel assured that they are repaid or remunerated adequately. (See *Connecting East Asia: A New Framework for Infrastructure*, 2005).

9. In India, user charges have not been a constraint in financing operation or capacity creation in sectors such as airports, ports, telecom and to a large extent, railways.

and public scrutiny are more important with private sector participation than without, to make tariff levels and service standards socially acceptable. Finally, the private sector needs to be convinced that adequate individual and institutional capacity exists in the public sector to carry out the new frameworks effectively.

Challenges Due to Capacity Constraints for PPPs

A third set of challenges emerge from the need to create capacity for PPPs. The most significant challenge relates to skill-building. This is not just a question of shortage of skills in the public sector in an absolute sense but one of an imbalance between public and private partners. Simply put, public authorities are wary of being taken for a ride by private contractors. Further, if public authorities partner private parties through contracts that turn out to be flawed, public sector managers lose confidence in the approach. Secondly, for PPPs to succeed, there is a need to create champions in all participating organisations and to ensure that capacity building is ongoing and responsive to an inevitable change in interest amongst politicians during the (typically long) contract periods.

Political Economy and Governance

Does the political economy currently obtaining in India allow an appropriate governance response? To answer this question, it would be appropriate to examine the tensions and conflicts that characterise India's political economy and the way they influence governance response, with some examples. Broadly, we identify four different types of conflicts that have special relevance for the infrastructure sector. The effective and more systematic resolution of these tensions, we believe, would constitute good governance and holds the key to progress in the sector.

Conflicts between Tiers of Government

- Because of high distribution inefficiency in the power sector, the GoI-owned National Thermal Power Corporation's (NTPC's) receivables from state government owned state electricity boards (SEBs) had risen to bizarre levels, hurting NTPC's commercial viability. The GoI responded by bringing into force a Tripartite

Agreement (between GoI, the RBI and the states) which entailed an one-time securitisation of electricity over-dues and authorised an intercept of the centre's fiscal transfers to a state in the event of a default by the state's SEB. This has succeeded in resolving the tension between centre and states in this respect, but has created new tension elsewhere (see below).

- Royalty on coal is determined by the central government, but constitutes a source of revenue for states. Not satisfied with the royalty set by the GoI, some coal rich states have additionally levied cess on the mineral bearing land raising thereby the cost of thermal power producers. This has undermined the GoI's attempts to keep the cost of power provision under control.
- Most urban local bodies depend on state government agencies to create capacity for water and sanitation services for their residents, even though the local bodies are responsible for the provision of these services. This is so, because the ULBs generally do not have the technical and managerial capacity to carry out this function. In the process, ULBs lose control over the way their own funds are spent and often pay for the inefficiency of state government agencies. Further, ULBs are rarely consulted by the state-level agencies in matters relating to design, location etc. of the water works/sewage treatment plants, which leads to a lack of ownership on the part of ULBs for their own assets.

Jurisdictional (Inter-ministerial and Inter-departmental) Conflict

- Many private power projects have been delayed due to inter-ministerial wrangling: for example, between the Ministry of Power and the Ministry of Environment and Forest. Several port projects have also been delayed for years for similar reasons.
- The promenade in Juhu (Mumbai) took an unduly long time to get developed, because the Airport Authority of India (who owned the land), the Brihanmumbai Municipal Corporation and the Collector of that area, who had decision-making authority relating to different segments of the project, could not converge to a single objective for a long time.

- The Railways and the National Highways Authority of India take tariff decisions individually without much attention to inter-modal connectivity and competition. For example, tariff setting by Railways is often based on political considerations, although they can potentially impact the viability of private investments in the highway sector.

Public *versus* Private

- Several state governments have tended to abdicate their responsibility of consolidating land (free of regulatory encumbrances such as environmental clearances) for infrastructure projects to the private sector.[10] Leaving the burden of land acquisition to the private sector leads to inappropriate risk sharing and forces the private sector to compensate the land owners in a nontransparent manner. It also encourages all manners of rent seeking behaviour (as the private sector begins to seek regulatory dispensation), which hurts infrastructure development. Examples of this phenomenon can be found in power projects in recent years, although Ultra Mega Power Projects have been an exception.
- Ever since the private sector has been allowed to provide infrastructure, private operators have been finding themselves in competition with incumbent public sector providers. Tension arises—often justifiably—from (the private enterprises') suspicion that the government favours the public sector organisations by influencing regulation, redesigning policies etc. The Tripartite Agreement for example assures payment securities to public sector generating utilities, but there is no similar initiative for the private sector generators. Similarly, the public sector telecom companies—BSNL and MTNL—were exempt from paying license fee until the last financial year, while the private companies were not.

---

10. This trend is likely to accelerate after the experiences of the West Bengal Government in Singur. There is a growing body of opinion that suggests that it would be easier and less controversial to allow the private sector to consolidate land (through 'market solutions').

Urban *versus* Rural

- Tension has historically arisen because of the need to accommodate politically influential rural constituency. This has, for instance, led to extreme reliance on cross-subsidisation with commercial and urban consumers of electricity paying disproportionately high tariffs *versus* rural consumers.
- The distribution of the gains from infrastructure development between rural and urban areas has been a source of tension. For example, as the urban boundary expands on account of population growth, city development authorities acquire rural land from farmers at a cost that is calculated on the basis of its agricultural use without the premium reflecting proximity to urban centres. The development authorities service it with basic infrastructure and either lease (or auction) it to developers or directly to urban residents. In the process, the development authorities and/or private developers make huge windfall profits, while farmers get very little.

Response of Governance to Reforms

Let us now examine some instances of how governance has responded to reform initiatives, drawing mainly from the experience of the sectors worst affected by political economy considerations, namely the power sector and the urban sector.

- Independent power sector regulators have been created by most states *inter alia* to make the utilities viable. Some of these have started using multi-year tariff frameworks and setting tariff levels on the basis of targeted T&D loss levels. The utilities fall short of their targets year after year and thereby incur commercial losses. Regulators continue to reprimand the utilities for their inaction, but to no avail. There is little that regulators can do to take the utilities or their CEOs to task.
- The Electricity Act 2003 has introduced the concept of open access, which would allow consumers to choose their respective generators and thereby bypass the state utility. It is expected that as open access is phased-in as envisaged in the Electricity Act 2003, competitive pressures would be created. With the

generation and distribution assets remaining predominantly with them, the state governments have tended to not only delay the phase-in of open access, but also render it ineffective to the extent possible. Although nearly three years have passed and most states have introduced open access regulations in line with the Central Act, there has been hardly any open access deal.

- While the 74th Constitutional Amendment has significantly expanded the expenditure responsibilities of urban local governments to make them function as the third tier of government, it has only urged states to devolve more taxation powers to them. However, there has been no such devolution in any state that would make ULBs financially competent to deliver the added responsibilities. As a result, ULBs in all states depend on transfers from their respective state governments. While this has resulted in erosion of fiscal autonomy, ULBs continue to suffer from severe financial crunch—despite transfers from state governments—and are often not in a position to provide the basic minimum services required of them.
- In Maharashtra, as in several other states, rent control laws introduced several decades ago still persist. These laws basically require rents to be fixed at 'reasonable' levels (called 'standard rents'); rents so fixed can never be changed, nor can the sitting tenants ever be evicted.[11] Even though the distortions caused by these laws are widely recognised, lifting rent control has been considered politically unfeasible due to its potential disruption. A bizarre outcome of this is that municipalities have been forced to repeatedly raise the property tax rates in response to the rising cost of (civic) service provision, since the tax base (standard rent) cannot be changed. In Mumbai for example the property tax rate for commercial properties has risen to over 300 per cent from 21 per cent in 1948-49!

---

11. There has been some liberalisation of rent control laws, but they continue to be highly distorting.

Assessment

Ever since India embarked on a strategy of infrastructure development with private sector participation, there have been new challenges for governance, which have not been met adequately because of the political economy prevailing in the country. The history of infrastructure development in India during this period is replete with examples of poor governance. Further, India's ability to implement reforms, and indeed its choice of reform options is constrained by the reality of our political economy and the quality of our governance. At the heart of the matter is the fact that the approach taken to infrastructure development, which is sought to be accelerated in the medium term, requires the government to give up its role as provider and regulator and accept the role of a facilitator. While the Government has been attempting to play the facilitating role, it is unwilling to give up its role as provider and regulator in all sectors.[12] The resistance is sometimes due to ideological reasons (e.g., privatisation of PSUs entails a compromise of workers' interests), other times due to political populism (e.g. free electricity to farmers yields political benefits) or attempts to protect the politicians' patronage networks that reforms may potentially undermine. Even public investment is allocated to different sectors or different segments of the same sector (e.g. maintenance *versus* new capacity creation) in a manner that would maximise political benefits.[13]

Recommendations

While theoretical, first best solutions are a useful beacon, reform initiatives must be designed and sequenced taking due account of the realities of political economy. Keeping this in view, we make the following recommendations to facilitate a more rapid infrastructure development. These are only indicative of what kind of solutions can be pursued under the current constraints and are by no means

12. In some instances, it has given up the regulatory role only grudgingly and has created a system where the new regulatory body has become an extension of the Government.

13. For example, many states are opting for metro rails for their cities because of prestige factors, even though more optimal and yet less expensive solutions are available.

comprehensive. Our recommendations relate only to the laggard sectors—that is sectors that have failed to attract adequate new investment or make past investment sustainable. These include power, roads and urban sectors.

Segregate Urban and Rural Power Supply

Segregation of urban and rural supply operations would be an important strategy to fulfill consumer expectations while enhancing utility accountability. Characteristics of urban and rural electricity distribution are very different, reflecting different client needs, expectations and abilities to pay, as well as different delivery challenges. Segregation would make subsidies more transparent and better targeted by eliminating the option of camouflaging theft through over reporting of non-metered subsidised agricultural consumption. For this reason, segregated supply *per se* is a better option than the current mode of supply, even though segregation would give the most optimal results if it is followed by private sector participation. Further, since it is easier in urban zones to focus efforts on reducing theft and on collecting revenues, segregation can potentially lead to higher private investment.[14] Implementation of segregation would have to be state-specific and could take different forms (creation of separate companies or Strategic Business Units (SBUs) or ring-fencing arrangements within the same company). Financial incentives may be needed upfront to facilitate segregation, followed by milestone based incentives linked to outcomes. Intense strategic communication would be required to convince that segregation does not entail a pro-urban bias.

Create Dedicated Institutes for Capacity Building

As long as infrastructure was provided entirely by the public sector, capacity building was not considered critical for investment or operation. With the shift in emphasis to private participation, particularly through PPPs, individual capacities of public sector managers and regulators in the newly created regulatory institutions has emerged as a constraint to carry out the new frameworks for investment and operation. The problem has been accentuated by the

14. Theft is generally concentrated in these zones.

government's attempt to scale up PPPs. One way to address this issue is to create dedicated institutes for capacity building.

The agenda of these institutes would be to:

- Strengthen the capacity of mainly the public sector organisations (in some cases that of financial institutions, and other stakeholders from the private sector and civil society also) so that they may more effectively design, assess, market and execute viable PPP projects.[15]
- Assist the development of regulatory skills in existing and potential regulatory institutions.
- Demystify the private sector's role in infrastructure provision. Demystification through accretion of knowledge and information helps dispel prejudice and allay misapprehensions of the functionaries of the state.
- Expose public sector organisations to best practices (national and international) to achieve the same and to build confidence by providing civil servants with successful precedents.

In setting up institutes of this nature, some infrastructure financing institutions would enjoy two major comparative advantages. First, they have accumulated substantial domain knowledge in private financing of Indian infrastructure. Second, they have well developed relationships with both government entities and prominent private sector sponsors. While these relationships have individually yielded benefits, there have not had many opportunities to exploit the synergies between them. These institutions would provide such an opportunity.

While the financing institutions can contribute to capacity building in terms of sharing their experience, apprising the public sector managers the needs of the financiers etc., they do not have the requisite skills to train personnel. It would therefore be appropriate for them to enter into partnerships with established academic/professional training institutes. IIMs, Xaviers Institute of Management, Institute of

15. This would range from introductory exposure to the concepts of PPPs (what, when, how, why and who) to the more detailed transactional and post-transactional management and monitoring skills. An important aspect in the initial training is 'expectations management' *viz.* a clear understanding of what PPPs can and cannot achieve.

Economic Growth, Administrative Staff College of India, National Institute of Public Finance and Policy are some of the potential candidates for this purpose. Many of them have long experience in training mid-career professionals.

Create an Overarching Legislation for Regulation

It is well known as to why autonomous regulatory institutions are critical for private sector participation. In sectors such as power, where such institutions have emerged, the experience has not been encouraging. Regulatory orders have tended to be inconsistent, delayed and patchy. The regulatory system in the transport sector has also been weak. While there is no autonomous economic regulator in case of National Highways, Railways and Airports, the regulation of Major Ports through the Tariff Authority for Major Ports is restricted to tariff setting. Further, there is no uniform approach to regulation, leading to an absence of standard regulatory principles and processes, with each Ministry following its own procedures. In case of NHAI for example, tariff setting is done by Government Committees through a process which is neither consultative nor based on detailed economic and market studies of transport networks. In other sub-sectors such as Railways, tariff setting has been subject to political and administrative considerations, leading to an uncertain environment in respect of the inter-modal attractiveness of railways *vis-à-vis* road transport. Private investment in the road transport sector can be potentially impeded if investors are not convinced about the consistency in the way the Railways sets its current and future tariff, because they can significantly impact the return on their investments.

To address the broader question of consistency in approach to regulation, there should be an overarching enabling legislation for regulation in India, which would set out:

- Role and functions of the regulators and their relationship with the executive and legislature.
- General objectives of regulation such as developing a mature and competitive market, ensuring universal access and providing consumer protection.
- Activities that need to be subject to independent regulation.

- Principles of regulations that promote: (a) long-term views of investment and maintenance and (b) efficient use of the service under consideration.
- Suitability of types of regulation (heavy-handed or light-handed) depending on industry structure.

This statute could be supplemented by sector-specific legislation which would set out sector-specific objectives, but maintain core institutional form across sectors.

Develop State Highways

State highways—which constitute 4 per cent of the road network, but carry 40 per cent of traffic—are grossly underfunded and under-maintained, leading to even higher requirement for investment. There are three major challenges facing the sector.

- The Public Works Department system, which is responsible for state highways, is outmoded and lacks not only clear objectives and focus but also modern technical and managerial capacity.
- The planning and management in this sector is ad hoc due to lack of adequate database (on road inventory, road condition and traffic characteristics) and data management systems. Barring one or two states, no state has a master plan for state highways.
- While the investment requirements are daunting, funding through the BOT model is appropriate only for some heavily trafficked state highways. Majority of traffic is non-tollable, slow-moving and local in nature. Further, in the absence of a medium term framework, adequate resources and technical and managerial capacity to carry out large scale PPP frameworks, private investment has naturally been limited and sporadic.

In this sector, the GoI could play a more active role in steering and monitoring the state highway sector by creating a nodal unit at the centre which would be responsible for the development of a common framework at the state level. The framework would encompass models for road development policy, state highway act, road funding, and establishment of state highway authorities. Such measures would provide clear guidance to states and reduce the time and effort necessary to initiate a medium term investment programme. At the state government level, the comprehensive reform initiatives undertaken by MP can be emulated by other states (Box 2.2).

Box 2.2

The Madhya Pradesh Model of State Highway Development

Some of the major initiatives taken by the Government of Madhya Pradesh (GoMP) are as follows:

- GoMP has significantly enhanced the funding for this sector.
- A wholly owned government company, the Madhya Pradesh Road Development Corporation (MPRDC) has been created, which has been notified as State Highway Authority. It has been entrusted with the responsibility of the entire highway sector and is currently implementing projects through BOT contracts for about 2000 km.
- A special bill for the highway sector has been passed.
- A computerised road database system has been developed for the state highway sector, which can generate reports for management information and decision making.
- Fully functional business processes have been developed for: (i) financial management and accounting; (ii) planning, budgeting, and programming; (iii) road safety; (iv) a management information system and (v) procurement.
- MPRDC has undergone extensive training and capacity-building programmes to adapt the new business processes and modern road management systems.

Introduce Incentives for Open Access

As stated earlier, states have been unwilling customers to the open access initiative. Although nearly three years have passed and most states have introduced open access regulations in line with the Central Act, there has been hardly any open access deal. States are apprehensive that with the introduction of open access regime, most High Tension (HT) consumers would desert SEBs in favour of other generators and in the process deprive SEBs of a source of buoyant revenue, cross subsidy surcharge notwithstanding. Further, states would have to cut cross subsidies drastically and thereby incur huge political costs. While some may argue that open access is mandated by law and therefore no incentive is necessary, the reality is that states will not adopt them in earnest unless they see significant and lasting 'net' benefits.[16] To tilt the balance between benefits and costs, incentives may be necessary.

The central government can provide this incentive in terms of allocation of power generated by central PSUs to states with relatively higher open access consumption. It may be noted that central PSUs account for over a quarter of total generation by utilities and supply about 30 to 40 per cent of power consumed in case of some states. It is reasonable to assume that the capacity addition in this segment in the next five years will continue to be more significant than in the state sector and private sector. Obviously, the central government is in a strong position to influence the state government's decisions, if it chooses to leverage the centrally generated power. Furthermore, allocation of power from NTPC plants (and other central sector thermal/atomic power stations) is determined on the basis of a formula devised by the central government (Box 2.3).[17] This implies that the GoI is within its rights to alter the formula to create incentives for open access.

Summary and Conclusion

The analysis in the paper leads to the conclusion that it would be feasible to translate the government's vision of high infrastructure investment in the medium term into reality. The task, however, would not be easy and will entail substantial efforts to strengthen the financial system and governance. While resource constraints are not insurmountable, the challenge lies in encouraging diversified and more effective intermediation of savings such that it meets the needs of infra development. Simple measures to facilitate the participation of financial investors for equity capital, kick-start domestic debt capital markets, and improve access to long term foreign debt financing would go a long way. The Government would have to play a moderate role in financing, but a much more enhanced role in creating appropriate institutions and improving governance standards. The latter role will be constrained by

---

16. States realise that the move is irreversible.

17. There is a similar, but not identical formula governing allocation of central sector hydel power.

Box 2.3

Formula Governing NTPC Allocation

- Fifteen per cent of capacity is to be kept at the disposal of the central government for meeting the urgent requirements of individual states in the regions from time to time.
- Ten per cent of the power is allocated to the state in which the power station is located; and
- The remaining 75 per cent of power is allocated among the states of the region (including the "Home State") on the basis of the share of energy consumed, and central plan assistance received by them in the preceding five years. The needs of the union territories are also met through appropriate allocations. The two factors—electricity consumed and central plan assistance—are given equal weights.

the political economy factors at least in the short to medium term. Nevertheless, considerable progress can still be made through better prioritisation of reform initiatives (e.g. state highways); and through creative, yet practical, design (e.g. the separation of urban from rural electricity distribution and incentives for open access). The harder problems pertain to pervasive institutional deficiencies and the full range of governance issues—eliminating the infrastructure deficit will require us to deal with these problems head on.

References

Ahluwalia, Montek S. (1998). "Infrastructure Development in India's Reforms", in I.J. Ahluwalia and I.M.D. Little (eds.), *India's Economic Reforms and Development: Essays for Manmohan Singh*. New Delhi: Oxford University Press.

Government of India (2006). *Union Budget (2006-07)*. New Delhi: Ministry of Finance.

———. (2005). *Report of High Level Expert Committee on Corporate Bonds and Securitisation*. New Delhi: Ministry of Finance.

Mohanty, Nirmal (2006). "Local Benefit Tax". Mumbai: IDFC. (*mimeo*).

RBI (n.d.) *Handbook of Statistics on the Indian Economy 2005-06*. Mumbai.

Singh, Manmohan (2007). Prime Minister's speech at conference on *Building Infrastructure: Challenges and Opportunities*. New Delhi. October.

World Bank (2006). *Financing Infrastructure: Addressing Constraints and Challenges*. Finance and Private Sector Development Unit South Asia Region.

———. (2005). Connecting East Asia: A New Framework for Infrastructure. Tokyo: Asian Development Bank, Japan Bank of International Cooperation and World Bank.

3

Innovating with Infrastructure

Maruti's Power-sharing Model and its Implications for Electricity Restructuring

SUMILA GULYANI

Introduction

Many developing countries are unable to provide their industries with a basic input—reliable electric power. Not only must industrial firms contend with insufficient electric power supply but also with its poor quality. In a country such as India, the quantity shortage or demand-supply gap makes it difficult for firms to get electric connections from public utilities; when firms do get connections the 'sanctioned load' is often lower than their demand; and they face frequent—scheduled and unscheduled—power cuts. In addition, the quality problem—in particular, fluctuations in voltage and frequency of power supplied—causes machine damages, material losses, and variations in product quality. Consequently, production volumes, manufacturing costs and output quality are all adversely affected.

To offset these negative impacts of poor public power, industrial firms in developing countries are increasingly opting for self-generation. However, self-generation is widely considered an inferior solution in the power restructuring literature. The majority of development practitioners, power technocrats, public and private electric utilities, and energy economists agree that self-generation is, at best, a 'second-best' solution for the following reasons. First, self-generation is supposedly high-cost relative to efficiently provided public power and it tends to use polluting fuels such as liquid hydrocarbons (World Bank, 1996). Second, users often invest in excess capacity which then sits idle and this represents a waste of national resources (Lee, Anas and Oh, 1996). Third, the exit of industrial users from public grids is problematic because it hurts the financial or commercial viability of electric utilities in developing countries—industrial firms are often the only paying customers and they help cross-subsidise provision to residential and agricultural users (World Bank, 1996). Finally, from the perspective of many energy economists, the 'optimal' solution to the power problem is for governments to encourage the emergence of electric power markets and to pursue models similar to the one adopted by the United Kingdom. In this 'model', private power companies bid to sell their power in a competitive 'spot market', and a public regulator sets the rules and incentives that are necessary for this electricity market to work well.

Few of these critiques take into account how industrial users themselves perceive the power problem and the efficacy of self-generation as a solution. This paper aims to do just that—it presents a case study of a self-generation system adopted by a large industrial user in India, and analyses how and why the firm devised this particular solution. This case is drawn from a broader study which examined 30 auto firms and 10 other manufacturing units in India to better understand firm-responses to poor public power supply (see Gulyani, 2001a). Methodologically, this paper differs from the majority of the power and infrastructure literature in the following ways. Unlike previous studies that have tended to take a macro-level and supply-side perspective on the power problem and its potential solutions, this paper examines these issues at the micro level and from a user/demand perspective. Further, this is one of the few studies that empirically examine how industrial firms in developing countries actually cope with—and manage to survive—serious problems in public power supply.

Specifically, this paper analyses the self-generation system adopted by India's largest car-maker—Maruti, and makes the following arguments. First, contrary to popular notions about the costs and technologies of self-generation units, Maruti's power plant is cost-effective and efficient, uses clean and safe fuels, and represents an excellent technology choice. Further, not only does Maruti's power plant offer a unit cost that is lower than the cost of public power, but it also provides power that is far superior in quality than that supplied by the public utility. Particularly striking is the finding that Maruti's low unit cost of generation is not unique—indeed, both primary and secondary data suggest that the unit costs of self-generation are far lower than previous studies suggest. Overall, industrial self-generation emerges as an effective and economical—rather than an inefficient and second-best—solution to the power problem.

Second, Maruti has devised innovative power-sharing arrangements, and the resulting system is more like that of an 'independent-power-producer' that sells power, or even a private mini-electric utility, rather than a 'captive' plant that serves only the firm's own demand for electricity. Maruti's success as a mini-electric utility suggests that industrial firms are power producers and not just consumers, and that they can compete with government utilities and specialised private-sector power producers in the emerging market for electricity.

These findings must be understood in the context of broader 'supply-side' developments that lie at the heart of—and serve as the basis for—the literature on electric power restructuring. Specifically, the restructuring literature argues that two fundamental changes are forcing revisions in how power services are provided.[1] First, changes in technology are reducing the economies of scale in power generation and distribution. And computers/information technology are creating unprecedented possibilities such as the ability to create 'spot markets' for electricity. Second, innovations in institutional arrangements and regulatory frameworks—often pioneered by and tested in advanced industrialised countries—are making it possible to 'unbundle' or separate electricity provision into its three component parts, that is, generation, transmission, and distribution. Once unbundled, it is feasible to allow different public and private entities to own each of the three components and to introduce competition in generation and distribution. Thus, it is now technically and institutionally feasible to not treat electric power as a natural monopoly and as a service that is exceptionally prone to market failure.

This research finds that the above technological and institutional changes, in combination with certain other developments, are altering not only the supply-side of the power industry but also the demand-

1. See, for example, Hunt and Shuttleworth (1996); Tenebaum, Lock, and Barker (1992); World Bank (1993, 1994); *India Infrastructure Report* (1996).

side of the equation. As scale economies in power generation fall, industrial users are finding that it is cheap to self-generate and lower their demand for a publicly provided service. Similarly, the new institutional arrangements—such as specialised 'take or pay' contracts and 'power purchase agreements' between the government and private providers—that facilitate unbundling and allow for a greater menu of supply-side solutions also create the space for a new set of user responses; thus, it is possible for industrial users to enter into new types of contracts and infrastructure deals with other firms as well as government agencies. Further, these changes have been accompanied by the emergence of sophisticated technology vendors—such as General Electric, Bharat Heavy Electricals Ltd. (BHEL), and Wartsila Diesel—that design, build, and sell generators and entire power plants tailored to the needs of individual users. These vendors are making it easier, both technically and financially, for industrial firms to switch to self-generation. In other words, the same supply-side developments that are revolutionising service provision and facilitating the creation of electricity markets are, simultaneously, altering industrial demand for public provision and old ideas about self-generation. These developments are also challenging received wisdom regarding transmission and distribution. This paper focuses on how these 'supply-side' developments are influencing demand, transforming old and new ideas about how electricity should be generated and delivered, and broadening the set of solutions available for addressing power problems in developing countries.

This paper is structured as follows. Section II presents details on the evolution and mechanics of Maruti's self-generation system. Section III analyses Maruti's unit cost of self-generation and compares it with alternative sources of electric power. Sections IV and V discuss the innovative power-sharing and wheeling system that the firm has devised, and highlight features that make the system work exceptionally well. Section VI presents the conclusions.

Maruti Starts with Generators and Upgrades to a Captive Power Plant

With an extraordinary 81 per cent market share in 1996-97, Maruti was indisputably India's largest car-maker (ACMA, 1997). Maruti was created, in 1982, as a joint venture between the Government of India (the majority share-holder) and the Suzuki Motor Company of Japan. When Maruti started full-scale production in 1984-85, the only significant infrastructure-related investment that the assembler decided to make was in six power generators. These were to provide eight megawatts (MW) of emergency back-up power when there was a disruption in supply from the public utility, Haryana State Electricity Board (HSEB). Within a few years of commencing operations, however, Maruti's managers realised that their power generators were not enough. The shortfalls in, and unreliability of, the power supply was such that Maruti was running its generators almost continuously. The assembler needed more power, and more reliable power. Maruti decided to invest in a self-generation system or a 'captive' power plant. Self-generation systems are often referred to as 'captive' plants because they are usually set up by an individual firm or institution to meet solely its own requirements.

In 1990, Maruti started work on its own power plant—a 20 MW gas turbine (GT)—which commenced operation in 1993.[2] The second and third generating units, of 20 MW capacity each, became operational in 1995 and 1997. In late 1997, a fourth 20-26 MW unit was in advanced planning stages. The capital costs of the first three units, in their respective years of construction, were about US$ 19 million for GT-1, and US$ 15 million each for GT-2 and GT-3.[3]

Even as Maruti was building up its power generating capacity, the electricity situation in the country was worsening, and the situation in Haryana, the assembler's home state, was particularly bad. The World Bank (1996: 48) notes that system losses in Haryana were reported at 33 per cent but were probably closer to 40 per cent; the

2. For much of the information on Maruti's power system, I rely on company data and multiple personal interviews with a manager in Maruti's EMU Department, that is, the unit responsible for managing the system.

3. The following exchange rates have been used: Rs. 31.36/US$ for GT-1, Rs. 33.46/US$ for GT-2, and Rs. 35.5/US$ for GT-3. These are exchange rates for the fiscal years 1993-94, 1995-96 and 1996-97, respectively (*Source*: IMF statistics cf. World Bank 1997). Expenditures on gas turbines and all other costs presented in the paper have been converted into US dollars for ease of reference (and not because they entail foreign exchange outlays). In the rest of this paper, I use an exchange rate of Rs. 35/ US$ because most of the cost data presented hereafter is for the year 1996-97.

plant load factor on thermal plants averaged 44 per cent (well below India's average); and every year 27 per cent of the distribution transformers failed because of overloading. In addition, unserved demand in Haryana increased from 9 per cent in 1993 to 25 per cent in 1996, representing a cost to the economy of at least US$ 530 million (Ibid).

Selecting Gas Turbines—A Technology that has Revolutionised Power Generation

It was in 1990 that Maruti first decided to opt for a gas turbine that would be operated in cogeneration mode. In doing so, it selected a relatively new 1980s technology that is now accredited with having revolutionised power generation and, indeed, the power industry as a whole. Hunt and Shuttleworth (1996) argue that it is because of combined cycle gas turbines (CCGTs) that generation is no longer considered a natural monopoly.

Gas turbines have several advantages. First, the capital and operating costs of gas turbine generators are low. Second, gas is a clean fuel—much cleaner, for example, than coal. Third, if operated in combined cycle or cogeneration mode, gas turbines not only produce electricity but also heat or steam or hot air that can be used for other industrial processes.[4] Fourth, gas turbines are efficient, and they can achieve even higher efficiency levels when operated in a combined cycle or cogeneration mode.[5] Fifth, they are versatile—although natural gas is clearly the superior and cheaper fuel for CCGTs, these

4. Maruti's first unit is operated in co-generation mode to provide steam and power, and achieves a 60 per cent efficiency level. The second unit is operated as a gas turbine and the efficiency level is, hence, a low 27 per cent. The fourth unit is planned as 20-26 MW steam turbine which can help raise the efficiency of the system. With the steam turbine Maruti plans to run its entire system as an 86 MW combined-cycle plant.

5. Specifically, if gas turbines are operated in a simple-cycle mode they can achieve efficiency levels of 30-38 per cent. If a steam turbine is added and they are operated in a combined-cycle mode—that is, as a CCGT—they can achieve up to 60 per cent efficiency. Full recovery of heat produced can enhance their efficiency even further (Casten 1995). By comparison, coal-fired thermal power plants achieve efficiency levels of 29-34 per cent. Casten (1995), notes, for example, that the total delivered efficiency of electricity from all US thermal plants, including nuclear, has remained at 30 per cent.

can be operated on a variety of different fuels (such as naphtha and high-speed diesel) in the event that gas is unavailable. It is relatively easy, and fast, to reconfigure these generating units to accept a different fuel. In other words, CCGTs are efficient, and versatile plants for generating electricity that can simultaneously meet an industrial user's steam or hot air requirements.[6]

Negotiating Access to Natural Gas

Before deciding on gas turbines, Maruti needed to ensure access to gas. This was an issue because neither Maruti's industrial area, located 25 km from downtown Delhi, nor the capital city of Delhi have provision for piped gas. Further, gas allocations were controlled by the Gas Authority of India Limited (GAIL), a public agency; most of the gas was earmarked for the production of subsidised fertiliser for the agricultural sector. Maruti's managers, however, reached an agreement with GAIL.[7] GAIL would build a special extension from its existing pipeline to the assembly plant. Maruti would pay not only for the gas but also for the dedicated pipeline in the form of a monthly lease fee over a period of about 10 years (that is, until the year 2002). Further, the gas would be supplied under a 'take or pay' contract—Maruti would pay for a fixed amount of gas in its contract, even if actual gas consumption was lower.[8] In January 1997, the minimum gas charge was US$ 0.8 million per month and was scheduled to increase to US$

---

6. CCGTs are the also technology of choice for newer base load plants in the United States and virtually all new capacity in the United Kingdom is in CCGTs (Tenebaum, Lock, and Barker 1992). In the United Kingdom, about 20,000 MW of gas-fired capacity has been installed since 1989, and it accounts for a third of the nation's total generation capacity of 60,000 MW (*The Economist*, 3/28/98).
7. This deal was facilitated by the following circumstance. GAIL's trunk pipeline was ready and it had gas, but there was little off-take of gas by various downstream fertiliser plants, that is, its intended customers. This discussion of the deal between Maruti and GAIL is based on personal interviews (on July 24, 1996, and February 13, 1998) with Mr. R.C. Bhargava, the Managing Director of Maruti from 1985 till August, 1997.
8. Maruti is required to pay for at least 80 per cent of the long-term commitment which, in January 1997, was 0.35 million metre cube per day (mmcd) and was scheduled to increase to 0.5 mmcd in March, 1997.

1.1 million in March, 1997.[9,10] The pipeline lease fee amounted to an additional US$ 0.17 million per month.[11]

Overall, Maruti appears to have devised a good technical solution to the power problem and used its political clout to ensure access to gas. However, commenting on the overall efficacy of the solution devised by his firm, Maruti's Japanese Joint Managing Director (JMD) noted, "[this solution to the power problem] costs us more but we've solved the problem" (Personal interview, June 14, 1996). Although in his comment the JMD appears to confirm conventional notions that captive generation is more expensive, the discussion in the following sections demonstrates that this is not the case. To evaluate the claim that it costs 'more' we need to answer the questions—compared to what? And what is Maruti's cost of generation?

Maruti's Cost of Self-Generation: Demolishing the Myth of 'High Costs'

During 1996-97, Maruti's average cost of self-generation was US$ 0.08 per unit for its 40 MW system as a whole. This includes the cost of operating two turbines (GT-1 and GT-2) but not the third because the latter came on-line in the next fiscal year.[12] An analysis of Maruti's operating expenditures on power generation in 1996-97, show that the actual variable costs amounted to an average of US$ 0.047 per unit

9. In January 1997, the price of gas for Maruti was US$ 0.10 (Rs. 3.50) per cubic metre. According to the ex-CEO of GAIL, unlike many of its other customers, Maruti does not receive any subsidy on the gas that it purchases (Personal interview, Mr. K.K. Kapur, ex-Managing Director, GAIL, July 20, 1997)

10. In September 1997, the government announced changes in its gas policy (*Economic Times*, September 16, 1997). It raised the price of gas from Rs. 1850/mcm to Rs. 2200/mcm. The government also to decided to gradually eliminate the price controls on gas and to peg domestic gas prices to international prices. The price reform was to be phased in over a three year period from 1997-2000. This meant that domestic gas prices would be adjusted more frequently (say on a monthly basis) to reflect international rates, and would be pegged at 55 per cent, 65 per cent and 75 per cent of the international prices in 1997-98, 1998-99 and 1999-2000; by April 2000, domestic gas prices would fully reflect international rates.

11. The pipeline lease fee is a fixed fee that increases at the rate of 3 per cent per year. In local currency, the construction costs of the pipeline amounted to Rs. 620 million, in 1991. In January 1997, Maruti was paying a monthly lease fee of Rs. 6.0 million for the pipeline.

12. The Indian fiscal year runs from April 1 to March 31.

(see Appendix A 3.1). According to the manager in Maruti's energy department, the fixed costs amounted to an estimated US$ 0.032 per unit.[13] Although we use US$ 0.08 as Maruti's cost, it is important to note that the assembler's cost may actually be somewhat lower.[14]

In October 1997, Maruti was negotiating with HSEB on a 'fair' price at which it could sell the surplus power from its gas turbines to the power-short state electricity grid. For these price negotiations, Maruti's energy department calculated the cost of electricity from two alternatives: (a) the annualised cost of electricity if its three gas turbines are operated as a 60 MW simple cycle plant; and (b) the annualised cost from a 86 MW combined cycle plant, assuming that a steam turbine of 26 MW is added to the system. For these calculations, Maruti assumed a (relatively high) discount rate of 12 per cent, and a (relatively short) plant life of 15 years. Further, and in contrast to the cost calculations in the previous paragraph, Maruti built in a rate-of-return of 16 per cent on its equity. The results were as follows.

The first option, a 60 MW simple cycle plant, would result in a uniform ('levellised') tariff or price of US$ 0.093 per unit. The second option—an 86 MW combined cycle plant—would result in a lower uniform tariff of US$ 0.088 per unit. That is, despite the fact that HSEB was likely to push for lower prices, Maruti started its negotiations with a unit price of US$ 0.088-0.093 or, for simplicity, US$ 0.09 per unit. Thus, Maruti's unit price of US$ 0.09 also appears to represent an upper bound and it may be possible for Maruti to supply power profitably at somewhat lower prices.

In the next three subsections, we compare Maruti's: (a) proposed price of US$ 0.09 per unit with electricity prices offered by private and public sector power generation projects at the time; (b) generation

---

13. The fixed costs were calculated by Maruti's energy department using an interest rate of 16 per cent, and the following depreciation rates: 11.31 per cent for GT-1, and 15.83 per cent for GT-2.

14. Calculation of fixed costs entails assumptions on the interest and depreciation rates, and the life of the plant—the final costs are relatively sensitive to these assumptions. Maruti's assumptions were conservative in that the assembler uses a short plant life and a high discount rate—this means that the fixed cost of US$ 0.032 may have represented an upper bound.

costs of US$ 0.08 per unit with the costs of self-generation that a World Bank supported study finds in its surveys of industrial firms in Nigeria and Indonesia; and (c) unit cost of self-generation with the price of public power, as well as the quality of power from these two sources.

The Price of Electricity from Maruti Compares Favourably with that from IPPs

The World Bank (1994; 1996) and the literature on power restructuring valourises generation projects set up by independent power producers (IPPs) such as the Enron Corporation (USA), Hopewell (Hong Kong), and Reliance Power (India). IPPs are firms that specialise in the energy business—they finance, build and operate generation plants, and usually supply electricity to the public grid under contract from the government. According to the World Bank, while IPP projects—particularly those selected through a competitive-bidding process—are an ideal way of adding capacity and ensuring that the generation segment of the power industry is competitive and efficient, self-generation systems are high-cost and short term solutions. The data presented in Table 3.1 challenges this notion; it suggests that self-generation systems set up by industrial firms like Maruti can be as competitive as IPPs on costs and that they offer some additional advantages as well.

Specifically, Table 3.1 compares Maruti's costs with the capital costs and unit prices reported for 'fast track' power generation projects that were under negotiation in India in late 1996. It shows that the average unit price from nine of these projects—proposed by specialised power producers (both private and public)—was US$ 0.07 per unit, that is, the same as what some authors (e.g. Lee, Anas and Oh, 1996) estimate to be the 'internationally competitive' price of power generation. At US$ 0.09 per unit, Maruti's proposed price is somewhat higher than most. On the other hand, it is exactly equal to at least one of these competitive IPPs (i.e. CMS-Neyveli). And Maruti's capital cost per MW is substantially—or about 40 per cent—lower than the average cost for 11 of these power generation projects.

Table 3.1 also shows that Maruti is not the only firm with competitive costs of generation and, more broadly, that generation projects do not appear to display significant economies of scale. The final three rows of Table 3.1 show that Maruti's unit cost and capital expenditure are similar to that of two other industrial firms (Daewoo Motors and Arvind Mills). Strikingly, a firm with a self-generation capacity of 4 MW reports similar (rather than substantially higher) unit costs as firms with 37 MW and 60 MW of capacity. Further, with its three 20 MW gas turbines, Maruti achieves a unit cost that is similar to, or only slightly higher than, the prices being offered by Independent Power Producers (IPPs) with generating capacities of 250 MW to 1000 MW.

Overall, Maruti's self-generation system results in capital costs and unit prices that are highly competitive relative to those offered by various 'specialised' producers including IPPs. Maruti's system and, arguably, similar generation projects developed by other industrial firms offer two additional advantages over IPPs. First, unlike most IPPs, Maruti and other industrial firms do not receive any potentially expensive 'guarantees' from sovereign and state governments that help reduce project risks and, hence, the unit prices offered by these projects. Indeed, the IPP prices shown in Table 3.1 tend to exclude the cash expenditures incurred by the government on land and infrastructure for the project, and hide the fact that the various government guarantees—such as 'take or pay' contracts and buffers against foreign exchange fluctuations—may translate into significant financial costs for the government. Second, generation projects undertaken by firms like Maruti come on-line much faster than those negotiated with IPPs. IPPs tend to take much longer not only because they are larger in size but also because they tend to involve protracted and controversial negotiations between the government and private sector energy firms.

By contrast, if the government were to buy power from industrial firms like Maruti, it would get it almost immediately, with minimal negotiations or transaction costs, without incurring any capital expenditures, and without bearing any foreign exchange risk. As we will see shortly, the HSEB did just that and paid Maruti a tariff of only US$ 0.04 per unit.

Table 3.1

Self-generation versus Fast Track Projects and IPPs under Negotiation in India in 1996

	Project	Size MW	Capital Cost Rs. Mill/MW	Price of energy Rs./KW	Price of energy US$/KW[(a)]
		(1)	(2)	(3)	(4)
1.	Spectrum-Godavri	208	36.0	1.87	0.053
2.	NTPC-Faridabad[(b)]	-	30.0	2.12	0.061
3.	Torrent-Gandhar	654	42.7	2.17	0.062
4.	GVK-Jegurupadu	216	35.2	2.21	0.063
5.	AES-Ib Valley[(c)]	420	48.2	2.39	0.068
6.	Enron-Dabhol[(d)]	695	44.9	2.40	0.069
7.	Congentrix-Mangalore[(c)]	1000	50.8	2.59	0.074
8.	NTPC-Kayamkulam[(b)]	-	32.0	2.61	0.075
9.	CMS-Neyveli	250	45.0	3.10	0.089
10.	NTPC-Gangadhar	648	35.3	-	
11.	Ashok Leyland-Vizag[(c)]	1000	58.1	-	
	Average (No. of Data Points)	566 (9)	41.7 (11)	2.38 (9)	0.068 (9)
12a.	Maruti-Option 1	86	32.0	3.10	0.089
12b.	Maruti-Option 2	60	30.2	3.25	0.093
	Industrial Self-generation Units			Unit cost (not price) of self-generation	
13.	Maruti	60	30.2	2.84	0.080
14.	Daewoo Motors	37	29.7	3.10	0.088
15.	Arvind Mills	4	30.6	2.75	0.079

Notes : (a) Assuming an exchange rate of Rs. 35/US$.

(b) Average cost escalation for all NTPC projects completed in 1991-94 was around 70 per cent.

(c) Coal Powered Projects.

(d) After removing costs of additional infrastructure, capital costs for Enron were Rs. 36.5 million/MW.

Source: Rows 1-11, Data from Ministry of Power and Dabhol Power Company, as presented in Exhibit 1, Case 9-596-100, Harvard Business School (1996). Reproduced by permission. Copyright 1996 by the President and Fellows of Harvard College.

Rows 12-15, Based on data collected from the headquarters of the respective firms.

Maruti's Low Cost of Generation is not Unique—A Comparison with Nigerian and Indonesian Firms

At first glance, the fact that Maruti and at least two other industrial firms in India can generate at a cost as low as US$ 0.08-0.09 per unit appears to be both surprising and unique. In fact, this observation seems to conflict sharply with the findings of a set of studies or industry surveys conducted under the aegis of the World Bank. This set of studies—one of few empirical research studies of firm-level infrastructure problems and solutions in developing countries—strongly supports the view that self-generation by industrial firms is substantially more expensive than the power supplied by efficient utilities and competitive private power producers. These studies, conducted in 1988 and 1992, examined infrastructure expenditures of a total of 790 firms in three countries—Nigeria, Indonesia and Thailand.[15]

Anas and Lee, the primary authors of the above set of micro-studies, find that the average cost of privately produced power is ten to thirty times higher than the price of publicly provided electricity (Anas and Lee, 1989; Lee and Anas, 1992; Lee, Anas, and Oh, 1996; Anas, Lee and Murray, 1996). However, a closer examination of Anas and Lee's data shows that firms with 'larger' generation capacities had lower costs—indeed, among the least-cost generators the unit costs were 10 to 30 times lower than the average unit costs calculated for a particular country. In their Indonesia sample the average cost of self-generation, in 1992, across 182 firms was US$ 2.14, but 23 firms (13 per cent of the sample) had generation costs in the range of US$ 0.06-0.08/unit (Lee, Anas and Oh, 1996: Table F10).[16] Similarly, in Nigeria, in 1988, 12 firms (7 per cent of 164 firms) had unit costs in the US$ 0.07-0.08 range.

---

15. The survey in Nigeria was conducted in late 1988 and covered 179 firms. Similar questionnaires were, then, developed for Indonesia and Thailand and the surveys were conducted in the latter half of 1992. The surveys covered 290 firms in Indonesia and 300 firms in Thailand. (See Lee, Anas and Oh 1996: 5-6, for information on the data).

16. 1 Mwh=1000 kWh=1000 units. A kilowatt-hour is the amount of energy consumed/produced in one hour.

It is because they average the costs over dramatically different technologies and sizes of electricity generation that Anas and Lee come up with almost astronomical costs of self-generation. In the Indonesia sample, for instance, costs are averaged across firms with generation ranging from only 4 Mwh to more than 500 Mwh of electricity. In terms of technology, they appear to be aggregating small diesel or battery-operated generators for running light bulbs or a small machine, on the one hand, with 'captive' power plants including, perhaps, CCGTs, on the other.

Anas and Lee's own data, hence, reveals a total of, at least, 35 firms (10 per cent of the combined sample) in Nigeria and Indonesia with generation costs that were similar to Maruti's. In other words, Maruti's generation cost of US$ 0.08 per unit is not an exception. Indeed, since Anas and Lee's surveys in Nigeria (1988) and Indonesia (1992), power generation technology has moved rapidly, making it increasingly more affordable for larger numbers of industrial users to install efficient and low-cost self-generation units.

Self-generation Provides Superior Quality at Low Costs

How do Maruti's costs compare with the unit price charged by the public electricity utility, and is this difference the only factor influencing the firm's 'make or buy' decision? Most of Maruti's cost-benefit calculations regarding self-generation were done when the tariff for public power was US$ 0.07 or less. That is, Maruti decided to opt for self-generation even when the cost of public power was lower than the estimated cost of self-generation. In its decision to self-generate electricity, Maruti was opting to pay slightly more than the price of public power but for a higher level of service, in particular, adequate quantity, excellent quality, and exceptional reliability of power. By 1996 HSEB had raised its tariffs to US$ 0.09 per unit and the power supply situation in the state has worsened.[17] Maruti, therefore, ended up paying less for better quality power and for a level of service that is far superior to that provided by HSEB. Overall,

17. HSEB's revised rates came into effect in August, 1996—the average tariff for industry in this area increased from US$ 0.07 to US$ 0.091 (Rs. 3.19) per unit. The tariff for industry is significantly higher than it is for agriculture and residential consumers-industry cross-subsidises consumption in other sectors.

Maruti is more quality-sensitive than price-sensitive as a power consumer, and newer self-generation technologies allow it to retain control over power quality—and, thereby, greater control over its manufacturing process—without raising costs.

Self-generation as a Preferred Alternative

In summary, I have argued that Maruti's:

a) proposed unit price of US$ 0.09—that is, the price (cost + 16 per cent return) that Maruti is trying to negotiate from the public utility (HSEB)—is somewhat higher than the estimated internationally competitive price of power generation which is US$ 0.07/unit;

b) proposed price of US$ 0.09 is equal to or higher than the actual prices offered by nine 'fast track' power projects but, in contrast to these IPP projects, Maruti's system does not entail any capital expenditures by, or potentially expensive guarantees from, government;

c) generation costs of US$ 0.08 per unit are lower than the price of public power even though the quality of power is far superior, and

d) low generation costs are not unique—indeed, they are very similar to those of about 35 other 'larger' producers in Indonesia and Nigeria studied by Anas and Lee.

These findings suggest that it makes economic sense for industrial firms in developing countries to self-generate because they gain access to good quality power—usually far superior in quality as compared to public supply—at relatively low costs. It is important to note, however, that even in advanced industrialised countries where utilities provide high quality and highly reliable power, industrial firms often find that the economics are in favour of self-generation. For example, in the United States, self-generation by industrial firms increased four-fold over 12 years—it rose from about 100 billion kWh in 1984, to an estimated 400 billion kWh in 1996 (Cambridge Research Associates cf. *The Economist*, 3/28/98: 61). In 1996, self-generation by American industry represented about 35 per cent of total industrial demand (Ibid).

Overall, industrial users in developing countries are increasingly likely to self-generate both because they cannot rely on public/private utilities for adequate quantity or quality of power and because it is getting easier and cheaper to self-generate. Indeed, self-generation may emerge as a preferred and first-best—rather than back-up or second-best—source of electric power for industrial users. The next section discusses an innovative power-sharing arrangement which indicates how the trend towards self-generation can be exploited—by governments of developing countries—to create broader social benefits.

'Excess' Generating Capacity and Maruti's Power-Sharing Arrangements

In fiscal year 1996-97, when its installed capacity was 40 MW, Maruti's generation capacity exceeded its power requirements—indeed, Maruti needed only about half of its total installed capacity. Maruti's third and fourth generating units were to add 40 MW of capacity, doubling the firm's power generating capacity, at an estimated cost of US$ 29-35 million. The planned increase in generating capacity was expected to surpass the increase in demand associated with completion of its new assembly plant (Plant III).

Why would a firm as cost-conscious as Maruti invest in expensive generating capacity that is likely to be substantially in excess of its needs?[18] The answer is that Maruti had developed power-sharing arrangements, and was intentionally expanding capacity so that it could help solve the power problems of its suppliers. In 1996-97, Maruti consumed 51 per cent of the electricity that it generated and sold the remaining or 'surplus' 49 per cent to three types of 'customers' (Figure 3.1). This means that Maruti's plant is no longer a 'captive' unit that serves only Maruti's demand. Indeed, it supplies power to: (a) its joint-venture firms that are in its immediate vicinity; (b) the state electricity grid; and (c) other firms that supply components for its cars. Maruti has a different arrangement with, and reason for serving, each one of its three customer categories.

---

18. One of the usual reasons for overcapacity is to ensure backup in case of a breakdown in one of the turbines. Theoretically, Maruti could get backup capacity from HSEB but tends not rely on it.

Figure 3.1

Maruti's Power Sharing Arrangements

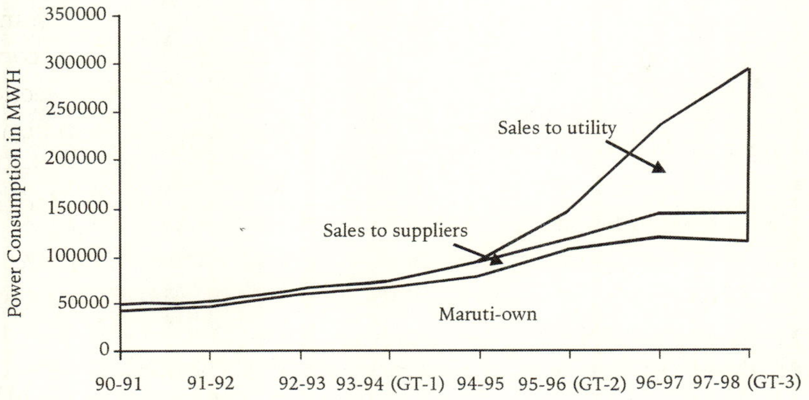

Supplying Power to Adjacent Joint Venture Component Suppliers

Maruti supplies power to five of its joint venture (JV) suppliers. These are dedicated suppliers and Maruti holds equity in these firms. In terms of location, these five firms share a boundary wall with Maruti's plant..The JVs have been receiving power from Maruti since its gas turbines first commenced operations in 1993. The fact that the JVs are both organisationally and physically a part of Maruti undoubtedly made it easier for the assembler to obtain HSEB's permission to supply electricity to these firms. According to Maruti's managers, it made sense to solve the power problems of its key partners along with its own, particularly, because their demand was relatively small. Although Maruti meets their full demand for electricity, these JVs together account for only a small fraction of the power that the assembler generates—in 1996-97, the JVs accounted for 6.0 per cent of the total electricity generated by Maruti. For this they paid a tariff of US$ 0.093 per unit or about 16 per cent more than the cost of US$ 0.08 per unit, calculated previously as the total cost of generation. The JVs consider this to be an excellent arrangement—affordable, efficient, reliable and problem-free.

Selling Electricity to the State Grid

A second customer for Maruti's excess power generation capacity is the HSEB itself. Until October, 1995, only one of Maruti's 20 MW turbines was in operation and the assembler was relying, to a small extent, on electricity from HSEB. By December, 1995, Maruti's second 20 MW gas turbine was on-line and Maruti started selling power to HSEB almost immediately; it did not idle its generating capacity at all. In August 1996, Maruti was deploying 20 MW, or half of its installed capacity, to supply power to the HSEB grid. This power was supplied 24 hours a day and Maruti was able to increase supply to 23 MW during peak load periods.[19] Given that demand outstrips supply by about 25 per cent in Haryana State as a whole, Maruti's power provides invaluable capacity to the local public grid[20]—sufficient to meet about 30 per cent of Gurgaon district's industrial power requirement. During fiscal year 1996-97, HSEB purchased a remarkable 38 per cent of Maruti's total generation—this means that HSEB bought about 90,000 Mwh of electricity from Maruti in that year. Unlike in the United States and several other countries, this is a relatively rare arrangement in India. In fact, such an option became possible only in 1995 when the government first introduced power reforms that allowed and encouraged private producers to supply power into government-owned transmission grids.[21]

Although HSEB was pleased to use Maruti's excess power to supplement its own supply, it drove a hard bargain on the price. HSEB argued that they should not have to pay anything for the power since it is like a 'sunk cost' for the firm—Maruti has a take-or-pay contract for gas, prefers to run its power plants continuously (even though it operates only two full shifts at the assembly plant), and would, hence, incur the cost whether or not it supplies the power to HSEB. Eventually, HSEB agreed to pay US$ 0.04 per unit—that is, the price

---

19. Peak periods are 9 a.m.-11.30 a.m., and 6 p.m.-8.30 p.m.

20. HSEB's capacity shortage is evident from the following example. On January 7, 1997, HSEB announced a 10 day power cut for industrial units in Faridabad that consume more than 1 MW of power. About 220 units were affected and were forced to rely entirely on their own generation during this period (*Times of India*, January 7, 1997).

21. It is worth noting that public utilities in other states have tended to oppose such arrangements.

at which it could have (theoretically) purchased power from the (capacity-starved) national grid.

This is an advantageous deal for both parties. HSEB gets access to additional and reliable power supply at a price similar to that from the national grid. In addition, the overall demand-supply gap is lowered and, thereby, so is the total investment outlay required. Maruti gets to recover at least part of its cost of power—the agreed unit rate is approximately equal to the cost of gas per unit of electricity generated. Thus, even the lowest tariff that Maruti charges from its most difficult (or most demand elastic) customer covers, at the very least, the cost of gas that Maruti has to incur, given its take-or-pay contract with GAIL. Supplying power to the public grid allows Maruti to achieve a high plant load factor and recover its sunk costs on gas. In 1997, Maruti was trying to negotiate with HSEB for better prices and for a medium-term power purchase agreement—it was arguing that HSEB should treat it as any other IPP (even though Maruti does not specialise in the power business).

Expanding the Customer Pool to include Additional Component Suppliers

In 1997, Maruti was extending its base of power customers to include a third category of users—that is, its other (non-JV) auto component suppliers located within a 15-20 km radius. This strategy offers two advantages. First, solving the power problems facing its suppliers has benefits for Maruti (see Gulyani, 2001a). Second, its component suppliers are willing and able to pay higher tariffs as compared to HSEB, and this helps Maruti recover its full costs of generation. Initially, Maruti decided to connect these suppliers to its own system because it had some excess capacity. Now, however, Maruti is well aware that it is a low-cost producer of highly reliable electricity—a valuable input—and is using this as part of a broader competitive strategy (Gulyani, 2001a; 2001b).

By March 1997, the number of component suppliers that receive power from Maruti had increased from five to 15 firms and this number continues to grow; Maruti was expecting to connect an additional 20 suppliers in the near future. In 1996-97, these firms accounted for 5.0 per cent of Maruti's total generation and paid the same tariff (US$ 0.09 per unit) as the JV firms.

India's Largest Car-Maker Runs an Efficient Mini Electric Utility

This section examines various components of the 'Maruti mini-electric utility'—the transmission and distribution arrangements, the billings and collection systems, the cost of generation and the associated tariff structure. Then, it summarises why this is an excellent system and what it appears to suggest with respect to improving power supply for industry.

Transmission and Distribution Arrangements

The plan for implementation of the transmission and distribution system agreed upon by the various players—the component suppliers, HSEB and Maruti—was as follows. Maruti would be responsible for the distribution system required to connect component suppliers in its immediate vicinity (1-2 km distance). After obtaining requisite clearances from government agencies, Maruti put in 11 KV underground cables to connect firms in its vicinity. HSEB would construct a dedicated 66 KV, 12 km long transmission line necessary for Maruti to connect more distant suppliers; it would use its eminent domain power to acquire the right-of-way for this dedicated transmission line. The capital costs of the transmission line, including the land compensation costs, would be borne entirely by Maruti and its suppliers. Once built, this transmission line would connect Maruti to a sub-station located at one supplier's factory (Rico). Again, Maruti would be responsible for the underground cables required for connecting other suppliers in this area to the sub-station at Rico—that is, the local distribution system.[22]

This arrangement represents a special case of power 'wheeling'. Usually, electricity generated by an independent power producer is 'wheeled' or transported, for a fee, over transmission lines owned or

22. Implementation progress was, however, slower than Maruti had anticipated. Although Maruti deposited the requisite funds with HSEB in early 1996, in November 1997, HSEB was yet to complete the line. The delays were, allegedly, partly due to problems with land acquisition, and partly due to the fact that the transmission line crosses several jurisdictions and involves different HSIDC offices.

managed by an entity that is different from the power producer herself.[23] In this case, however, the private firms have opted for a dedicated line (a capital-expensive alternative)—rather than opting to wheel electricity over the HSEB grid for a small charge—to ensure that the quality of electricity remains high. If Maruti were to input good quality power into the public grid, its customers at the other end would not get the same good quality electricity. This is because the quality of power that a user receives depends on the quality of the transmission infrastructure and on the quantity and quality of power in the public grid as a whole. (For example, at peak demand the grid is overloaded and voltage in the entire system tends to drop.)

How Component Suppliers Buy a Share of the Maruti Power System

Maruti and its industrial customers share the capital cost for both the distribution lines put in by Maruti and for the dedicated transmission line constructed by HSEB. These industrial customers will pay Maruti directly for the initial capital costs and, subsequently, for the electricity that they consume. In other words, the component suppliers are buying a share of the total power project in proportion to their demand. Maruti and all of these industrial firms, then, get access to better infrastructure and they actually pay the direct costs of the capital investments and service improvements.[24]

---

23. Tenebaum, Lock, and Barker (1992) define wheeling as "the unbundled transportation of electricity over high and low voltage lines." They note that in the United States, it is categorised into "retail" and "wholesale" wheeling and the category depends on the customer that receives the electricity. In the US, the policy debate on wheeling has been limited to (or focused on) wholesale wheeling. In Europe, wheeling is referred to as third-party access (TPA) and encompasses both retail and wholesale wheeling. Both forms of wheeling are under intense debate in Europe.

24. The following serves as an example of how and why the deal is attractive for Maruti's component suppliers. It also provides some insight into how the public electric supply system currently tends to work or, rather, not work. KML is a seats supplier located about 15 km from Maruti's plant. KML started operations in 1994, but does not have an electricity connection from HSEB. There is a waiting list for HSEB connections, and because KML is located in a non-priority area—it is not located, for example, in a government-owned or zoned industrial complex—it is not astute to wait around for one. Thus, at the very outset the management decided to purchase three generators of 380 KV each, and start production. In October 1997, the firm was continuing to rely on these generators, which operate on high-speed-diesel, for 100 per cent of its consumption.

contd...

Billings, Collections and Enforcement

In this arrangement, Maruti serves as a generating company and a distributor. It also controls billings and collections and has designed the system to reduce risk of non-payment and minimise collection costs. Electricity dues are directly deducted from the payments that the suppliers are to receive from Maruti for the auto components that they supply. At the same time, Maruti also has an incentive to provide reliable service to its component suppliers because any disruptions at supplier plants can directly, and almost immediately, hurt production planning and quality at its own assembly plant (see KML example in footnotes). Maruti has also been successful in collecting dues from HSEB, despite the fact that the latter, like most other SEBs, is in poor financial condition. It has done so by establishing a revolving credit mechanism and threatening to cut off supply if HSEB defaults on payments—it seems that HSEB perceives this to be a credible threat (Personal interview, Mr. Bhargava, ex-MD, February 13, 1998).

The Tariff Structure, Revenues from Electricity Sales, and a 'Cross-subsidy' for HSEB

In 1996-97, Maruti consumed 51 per cent of its total generation and sold the remaining 49 per cent—about 116,000 Mwh of electricity —to HSEB and its component suppliers. Its industrial customers accounted for 22 per cent of the total electricity sold and for 38 per cent of Maruti's revenue from electricity sales. The HSEB accounted

...contd...

Under the Maruti electricity deal, KML would be one of the firms that is connected from the sub-station at Rico. KML would pay an estimated US$ 14,000-20,000 as its share of the capital costs of the transmission line and generation units. In addition, the firm had already incurred a capital cost of US$ 14,000 for transformers and cables required at or near its own plant. The firm sees this US$ 28,000-34,000 as the capital cost of connecting to, and buying a share in, the Maruti system. The firm will pay Maruti about US$ 0.09/unit for the power, but knows that the prices will be adjusted upwards as and when fuel or other costs rise. It is more than willing to incur these costs, first, because Maruti already has a proven track-record in delivering good quality power. Second, KML knows that Maruti has all the incentives to minimise disruption in service and maintain the quality—any disruptions at KML directly translate in to disruptions in Maruti's own production plans. The reason for the latter point is that KML is one of Maruti's two seat-suppliers and it supplies on a just-in-time basis which means that there is only a few hours of buffer inventory for seats at Maruti's own plant.

for as much as 78 per cent of the total electricity sold and 62 per cent of the assembler's sales revenue. Maruti charged its industrial customers US$ 0.093 per unit, or about 16 per cent more than its generation cost of US$ 0.08. By comparison, HSEB paid a tariff of US$ 0.043, about 10 per cent less than Maruti's variable cost of generation of US$ 0.047 per unit.

Overall, Maruti recovered the fixed and variable cost of generation on the power that it sold to its component suppliers, and appears to have designed a 'cross-subsidy' that helped recover the full variable cost of the electricity that it sold to HSEB. In other words, Maruti does better at recovering the costs of its power infrastructure than, perhaps, most electric utilities not only in India but the entire developing world. As the World Bank (1994: 47) notes, public electric utilities in the developing world are, on average, net money losers—their revenues cover only about 60 per cent of their total cost.

Summarising the Features of and Insights from the Maruti 'Model'

In summary, Maruti and HSEB have put together a service production, delivery and collection arrangement that is innovative both in financial and institutional terms. First, the industrial users pay for the direct capital costs of improvements in (or expansion of) the physical infrastructure to gain access to improved service. Second, the tariff levels are such that the industrial users pay the full fixed and variable costs of power generation and the government pays, at least, the cost of fuel for surplus power directed to its grid. Indeed, the industrial users appear to be cross-subsidising the HSEB and its poorer customers—this ensures that the arrangement is financially sustainable. Third, the billings and collections arrangement with its industrial customers ensures a 100 per cent collection of user fees (or electricity bills), at little additional cost to Maruti. Fourth, it allows Maruti to achieve a plant load factor of about 70 per cent—comparable to that of the National Thermal Power Corporation, equal to or better than the average achieved by the best performing state electricity boards, and far better than the all-India average of 55 per cent for the 19 SEBs (*India Infrastructure Report 1996*, Vol.3: 92).

On a broader level, the Maruti case challenges some widely held notions regarding transmission and distribution systems, and the appropriate institutional mechanisms for restructuring service delivery. First, it brings into question conventional ideas about the high costs and large scale economies entailed in transmission and distribution and suggests that entry barriers may be lower than previously anticipated. Second, it indicates that it may not be easy to maintain quality of power in an unbundled system where different entities control generation, transmission and distribution. Third, it shows that certain industrial users are highly quality sensitive and new developments in the power sector are making it feasible for them to invest in their own transmission and distribution networks to ensure access to high quality power. From an electricity reforms perspective, these findings raise important questions—whether service provision can be unbundled without sacrificing quality, who should be allowed to compete in the electricity market, and how the demand for exceptionally high quality electricity should be met.

Conclusion

In contrast to previous studies that find the average cost of self-generation to be several times higher than the price of public power, this research finds that Maruti and some other firms in India are able to self-generate electricity at unit costs that are comparable to, and often lower than, the price of public power for industrial users. Not only does self-generation provide electricity at relatively low costs, but also provides electricity that is far superior in quality and reliability as compared to that supplied by most public utilities.

The key reason why these firms are able to generate at low costs is that economies of scale in generation have fallen dramatically and are continuing to fall; a technological revolution is well underway.[25] These changes in technology—combined with the emergence of sophisticated equipment vendors that design, build, and sell generators and power plants tailored to the needs of individual users—are making it easier and cheaper for firms to opt for self-generation. Consequently, an increasing number of industrial firms in

---

25. See *The Economist* (August 5-11, 2000); the cover story of that issue proclaims the arrival of the "The Electric Revolution" and argues that it may well be as exciting as the one that has occurred in telecommunications

developing and advanced industrialised economies are shifting to self-generation as their preferred option.

From a public policy perspective, however, Maruti's innovative power-sharing arrangement is a solution that works significantly better than captive self-generation. The sharing arrangement minimises the problem of idle generation capacity and, thereby, offsets a major drawback associated with captive generation. More importantly, the power-sharing system creates benefits that spillover to other firms and stakeholders.

Specifically, the power-sharing and wheeling arrangements that Maruti has developed with its auto component suppliers and the Haryana State Electricity Board result in a 'win-win' situation for all players. The sharing mechanisms help reduce the unreliability in Maruti's supply chain and, thereby, improve its competitiveness. They also improve the load factors and lower the generation costs of Maruti's power system. The auto component suppliers get access to exceptionally high quality power and reliable service at prices that are similar to that from the public utility. For the state electricity board, the deal reduces the shortfall between supply and demand in its system – it directly meets the demand of the industrial firms that are part of the power-sharing arrangement, and it supplements the capacity-starved public grid at a low unit price. In contrast to a contract with a specialised independent power producer, HSEB has gained access to power without waiting for several years for the project to come on-line, with minimal negotiations or transaction costs, without incurring any capital expenditures, and without bearing any foreign exchange risk. Public utilities and state electricity boards would do well to lock-in such sources of electricity with power purchase agreements. On a broader level, this case suggests that industrial firms are important players in the electricity business not only because they are large customers but also because they can compete with public utilities and specialised private sector power producers in the emerging market for electricity.

On their part, governments can exploit the trend towards self-generation to create broader social benefits. Governments can leverage private firm-level investments in power generation to increase capacity in the public grid. They can also facilitate power-sharing or 'wheeling' among firms and use it as one mechanism for meeting niche demand for exceptionally high quality power. Indeed, the Maruti power-sharing arrangement represents a highly effective 'model' that policy-makers and other firms can seek to emulate and replicate. It suggests, for example, that it may be feasible and desirable to treat industrial cluster as independent infrastructure districts and allot service provision franchises either for a package of services or for a single service, such as power (Gulyani, 2001a). The model offers, perhaps, an easier step towards ameliorating the power problem and catalysing reform in the power sector in India—'easier' as compared to waiting for a radical restructuring of public utilities and a disbanding of the state electricity boards altogether.

References

ACMA (Auto Component Manufacturers Association) (1977). *Automotive Industry of India: Facts and Figures, 1996-97.* Delhi.

Anas, Alex and Kyu Sik Lee (1989). "Infrastructure Investment and Productivity: The Case of Nigerian Manufacturing", *Review of Urban and Regional Development Studies,* 2.

Anas, Alex, Kyu Sik Lee, and Michael Murray (1996). "Infrastructure Bottlenecks, Private Provisions, and Industrial Productivity: A Study of Indonesian and Thai Cities", Policy Research *Working Paper* 1603. Washington DC: The World Bank. May.

Casten, Thomas (1995). "Whither Electric Generation? A Different View", *The Energy Daily,* September 7.

Diamond, Derek and Nigel Spence (1989). *Infrastructure and Industrial Costs in British Industry.* London: H.M.S.O.

Economic Times (1997). "Gas Pricing Deregulated", *Economic Times,* Delhi, September 16.

———. (1997). "Natural Gas to Cost 22 per cent more from Today", *Economic Times,* Delhi, September 30.

Government of India (1996). *Economic Survey 1995-96.* Delhi: Ministry of Finance.

———. (1996). *India Infrastructure Report: Policy Imperatives for Growth and Welfare.* Report of Expert Group on The Commercialisation of Infrastructure Projects (Dr. Rakesh Mohan, Chair) for The Ministry of Finance, Volumes 1, 2 and 3. Delhi: Thomson Press.

Gramlich, E.M. (1994). "Infrastructure Investment: A Review Essay", *Journal of Economic Literature,* Vol. XXXII, pp.1176-1196, September.

Gulyani, Sumila (2001a). *Innovating with Infrastructure: The Automobile Industry in India,* Basingstoke and New York: Palgrave-Macmillan.

———. (2001b). "Effects of Poor Transportation on Lean Production and Industrial Clustering: Evidence from the Indian Auto Industry", *World Development,* Vol. 29(7), July 2001.

———. (1999). "Innovating with Infrastructure: How India's Largest Carmaker Copes with Poor Electricity Supply", *World Development,* Vol. 27(10), October.

Harvard Business School (1996). *Enron Development Corporation: The Dabhol Power Project in Maharashtra, India (B)* by Krishna G. Palepu, V. Kasturi Rangan, and Sarayu Srinivasan. Case 9-596-100. Boston, MA: Harvard Business School. December 16.

Hunt, Sally and Graham Shuttleworth (1996). *Competition and Choice in Electricity.* Chichester and New York: John Wiley & Sons.

Jimenez, Emmanuel (1995). "Human and Physical Infrastructure: Public Investment and Pricing Policies in Developing Countries", in J. Behrman and T.N. Srinivasan (eds.), *Handbook of Development Economics* 3. Amsterdam: Elseiver.

Lee, Kyu Sik, Alex Anas and Gi-Taik Oh (1996). "Costs of Infrastructure Deficiencies in Manufacturing in Indonesia, Nigeria, and Thailand", *Policy Research Working Paper* 1604. Washington DC: The World Bank. May.

Lee, Kyu Sik, and Alex Anas (1992). "Costs of Deficient Infrastructure: The Case of Nigerian Manufacturing", *Urban Studies,* Vol. 29(7).

Maruti Udyog Limited (1996, 1997). *Company Annual Reports.* Delhi: Maruti Udyog Limited.

Tenebaum, B.T., R. Lock and J. Barker (1992). "Electricity Privatisation: Structural, Competitive and Regulatory Options", *Energy Policy,* December.

The Economist (1998). "The Electricity Business: Power to the People", *The Economist,* March 28-April 3.

———. (2000). "The Electric Revolution", *The Economist*, August 5-11.

Venkataramani, Raja (1992). *Japan Enters Indian Industry: The Maruti-Suzuki Joint Venture.* Delhi: Radiant Publishers.

Wall Street Journal (1995). "Enron Project is Scrapped by India State", *Wall Street Journal,* August 4.

World Bank (1993). "The World Bank's Role in The Electric Power Sector", A World Bank *Policy Paper*. Washington DC: The World Bank. December.

———. (1994). *World Development Report: Infrastructure for Development.* New York: Oxford University Press.

———. (1996). *India: Five Years of Stabilisation and the Challenges Ahead,* A World Bank Country Study. Washington DC: The World Bank. December.

———. (1997). *India. 1997 Economic Update: Sustaining Rapid Growth*, Report No. 16506-IN. Washington DC: The World Bank. May 30.

Appendix A-3.1

Maruti's Power System: Output, Costs and Sales (1996-97)

	Apr. 1996	*May 1996*	*June 1996*	*July 1996*	*Aug. 1996*	*Sept. 1996*	*Oct. 1996*	*Nov. 1996*	*Dec. 1996*	*Jan. 1997*	*Feb. 1997*	*Mar. 1997*
A Maruti Consumption-MWH	7188	11138	11766	12677	12165	10877	8483	8535	9045	8977	8518	10408
B Sale to Joint Venture Suppliers-MWH	1020	1163	1126	1267	1033	1151	1100	1105	1103	1133	1041	1046
C Sale to Other Suppliers-MWH	848	967	1148	1198	1298	1006	939	1022	975	1052	854	986
D Sale to HSEB-MWH	4094	5079	4990	5363	5445	5144	6204	10189	14021	3954	12664	13064
E Actual Generation (A+B+C+D)-MWH	13151	18348	19029	20505	19942	18179	16726	20851	25144	15117	22658	25583
F Projected Generation GT (2X19.30)-MWH	20844	28718	27792	28718	28718	27792	25013	27792	28718	27792	25939	28718
G Standby Diesel Generator (actual)-MWH	915	672	96	3	25	5	46	793	990	2002	1187	1187
H Total Projected Generation (F+G)-MWH	21759	29390	27888	28721	28743	27797	25059	28585	29709	29794	27126	29905
I Plant Load Factor[2]	60%	62%	68%	71%	69%	65%	67%	73%	85%	51%	84%	86%
J Gas Consumption-NM3	5655657	7876519	8484507	8964003	8677606	8328346	7596755	8870391	10484715	3100316	9320198	10398583
K Gas Charges-Rs./NM3	4.10	3.68	3.47	3.44	3.46	3.48	3.71	3.03	2.94	2.87	2.78	2.69
L Expenditure on Gas (J*K)-Rs.'000	23207	29003	29434	30826	30039	28956	28154	31600	35443	14819	31965	38504

Contd...

...contd...

	Apr. 1996	*May 1996*	*June 1996*	*July 1996*	*Aug. 1996*	*Sept. 1996*	*Oct. 1996*	*Nov. 1996*	*Dec. 1996*	*Jan. 1997*	*Feb. 1997*	*Mar. 1997*
M Expenditure on Diesel-Rs. '000	1769	1312	210	19	86	18	118	1911	2185	26482	2439	2827
N Gas+Diesel expenditure (I+K)-Rs. '000	24976	30315	29644	30845	30125	28974	28272	33511	37628	41301	34404	41330
O Fuel cost per unit (N/E)-Rs./kwh	1.90	1.65	1.56	1.50	1.51	1.59	1.69	1.61	1.50	2.73	1.52	1.62
P Revenue from HSEB-Rs. '000	6141	7619	7484	8045	8168	7716	9306	15284	21031	6228	19946	20576
Q Revenue from Suppliers-Rs. '000	6072	6923	7389	8012	7575	7010	6627	6912	6755	7103	6158	6605
R Total Sales Revenue (P+Q)-Rs. '000	12214	14542	14873	16056	15743	14727	15933	22196	27786	13331	26103	27181
Projected Peak Load-MW			40.7			45.7						
Actual Peak Load-MW			38.1				35.0	46.7	45.0			

Note: HSEB paid a price of Rs. 1.5/kWh and suppliers paid Rs. 3.25/kWh.

Source: Company Data.

4

Growth and Non-traded Sectors

The Scope of India's Infrastructure

AVIK CHAKRABARTI

Introduction

The significance of non-traded sectors, discovered by Ohlin (1929) in his criticism of Keynes' (1929) views on the German transfer problem[1] and subsequently illuminated by many prominent economists, continues to draw our attention even in today's increasingly integrating world. There exists a host of services (e.g. infrastructure, education, health, utilities etc.) that are not traded across the borders, either because they simply cannot be traded or because barriers (economic and/or political) to trade are prohibitive. Services liberalisation offers a potential source of welfare gain as the performance of service sectors and policies affecting their performance are likely to have important consequences for trade volumes, the distributional effects of trade, and economy-wide growth.[2] With this backdrop, in this paper, I will focus on the incentives and constraints

1. Keynes and Ohlin agreed that a transfer would inevitably result in a re-allocation of resources between the traded and non-traded sectors. However, Keynes had argued that the presence of non-traded sectors would shift resources away from the non-traded sector into the exporting sector to exacerbate further the donor's terms of trade deterioration as a result of a transfer. Ohlin, in contrast, saw no reason for a movement in the terms of trade and expected only opposing changes in the prices of traded sectors relative to those of nontraded sectors for the donor and recipient.

2. The competitiveness of firms in open economies is determined in part by access to low-cost and high quality services. One of the stylised facts of economic development is that the share of services in GDP and employment rises as per capita incomes increase. In the lowest-income countries, services generate about 35 per cent of GDP. This rises to over 70 per cent of national income and employment in OECD countries.

that India's infrastructure seemingly projects on her growth prospects.[3]

The rest of the paper is organised as follows. In the next section, I discuss the economics of non-traded sectors with emphasis on infrastructure services. Section III outlines the evolution and current state of India's infrastructure *vis-à-vis* the rest of the world. In section IV, I describe the data used for analyses, explain the econometric method, and report the results. Section V concludes.

The Economics of Non-traded Sectors

The services of non-traded sectors must have their markets cleared locally, and in this respect, differ fundamentally from traded sectors[4] for which local excess demand or supplies can be accommodated in the world markets. Services that are traded internationally can be provided in another country at some cost. In principle, therefore, the providers from different countries compete with each other in such traded sectors. In contrast, non-traded services have to be provided locally and do not involve competition among international providers. In addition, non-traded services such as infrastructure—including telecommunications, electricity, water and sewerage, natural gas, and transportation—reflect some unique economic characteristics, which make them a natural target for government intervention yet render them difficult to regulate in the public interest. These features[5] include a) extensive economies of scale and scope that generally lead to market concentration and inhibit competition; b) large sunk costs relative to fixed and variable costs; and c) services deemed essential to a broad range of users, making their provision and pricing politically sensitive.

While there is no denying the fact that 'it was all in Marshall', traditional economic theory postulated growth as a function of

3. Ianchovichina and Kacker (2005) forecast that the largest real per capita GDP growth dividend, for countries (including India) that together account for nearly 80 per cent of the developing world's GDP, is likely to come from sustained improvement in infrastructure.

4. Chakrabarti (2004) identifies the role of asymmetries in adjustment costs for traded sectors.

5. See also Spiller and Savedoff (1999).

increases in the quantity and productivity of primary inputs with negligible role to non-traded services. The significance of non-traded services in the growth and development of an economy, that has increasingly become evident in international data, continues to be debated by many. An important economic characteristic of many such services is their 'facilitating' (i.e. supporting finer specialisation) role. The growth of intermediation services is an important determinant of overall economic growth and development as much of this intermediation activity facilitates transactions through space (transport, telecommunications etc.).

Several empirical studies have investigated the linkages between services, services liberalisation, and economic growth. Empirical explorations of the effects of infrastructure on growth have been characterised by ambiguous (countervailing signs) results with little robustness.[6] A number of explanations of the contradictory findings have been proposed. These range from the crowding out of private by public sector investment, non-linearities generating the possibility of infrastructure overprovision, simultaneity between infrastructure provision and growth, and the possibility of multiple channels of influence between infrastructure and productivity improvements.[7]

Aschauer (1989a, 1989b), Easterly and Rebelo (1993), Canning *et al.* (1994), Sanchez-Robles (1998) have found high returns to infrastructure investment. Among relatively recent contributions, Fink *et al.* (2002) assessed the impact of policy reform in telecommunications on sectoral performance using a panel data set for 86 developing countries across Africa, Asia, the Middle East, Latin America and the Caribbean over the period 1985 to 1999. They observed that both privatisation and competition led to significant improvements in performance, but that a comprehensive reform programme, involving both of these policies supported by an independent regulator, produced the largest gains. Esfahani and Ramirez (2003) provide cross-country estimates reflecting that the contribution of infrastructure services to GDP is substantial and, in general, exceeds the cost of provision of those services. Eschenbach

6. See Munnell (1992), Tatom (1993) and Gramlich (1994).

7. See Fedderke and Bogetic (2006).

and Hoekman (2006) investigated the impact of changes in services policy, including liberalisation, on economic performance over this period for a sample of 20 transition economies during 1990–2004. They found that changes in policies towards infrastructure services, including telecommunications, power and transport, are statistically significant explanatory variables for the post-1990 economic performance of the transition economies in the sample. Arnold *et al.* (2006), in a firm-level study focusing on Africa that uses data from over 1,000 firms in 10 sub-Saharan African economies, found a statistically significant positive relationship between firm performance and the performance of service input industries for which data was collected through enterprise surveys (including access to communications and electricity). Fedderke and Bogetic (2006) analysed a panel data of South African industries during 1970–2000 to conclude that the impact of infrastructure capital on growth is not only positive, but of economically meaningful magnitudes.

The Global Positioning of India's Infrastructure

For much of the 20th century, India, like most countries, relied on government ownership and regulation to promote socially equitable access to infrastructure services using mechanisms such as non-exploitive pricing, non-discriminatory coverage, and universal service. Reflecting infrastructure's strategic importance and concerns about monopoly power, it was widely believed that these sectors could not be entrusted to the signals, motivations, and penalties of free markets. In addition, most governments were convinced that state resources were required to finance large investments in service coverage. Infrastructure's enormous economic importance, a desire to protect the public interest in industries supplying essential services, and concerns about private monopoly power led governments to conclude that control over these services could not be entrusted to the motivations and penalties of free markets. But in recent decades this consensus has changed, resulting in far reaching restructuring, privatisation, and other reforms of crucial infrastructure sectors and services.

During the 1950s vertically integrated, state-owned infrastructure became the industry model for electricity, telecommunications, water, natural gas, and railways and other transportation services. Since the early 1980s, however, the monolithic model has proven increasingly unsuited to dramatically changing conditions in both industrial and developing countries. As a result there has been a worldwide reassessment, led by the examples set by the US, UK and the EU, of public policies for infrastructure. In a globalised economy, poorly performing state-owned infrastructure providers were increasingly seen as constraining economic growth and undermining international competitiveness. Developing countries simply could not continue to absorb the fiscal burden of these enterprises. It became evident to policymakers that the problems of public enterprises could be solved only by implementing radical structural changes and realigning the roles of the government and the private sector. Proponents of deregulation argued that unleashing competition among service providers would lower inflation and restore productivity growth. At the same time, concerns about the energy crises and environmental protection facilitated the introduction of economically efficient pricing, which was expected to discourage wasteful consumption.[8]

As such, balancing the roles of the private[9] and public sectors (which presumes an effective legal and regulatory framework, strong political will demonstrated by a clear government commitment for a long-term partnership, transparency in the procurement bidding process, a positive lending environment and guaranteed cost recovery) has become an integral part of nearly every infrastructure reform programme around the globe. India's Prime Minister Dr. Manmohan Singh has recently (2006) confirmed his government's commitment to developing infrastructure in India through the use of public-private

8. See also Joskow and Noll (1994), Noll (1999) and Kahn (2001).
9. See Chakrabarti and Heywood (2004) for a spatial model in which a foreign firm and local government behave strategically in setting a local equity requirement. Contrary to simple intuition, larger equity requirements may increase economic efficiency but this conclusion is highly sensitive to the vertical structure of the foreign firm. When the foreign firm has monopoly power in both foreign (upstream) and domestic (downstream) markets the optimal equity requirement is zero. Surprisingly, the introduction of domestic competition upstream causes the government to adopt an LER which lowers economic efficiency.

partnerships (PPPs):[10] "It is imperative that we explore avenues for increasing investment in infrastructure through a combination of public investment, public-private partnerships and occasionally, exclusive private investments wherever feasible... Among these, the PPP approach is best suited for the infrastructure sector."[11]

India experienced an economic growth of 9.3 per cent for the first quarter of the 2006–07 fiscal year.[12] In comparison, the figures released by the Ministry of Commerce & Industry on the growth of core infrastructure industries in May 2006–07 recorded a slowdown in production. India's current state of infrastructure reveals many weak links that threaten to hobble its economic growth. For instance, Indian

---

10. One variant of PPPs is a "build-operate-transfer" arrangement in which the private company operates a toll road or other facility until it has recovered its investment and made a profit, then turns it over to the government. In other cases, the builder gets a partial capital subsidy from the government. An example is the new 62-mile, six-lane expressway that replaced a potholed stretch of National Highway 8 from Jaipur in the Rajasthan desert to Bombay. The project, led by Larsen & Toubro Ltd. and Hyderabad's GVK Industries, cost $141 million, with $49 million provided by the government.

11. There are several issues confronting a complete transfer of financing infrastructure from the public to the private sector. First, the ability of the private sector to respond to the needs of low-income households is limited given the profit-oriented nature of the former. Without some form of targeted subsidies, the poor will barely have access to basic infrastructure. Second, financing infrastructure is often a long-term process when compared with other sectors of the economy. Consequently, the private sector may be unwilling to undertake such risk, as the long gestation period may adversely affect returns on investment. Third, the private sector does not adequately account for externalities associated with infrastructures except when government financing is involved. As such, the public sector is likely to continue to be a major player in the provision of infrastructure.

12. Out of the 17 industry sectors, 8 sectors have posted higher growth in production. These sectors include other manufacturing industries (32.3 per cent), basic metal and alloy industries (20.5 per cent), transport equipment (22.0 per cent), machinery and equipments (15.4 per cent), non-metallic mineral products (15.1 per cent), paper products (12.0 per cent), rubber plastic petroleum and coal products (8.7 per cent) and man made textile products (7.3 per cent). Of the remaining 9 industry sectors, growth fell in 4 sectors namely beverages and tobacco, cotton textiles, textile products and chemical products while the other 5 sectors wood, leather, jute, food products and metal products registered negative growth. All of the use based industry categories, the capital goods, basic goods and intermediates achieved higher growth rates of 22.9 per cent, 8.8 per cent and 9.1 per cent respectively compared to the growth rates registered in the corresponding quarter of the last fiscal year. While there has been a sharp slowdown in the production of consumer non-durables since the beginning of 2006-07, higher growth in production could be seen in the consumer durables category during the first three months of the current fiscal year.

cities currently contribute as much as 70 per cent of her GDP and over 500 million people are expected to live in urban India by 2020. However, about 15 per cent of the urbanites do not have access to safe drinking water and about 50 per cent are not covered by sanitary facilities. The Central Public Health Engineering (CPHEEO) has estimated the requirement of funds for 100 per cent coverage of the urban population under safe water supply and sanitation services by the year 2021 at US$ 41.16 billion. Estimates by Rail India Technical and Economic Services (RITES) indicate that the amount required for urban transport infrastructure investment in cities with a population 100,000 or more during the next 20 years would be of the order of US$ 49.28 billion.

India's infrastructure has been subject to chronic underinvestment causing significant deterioration in service quality and seriously undermining providers' ability to respond to new demands and expand service. Compared with China's infrastructure spending of 20 per cent of its GDP, India currently spends only about 6 per cent. It is not surprising that Dr. Shankar Acharya, former Chief Economic Adviser to the Government of India, is convinced that that India is yet to be in "China's league": electricity production in China is nearly 3 times higher than in India; tonne-kilometres of freight hauled on railways is about 4.5 times greater; air-freight tonne-kilometres flown in China is nearly 10 times higher; container traffic shipped through ports is an astonishing 16 times more in China.[13] In order for India to maintain its current growth momentum, the Confederation of Indian Industry (CII) estimates that the nation calls for US$ 330 billion of investment on infrastructure over the next five to seven years.

In a recent (2006) interview, Dr. Montek Singh Ahluwalia, Deputy Chairman of India's Planning Commission, anticipated that resources can flow into India's infrastructure in the form of foreign direct investment (FDI) or from domestic savings or through market borrowings. If the nation reflects the right environment, all the

---

13. There are reasons for some to believe that India is likely to emerge as a more fertile ground for investment than China: India is a functioning democracy with respect for property rights and the rule of law; India is now emerging on the global stage and playing classic balance of power politics; India's capital markets are better organised than China's; and India is a relatively youthful nation with half of its population under 25 years of age.

domestic investment can be absorbed in infrastructure, which will make room for FDI in other sectors and vice versa. Hence, he pointed toward the need for two distinct yet related kinds of policies: the general policies that will make India an attractive destination for investment[14] and another, more specific, one for infrastructure.

Data, Estimation and Results

In this section, I will employ recently developed techniques of multivariate heterogeneous panel cointegration analyses to capture the association between growth and infrastructure. The data set used in this analysis contains annual observations spanning 78 countries over the period from 1961 to 2000 and is extracted from the *World Development Indicators (WDI), 2005* and *Penn World Tables* (Table 5.6.). Summers and Heston's (1991) Penn World Table summary assessments of the quality of countries' data are used to identify countries with the lowest quality (D-graded) data.

The first step in applying any cointegration technique is to test for non-stationarity in the data. For this the cross-sectionally augmented Im-Pesaran-Shin (CIPS) panel unit-root test[15], based on the simple averages of the individual cross sectionally augmented Dickey-Fuller statistics, is used. The main advantages of this approach are a) it incorporates potential cross-section dependence; and b) it allows (since it does not directly pool the autoregressive parameter in the unit root regression) for the possibility of heterogeneous coefficients of the autoregressive parameters under the alternative hypothesis that the process does not contain a unit root. To use the CIPS test the following equations are estimated:

---

14. See Chakrabarti (1999. 2001, 2003) on a host-country perspective on the determinants and spatial distribution of FDI in a strategic environment.

15. See Pesaran (2005). The CIPS test statistic is a generalisation of the IPS test statistic, originally proposed by Im, Pesaran, and Shin (2003), that incorporates potential cross-section dependence. Chang (2002) had proposed a non-linear instrumental variable approach to deal with the cross section dependence of a general form and established that the individual Dickey-Fuller (DF) or the Augmented Dickey-Fuller (ADF) statistics are asymptotically independent when an integrable function of the lagged dependent variables are used as instruments. In this paper I have chosen not to implement this test since it can be shown, using Monte Carlo techniques, that Chang's test is grossly over-sized for moderate degrees of cross section dependence even when the sample contains a relatively small number of countries.

(1A) $\Delta Y_{it} = \mu_{1i} + \lambda_{1i} Y_{i,t-1} + \theta_{1i} f_{1t} + \varepsilon_{1it}$

(1B) $\Delta X_{it} = \mu_{2i} + \lambda_{2i} X_{i,t-1} + \theta_{2i} f_{2t} + \varepsilon_{2it}$

$(i = 1,2,...,N;\ t = 1,2,...,T)$

where Y is the residual[16] per capita GDP growth rate and X is the proxy for infrastructure (measured by the number of telephone mainlines per capita in a country[17]), f_t is the unobserved common effect proxied by a linear combination of the current and lagged cross-sectional averages of the dependent variable and ε_{it} is the individual specific (idiosyncratic) error.

The null hypothesis $(\lambda_i = 0, \forall i = 1,2,...,N)$ of a unit root is then tested (against the alternative hypothesis: $(\lambda_i < 0, i = 1,2,...,N_1)$ and $\lambda_i = 0, i = N_1 + 1, N_1 + 2,....,N)$ using the CIPS statistic:

$$CIPS(N,T) = \frac{1}{N}\sum_{i=1}^{N} t_i(N,T)$$

where t_i (N,T) i is the cross-sectionally augmented Dickey-Fuller test statistic for the i-th country. In the next step γ is estimated from the following equation and the null of no cointegration is tested:

(2) $Y_{it} = \alpha_i + \beta_t + \gamma X_{it} + e_{it}$

$(i=1,2,....,N;\quad t=1,2,...,T)$

16. The residual is obtained from regressing per-capita GDP growth rate on education, financial depth, openness, government burden and inflation. Education is measured as the ratio of total secondary enrollment to the population 25 years or older. Financial depth is computed as the ratio of M2 to GDP. Openness is the residual of a regression of the log of the trade (exports and imports) to GDP ratio on the logs of area and population, and dummies for oil exporting and landlocked countries. Government burden is measured with the ratio of government consumption to GDP. There is a host of other variables (political instability, life expectancy at birth, distance from the equator and shares of primary products in GDP) that have appeared in the empirical studies as determinants of growth but turned out to be statistically insignificant in our regression.

17. Telecommunications services offer a source of natural experiment for infrastructure since they have historically been provided through government monopolies and been an important source of state revenue. As a result of changes in telecommunications technologies the 'natural monopoly' argument for state ownership or control has been eroded, and many countries now allow competition, but often restrictions are maintained on ownership and access to networks. The inferences are not sensitive to alternative proxies of infrastructure, such as power, energy, and transport facilities. See Table 4.4 for the current state of India's telecommunication network.

where α_i represents any idiosyncratic fixed effect that differs across countries, β_i represents any effect common to all countries and e_{it} is the error term capturing unmeasured shocks.

Table 4.1

Panel Unit Root (CIPS) Test

Variable	*p =1*	*p =2*	*p =3*	*p =4*
Y	– 3.392	– 3.811	– 2.821	– 2.801
X	– 3.963	– 3.248	– 2.872	– 2.441

Notes:

(i) All statistics are based on AR(p) specifications in the level of the variables with $p \leq 4$, for the largest balanced panel contained in the sample.

(ii) The critical values are – 2.19 for 1 per cent, – 2.08 for 5 per cent, and – 2.02 for 10 per cent, levels of significance.

Table 4.1 reports results from the CIPS panel unit root tests for each variable. It provides evidence that both per capita GDP growth rate and the proxy for infrastructure suffer from non-stationarity: the null hypothesis of a unit root cannot be rejected consistently.

Cointegration tests and Fully Modified Ordinary Least Squares (FMOLS)[18] estimation techniques for heterogeneous panels, developed recently by Pedroni (1999; 2000), are employed due to several distinct advantages.[19] First, it combines information from the time series dimension with that obtained from the cross section of units making inference about the existence of cointegration more efficient than pure time series-based tests given their well-known power deficiencies. Second, it provides efficient estimation of a long-run relation among variables even in cases where consideration of the time dimension alone would lead to the regression being characterised as spurious. This has been discussed by Phillips and Moon (1999), Engel and Granger (1987) and Granger and Newbold (1986). Third, it allows (using the asymptotic properties of non-stationary panels) for

18. The panel FMOLS estimation technique applied in this paper is outlined in the technical appendix.

19. It is well known that standard OLS or 2SLS results can suffer from 'spurious regression' problems when data are non-stationary.

considerable heterogeneity[20] among individual members of the panel, including heterogeneity in the long-run cointegrating vectors as well as in the dynamics associated with short-run deviations from these cointegrating vectors. Fourth, the method simultaneously corrects for serial correlation, endogeneity and sample bias (asymptotically).

Table 4.2 presents the results from panel cointegration tests of the null of no cointegration among the variables. The rows report the computed values of the panel test statistics, following Pedroni (1999), that are classified into two categories: within-dimension and between-dimension. Rows labeled 'within-dimension' report the computed value of the statistics based on estimators that effectively pool the autoregressive coefficient across different countries for the unit root tests on the estimated residuals. Rows labeled 'between-dimension' report the computed value of the statistics based on estimators that average individually estimated coefficients for each country. The statistics are calculated 'without time dummies' as well as 'with time dummies' where the latter is intended to pick up any common disturbances affecting all countries in the panel.

The asymptotic distribution of each of the statistics is normal with zero mean and unit variance. Under the alternative hypothesis the variance ratio statistic diverges to positive infinity and consequently the right tail of the normal distribution is used to reject the null hypothesis. Each of the other statistics diverges to negative infinity under the alternative hypothesis and consequently the left tail of the normal distribution is used to reject the null hypothesis. Clearly per capita GDP growth rate and the proxy for infrastructure are cointegrated: the null of no cointegration is rejected at one per cent level using any of the test statistics with or without the inclusion of time dummies.

---

20. Inferences can be made regarding common long run relationships that are asymptotically invariant to considerable degree of short run heterogeneity prevalent in the dynamics. In particular, two key sources of heterogeneity are captured in this analysis. One source of heterogeneity manifests itself in the familiar fixed effects form. These reflect differences in mean levels among the variables of different countries in the panel and are modeled by including country specific intercepts. The second source of heterogeneity comes from differences in the way countries respond to short run deviations from equilibrium cointegrating vectors that develop in response to stochastic disturbances. This is modeled by allowing the associated serial correlation properties of the error processes to vary across sectors.

Table 4.2

Panel Cointegration Tests

Test Statistic	*Without Time Dummies*	*With Time Dummies*
Within-dimension		
variance ratio statistic	9.17	5.88
rho statistic	- 9.80	- 6.94
Phillips Perron t-statistic	- 9.07	- 8.07
ADF t-statistic	- 10.20	- 10.32
Between-dimension		
rho statistic	- 8.21	- 8.25
Phillips Perron t-statistic	- 8.44	- 9.93
ADF t-statistic	- 11.97	- 11.90

Notes:

(i) The within-dimension test statistics are based on estimators that effectively pool the autoregressive coefficient across different members for the unit root tests on the estimated residuals.

(ii) The between-dimension test statistics are based on estimators that average the individually estimated coefficients for each country.

(iii) The first of the four statistics is a type of non-parametric variance ratio statistic. The second is a panel analogue of the Phillips and Perron (1988) rho-statistic. The third is a panel analogue of the Phillips and Perron (1988) t-statistic. The fourth is a panel analogue of the Dickey-Fuller t-statistic.

(iv) The asymptotic distribution of each of the four statistics is normal with zero mean and unit variance. As such the standard normal table provides the critical values.

Table 4.3 reports results from FMOLS estimation of equation (2).[21] The calculated value of the t-statistic, under the null hypothesis that a coefficient is zero, is provided within parentheses.

The first row of the table presents results for the full panel of 78 countries. Row 2 presents results for the largest balanced panel contained in the sample. Row 3 reports results from a panel that excludes major oil-producing countries because the bulk of their recorded investment is in the extraction of existing resources (not value added). To address the issue of potential data quality problems row 4 presents results obtained after excluding the countries with the

21. The estimates are strikingly similar with and without time dummies. The results are reported from estimation with time dummies in order to allow potential cross-sectional dependencies.

poorest data from the sample. Specifically, only countries that are assigned a grade better than 'D', on the Penn World Table's summary assessments of the quality of countries' data, are included. Rows 5 and 6 report results separately for OECD and non-OECD economies.

Table 4.3

Fully Modified Ordinary Least Squares (FMOLS) Estimates

	Panel	*Estimate*
I.	Full (78 countries; 1961-2000)	0.44 (24.58)
II.	Largest Balanced Panel Contained in the Sample (46 countries; 1961-1998)	0.41 (19.65)
III.	Non-oil-producing (55 countries; 1961-2000)	0.43 (34.28)
IV.	Non-D-graded (66 countries; 1961-2000)	0.59 (33.04)
V.	OECD (20 countries; 1961-2000)	0.57 (24.04)
VI.	Non-OECD (58 countries; 1961-2000)	0.73 (17.02)

Notes:

(i) The calculated values of the t-statistic are indicated within parenthesis.

(ii) The asymptotic distribution of the t-statistic is normal with zero mean and unit variance. As such the standard normal table provides the critical values.

The following inferences are drawn from the Table. First, the panel estimates exhibit a significant positive association (ranging from 0.41 to 0.73) between per capita GDP growth rate and the proxy for infrastructure. This is consistent with most of the earlier findings. The estimated coefficient is even stronger for the select group of countries that pass the test of the Penn World Table's summary assessments of data quality as well as for the group of non-oil-producing countries. The estimates do not differ significantly from that of the balanced panel. Second, the growth-infrastructure association is higher for the group of non-OECD countries than the OECD countries. The hypothesis that the estimated correlations are equal for the two groups is rejected (the t-statistic is 8.71) in favour of the alternative hypothesis that the estimated association is significantly higher for OECD countries, at 1 per cent level of significance. Finally, the possibility of cross-sectional dependency, which is particularly relevant for the growth-infrastructure relationship, has been incorporated in this analysis by employing the CIPS panel unit root test by Pesaran (2005) and in the form of including common time dummies in the panel cointegration and the FMOLS estimation techniques. It may be noted that while the inclusion of common time dummies captures a broad class of cross-sectional dependencies (such as, if growth or infrastructure tends to be driven by a common disturbance) there are likely to be other forms of dependency that time dummies cannot control. In particular, if there are dynamic feedback effects that exist between the variables of different countries, these cannot be controlled simply by using time dummies. It is worthwhile to note though that, based on the strong evidence from the individual country test results, a relatively simple method of inference can be used to conclude if the results are sensitive to the likely presence of other such forms of cross-sectional dependencies. To see this, note that according to the Bonferroni inequality constraint, the marginal significance level, P, for a rejection of the null hypothesis applied to a panel of N countries is such that $p \leq \sum_{i=1}^{N} p_1$, where p_i is the marginal significance level of the tests applied to W"the individual members of the panel: $p_i = \frac{P}{N}$ can be used as a criterion to set the rejection level, in which case we require $p_i \leq 0.03$ for any one member of our sample to reject the null as applied to the panel as a whole at the 10 per cent level. Following Maddala and Wu (1999), this type of test does not rely on the independence of the individual tests, and is thus invariant to the presence of any form of cross sectional dependency. For the normal distribution, absolute Chakrabarti: Non-Traded Sectors and Growth 15 values of the t-statistic in excess of 4.0 are sufficient for $p_i \leq 0.003$. In our sample, the individual FMOLS tests produce 43 such cases, leading to the conclusion that no degree of cross-sectional dependency would be sufficient to overturn the key inferences of this analysis.

Conclusion

It is evident that a developing economy like India is likely to gain from sustained expansion of investment in and improved performance of her infrastructure sectors. Institutional capabilities and organisational reforms that lend credibility and effectiveness to government policy are likely to complement her growth momentum through expanded infrastructure investment. In particular, the high rates of urban growth experienced in India will require significant investments in infrastructure if cities are to perform their various production and service activities in a manner consistent with the principles of sustainable development. With Indian cities being at the forefront of socioeconomic transformation and given the backlog and state of deficient infrastructure characterising these cities, increasing the level of investment in infrastructure should be a major policy thrust.

However, it is crucial for the policymakers of the 'world's fastest growing, free market democracy' to distinguish the 'hypes' from the 'facts' in order to guard the nation from missing her shot at converting global interest into investment, jobs and development. While it is not sensible to design a common set of recommendations uniformly applicable for all infrastructure sectors, it goes without saying that reforms should be directed toward drawing resources into expanding, modernising, and improving infrastructure facilities and services. Fair competition should be promoted by lowering entry barriers and giving entrants access to network infrastructure. Innovations must be facilitated by focusing on goals to be achieved and giving operators and investors the leeway to introduce more efficient technologies and innovative service arrangements. At the same time, it is necessary to recognise that infrastructure is critical for growth through expansion of production and trade but absent adequate complementary investments, infrastructure alone is not likely to build the 'road' for moving jobs to people in a world where people increasingly keep moving to jobs. Finally, it is important not to overlook the pressing needs for designing and effectively implementing adequate governance mechanisms, the conspicuous absence of which continues to draw media and political attention, to compensate those adversely affected by the transformation of infrastructural services.

Table 4.4

Growth of India's Telecommunication Network

(in million)

	Fixed Line (including WI.L fixed)	*Cellular Mobile Phones (including WI.I. Mobile)*	*Total Phones*
1996-97	14.5	0.3	14.9
1997-98	17.8 (3.3)	0.9 (0.5)	18.7 (3.8)
1998-99	21.6 (3.8)	1.2 (0.3)	22.8 (4.2)
1999-00	26.8 (5.2)	1.9 (0.7)	28.7 (5.8)
2000-01	33.0 (6.2)	3.6 (1.7)	36.6 (7.9)
2001-02	39.1 (6.2)	6.4 ((2.9)	45.6 (9.0)
2002-03	41.5 (2.4)	13.0 (6.6)	54.5 (8.9)
2003-04	42.6 (1.1)	33.6 (20.6)	76.2 (21.7)
2004-05	45.9 (3.3)	52.2 (18.6)	98.1 (21.9)
2005-06	46.7 (0.8)	93.04 (40.8)	139.8 (41.7)
2006-07 (Apr.-July)	47.4 (0.6)	111.2 (18.2)	158.6 (18.8)

Source: Telecom Regulatory Authority of India.

Technical Appendix

Fully Modified Ordinary Least Squared (FMOLS) Estimation

The panel FMOLS technique, developed by Pedroni (2000), is a method for estimating and testing hypotheses for cointegrating vectors in a dynamic time series panel. It augments the conventional panel Ordinary Least Squares (OLS) technique by applying the same principle underlying the semi-parametric correction for the OLS estimator used by Phillips and Hansen (1990) to develop the time series FMOLS estimator. The panel FMOLS estimator is essentially the simple average of the time series FMOLS estimates. The same is true for the t-statistic. Let y be the dependent variable and x be the vector of m explanatory variable(s). The panel FMOLS technique involves the following steps:

1. Construct $(y_{it} - \bar{y}_t)$ and $(y_{it} - \bar{y}_t)$

   where $\bar{y}_t = \frac{1}{N}\sum_{i=1}^{N} y_{it}$ and $\bar{x}_t = \frac{1}{N}\sum_{i=1}^{N} x_{it}$.

2. Estimate $y_{it} = \alpha_i + \beta_t + \gamma x_{it} + e_{it}$ $(i = 1,2,....,N;\ t = 1,2,....,T)$ where α_i represents any idiosyncratic fixed effect that differs across countries, β_t represents any effect common to all countries and eit is the error term capturing unmeasured shocks.

3. Use the estimated residuals $(\mu_{it} = y_{it} - \hat{y}_{it})$ from step 2 and the differences of each regressor $(\varepsilon_{it} = x_{it} - \bar{x}_t)$ to construct a vector error series $\xi_{it} = [\mu_{it}^{'}\ \varepsilon_{it}^{'}]^{'}$.

4. Apply the Newey-West (1987) long run covariance matrix estimator to the vector ξ_{it} to generate long run covariance matrix Ω_i and the auto-covariance matrix Γ_i .

5. Construct matrix L_i by applying Cholesky triangularisation to Ω_i .

6. Construct an estimate of the standard contemporaneous covariance matrix Ω_i^0 for the elements of it ξ_{it} similarly partitioned.

7. Let Ω_{11i} be the far upper right scalar element and Ω_{22i} be the lower m×m partition of the $(m+1)\times(m+1)$ long run covariance

matrix Ω_i;Ω_{21i} corresponds to the remaining m elements in the column below Ω_{11i}. The same mapping applies to the partitions of the $(m+1)\times(m+1)$ auto-covariance matrix Γ_i. A superscript '0' is used when a covariance or auto-covariance is "contemporaneous". Construct a serial correlation correction term λ_i as $\hat{\lambda}_i = \hat{\Gamma}_{21i} + \hat{\Omega}^0_{21i} - \frac{\hat{L}_{21i}}{\hat{L}_{22i}}\left(\hat{\Gamma}_{22i} + \hat{\Omega}^0_{22i}\right)$.

8. Construct $y^*_{it} = (y_{it} - \bar{y}_i) - \frac{\hat{L}_{21i}}{\hat{L}_{22i}}\Delta x_{it}$ where $\bar{y}_i = \frac{1}{T}\sum_{t=1}^{T} y_{it}$.

9. Construct the cross-product terms between y^*_{it} and $(x_{it} - \bar{x}_i)$ where $\bar{x}_i = \frac{1}{T}\sum_{t=1}^{T} x_{it}$.

10. The panel FMOLS estimator is given by:

$$\hat{\gamma} = \frac{\sum_{i=1}^{N} \frac{1}{\hat{L}_{11i}\hat{L}_{22i}}\left(\sum_{t=1}^{T}(x_{it} - \bar{x}_i)y^*_{it} - T\hat{\lambda}_i\right)}{\left(\sum_{t=1}^{N} \frac{1}{\hat{L}^2_{22t}}\sum_{t=1}^{T}(x_{it} - \bar{x}_i)^2\right)}$$

The t-statistic is given by:

$$t = \frac{1}{\sqrt{N}}\sum_{i=1}^{N} \frac{1}{\hat{L}_{11i}\sqrt{\left(\sum_{t=1}^{T}(x_{it} - \bar{x}_i)^2\right)}}\left(\sum_{t=1}^{T}(x_{it} - \bar{x}_i)y^*_{it} - T\hat{\lambda}_i\right)$$

In sum, this FMOLS technique allows for considerable heterogeneity across individual members of the panel. In addition to producing asymptotically unbiased estimators, it also produces nuisance parameter free standard normal distributions.

References

Arnold, J.M., A. Mattoo and G. Narciso (2006). "Services inputs and firm productivity in Sub-Saharan Africa: Evidence from Firm-level Data", *World Bank Policy Research Working Paper* No. 4048.

Aschauer, D.A. (1989a). "Is Public Expenditure Productive?", *Journal of Monetary Economics*, Vol. 23: 177–200.

———. (1989b). "Does Public Capital Crowd Out Private Capital?", *Journal of Monetary Economics*, Vol. 24: 171–88.

Canning, D., M. Fay, and R. Perotti (1994). "Infrastructure and Growth", in M. Bsaldassarri, M. Paganaetto and E.S. Phelps (eds.), *International Differences in Growth Rates*. New York: St. Martins Press.

Chakrabarti, A. (2004). "Asymmetric Adjustment Costs in Simple General Equilibrium Models", *European Economic Review*, Vol. 48(1): 63–73.

———. (2003). "A Theory of the Spatial Distribution of Foreign Direct Investment", *International Review of Economics and Finance*, Vol. 12(2): 149–169.

———. (2001). "The Determinants of Foreign Direct Investment: Sensitivity Analyses of Cross-Country Regressions", *Kyklos*, Vol. 54(1): 89–113.

———. (1999). "17. Foreign Direct Investment & Host Country Interaction", *Export-Import Bank of India Occasional Paper* No. 69: 1–27.

Chakrabarti, A. and J. S. Heywood (2004). "Foreign Investment, Vertical Integration and Local Equity Requirements", *Economica*, Vol. 71: 559–574.

Chang, Y. (2002). "Nonlinear IV Unit Root Tests Under Cross Sectional Dependence", *Journal of Econometrics*, Vol. 110: 261–92.

Dickey, D.A., W.R. Bell, and R.B. Miller (1986). "Unit Roots in Time Series Models: Tests and Implications", *The American Statistician* Vol. 40: 12–26.

Easterly, William, and Sergio Rebelo (1993). "Fiscal Policy and Economic Growth: An Empirical Investigation", *Journal of Monetary Economics*, Vol. 32, pp. 417–458.

Engel, R.F. and C.W.J. Granger (1987). "Cointegration and Error-Correction Representation: Estimation and Testing", *Ecnometrica*, Vol. 55: 251–276.

Eschenbach, F. and B. Hoekman (2006). "Services Policies in Transition Economies: On the European Union and the World Trade Organisation as Commitment Mechanisms", *World Bank Policy Research Working Paper* No. 3951.

Esfahani, H.S. and M.T. Ramirez (2003). "Institutions, Infrastructure, and Economic Growth", *Journal of Development Economics*, Vol. 70: 443–77.

Fedderke, J. W. and Z. Bogetic (2006). "Infrastructure and growth in South Africa: Direct and Indirect Productivity Impacts of 19 Infrastructure Measures", *World Bank Policy Research Working Paper* No. 3989.

Fink, C., A. Mattoo, and R. Rathindran (2002). "An Assessment of Telecommunications Reform in Developing Countries", *World Bank Policy Research Working Paper* No. 2909.

Gramlich, Edward M. (1994). "Infrastructure Investment: A Review Essay", *Journal of Economic Literature*, Vol. 32: 1176–96.

Granger, C.W.J. and P. Newbold (1986). *Forecasting Economic Time Series*. New York: Academic Press.

Ianchovichina, E. and P. Kacker (2005). "Growth trends in the Developing World: Country Forecasts and Determinants". *World Bank Policy Research Working Paper* No. 3775.

Im, K.S., M.H. Pesaran, and Y. Shin (2003). "Testing for Unit Roots in Heterogeneous Panels", *Journal of Econometrics,* Vol. 115: 53–74.

Joskow, P. and R. Noll (1994). "Deregulation and Regulatory Reform during the 1980s", in M. Feldstein (ed.), *American Economic Policy during the 1980s.* Chicago, Ill: University of Chicago Press.

Keynes, J.M. (1929). "The German Transfer Problem", *Economic Journal,* Vol. 39, pp. 1–7.

Kahn, A. (2001). *Whom the Gods Would Destroy, or How Not to Deregulate.* American Enterprise Institute-Brookings Joint Center for Regulatory Studies, Washington D.C.

Maddala, G.S. and S. Wu (1999). "A Comparative Study of Unit Root Tests with Panel Data and a New Simple Test", *Oxford Bulletin of Economics and Statistics,* Vol. 61, pp. 631–652.

Munnell, A.H. (1992). "Infrastructure Investment and Economic Growth", *Journal of Economic Perspectives,* Vol. 6: 189–198.

Newey, W. and K. West (1987). "A Simple, Positive Semi-Definite, Heteroskedasticity and Autocorrelation Consistent Covariance Matrix", *Econometrica,* Vol. 55: 703–708.

Noll, R. (1999). *The Economics and Politics of the Slowdown in Regulatory Reform.* Washington DC: American Enterprise Institute-Brookings Joint Center for Regulatory Studies.

Ohlin, B. (1929). "The Reparation Problem: A Discussion. I. Transfer Difficulties, Real and Imagined", *Economic Journal,* Vol. 39: 172–78.

Pedroni, P. (2000). *Fully Modified OLS for Heterogeneous Cointegrated Panels Advances in Econometrics* 15: 93–130.

————. (1999). "Critical Values for Cointegration Tests in Heterogeneous Panels with Multiple Regressors", *Oxford Bulletin of Economics and Statistics,* Vol. 61: 653–670.

Pesaran, M.H. (2005). "A Simple Panel Unit Root Test in the Presence of Cross Section Dependence". Cambridge University. *(mimeo).*

Phillips, P.C.B. and B. Hansen (1990). "Statistical Inference in Instrumental Variables Regression with I(1) Processes", *Review of Economic Studies,* Vol. 57: 99–125.

Phillips, P.C.B. and H. Moon (1999). "Linear Regression Limit Theory for Nonstationary Panel Data", *Econometrica,* Vol. 67: 1057–1111.

Sanchez-Robles, B. (1998). "Infrastructure Investment and Growth: Some Empirical Evidence", *Contemporary Economic Policy,* Vol. 16: 98–108.

Spiller, P., and W. Savedoff (1999). "Commitment and Governance in Infrastructure Sectors", in F. Besanes, E.M. Uribe, and R. Willig (eds.) *Can Privatisation Deliver? Infrastructure for Latin America.* Baltimore, Md.: Inter-American Development Bank and Washington DC: The Johns Hopkins University Press.

Tatom, J.A. (1993). "The Spurious Effect of Public Capital Formation on Private Sector Productivity", *Policy Studies Journal,* Vol. 21: 391–95.

5

Enhancing the Flow of Credit and Managing Risks in Agriculture

NACHIKET MOR, D. CHATTANATHAN and RAJIV PANTHARY

Introduction

Agriculture sector is a key component of the Indian Economy. Even though the contribution of Agriculture in overall GDP of the country has declined[1] from 44.5 per cent in 1970-71 to around 20.0 per cent in 2005-06,[2] agriculture continues to be the principal source of livelihoods for around 62.0 per cent of the country's population.[3] In the last decade while the Indian economy has done quite well overall,[4] achieving a Compounded Annual Growth Rate (CAGR) of over 6.0 per cent, agriculture has remained sluggish with a CAGR of only 2.0 per

1. During the 54 years of Planning between 1950-51 and 2004-05, the share of agriculture in GDP has fallen by more than half from 59 per cent to 24 per cent, whereas the share of industry has almost doubled from 13 per cent to 25 per cent and the share of services has increased from 28 per cent to 51 per cent. The steep fall in the share of agriculture in GDP is due to the fact that its growth rate at 2.7 per cent per annum has been less than half of the growth rates of 5.6 per cent per annum for industry and 5.7 per cent per annum for services (*http://www.organiser.org/dynamic/*).
2. *Economic Survey 2004-05*; *The Pioneer*, March 19, 2006.
3. *Economy Overview* in *http://www.economywatch.com*.
4. India is the fourth largest economy as measured by purchasing power parity (PPP), with a GDP of US $3.36 trillion. When measured in USD exchange-rate terms, it is the tenth largest in the world, with a GDP of US $691.87 billion (2004). India was the second fastest growing major economy in the world, with a GDP growth rate of 8.1 per cent at the end of the first quarter of 2005-06. ("Economy of India", *Wikipedia*).

The views expressed in this note are entirely those of the authors and do not in any way reflect the views of the Institutions with which they are associated. The authors would like to thank Madhavi Soman, Professor Jessica Wallack, Ajun Uppal, Manish Khera, Bindu Ananth, Madan Sabnavis, Praveen P.A., Neha Agarwal, Rupalee Ruchismita for their assistance in preparing this note.

cent. Given the strong backward and forward linkages of agriculture with the overall Indian economy and its sheer scale, a strong growth in agriculture (at the rate of 4.0-5.0 per cent per annum) has the potential to catapult the Indian economy to well past a 10.0 per cent growth trajectory.[5] A stronger growth in agriculture would lead to higher income for farmers, generate more employment opportunities and sharply reduce poverty. It is our belief that for India, a rapid growth in the rural economy overall, and within that of agriculture, is highly feasible[6] and may hold the key to addressing India's problems of growth and poverty eradication—unlike in the rest of the region

---

5. "In two to three years, India should be targeting 10 per cent growth if its savings rate improves, agricultural output increases, and infrastructure is substantially upgraded", Prime Minister Shri Manmohan Singh at the *India Economic Summit* (November, 2005). It may be noted that 1 per cent growth in agriculture would translate to only 0.2 per cent growth in overall economy as agriculture's share in the overall economy is around 20 per cent. In real senses even if agriculture grows at the rate of 4-5 per cent from current level of less than 3 per cent the impact on economy will not be more than additional 0.4-0.5 per cent in overall economy growth. Therefore growth in agriculture has to be complemented with growth in infrastructure facilities, growth in savings rate besides higher growth in services and industries segment. However even a 1 per cent additional growth in agriculture is desirable as it directly impacts the employment and poverty levels in the countryside. The spread effects of doubling of agricultural growth are greater due to the multiplier effect of agriculture in the overall economy. It has been estimated that one incremental percentage growth in agriculture leads to an additional income generation of Rs. 100.00 bn in the hands of the farmers thereby increasing their disposable income and ultimately, their purchasing power.

6. On the one hand, India's position as a production base for most 'dry' commodities such as wheat, rice and maize may be unattractive because of small farm holdings, high volatility in rainfall patterns, low levels of mechanisation and the high levels of subsidies offered by international producing nations to their own farmers. Conversely, it is possible that horticulture in India could yield handsome returns. In fact, while overall growth of agricultural production has languished at below 2 per cent, horticulture already increased it's contribution to 28 per cent of AGRI GDP and 54 per cent of the export share of agriculture, all from a cultivated area share of 8.5 per cent only (extracted from the PM's speech to the *Agricultural Summit* on April 9, 2005, at New Delhi). Traditionally, it has suffered primarily due to a lack of customer focus, outdated varieties and huge wastage of 25-30 per cent of output due to a poor supply chain of pre-cooling units, cold storage, refrigerated transport. However, this could be poised for a dramatic change. The growing popularity of tropical fruits, organic farming and semi-processed (cleaned, pre-packed and pre-cut) fruits and vegetables could work in India's favour as they enable us to take advantage of a high labour component to become a competitive force. The willingness of the international customer to pay a premium for these offerings make investments in the required certification, irrigation and other infrastructure necessary for the development of both the fresh, as well as processed, fruits and vegetable sector well worthwhile. For example, expensive oils such as Menthol and Patchouli have very manual processing requirements, which once again provide a source of competitive advantage to India.

where urbanisation and growth in manufacturing have been the principal drivers.[7]

However, for this to happen, key ingredients would be an adequate supply of credit and the availability of tools for the management of considerable risks that agriculture is exposed to. Repeated attempts have been made in the past to ensure this. In the area of credit this has been attempted by promoting rural co-operative banks, nationalisation of banks, rural-urban branch ratio restrictions along with a high priority sector requirement imposed on banks,[8] promotion of regional rural banks and most recently the development of the Self-Help-Group (SHG)-Bank Linkage model. In the area of risk management, the principal instruments have been a Minimum Support Price (MSP) programme[9] and a highly subsidised Crop Insurance

7. Jones (2006).

8. Banks in the past have generally failed to meet the requirements of priority sector advances. Over the period from 1991-92 to 1996-97, the levels achieved by the public sector banks ranged between 30 per cent and 35 per cent—this despite the fact that the bulk of such lending is promptly re-discounted by NABARD, SIDBI, or one of the other DFIs. Even though priority sector advances situation has improved in the current context, agriculture lending by banks continues to lag. For instance, as on March 2005, 13 banks out of 27 PSU banks achieved the 18 per cent agriculture-lending target while only 1 out of 30 private sector banks met the 18 per cent lending mark. However, when we analyse the priority sector lending (40 per cent of NBC) targets then we find that only 2 banks out of total 27 PSU banks were unable to achieve the 40 per cent benchmark while 11 private sector banks out of total 30 private sector banks failed to reach the 40 per cent priority sector lending target milestone. (*RBI Statistics*)

9. The Agricultural Price Policy being followed in India from 1965 onwards is generally known as the minimum support price policy. Currently, the Union government fixes minimum support prices of as many as 24 agricultural commodities, based on the recommendations of the Commission for Agricultural Costs and Prices (CACP). The main objectives of the minimum support price policy are to provide incentive to the farmers for adopting improved technology and for developing a production pattern broadly in the light of national requirements—and also to ensure rational utilisation of land, water and other production resources.

   Panthary (2005) argues that controls and subsidies in the agriculture sector have failed to reach the targeted beneficiaries and at the same time have become heavy burden to the state economy. Minimum Support Price is another distortion that has led to over production of food grains despite burgeoning food grains stocks with FCI. It has also stifled diversification to other remunerative and market demanded crops with the result that we have even resorted to exports at a lower price. Right strategy could be to restrict the open procurement of food grains to the minimum required for food security purposes. Dismantling of the unlimited procurement or a balanced

Contd...

programme.[10] While a few of these steps have experienced a measure of success, for the most part these have failed to meet their objectives and the gap between what is required and what is available remains large.[11] For example, against a projected flow of Rs. 7,365.70 billion of institutional credit to agriculture and allied activities for 2002-2007, in the first three years of the tenth plan the institutional credit flow is estimated to be only Rs. 2,500.60 billion.

It is our belief that in order to deliver on the promise of agriculture and to set it firmly on a longer term growth path, fundamentally different approaches from the ones that have been taken in the past are called for. In our view, merely changing ownership, imposing regulatory requirements, launching subsidised but poorly designed products, providing refinance at low rates of interest and exhorting financial services providers to do more in rural India is unlikely to achieve much if the preconditions for an orderly functioning of these markets are not put in place first. The creation of these preconditions is likely to take time but in our view offers the only way forward if one wants to place the entire rural credit and risk management system on a firm footing, allowing it to become a strong partner in the delivery of the risk management products and services and credit required for the growth of agriculture.

In the following paragraphs we will attempt to list and describe a comprehensive set of interventions that in our view will create the necessary preconditions.

...contd...

reduction would in itself lead to crop diversification besides huge savings for the public exchequer. The savings in turn could be utilised for creating targeted and better-managed safety net for the poor or for creation of infrastructure facilities such as provision of all weather roads, link roads from villages to markets, rural electrification etc.

10. Skees, Hazell and Miranda (1999) observe that the financial experience with publicly provided; multiple-peril crop insurance has been disastrous. In all cases, programmes are heavily subsidised and governments not only pay part of the premium, but also most of the delivery and service costs, and they cover aggregate losses even when the losses exceed targeted levels over long periods of time.

11. RBI could play an important role here in encouraging management of banks to ensure that they focus on the availability of loans for the poor rather than on low interest rates that only result in the exclusion of the poor from the banking system (Sinha, 2000).

Development of a Comprehensive Rural Information System

The importance of developing a comprehensive rural information system cannot be overemphasised. Country after country (both rich and poor) in which well functioning credit delivery systems exist, are underpinned by such information systems. The development of such a system would require the following steps to be taken.

Smart Card

Introduction of a biometric (thumb-print) smart card for each and every individual farmerborrower with a Unique Identification Number. The cost of issuance of this smart card is a one-time cost (ranging between Rs. 50 to Rs. 100 per farmer) that can be shared between banks, government (state or central) and the farmer himself. This smart card could be used to keep track of the farmer's: (a) lending records; (b) savings records; (c) production records; (d) insurance records; (e) health records; (f) ration card information and (g) land records (e) other similar applications.[12] Nigeria has recently completed the complete identification of its population of 60 million in a record time of 6 weeks and is in the process of issuance of such biometric smart cards. In Bolivia,[13] Smart Automatic Teller Machines have been installed, which are serving 43,000 clients who live mostly in rural or semiurban settings. These SATMs are unusual in that they incorporate fingerprint readers for client verification rather than use PIN technology. They also use voice instructions in three languages to assist illiterate or semi-literate users.

A new company Financial Innovations and Network Operations (FINO) which has been launched by a few former ICICI Bank executives with some financial support from ICICI Bank has developed a full

12. In South Africa, fingerprint-based digital biometrics have been used in the delivery of pension benefits The system involved the prior digital registration of fingerprints which were then stored on a card bearing a magnetic strip and on a central database. From 1999, multi-function smart card are being used through which instead of a direct cash payment, pensioners now receive a credit directly onto their smart card, which can then be used immediately to draw cash from an adjacent cash dispenser. (Breckenridge, 2002).

13. Whelan, Steve. *Building Financial Systems for the Poor.* With contributions from CGAP Staff and exchange, LLC in CGAP.

capability to issue these smart cards and is in the process of issuing biometric e-pass books to ICICI Bank's 3 million rural customers in the next few months.[14] If NABARD and a few other banks were to co-invest in FINO and participate in its governance, it would become possible for FINO to issue such cards to all the clients of all banks (including Regional Rural Banks (RRBs) and Co-operative Banks).[15]

Credit Bureau

In the rural context, getting borrowers' credit history information is very difficult, resulting in information asymmetries, which makes it difficult for the lending agencies to make accurate credit risk assessment. Development of a credit bureau for rural India, which makes use of the smart card and is able to return a credit score to any potential lender who is registered with the Bureau, can lead to accelerated growth of rural credit. FINO has the capacity to store and manage the data and could easily partner with a specialised credit-tracking organisation to develop this capability.[16] If NABARD joins hands with FINO, this whole process could be further facilitated, since it enjoys the confidence of the entire rural finance industry and already has a significant amount of historic data available to it. There is a great deal of academic work that suggests that the introduction of such a bureau could have a transformational effect.[17] The Rural

---

14. Annexure A.5.1 has a full discussion of FINO and its current capabilities.

15. Bekier and Nickless (1998) suggest that governments can play an important role in influencing switching over to electronic forms of transactions. Government can rather drive the change by using electronic systems for their own transactions—by making social security payments through rechargeable smart cards, for example, or providing telephone banking facilities for community services. We feel that the application of the same in India will not only help control transaction costs but also usher higher efficiency and transparency in banking transactions. Government could consider paying wages to workers participating in anti-poverty programmes, employment programmes (recently launched 100 days assured employment scheme) through electronic means; this will offer banks sizable floats for recycling to farmers at low cost.

16. We understand from FINO that there are a few agencies having credit information services for credit tracking in rural areas.

17. Rajan and Zingales (2003) emphasise the importance of credit information sharing in expanding access to finance, especially for those who are unable to provide collateral. They deduce that, Credit bureaus help the poor build credit histories that they can then use to shop around for the best and most appropriate financial services available, turning their reputation—defined in a formal credit history—into collateral

contd...

Credit Bureau would allow the entire branch networks of banks of all types to become fully active since a fairly mechanical lending process would then be adequate to deliver credit and even nontraditional lenders such as tractor, pesticide and fertiliser dealers could directly start to vend credit on the basis of this information as agents of commercial banks. The existence of this information would also allow a good assessment of the true extent of credit risk in rural lending and through a cross mapping of this with borrower profile and systemic developments (such as rainfall patterns), allow the development of rational pricing strategies and good risk management products.

Management and Recovery of Transaction Costs

High transaction and supervisory costs involved in rural lending is a major constraint in rural credit. The small size of seasonal agricultural credit, wide geographical spread, poor transport and communication infrastructure results in higher transaction costs for rural banking. The strategies suggested below could be employed to address the issue of high transaction and supervisory costs.

...contd...

to access financial services. As credit histories and credit bureaus develop, they facilitate other types of business transactions; for example, poor entrepreneurs can use their credit history as references for business relationships with suppliers and other business connections.

Robin Young, Senior Development Specialist, Development Alternatives Inc. in the article "Credit Bureaus in Latin America: Expanding Financial and Other Services to the Base of the Pyramid" reveals that financial institutions and other firms that use credit bureaus are reaching new markets that in many cases are more profitable than traditional client segments. Perhaps most important, poor people gain access to financial services at better terms and conditions than were previously made available to them.

In her comprehensive literature review for *Credit Reporting Systems and the International Economy,* Margaret Miller notes that "information sharing is associated with higher levels of lending in relation to gross national product (GNP) as well as lower default rates." Inessa Love and Nataliya Mylenko of the World Bank, in their empirical study of credit bureaus' impact on credit markets, found that the presence of private credit registries "is associated with lower financing constraints and higher share of bank financing. Small and medium firms tend to have higher share of bank financing in countries where private registries exist and stronger rule of law is associated with more effective private credit registries." They found that 49 per cent of small firms report credit constraints in countries without a credit bureau, compared with only 27 per cent in countries with one, and the probability of obtaining a loan improves from 27 per cent in countries without a credit bureau to 40 per cent in countries with one. The increasing numbers of bankers and other lenders buying private credit bureau reports as part of their credit appraisal process indicate that they are relevant for decision making among lenders.

Automation

One of the important reasons for the failure of many providers of rural finance has been their inability to properly manage their operations in a cost effective manner. Automation through the creation of a Banking Platform that offers its services to co-operative banks, regional rural banks and scheduled commercial banks on an Application Services Provider (ASP) basis would be cost effective and will be well managed by professionals. While a few Rural Financial Institutions (RFIs) in India have grown to scale but individually, none of the RFIs have resources to invest in development of unique software or systems for their exclusive use, as this would involve high upfront costs, even if it were to scale its operations extensively.[18] In the meanwhile, the lack of efficient systems acts as a deterrent to growth. Therefore, creation of a sectoral IT resource for RFIs presents itself as the most workable solution. Such a sectoral resource could be shared across RFIs, thereby improving their capacity to scale up in terms of reach and range. The common solution would provide RFIs with a ready platform to achieve reasonable size and scale without incurring heavy capital expenditure. A brief on shared technology platform has been put as Annexure A.5.2.

There are a number of examples of banking systems adopting this approach so that a low cost and relatively rapid migration to high quality banking systems can take place.[19] FINO has been built as a platform to provide exactly these services to Rural Financial Institutions (RFIs) and is currently in the process of being rolled out to three different types of RFIs including a cooperative bank, one scheduled commercial bank's rural operations and a non-bank finance company operating as a lender in rural India. The automation effort

---

18. An indicative quote for a single medium scale deployment is put at Rs. 95 million. This covers the cost of the hardware platform, network connectivity, setting up of the data centre, facilities management and managed IT services that come up to Rs. 65 million.The cost of the solution license, customisation and integration is estimated at Rs. 30 mn.

19. Firpo (2005) suggests that reaching out to the poor requires use of innovative technology. However, creating separate solution for each institution is neither sustainable nor scalable. She argues that shared infrastructures and common standards can significantly lower the costs of providing financial assistance to the

contd...

being undertaken by FINO combines the benefits of the card platform developed earlier in the form of a multi-account debit card and a number of new and existing Point-of-Sale (POS) terminals to ensure that card-holders are able to access a full suite of high quality financial services even from very small RFIs.

Similarly, village based transaction point for servicing the financial needs of the poor could be created.[20] However, if this channel is set up primarily to deliver the financial services, the costs of serving the clients will be prohibitive. There is a need for a shared services network that can recover the servicing costs over multiple applications. Internet based kiosks can be one such transaction point. Such a channel can provide e-governance applications, agriculture extension services, Internet[21] connectivity, telemedicine and health diagnostics lab, crop diagnostics, education and entertainment, recruitment/employment centre and financial services like life and health insurance. Through these one-stop shops consumers in even remote parts of the country can participate in mainstream economic activity at low costs.

...contd...

rural populace. Such sharing is required to increase the number, and reduce the costs of access, points through which a client can obtain financial services. Even in the urban context, Business models have changed to allow cooperation and competition to co-exist as financial actors are building shared infrastructures to reach a growing customer base. For example, initially, banks issued their own credit cards for use within exclusive merchant agent networks. This exclusive strategy, however, dampened any chance to get scale as it was proving unsustainable for the issuing banks. Bank of America finally broke this logjam when under the leader leadership of D ship Dee Hock, it developed the VISA model—a shared network owned now by more than 20,000,000 member banks from around the world. Within the VISA model, member banks agreed to establish a common architecture with standards adhered to by all members that would permit shared technologies to be developed that could settle financial transactions among a large number of merchants and banks.

In the US, banks share the costs of the infrastructure elements, including technology investments that are too expensive for any single player, yet they continue to compete on differentiated services. The breaking of walls between the banks in turn has permitted shared technologies to be built that could enable scaling up of the industry while also improving the services delivered to a rapidly growing customer base.

20. Ruchismita, Rupalee, *Catalytic Funding to Scale Micro Finance in India.*

21. ITC's e-*Choupal* is a good example of how they can serve as procurement and purchase points and facilitate price discover mechanisms for the farmers, eliminating the need for middlemen. The ITC hub has now also become a distribution channel for its consumer goods division.

Recovery of Transaction Costs

High transactions costs coupled with tight interest rate restrictions imposed on Banks have, not surprisingly, led to a high degree of exclusion particularly of the small and marginal farmer for whom not only are the costs higher but the extent of problems imposed by adverse selection, moral hazard, high transaction intensity, low levels of equity and higher exposure to systemic risks such as failure of rainfall result in much higher levels loss levels from a bank's point of view. It is estimated that typically, for the aforesaid marginal farmer where the loan size would be below Rs. 10,000, the basic transactions costs per farmer on the annual loans averages about Rs. 500-600 or higher. This is of course assuming about 50-60 number of interactions/transactions (if weekly collections) with farmer (typically involving stages such as, application, sanction, disbursement and collection). The above transaction costs includes service (comprising of sales/credit/sanction/collection), stationery/documentation, stamp duty and other ancillary costs etc thus translating to a transaction cost of about 5-6 per cent or higher on a loan size of about Rs. 10,000.[22] If we account for an additional 6 per cent of average risk charge for farmer loans, and a component of cost of funds of 10 per cent for the bank, then even with a minimum spread the lending rate would need to be around 25 per cent per annum. In our view, the imposition of interest rate caps at 10-12 per cent has directly been responsible for the high degree of exclusion[23] that is observed because such interest rates make it viable to serve only the larger and

---

22. However such costs up to a certain level can be brought down in percentage terms to about 3 per cent-4 per cent for non-marginal farmers, when the average loan size increases to Rs. 15,000 to Rs. 25,000.

23. Priya Basu from World Bank in an article in *Economic Times* (March 20, 2006) writes that interest ceilings tend to reduce the supply of credit to the poorer section of society as formal lending gets concentrated towards less riskier or bigger farmers. Interest caps have also led to lack of transparency in the formal rural lending as in some cases various service charges, application fees are charged making the true cost of borrowing to be higher than the stipulated rates. Priya argues that a far more effective way for government to ensure low interest rates for poor is by fostering healthy competition within the financial sector. Vikram Akula, CEO of SKS Micro finance in an article in *Economic Times* (March 20, 2006) also point towards a similar fact by stating that in countries like Columbia and Tunisia where interest caps are imposed the poor have actually received only a quarter of finance than did the poor in countries like Bolivia and Morocco with no interest caps.

richer borrowers.[24] While continuing efforts to research the drivers of these costs need to go on, the whole interest rate paradigm would need to be examined carefully to allow full recovery of the attendant risk charges and transaction costs.[25]

Investments in POS and Digital Money Infrastructure

Investments in POS and Digital Money Infrastructure and Fiscal Incentives for Movement away from Cash and Cheque on a System Wide Basis

Research by McKinsey[26] suggests that it is not the number of people or the number of branches that are the drivers of high costs in a financial system. Movement away from cash towards digital money holds the key to sharply lowering the transactions costs associated with rural finance and also allows the improvement of information management. The current fiscal structure seeks to tax the use of cards thus making it more desirable to stay with cash as the principal means of exchanging value. If, instead, as in the case of South Korea strong incentives were provided on all transactions that take place without the use of cash, the savings on transactions costs would be quite large. As mentioned earlier, FINO has developed the capability to issue Biometric Debit Cards and Smart Cards but would need a national infrastructure of Point of Sale (POS) Terminals at various sales locations that can read these cards and transmit the information to FINO's central database. While FINO is attempting to develop commercially self-financing ways of putting these POS Terminals in place, if a consortium of banks, supported in part by a

---

24. Also refer Sinha (2000) where he argues how interest rate caps have led to the exclusion of the poor by lending agencies.

25. Prahalad and Hammond (2002) argue that the issue is not just cost, but also quality—the quality of water, the range and fairness of financial services, the variety and quality of food. The current informal system that serves poor communities is not only unorganised but also full of inefficiencies and intermediaries or middlemen who exploit those inefficiencies. Creating real markets among the poor—with adequate information, competition, and choice—can change the situation. Allowing the benefits of organisation, logistics, information technology, and scale to bear upon the problem can lead to a 'win-win' solution. If we can remove the inefficiencies of the unorganised sector, we will find an attractive market—for consumers and for firms.

26. Bekier and Nickless (1998).

one-time subsidy from the Government, can allow FINO to roll these POS terminals out faster, it would allow a reduction in transactions costs and better information management that much sooner, directly resulting in a reduction in interest rates.

Creation of New Rural Financial Institutions (RFIs)

Creation of New Rural Financial Institutions and Financial Services Infrastructure

The existing rural financial services architecture suffers from several problems and has not been able to scale up to meet the challenges of rural finance and has particularly excluded the landless labourer and the small and marginal farmer from its service net. A few of the strategies suggested below can help address some of these issues and enable better access to financial services by all segments of population in the rural areas.

Creation of 200 New RFIs in the Private Sector

These would ideally be structured as Non Deposit Taking Micro Finance Non-Bank Finance Companies (MF-NBFC–ND) and be regulated by the Reserve Bank of India. They would each have a minimum capital base of Rs. 20 million and would be formally registered with the RBI. Each would seek to serve approximately 3 districts of the country and would have the capacity to serve about 0.5 million households and build an asset base of Rs. 5 billion. Together these RFIs could therefore serve 100 million households and hold an asset base of Rs. 1,000 billion. Against a requirement of at least 200 MFIs, there are very few MFIs,[27] which have achieved a measure of scale-up and most, despite a very good track record of performance, have not been able to increase the size of their operations.[28]

ICICI Bank, by March 2006, has built partnerships with 100 such RFIs, which it has helped promote/grow in size. In order to facilitate

27. There are approximately 30 mature MFIs with a combined outreach of less than 3 million households.

28. The MFI sector has together cumulatively disbursed funds approximating Rs. 3000-3500 million (USD 60-70 million) (Ananth and George, 2003).

this, a number of the guidelines that are sought to be applied to investment in regular NBFCs (including from foreign sources) and loans to NBFCs would need to be relaxed for this class of NBFCs. For instance RFI could be allowed to access funding from foreign sources (donor agencies) routed through Micro finance investment funds like Aaviskaar and Lok Capital.

Non-Deposit Taking RFIs

A critical design flaw in the current RFIs is the fact that they have been permitted to access deposits directly on their balance sheet from their clients because their mandate has been to be largely self-financing. The high risk environment, the concentrated asset exposure, high borrowing cost induced adverse selection of borrowers, have all inevitably led to the gradual failure of these self-financed institutions and has directly led to problems associated with depositor protection. All of ICICI Bank's current RFI partners (as well as a number of main-stream NBFCs such as TVS Finance, Sundaram Finance and Chola Mandalam Finance) use securitisation of assets both to generate resources for lending as well as to diversify the risks on their balance sheet. Since the securitised assets are bought by larger financial institutions and eventually by the capital markets, they serve to act as internal regulators of the RFIs ensuring that on an ongoing basis these RFIs are managed well. ICICI Bank supported the creation of FINO in large part to serve these new RFIs. RBI has also recently issued guidelines on securitisation[29] making it very feasible for this form of fund-raising to be scaled up even by smaller institutions. The suggestion therefore is to not to permit this new class of MF-NBFC–ND (referred to above) to mobilise deposits from the public but raise funds only from QIBs (Qualified Institutional Buyers.)

Full Service RFIs

While these RFIs (MF–NBFC–ND) will be able to freely offer loans from their balance sheets and act as credit agents of banks, through partnerships with Insurance Companies and Banks using the bancassurance model for insurance, the banking correspondent model

29. RBI No. 2005-06/294 DBOD.NO.BP.BC.60/21.04.048/2005-06 dated February 1, 2006.

for deposit taking and cash management services and Direct Business Catalyst[30] (DBC) model for investment services, these entities can offer the full suite of financial services to their clients. But since the insurance and deposit risks would now be taken on the balance sheets of much larger and well capitalised and more directly regulated financial intermediaries, the design flaw mentioned earlier would be largely absent.

Removal of Branch Licensing for Rural Branches of SCBs

In a country with over 600,000 villages, the number of financial service access points needs to increase very sharply. Each Scheduled Commercial Bank (SCB),[31] as it seeks to roll out its rural finance strategy would be desirous of putting in place a hybrid channel strategy involving a combination of branches and agents. However, for this to proceed apace, it would be imperative to remove all branch licensing requirements[32] for branch and ATM licensing (or putting it on automatic approval route) for branches and ATMs to be placed in designated non-urban centres (rural and semi-urban).

Permission to Cooperative Banks and Regional Rural Banks

Permission to Cooperative Banks and Regional Rural Banks to deal with the market and other banks

There are several formal and informal restrictions imposed upon the Co-operative (Co-op) Banks by the respective states in which they

30. DBC (Direct Business Catalyst) is a localised and personalised face of online trading portals (such as ICICIdirect) to the customers. DBCs, as facilitators, provide investment convenience to customers who are not net savvy and need guidance from an expert to help them with their investments. Further, DBC acts as authorised person on behalf of the client and acts as sub broker to such online portals. (*Source:* Internal note by ICICI Web Trade).

31. Scheduled Commercial Banks constitute those banks, which have been included in the Second Schedule of Reserve Bank of India (RBI) Act, 1934. RBI in turn includes only those banks in this schedule, which satisfy a few criteria laid down, vide section 42 (60) of the RBI Act. Being a part of the second schedule confers some benefits to the bank in terms of access to accommodation by RBI during the times of liquidity constraints. At the same time, however, this status also subjects the bank to certain conditions and obligation towards the reserve regulations of RBI.

32. Section 23 of the Banking Regulation Act, 1949 requires banks to obtain the prior permission of the RBI to open any new branch or shift a branch to a location outside of the city, town or village where it is originally located. Accordingly banks can open new branches only after obtaining specific authorisation from the RBI.

are registered and on the Regional Rural Banks (RRBs). Giving them a certain measure of operating freedom would, we feel, considerably enhance their effectiveness:

- Co-op banks/RRBs should also be permitted to purchase investment grade credit portfolios even if underlying assets are situated outside their jurisdiction. This will allow them to diversify their risks on the lending side—this would be imperative if they are to continue to be permitted to raise deposits from their own jurisdiction.
- The Co-op banks/RRBs should also be permitted to freely sell their assets to bring in liquidity and manage risks using assignment, securitisation and Inter-Bank Participation Certificates (IBPCs) as channels. This would help them increase exposure in their jurisdiction area by selling existing assets to other banks and using the funds thus generated to create more loans. The Co-op Banks and RRBs have strong loan origination capabilities in their command area but do necessarily have the lowest cost of funds or in some cases are liquidity constrained. The permission to sell/securitise their assets would free them from these constraints and place them at par with the MF-NBFC–ND mentioned earlier.

Better Market Risk Management

Market risks are a result[33] of both variations in supply and demand for crops that are not subjected to binding price controls and from the inability of controlled markets to respond timely and efficiently to changes in the market conditions. Variation in the market price fetched by the farmers is a reflection of the market risk. Market risks may be due to factors affecting timely delivery of produce to markets or the quality of the produce (e.g. poor feeder roads and storage/transport facilities in combination with perishable, bulky produce), as well as to changes in the demand or price (due to factors such as glut in the market at the time of harvest or lack of demand due to change in the consumption pattern). We discuss below a few strategies, which in our opinion will help address some of the market risk issues.

---

33. Hollinger, 2004.

Warehouse Finance

Warehouse finance clearly represents an opportunity to give the farmer access to cheap finance on a post-harvest basis as well as allow him the opportunity to not be subjected to distress sale situations. This has enormous benefits for the small farmer because the large farmer is often able to hoard the commodity in case he has higher price expectations. It is the small farmer that needs to sell as soon as the crop is harvested. The warehouse receipt needs to be made a negotiable instrument. In the current form, banks are reluctant to lend to the small farmer, and when they do, lend at high interest rates. However, if the goods are sold forward on a futures exchange such as National Commodity and Derivatives Exchange Ltd. (NCDEX) where the goods are deposited in a warehouse (an electronic warehouse receipt is issued) and graded appropriately. As the goods are certified, there is no question on the grade and quality of the good. As it is sold in the futures market, the value of the future proceeds is fixed. The bank now does not carry any risk on such loans and can lend at a lower interest rates. Clearly, the farmer's holding power now increases, as he does not have to resort to distress sale any longer. Annexure A.5.3 contains a brief from the National Collateral Management Services (NCMSL) on the current state of warehousing in India and pointers to the future direction for enhancing warehouse-based finance.

Improved Price Discovery

Improved Price Discovery through Exchanges and Automated Auction Markets

One key driver of value for farmers in general but specifically for improving access to finance is the development of national warehouse receipt/spot market for both dry and wet goods. An NCDEX type platform[34] for limit-order matching type trades and a SAFAL type

34. Futures exchanges, which already have the platform for efficient price discovery can actually also get into spot trading. Today the farmer has a bundled product in the *mandi*: price information, decision to sell, physical delivery and financial realisation. Quite clearly he does not really have an option once he goes to the *mandi* where he has to sell the product at the offered price. But if we look at the NCDEX solution: the farmer views various spot prices (polled by NCDEX) in his village and decides where he has to sell his goods. He then goes to the terminal (there are over 8000 in the country today) and places the order. Once the order is placed, he moves to the mandi of his choice and delivers the goods. Financial realisation is instantaneous once his commodity account is certified and the payment received from the buyer. For this the APMC laws need to be changed to permit futures exchanges to trade in commodities.

platform for Dutch and English Auctions are essential for these markets. All of the *Mandi's* need to be electronically linked to these exchanges and prices made available to all the farmers. Through the whole Village Knowledge Centre proposal (and other similar internet based initiatives) trading platforms need to be extended to the farthest corners of the country. In case of SAFAL, since there is need for a much larger market yard infrastructure in other parts of the country as well, there is a need to promote the creation of a number of such markets but all with both physical and on-line auctioning capability (including from overseas) so that price discovery can happen on a local as well as national and global[35] basis.

Restructure the Minimum Support Price (MSP) Mechanism

While there is no doubt that in the process of transition and in the face of enormous subsidies offered by other countries to their farmers there is a need for some form of subsidisation to the small farmer, it needs to be examined if the MSP is the best way to offer this. Putting in place a more transparent and effective mechanism of giving direct support to the farmer would serve the interest of the farmers more than the present system of MSP. For instance, weather futures[36] (temperature-related weather derivatives), could be seen as alternative to crop insurance and even MSP by way of option trading by farmers wherein government could think in terms of paying the options premium on behalf of the farmer. A few alternative mechanisms to MSP that could be administered through commodity exchanges have been discussed separately in Annexure A.5.4.

---

35. The concept of an offshore exchange similar to the offshore banking unit could be permitted so that global price discovery can happen right here in India. Then those entities that are permitted to access international exchanges can trade with these offshore exchanges, which are physically, located right here in India.

36. According to UNCTAD's global expert on commodity futures Lamon Rutten, weather futures are a good example of product innovation. "Weather futures are important and cheaper than crop insurance which is important to make the agriculture sector cost-effective under the WTO regime." Weather futures were first traded on the Chicago Mercantile Exchange (CME) in the year 1999 and since then they have picked up significant volumes. It has also started trading in the Euronext-London International Financial Futures Exchange (LIFFE). NCDEX intends to launch this facility in the country soon.

Banks to be Permitted to Trade Agricultural Commodities

Since there is an expectation that banks will: (a) provide large amounts of finance against crop risk and (b) extend outreach of financial services deep into rural India, it is imperative that they be permitted to trade these commodities directly on their own balance sheet (both domestically and cross-border) so that they can hedge out the risks that they already incur on their balance sheet, provide a larger proportion of current value as commodity finance to the small farmer and offer simpler financial products such as commodity forward contracts to those farmers that cannot afford to trade in the minimum lot sizes of the national exchanges—the current permissions make it impossible for the small and marginal farmer and the farmer without direct exports (but with similar price risks) to access these risk management instruments. In many situations buyers or sellers may need fixed price situations rather than attempt to engineer them through hard-to-enforce contract-farming frameworks it may be better to allow financial intermediaries to launch longer-term fixed-floating commodity swap markets. Banks can act as an aggregator here and represent the farmers on the exchanges on a fee basis. Farmers would thus be able to trade on the exchanges. Further, by covering the farmer, the banks are also able to ensure that the credit risk in lending to the farmers is mitigated by selling on futures exchanges.

Management of Rainfall Risk

The Indian farmer is more affected by weather than his counterparts in many parts of the world. Dependency on rainfall continues to be high. We discuss below a two-pronged strategy of mitigating rainfall risk and of augmenting irrigation and water markets for higher efficiency in water use.

Need for More Weather Stations

Weather insurance[37] contracts have already been launched in a

37. Weather insurance has multiplier effect on the economy as it enables access to factors of production. Adequate protection offered through the weather insurance product enhances the risk taking capacity of the farmers, banks, microfinance lenders and agro-based industries. This in turn would result in boosting the entire rural economy.

contd...

limited way in the country. Along with Price Risk the risk of rainfall failure (or excess rainfall) is the biggest driver of systemic shocks for the farmer. While ICICI Lombard has worked hard to develop the basic contract design along with the Commodity Risk Management Group (CRMG) of the World Bank and now a few other insurance companies, notably, IFFCO-Tokyo and AIC have also launched a similar contract, the availability of high quality and automated rain gauges remains a substantial problem leaving the farmer who has bought this insurance contract very highly exposed to basis risk. Investment by government in setting up of weather stations[38] across the country would enable the farmers to protect themselves from the vagaries of nature. This would also enhance the flow of credit to agriculture as the basic crop risk is mitigated to a large extent. NCDEX through National Collateral Management Services limited (NCMSL) is setting up such weather stations in few parts of the country. As of now NCMSL has installed 88 weather stations in 10 states. The presence of these weather stations will also improve the quality of forecasts that the Meteorological Bureau is able to make. Annexure A.5.5 gives a brief on the importance of weather stations and its utility in the weather insurance context.

Irrigation and Water Markets

There is an urgent need to develop local markets for water in which there is private interest in developing deep tube wells and irrigation projects. The Electricity Act has permitted wholesale purchase of electricity and resale by private entrepreneurs. In a similar manner if this is permitted for water it will become possible for banks to enter as financiers of irrigation projects in a manner that does not

---

...contd...

Further, as the product is developed on the foundation of universally acceptable parameters, it is easier to transfer the risk to international financial markets through reinsurance. This allows for global pooling of risk and thereby more competitive 'portfolio adjusted' pricing for the insurer and ultimately for the farmers. (*Source*: Internal Paper by ICICI Lombard.)

38. By installing modern weather stations, data on various weather parameters can be collected e.g. rainfall, sunshine, air temperature (maximum and minimum), air pressure, wind speed, relative humidity and dew points. This could be used for regular and timely weather data collection by expanding and strengthening network of weather stations to meet the requirements of not only weather insurance but also to provide real time data to the government and agriculture departments and the farming community.

have recourse to the Government. A paper by Professor Mark Rosenzweig[39] and Professor Andrew Foster that suggests this approach may also lead to better use of water and even to the private financing of watershed development work.[40] The current approach of the Government directly financing irrigation projects from its budget or through Special Purpose Vehicles does not lend itself to financing by banks and is therefore limited to the extent of resources that the state governments are able to deploy. While the experiments with Water User Associations using an SHG format have been noteworthy they have not yet been able to scale to the extent expected barring a few select pockets—it may be useful to carefully examine why this has happened. BASIX and PRADAN have been engaged in this task for a number of years and may be able to provide some useful inputs. Several countries, including parts of India have experimented with innovative approaches in water (including irrigation) segment, a few of which are discussed in Annexures A.5.6 and A.5.7.

Creation of Complementary Infrastructure

The pace and pattern of agricultural development is largely conditioned by the growth of infrastructure facilities relating to roads, electricity, etc.[41] Thorsten Beck, Asli and Maria in a study on the banking sector spanning 99 countries find that better infrastructure reduces the cost of banking service delivery and makes the extension of bank outlets more cost-effective, thus increasing the use of banking services. Stephen Jones[42] in a recent study points out that there is strong international evidence[43] to suggest that infrastructure

39. Foster and Rosenzweig (2005).

40. An example of such a model is the work done by the N.M. Sadguru Development Foundation: *www.nmsadguru.org*. This is an NGO which has done some outstanding watershed work but on a limited scale as they do not have the resources to scale this. The challenge is to convert this into a corporate model, which can be financed by banks.

41. Beck, Demirguc-Kunt and Peria (2005).

42. Jones (2006).

43. Cook (2003) summarising studies (as quoted in Stephens Jones paper) on China, India, Thailand and Indonesia on determinants of rural poverty reduction concludes that the consistent finding is that investment in roads and education have been the main drivers of rural poverty reduction (with agricultural research and development also important in those studies where it has been examined). The poverty impact of irrigation and power investments has been positive but significantly smaller.

investment is central both for accelerating growth and for reducing inequality and making growth patterns more pro-poor. The paper further highlights that in terms of direct impact on the poor, water and sanitation services (mainly through their impact in improving health outcomes), roads, Information and Communication Technologies (ICT), and electric power have greater significance. A FAO study points out that, lack of investment in rural infrastructure gradually shifts comparative advantage of an area back towards subsistence production at very low-income and little multiplier to the rural non-farm sector. FAO study quotes from Winters[44] study that "the transaction costs of trade with remote villages are often so great that it can be cheaper for grain mills to buy from distant commercial growers than from small farmers located in the region." However, improved infrastructure also lowers the final cost of imports in the producing areas. We discuss below few possible approaches in building a strong, viable rural infrastructure network in select areas while Annexure A.5.8 generally discusses several innovative ways in which Rural Infrastructure may be financed.

Power

There is clearly a need for more power to be made available to farmers.[45] While there is slow progress happening in both the expansion of the grid and national generation capacity it should be possible to develop local power plants using renewable energy[46]

44. Winters (2000).

45. Presently, around 63 per cent of the rural households in the country remain un-electrified. The estimated cost of connecting the remote villages alone by power is placed at around Rs. 37.00 billion. An enabling provision has been made in the Electricity Bill 2001 permitting stand-alone systems (including those based on renewable sources of energy and other non-conventional sources of energy) for management of distribution of power in rural areas through panchayati raj institutions, users' associations, co-operatives and non-governmental organisations.

46. India's national electrification targets include providing electricity cover to all the villages by the year 2007 and to all the households by the year 2012. There is a special thrust on renewables for ushering last mile electricity connectivity in the country. Renewables also offer long-term ecological gains over conventional fossil fuels and compare favourably in per unit cost of production *vis-à-vis* conventional energy sources on a life cycle cost concept. The national targets therefore include 50,000 MW of the energy to be exploited by the year 2050 through renewable energy

contd...

sources such as biomass[47] wind and solar energy. A brief note from TERI[48] on renewables and Decentralised Distrbuted generation (DDG) in India has been put in Annexure A.5.9.

A pilot project done with NOIDA power (details enclosed in Annexure A.5.10) suggests that if high quality supply of power is combined with a loan for the purchase of a high quality (backed by warranty) the farmer is prepared to pay for the power. ICICI Bank has recently also opened dialogue with companies like Tata BP Solar, Shell

---

...contd...

sources. There are around 18,000 villages in the country where grid supplies are not possible/unviable and where renewables alone can be harnessed for providing electricity coverage. India has a large potential for renewable energy (RE), an estimated aggregate of over 100,000 MW. In addition, the scope for generating power and thermal applications using solar energy is huge. This provides ample opportunities to entrepreneurs, business associations at the village level.

47. Decentralised Energy Systems India (DESI) Power, has launched an innovative programme called EmPower Partnership Programme (EmPP). EmPower Partnership Programme, links employment and power for the sustainable development of the village and rural areas. DESI Power's business model involves building small scale (50 KW to 500 KW) biomass gasification based power plants in remote villages with direct association of local partners (NGO/*Panchayat*/co-operative) who own and operate the plant while technical help is provided by DESI Power which also takes up small equity in the project. The village level biomass projects by Desi Power are of small scale and typical examples of distributed generation, transmission and distribution, which is being mooted for last mile village power connectivity. The projects set up by DESI power are need based where demand of power has emanated from the locals themselves (in view of either lack of grid connectivity or reliable/ negligible grid supply) and particularly the local entrepreneurs/ farmers having own micro enterprises/using irrigation pump sets who can afford to pay reasonable cost for supply of reliable/quality power. Currently these local industries entrepreneurs (shop owners, etc.) and users of irrigation pump sets are using diesel based gensets—the supply from that is costing them Rs. 8-10/kwh (in addition to the capital investment) as against supply of power at Rs. 4.5-5.00/kwh from the pure gas based biomass projects of Desi Power. The replacement of fossil fuels power generation by small scale biomass gasification systems in these kind of projects also results in savings in Co2 emissions (unto 550 tonnes/year per 100 KW) leading to ecological gains besides creation of additional village level employment opportunities. The farmers are likely to benefit on account of assured buy back for biomass produced by them as also assured lower cost irrigation through pump sets powered by the biomass plant. Besides the same, supply of power in the villages is likely to trigger socio economic development in the near vicinity (for example in a biomass based project at Baharbari in Araria by the Desi power a small village level market came up within months of setting up of the power plant which is drawing power from the biomass power project.)

48. Please refer to website *http://www.teriin.org/* of The Energy Resources Institute (TERI).

Solar for making available cheaper solar PV (Photo Voltaic) systems to rural clientele. There is also the possibility of using very small hydro projects (5 KW) that would enable them to have a reasonable power supply to dry organic mushrooms, berries, and other high-value exports.[49]

Rural Roads

This is a clear need in rural India and there a strong role that banks can play in financing these roads. However, the whole process would be facilitated greatly if one could take a project finance approach towards the financing of these roads, identify potential bodies or organisations that may be willing to pay at least a part of the user charges that would be needed to pay for these roads. These could be organisations such as the local Mandi Board, a local dairy or even a local corporate. CRISIL has built a strong capability in this entire work and could be hired to develop these projects. There is also a need to develop a framework for prioritising the choice of roads in terms of which ones are more critical. Annexure A.5.11 discusses the current status of rural roads and provides several examples of how rural roads may be financed.

Supply Chain Infrastructure

In the era of globalisation, competition is no longer among firms, but among supply chain networks. The agriculture supply chain network in India is characterised by inefficiency and exploitation at different levels. To unblock real values of agriculture, the focus must be on the entire supply chain network and not just the production aspects.[50] Area specific commodity approach to fixing the complete chain is the most appropriate strategy whether it is mango in UP, litchi in Bihar, pineapple in Tripura, oranges in Nagpur, Apples in

---

49. Suggested by Professor Jessica Wallack.

50. R. Balakrishnan, Executive Director, NABARD in a *Business Line* Article (April 7, 2006) opines that an effective supply chain network calls for intensive collaboration among producers, processors, logistics providers, wholesalers and retailers to supply products demanded by the domestic and international customers in a cost effective manner. The same needs to be complimented with horizontal collaboration among policymakers, researchers, extension agencies, technology companies and financial institutions.

Himachal or poultry in Tamil Nadu. Typically the chain is broken or is weak in several links, which could be related to production, technology or marketing aspects. Private participation, through contract farming and investment in infrastructure could be one of the strategies to overcome most of the supply chain lacunae.

For instance, analysis of supply chain of grapes in Nashik reveals lack of effective logistics infrastructure (which is customised to cater to the requirement of foreign markets) leading to lot of wastage, quality degradation and consequently lower price realisation by the farmers. Private participation could be explored for setting up a dedicated state of the art air cargo[51]-handling unit at Nashik[52] for the purpose of exporting fresh vegetables and fruits to the premium markets of EU. Himachal apples[53] is another case where integrated cold chains equipped with Controlled Atmosphere (CA) technology and an end-to-end supply chain (complete logistic and distribution network) could fetch better prices to the apples farmers in the domestic market segment.

Extension Services

Given the scale and size of rural India, location and demand specific innovations in extension delivery are called for effective dissemination of technology and for dissemination of real time market based information to the farmers. In a similar concept to the value chain approach, extension must be provided from an end-to-end

---

51. Kenya exports Rs. 5.00 bn worth of fresh vegetables like peas, beans, okra to Europe every year by air.

52. Nashik provides suitable agro climatic conditions for the cultivation of a number of vegetables and fruits throughout the year. Since the nearest airport with air cargo facility is at Mumbai and considering the perishable nature of these products it becomes necessary for setting up such a unit at Nashik with cold storage facilities.

53. ICICI Bank in its endeavour to finance complete supply chain network is financing setting up of an integrated cold chain equipped with CA technology and an end-to-end supply chain project of Adani Agri Fresh Limited (AAFL) in Himachal. The Cold Chain project will be focused on apples, as apples can be stored in CA stores for up to an year and differential between price at the farm gate during the peak season and that at the endconsumer level during the off-season is very large (more than three times) leaving plenty of scope for greater value addition and sharing of efficiency gains between the consumer, the producer and the company. The company will also be providing its services to farmers, traders and agents for storage, logistics and marketing thereby reducing storage and commodity risks while improving asset utilisation.

perspective covering from preproduction[54] to production to the marketing stage. Some of the strategies could be crop/commodity specific extension, group based extension, private extension through input companies and extension in form of Public Private Partnership (PPP), extension through usage of ICT like interlinking of *mandis*. A few approaches in extension have been discussed separately in Annexure A.5.12.

An effective extension system needs to have strong inter linkages with R&D. Investment in creating need based and efficient R&D infrastructure needs to be an integral part of the extension paraphernalia. Even as new R&D centres are promoted on private mode, co-sharing of public R&D facilities with industry could be allowed to unlock higher values out of existing public infrastructure as well as to attract private participation in market based research activities.

Conclusion

The above note outlined several steps that can be taken relatively quickly in the following areas:

1. Development of a Comprehensive Rural Information System.
2. Management and Recovery of Transaction Costs.
3. Creation of New Rural Financial Institutions and Financial Services Infrastructure.
4. Better Market Risk Management.
5. Management of Rainfall Risk.
6. Creation of Complementary Infrastructure.

It is our view that these steps, particularly the first five are absolutely critical if the business of rural finance has to be put on a firm footing. If these steps are taken immediately then over the period

54. Pre-production extension to include information on right variety, right seed, right soil and planning of land mix etc. Production based extension to include right usage and timing of inputs and availability of credit while marketing extension to include right time to sell, information on storage options and warehouse receipts based funding, prevailing market prices including help to farmers in participating in commodity trading to receive better prices.

of the next five years an orderly rural financial system would evolve providing a full range of financial services to rural audiences and leading to a reduction in interest rates without leading to high level of exclusion.

ANNEXURES

Annexure A-5.1

Financial Innovations and Network Operations (FINO)

Background to the Initiative

There is a distinct lack of access to financial services in the country for the poor people with some estimates putting the overall number of unbanked at over 500 million. While several initiatives have been taken on this front in the past including nationalisation of banks, creation of Regional Rural Banks, etc, the situation has not improved on account of a variety of reasons. Financial services delivery in the rural scenario is characterised by high cost of delivery, lack of banking infrastructure and poor communication facilities. High illiteracy levels and lack of financial awareness further compounds operational challenges in validating the customer and in the need to provide the customer with assisted banking. Technology while having transformed banking for the urban educated, its impact has been largely unfelt in case of the rural customer as well as the urban micro customer.

The micro finance institutions (MFIs) that are active in this market space often work with rudimentary technology systems which while useful in providing low cost solutions for their small requirements, are becoming an impediment in their growth since these do not provide scale in number of transactions, customers handled and product breadth, and also at the same time do not create a credible auditable transaction trail. High capital costs for new systems and inefficient operating models act as significant entry barriers for scaling MFI operations.

Additionally, the issue of uniquely identifying the end customer has remained a challenge in this market. Various card-based solutions that rely on PINs and connectivity have failed to show the desired impact. The need is for more robust solutions that provide foolproof customer identity, which are based on traits that an individual bears and are not based on customer's memory.

To increase reach and scale, it is essential to expand the transaction capture points out from the branches and into the field. Even though this has been managed to a large extent by manual processes performed by human agents, the need is to automate the last-mile transaction capturing to achieve greater operational efficiency.

ICICI Bank has, on the insistence of several MFIs and with support of a few sectoral players like Consultative Group to Assist the Poor (CGAP) (under the World Bank), Grameen Foundation USA and Small Industrial Development Bank of India (SIDBI), taken a lead to facilitate a robust IT and Services Backbone (backbone) for use by various MFIs and other players in the unbanked market-space.

The technology platform will be offered by a separate company on a utility model. The backbone—built using the best-in-class solutions—is envisioned as a common sectoral resource and is positioned as a technology utility service that will be shared by any institution that forms a part of the initiative. The backbone would facilitate these entities to offer not only credit but also other financial services—liabilities and investments, where they may not be the principal, but only market these products. While the scoping of the system is being done for MFIs, the system would have capabilities to serve the requirements of other micro-agencies as well (co-operative banks, local agents, etc.).

The Solution Offering

1. *Core product engine*: The core banking engines cover the entire life cycle of product activities on both the asset and liability sides required by the customers. While this system would have the complete functionalities of a large-scale banking set-up, it would be offered to these entities at an affordable cost. In order to address the connectivity issues of remotely located branches, the system has been designed to enable branch operations in off-line mode with periodic uploads into the central back-end engine whenever connectivity is available.
2. *Distribution channel*: Since the country does not have any national identification set-up and the customer segment in question, does not have requisite documentation for unique identification, biometrics provided the answer for uniquely identifying the customers. Since most of the customers are illiterate, biometrics would also help in validation without the use of signatures or PINs, which would be necessary for them to operate their accounts. Hence these customers are proposed to be issued smart cards for operating their accounts, which would also carry their biometric fingerprints, which would be used to authenticate them for the transactions. Further, the use of smart cards can make it possible to conduct financial transactions in the off-line mode thus obviating the need of relying on the uncertain always-available connectivity. The company would thus issue smart cards on behalf of

the principal(s), set-up Points of Transactions (PoTs) and provide mobile devices to enable last-mile transaction capabilities.

3. *Credit Bureau Services*: The availability of authorised customer identity and transaction data presents the requisite raw material to offer a comprehensive suite of credit bureau services that facilitate improved credit decision-making process. These services would be available to all the participating entities.
4. *Innovation*: Innovation—both in products and processes—is the underlying theme uniting the three service pillars that allows the backbone to remain in sync with developments worldwide and avoid obsolescence. The company would continue to work on and develop innovative solutions to serve this market more effectively.

Annexure A-5.2

Shared Technology Platforms[55]

Information Systems as a Tool for Financial Leverage

One of the key challenges to scaling up of existing MF operations and creating new entities is the existence of a robust technology platform. A good technology platform requires substantial investment and acts as a significant entry/scale up barrier for most organisations. ICICI Bank, at the insistence of its partner MFIs, has taken an initiative to build a robust sectoral IT resource for micro finance sector to support the operations of MFIs. The technology platform will enable MFIs to become an aggregator of various financial services for its client base in a specified geography.

This would increase the load of data management on the MFI and would require systems capable of dealing with a very large number of transactions per day,[56] quick update and validation mechanisms, traceability, aggregation and drill down to the lowest level. Some of the key aspects where a strong technology platform will add value to the microfinance operations are:

- Reduce transaction cost
- Data available in soft copy
- Facilitate thorough appraisal of MFIs for enhanced funding
- Capability to interface with multiple peripherals, including ATMs, PDA, mobile phones, use of POS terminals, etc.

55. *Source*: Catalytic Funding to Scale Micro Finance in India by Rupalee Ruchismita.
56. Microfinance is associated with low value, high volume transactions.

- Better data management and reporting capacities
- Duplicate data available reducing possibility of loss of valuable data
- Standardisation of data for the sector, while continuing to provide flexibility at the front end.

This platform would address the long-term automation needs of the MFIs. The platform while being designed to be in line with the latest technologies will also be scalable and flexible for future modifications. This would be an end-to-end solution automating the entire chain of MFI activities.

A Centralised Core Banking backbone with connectivity to the MFI branches and branch level systems would form part of the systems level automation. This application would be hosted on shared hardware located at a centralised location. The data would have logical separation to prevent unauthorised use of data by any other individual/entity. Since both the software and the hardware will be shared, the cost of the system per user will drop significantly. This high quality shared technology platform can be used by MFIs as well as by Cooperative Banks and Regional Rural Banks and could solve multiple problems that the financial institutions working for the sub-prime sector face.

Wipro,[57] Infosys,[58] I-Flex,[59] 3iInfotech[60] and others are in the process of developing such a platform at an estimated fixed cost of USD 23 million. Apart from initiating the project, an effort is underway to raise sufficient funding for the project, with a view to largely subsidise the cost of accessing the technology platform. While several sources would be needed to completely fund this, a contribution to such a platform could go a long way in helping the IT platform achieve financial closure. In addition, field automation can be achieved through provision of multi application smart cards; this could potentially be the same cards as discussed above, to the customers and access through handheld devices at the agent level/POS devices at various other locations.

Annexure A-5.3

Warehousing in India and Future Pointers[61]

Current Status

In the initial period, the approach of the Indian Government towards the

57. *www.wipro.com.*
58. *www.infosys.com.*
59. *www.iflex.com.*
60. *www.3i-infotech.com.*
61. Note by Praveen PA, NCMSL.

warehousing sector in India was to provide the capacity required for buffer stock and operational stock of foodgrains to maintain the public distribution system and general warehousing. The approach was to provide scientific storage capacity and reduce dependence on the capacity under cover and plinth. Due to this reason and on account of the large investments needed in building of cold storages, the sector was dominated by the Central government and the State Government. The participation of the private sector was a miniscule percentage of the entire warehousing capacity of the country.

According to the latest FCI estimate Punjab has the highest storage capacity followed by Andhra Pradesh, Uttar Pradesh and Haryana, while Sikkim and the other NE states have the least storage capacity. The major player FCI has 24.33 million tonnes (owned and hired) of storage capacity in over 1451 godowns all over India.

There are three agencies in the public sector which are engaged in building large scale storage/warehousing capacity namely, Food Corporation of India (FCI), Central Warehousing Corporation (CWC) and 17 State Warehousing Corporations (SWCs). While the capacity available with FCI is used mainly for storage of foodgrains that with CWC and SWCs is used for storage of foodgrains as also certain other items. The position of storage/warehousing capacity available with the FCI/CWC/SWCs is given in the table below:

(in Million Tonnes)

Storage Capacity	*Covered*	*Cap*	*Total*
Owned	12.82	2.21	15.03
Hired			
Central/State Agencies	0.73		0.73
CWC/SWC	8.32		8.32
Others	1.8	1.36	3.16
Total	23.67	3.57	27.24
Storage Capacity Utilisation	Covered		Cap
Range	35-68%		18-55%
At The End of The Year	50%		18%

Source: *FCI Annual Report 2003-04.*

Significant unutilised capacity is mainly due to the increased off-take notably for export purpose.

With a view to encourage widespread distribution of the warehousing infrastructure across public and private sectors, the Central Government encouraged the construction/renovation of rural warehouses through a Capital Investment Subsidy Scheme, the Grameen Bhandaran Yojana in 2001-02 which was administered by the National Bank for Agricultural and Rural Development (NABARD). During the Tenth Five Year Plan (2002-2007) the FCI and CWC propose to construct an additional storage capacity of 4.55 lakh MT and 9.37 lakh MT respectively.

Regulatory Structure

The warehouses in India of the Central Warehousing Corporation (CWC) and State Warehousing Corporation (SWC) are currently regulated under the Warehousing Corporations Act, 1962 and the respective State warehouse laws. As per the current laws, the warehouse receipts are not negotiable, but only transferable unless the transferability is restricted by warehouseman. However, there are no prescribed standards for service quality, no uniform practice for quality verification and no accreditation body in the warehousing sector. Due to this reason, the warehouses, except government warehousing, are not relied upon by the banking sector for extending warehouse receipt finance.

Requirements for Strengthening the Warehousing Sector

Some Pointers

- Action plan and implementation of Negotiable Warehouse Receipt System is in progress which would have credibility with both the trading community as well as the banking system
- To augment the limited infrastructure and resources available with the Save Grain Campaign and in order to cover larger number of farmers/ villages, active collaboration and support both in terms of money and in kind was ensured from the State Governments, NGOs. *Gram Panchayats*, Corporate Houses like SAIL, TATA Steel, Joint Plant Committee (JPC) under the Ministry of Steel, etc.
- At present, Indian Grain Storage Management and Research Institutes (IGMRI) situated at Hapur (UP) and its field stations at Ludhiana (Punjab), Hyderabad (AP), and Jorhat (Assam) are carrying out research and training activities in the field of post harvest grain management. These institutions are organising various types of training programmes on all aspects of post harvest technology of foodgrains for the benefit of different stakeholders in the warehousing industry. The technology

developed by these Institutes is transferred to the farming community by the Save Grain Campaign and disseminated among farmers/farm women and also to the corporate level officers for adoption/ introduction in scientific storage of foodgrain.

- In order to make available efficient human resource in this field the premier management institutes are running cold chain and warehouse management courses and imparting training to the existing manpower.
- Private sector is also constructing storage facilities but due to its capital intensive nature and gestation period they are still on a small scale. But with cheap credit, and other favourable environmental conditions, more and more participation is expected. The enlarging commodity market is playing a strong stimulant in this way. It is estimated that about 20 million tonnes storage capacity is immediately required to fill up the vacant space (Agarwal, N.L). Uneven and inequitable distribution of storage facilities between States also need to be corrected soon.
- According to an estimate mere prevention of storage losses alone could feed 75 crores of people for a period of 11 months and 2 days. Existing storage capacity could only accommodate 31 per cent of the total agricultural produce and barely 10 per cent of the total fruits and vegetables (Puttamadiah, C).
- Doorstep storage facilities are required in the production-shed areas and also in the North Eastern states.

Keeping in view the requirements and future needs to encourage the confidence of the lenders in the credibility of the warehousing sector, the following steps should be undertaken:

- Technical standards should be established to encourage confidence in the warehousing infrastructure.
- The financial position of the warehousing company should satisfy certain minimum criteria to create stability of the warehouses.
- Managerial competence and good governance for credibility.
- Technology usage for web connectivity, networking, electronic commodity balances and trading and for ensuring connectivity with other logistics players, lenders, etc.
- Stable and reliable power source.
- Low cost and accessible grading and assaying facilities for ensuring that the goods accepted in the warehouses adhere to some minimum and objective criteria with respect to quality parameters.

Annexure A-5.4

Alternatives to Minimum Support Price through Exchange Mechanism[62]

Minimum Support Price Mechanism

The MSP programme of the government is analogous to an 'option' where the farmer has the right but not the obligation to sell the goods to the government at the MSP. At the time of harvest, the farmer can see the market price and then decide whether he can sell to the government (FCI) or not.

Alternative Possibilities through Commodity Exchanges like NCDEX

Within the realm of options, which are currently not permitted by the regulatory system, the commodity exchanges can provide a substitute for the same. Let us assume that the exchanges like NCDEX have a widespread warehousing reach so that all farmers have access to these exchanges. Alternatively all FCI warehouses become collection centres of the commodity exchange. Let us look at the various modalities.

The first issue is of course the one of quality. Farmers today do not pay attention to quality as they are assured of a good price by the government. Once they can trade on exchanges, then they can actually migrate to better quality of the crop, which can fetch a higher price. By growing this superior variety, they can then get into options trading and pay only an option premium. This premium can be paid by the FCI/government, which can eschew the cost of handling this entire set of food grains and still be better off as the subsidy element is reduced.

The second issue is where the FCI acts as an aggregator for the farmers and sells directly on the exchange for a better price and either does this gratis or charges a fee for the farmer where the farmer is willing to bear this cost because the price realised is higher than the MSP. In this case, the FCI warehouses would need to serve as the NCDEX warehouses and follow the same delivery processes as are prevalent on the exchange.

The third scenario is where the FCI decides to stop the open-ended procurement system where currently it is perforce compelled to pick up all the grains that are offered. Under the proposed dispensation, FCI will procure only that much as is required for PDS and food security (buffer stock).

---

62. Note from Madan Sabnavis, NCDEX (March 2006).

Subsequently all grains brought will be routed onto the exchange in the form of options. FCI will pay the premium and farmers can get a better deal. If the prices fall, then of course the FCI will take on the grains at the MSP.

In the last scenario, agencies like NCMSL can play a major role. Today a number of states are left out of the procurement process. NCMSL has procured rice for FCI this year in Orissa and MP. NCMSL can now be an aggregator and can get into options on the exchange directly and have FCI write these options and hence pay the premium. This way the operations of food procurement can be enlarged.

These are the various alternatives where commodity exchanges can fill in for the FCI.

Annexure A-5.5

Weather Stations Infrastructure for Index based Insurance[63]

Weather Insurance and Need for Accurate Information

The Indian farmer is more affected by weather than his counterparts in many parts of the world. In the last couple of decades, crop insurance has started assuming significant importance in the rural economy. While crop success or failure depends upon many factors, weather is predominant among them. Insurance companies are now looking at weather insurance itself as a product, which is directly relatable, measurable and appeals to the insurer, insured and the lender as a product the market is ready for.

However, weather insurance products can be structured only around reliable and verifiable data and the implementation is also dependent on availability of properly handled data sourced from tamper proof weather stations. Since the weather data decides the quantum of claim, if any, payable under the weather insurance, the accuracy of the data and secured environment under which the data is reported is very critical for its success.

Shortcomings of IMD Data

Till recently, all weather insurance contracts were written using IMD (Indian Meteorological Department) data, which has district level points of collection of weather data. However, it suffers from the following shortcomings:

63. Internal note by Neha Agarwal, ICICI Lombard.

1. Data recorded is not reported on time in many instances, which would result in delayed settlement of claims.
2. It has been noticed that there are huge gaps in reporting daily rainfall data even for major stations located at District Headquarters.
3. Weather stations are mostly located only at the District Headquarters and this data point is considered as the referral point for the whole district
4. Weather stations mostly are of vintage technology and do not have the capability to record and store data to ensure continuity of data.

Solution

Regular and timely weather data collection by expanding and strengthening network of weather stations to meet the requirements of not only weather insurance but also to provide real time data to the government and agriculture departments and the farming community.

By installing modern weather stations, data on various weather parameters can be collected e.g. Rainfall, Sunshine, Air temperature (Maximum and Minimum), Air pressure, Wind Speed, Wind Direction and Relative Humidity. ICICI Lombard is taking help of NCMSL in helping install such weather stations across the country. The current instrument that NCMSL uses for installation is 'Davis Instruments Cabled Vantage Pro2' which costs approximately Rs. 1.25–Rs. 1.5 lakhs. NCMSL in turn charges Rs. 4,800 per month from ICICI Lombard towards supply of weather data.

Till now, NCMSL has already installed 88 weather stations in 10 states across the country where Indian Meteorological Department's stations are either not present or are not functional. Besides for weather insurance, data from these stations are also being used for various modeling purposes.

High accuracy weather data find use in various industries. To further the benefits of these weather stations, it is important that Government supports such service providers and come forward to intensify the existing network of stations so that many more numbers of players can access the data at lower costs.

Annexure A-5.6

ICICI Bank Pilot Programme for Extending Finance to Organisations Supplying Low Cost Drinking Water Facilities in Rural Areas

Introduction

More than 1.00 billion people lack access to safe drinking water. Impure drinking water causes about 400 deaths per hour of children (below age 5), and hurts economic development. Water security has major implications for economic growth and public health. Together with transportation and electricity, it constitutes one of the three weakest components of Indian infrastructure. Studies show that investment in water purification and sanitation can reduce water-borne diseases by up to 75 per cent, many countries simply cannot spare the resources required to build capital-intensive, centralised water treatment facilities and distribution networks for their peri-urban and rural areas. India too is grappling with water related problems, which are more acute in rural areas where people rely on open wells, rivers, or lakes for their water supply. Studies have demonstrated the strong interlinkages between health and water. Access to clean water can do away/ mitigate several water borne diseases and consequently decrease spending health expenses.

Pilot by ICICI Bank

Routine use of bottled water, or fuel to boil drinking water, is unaffordable for the rural people. A robust effective and affordable technology, implemented in a financially viable model is needed for the rural poor. In its quest for developing commercially viable rural infrastructure models, ICICI Bank intends to support organisations providing low cost drinking water facilities to the rural poor. A few organisations like Naandi, Water Health International, and Water Aid are involved in providing water and sanitation facilities to the rural poor approached ICICI Bank in developing a commercially viable model of supplying drinking water to the rural poor.

Water Health International (WHI) has developed an innovative low cost water purification system that kills disease-causing microorganisms using ultraviolet light. It draws from the village water resources and its success derives from being community managed, which ensures equitable and efficient distribution of water at a very nominal price. Community water system developed by WHI can provide a village of up to 3000 people 10 litres of safe water per person each day, adding up to an annual water bill of approximately $2 per individual. The proceeds can cover the purchase of the UV system along with pumps, tanks, valves, controllers, civil structures, and maintenance. WHI has already done a few pilots of the model across the globe including few in Andhra Pradesh in India. In the absence of any other viable model of drinking water supply in rural areas, ICICI Bank is supporting the WHI for undertaking a few projects of supplying water to rural communities by levy of water charges. These projects will be of small scale and pilot in nature. Once the pilots are found to be successful, ICICI Bank would roll out similar facilities for other organisations and propagate the model across the country.

About Water Health International's Projects in India

Water Health International is a health-focused developer and manufacturer of innovative water purification and disinfection technology. The company is focused on providing technology and systems to deliver safe drinking water to the poor people who currently lack access to safe drinking water throughout the world.

WHI's novel and award-winning UV-based water purification and disinfection technology platform is modular and can be scaled easily to provide high quality drinking water to a broad range of population groups. The company is currently focused on providing systems to deliver affordable water to urban populations, and rural communities that lack access to municipal water supplies. Water Health's products are currently deployed in many countries around the world, including the United States and the Philippines.

WHI's decentralised systems require low capital expenditures and can be implemented quickly to meet longstanding needs of underserved populations. Water Health is currently working with Reddy's Naandi Foundation to install the company's community water systems in rural areas of India's state of Andhra Pradesh. While WHI is involved in building the systems and training community members to manage the daily operations and maintenance, Naandi is mobilising community interest in the programme with education programmes focused on safe water handling, sanitation, and hygiene to help communities fully realise the benefits of safe drinking water. WHI has formed a new company Water Health India that is solely dedicated to putting up community base water purification systems in different parts of the country.

Operational Structure

Water Health India will set up water purification facilities in different villages (basically the process will involve purification of water from available sources such as those from the local pond, lake. The capital cost of setting up purification facilities (one project) is estimated to be in the range of Rs. 2.0-

2.3 million. The proposed funding will be limited to Rs. 1.5 million per project while the balance will be contributed by Water Health India.

Purified water shall be sold to the rural consumers in 15 litre cans (capable of meeting a household daily requirement of water). Each can of Rs.15 litre will be priced at Rs. 1.50. Selling and collections will be done through a local agency, which shall be identified project wise, by Water Health India. The repayment of the loan will be through the project wise collections.

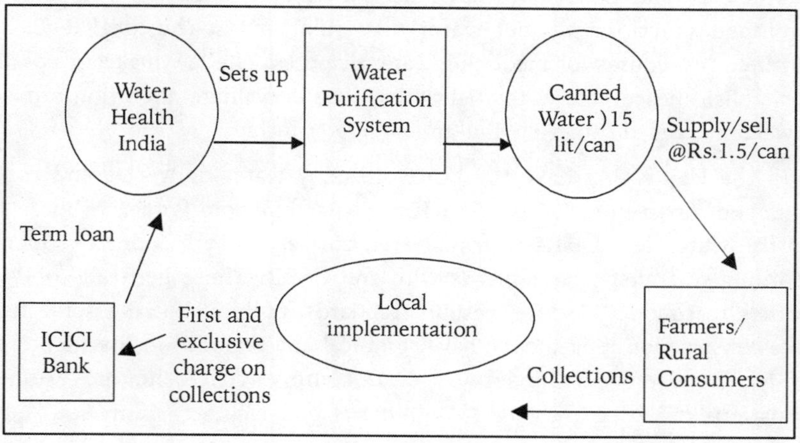

Annexure A-5.7

Other Experiments in Water Markets

Tradable Water Rights and Resource Allocation—Chile's Experience

Chile has also been a pioneer in ushering tradable water rights. The concept of tradable water rights was introduced in Chile in 1981. Under the system, while existing users of water were awarded property rights free of charge, the new property rights were sold through auction. The property rights covered under Chile's civil code can be freely traded in the open market and have legal value. The property rights having economic value can also be offered as loan collateral. The introduction of tradability of property rights has resulted in realignment of the consumption and use pattern of water. This has prompted farmers to adopt efficient irrigation systems such that their water consumption is reduced and the rights of the saved water can be sold to the city at higher prices. This has resulted in multiple benefits such as efficient utilisation of water, ecological gains from reduction in salinity due to excessive use of water The tradable water rights have also resulted in better water management by the water utilities.

Enabling Water Users Associations—China and US

In Hunan, China has legalised Water User Associations so that they can buy water and contract for construction of infrastructure. Enabled by a water law, the states in China have introduced a water extraction permit system; developed sanctions against water use violations at the local level and instituted procedures for mediating water disputes. The law makes it possible to establish measurable water rights that would facilitate allocation of water between sectors through buying and selling.

In the US, WUAs have the power to deny water deliveries and voting rights and can eventually take over land ownership from farmers who do not pay the water fee. Districts transferred to water users generally operate according to transfer agreements with the USBR. These generally obligate districts to conduct O&M at certain standards, build a capital reserve fund, make construction repayments, have technical and financial audits (done with USBR), have election observers, and comply with other government regulations.

Flexible System of Payment—South Africa

Prior to 2001 in Cato Crest, Durban, South Africa, a system of 'ground tanks' enabled the volume of water delivered to each household to be controlled by the local private entrepreneur. This was coupled with a flexible system of prepayment for water supplied; up-front payment could be made in full or in instalments. The system was self-regulating in terms of payment because people were required to pay in advance for the month, in order to receive an agreed volume of water. They knew what they were getting and could budget the cash flow accordingly. In Dolphin coast, a new tariff structure was introduced for the PPP; this created a tiered system of service levels and tariffs, which includes a 'lifeline' tariff of 10 kilolitres for low-income households.

Water Communities by Sewa in Gujarat

In addition to regular savings efforts promoted by SEWA, water user committees in about 25 villages in rural Gujarat have started separate Village Water Funds to be used for operations and maintenance expenses. Individuals contribute up to Rs 5 per month to the Water Fund. The sum collected in these Funds amounts to well over Rs. 1,00,000 in some villages.

Condominium Approach in Suez

Suez has utilised the 'condominium approach' for some projects in order to reduce the cost of access to service. Under this approach, households in a neighbourhood organise and agree to work together, providing their labour for excavation and filling work, as well as maintenance of the system once it is complete. To keep costs down, condominium systems use smaller pipe diameters, and pipes are buried in shallow trenches run through household lots or under sidewalks. The cost of condominium water connections has been shown to be less than 1/3 compared to conventional costs.

Indonesian Experience for Funding Maintenance of Irrigation Projects

A typical problem that has been plaguing almost all the developing nations is creation of public assets, which after a point of time deteriorate due to lack of operations and maintenance leading to colossal wastage of public funds spent on the assets. One of the novel ways to address this problem is by adopting the Indonesian approach for maintenance of irrigation projects. In collaboration with the World Bank and the Government of the Netherlands, the Government of Indonesia (GoI) has instituted an irrigation improvement fund (KIIF). The fund is set up at the district level using district and/or provincial funds and also loan funds/grant funds for start up. The funds are allotted among irrigation systems to federated Water User Associations (WUAs) that submit proposals for undertaking operations and maintenance work. The proposal includes the investment plan by WUAs to undertake maintenance work. A minimum standard of maintenance and quality provisions are stipulated and projects are allocated to the established WUA on the basis of criterion such as maintenance plan, WUA investment being put up, number of farm families to be benefited. We could also think in terms of adopting similar kind of model for ensuring upgradation and maintenance of our public assets by essentially involving the private sector and the stakeholders/locals.

Pani Panchayat Model

Innovations have also been made to maintain equity in the availability of irrigation water, through the Pani Panchayat model. Though the term refers to mobilisation of groups of farmers for the formulation and implementation of community irrigation projects, today it largely symbolises equitable distribution of water. The model, from the experiment of lift irrigation scheme in Naigaon in Maharashtra, is based on the fact that water is a common-pool resource therefore all the members in the village irrespective of land ownership could gain access to the utilisation of water resourced. Each member in the village was allocated water that would be sufficient to irrigate half an acre of area. These water rights were traded among the members for use. This enabled the landless to have equal rights over water and to enable to benefit from the common-pool resource.

Annexure A-5.8

Some Financing Models for Rural Infrastructure Projects

Infrastructure Funds

Projects that involve long-lived assets with long payback periods require low-cost, longterm finance. This type of finance is available only to governments and rated corporations. The inability to access low-cost capital holds back investment in much needed infrastructure. An infrastructure development fund could be constituted which could borrow from the government at concessional rates. The fund's role would be to provide a mix of loans and guarantees for loans originated by private lenders to infrastructure development projects. The fund could pool and securitise its loans to redistribute its portfolio and lower its borrowing costs. A fund on similar lines has been created in Australia in the form of the environment development fund.

Market-based Instruments

Market-based instruments (MBIs) are mechanisms for bringing a commercial focus and market-type disciplines to natural resource management. In Australia, MBIs are used in a number of policy settings including: greenhouse gas abatement, fishery management, salinity emissions, water entitlements and biodiversity enhancement. Two types of MBI with potential application to conveyance efficiency are environmental asset mechanisms and competitive tendering (auctions).

Environmental Assets

This model involves the government providing a legislative and planning framework for the creation of marketable assets or rights in the environmental outcomes from production or consumption decisions. The Renewable Energy

(Electricity) Act (2000) provides for the creation of a market in renewable energy credits (RECs). Under the Act, the production of renewable energy from sources such as wind and wave generation, and landfill gas, 'generates' RECs. RECs can be defined as negotiable instruments for acquitting obligations created in conventional energy production. Electrical energy retailers who operate in the Australian electricity market take on REC obligations when they sell retail electricity. Currently, retailers must offset 1 per cent of their sales by purchasing RECs. This will rise to 5 per cent by 2008. If retailers fail to acquit their REC obligations, they are 'fined' $40 for every MWh of REC not acquitted. The principal advantage of an environmental asset scheme over traditional approaches is that it provides incentives to seek least-cost solutions. It achieves this by creating a commercial focus and the market-discipline that comes with holding title to a valuable asset.

Apart from the renewable energy segment in India, environmental asset schemes would also seem to be technically feasible in the context of improving Water Use Efficiency (WUE) in irrigation conveyance systems. For example, the government might place a cap on water losses in a defined geographic area such as a catchment. (This could be achieved by changing legislation or perhaps through water management plans and/or conditions on irrigation district water licences.) Each irrigation district in a catchment could be assigned a share of water losses under the cap.

If a district invested in work to reduce losses below the baseline, 'credits' or environmental assets would be created. These could then be sold to other market participants to offset any increase in their water losses, say due to expansion in the area irrigated.

Competitive-tendering (Auction) Mechanisms

Competitive tendering as a price discovery mechanism can be used to improve the effectiveness of markets. The principal advantage of an auction over traditional methods is the price discovery element. An auction process involves government seeking bids from parties to provide specified services or undertake specified projects. Pre determined base technical and other quality standards are stipulated and bid is awarded on the basis of least cost.

In UK Private rail franchisees rights have been accompanied by the provisions of public grant subsides with the franchisee being awarded to the company requiring the lowest subsidy. At the same time strict quality and service obligations are put in place such that the infrastructure created is maintained in good working conditions. This has led to efficiencies in offering services to consumers with minimum and fixed drain on public resources.

FLDG based Funding

Another strategy for funding of large infrastructure projects could be by use of First Loss Default Guarantee Funds (FLDGs) by the Government.

RIDF Fund Utilisation[64]

A strategic options study could be done in all the states for preparing a master plan for rural road network and funds under the RIDF could be made available to finance only the identified projects. RIDF could also finance one time cost of such study, which must be done by experienced private consultants. The study could prioritise creation of such a network on the basis of desirability, social benefits, economic value etc. Similar approach could be adopted for creation of other facilities such as value addition centres, cool chain facility. This would enable utilisation of funds and creation of infrastructure in a systematic manner rather than in an *ad hoc* manner or under any influence from the vested forces.

Least Subsidy Model

In the UK, private rail franchisees rights have been accompanied by the provisions of public grant subsides with the franchisee being awarded to the company requiring the lowest subsidy. At the same time strict quality and service obligations are put in place such that the infrastructure created is maintained in good working condition. This has led to efficiencies in offering services to consumers with minimum and fixed drain on public resources. Similar strategy could be adopted to fund infrastructure projects in India with private participation

Bundling of Assets and Services

Bundling of assets and services is another option, which can attract private participation. This would require giving a catchment area under the control of the private sector such that he can draw his revenues from non irrigation activities as well-such as farming, setting up allied activities like processing unit, shops, etc. in the vicinity. This approach has been used in China and also is being used in the roads sector in India.

---

64. Panthary (2005).

Using Bonds for Raising Finance

Land Bank in South Africa and BAAC in Thailand are two examples, which have used the bond route for undertaking infrastructure and term loan projects. Land Bank issues bonds in the national capital market that closely match the terms and maturities of its term loan portfolio. Despite lending exclusively to agriculture and related activities, Land Bank has a sound history as a financial institution. Three factors are responsible for its good rating in the capital market: the bulk of the portfolio is relatively low risk, since it is lent to established medium- and large-scale commercial farmers; most of the portfolio is secured by mortgages on real estate; and government ownership provides an implicit guarantee of solvency in case of major external shocks.

BAAC also refinances a part of its medium- and long-term loan portfolio through bonds. Government ownership has certainly supported BAAC's success in mobilising commercial funds through deposits and bonds, though the Government has only stepped in once during the recent financial crisis. However, compared with Land Bank, BAAC finances mainly small- and medium-scale farmers, and its term loan portfolio is secured only through collateral substitutes and mortgages on land titles issued under the agrarian reform, with limited market value. BAAC's success in accessing capital markets is mainly attributable to the following key factors:

- development of a highly efficient lending technology based on joint liability groups, and a gradual diversification of loan products into term loans;
- a quasi-monopolistic position as the formal financier of loans with more suitable conditions, so that farmers wish to maintain creditworthiness with BAAC;
- high standards of staff professionalism and the existence of a 'firewall' that has largely protected the bank's operational autonomy from political interference; and
- national scale, which facilitates pooling of systemic risks.

Annexure A-5.9

Rural Electrification and Renewables[65]

Rural energisation and electrification has played a major role in the development of rural India (in enhancing agricultural productivity and

65. Note from TERI, New Delhi.

provision of lighting services for rural households). Today the forces of globalisation, free trade and instant connectivity provide new opportunities for the people living in rural India. However, to tap these opportunities and harness the potential of our resources (both manpower and natural resources), delivering quality infrastructure services has become essential and energy/ electricity services are amongst the most crucial of these services. However at present with a substantial increase in fossil fuel prices and the power situation in the country not being very encouraging, shortage in the delivery of energy/ electricity services has become critical. Growth in demand for power has outstripped supply with peak demand shortage being 12.2 per cent in 2005. Many parts of the country receive electricity for only a few hours a day, the quality of which is poor (backed up by TERI's own experience at the ground level). Today the average annual per capita consumption of electricity is 600 kilowatthours (one of the lowest in the world) and rural India (which houses over 70 per cent of the population) uses just 13 per cent of the available grid power.

To accelerate development of rural India, bring about greater energy security, inclusion of dispersed and remote communities in rural India as active members of the economy, there is a need for the provision of clean, high quality energy services. To achieve growth in the range of 8 per cent GDP growth, new decentralised mechanisms for the delivery of energy and power services need to be tapped.

Why DDG (Decentralised Distributed Generation)

DDG is not a new concept with DDG projects being actively implemented by industry for quite some time. DDG as a strategic approach which advocates the use of local natural resources for electricity generation. Through DDG, growing energy demand can be met through a practical, affordable, safe, and environmentally responsible way. DDG has the advantage of lowering T&D losses as the source of generation is located near the actual point of consumption, delivering reliable and efficient services to customers, reducing environmental pollution (associated with centralised thermal power stations) and decreasing the investment burden. DDG also provides the utilities the advantage of not committing large financial resources. DDG projects can be added incrementally whenever and wherever required. At the same time DDG projects are more cost effective to develop (according to S Mushtaq Khan (Frost & Sullivan, India, Feburary, 2006)) investments requirements go down by an estimated 50 per cent for DDG projects as compared to similar centralised generation project.

DDG in India

For a large and dispersed rural country like India, decentralised power generation systems, wherein electricity is generated at the consumer end thereby avoiding transmission and distribution costs, offers a better solution. DDG has the potential to bring about a paradigm shift in the rural economy. The Gokak Committee had gone into details about the concept of decentralised generation to meet the needs of rural masses. The main recommendations of the Committee are as under:

- The concept of Distributed Generation (DG) has been taken as decentralised generation and distribution of power especially in the rural areas. In India, the deregulation of the power sector has not made much headway but the problem of T&D losses, the unreliability of the grid and the problem of remote and inaccessible regions have provoked debate on the subject.
- The DG technologies in India relate to turbines, micro turbines, wind turbines, biomass, and gasification of biomass, solar photovoltaics and hybrid systems. However, most of the decentralised plants are based on wind power, hydel power and biomass and biomass gasification. The technology of solar photovoltaics is costly and fuel cells are yet to be commercialised.
- In so far as the 18,000 villages in remote and inaccessible areas are concerned, the extension of grid power is not going to be economical. Decentralised plants based on biomass, gasification of biomass, hydel power and solar thermal power and solar photovoltaic's are the appropriate solution for these areas. A decision with regard to the available options will have to be taken depending on the feature of each site/village.
- To improve the quality of power in villages which are already electrified it is recommended that these villages be encouraged to go ahead with the decentralised distributed generation (DDG).
- Though India has made considerable progress in adopting technologies based on renewable sources of energy these are not yet capable of commercial application on a large scale. However, with the price of fossil fuel prices sky rocketing, maturing of RE technologies (enhanced reliability and decreased costs) many such projects are expected to come up in the future.
- DDG provides a very effective tool for meeting rural electrification targets, reducing energy dependence on imported oil and gas and

tapping clean energy sources such as wind, solar, biofuels, fuel cells, micro-turbines and geothermal power. For example, the National Thermal Power Corporation (NTPC) has already started development of DDG projects for village electrification near their thermal power stations. In one such example NTPC in association with TERI set up a 10 kWe biomass gasifier system for electrification of Village Jemara, Chhattisgarh. This DDG plant provides electricity to 82 households for lighting, provides electricity for street lighting, lighting of the school, *Panchayat Ghar* and Shops. The management of the DDG project at the village level is with a local cooperative society called "Mahamaya Urja Utpadan Sahkari Samiti, Jemara."

DDG Technologies

The RET based power generation capacity in India is an estimated 50,000 MW capacity (200 billion kwh). India has a potential of about 100,000 MW of power generation from renewable energy sources and steps are underway to harness this potential and power generation from renewable sources is also increasing. The medium-term goal is to ensure electrification of 18,000 remote un-electrified villages, and achieve a minimum 10 per cent share, or around 10,000 MW, from renewable power in the overall power generation capacity to be added by 2012.

Over 4,000 MW of renewable power generation capacity has been set up in the country. Wind power generation alone accounts for around 2,000 MW, small hydro projects for another 1,530 MW and 640 MW from biomass resources. More than 10.5 lakh standalone PV systems aggregating to about 62 MW have been installed in the country. It is estimated that about Rs. 12,000 crores have been invested in the non-conventional energy sector so far. The details of specific areas are given in the following table.

Power from Bagasse

One of India's biggest agriculture industries, sugar cane has the potential of generating 3000 MW's of electricity. Most sugar mills consume about 25 per cent to 35 per cent of their bagasse for internal power generation. The rest 75 per cent can be burnt and the power generated can be sold to the SEBs. However, the SEBs initially offered only 0.6 Rs. per kWh which was insufficient for covering the capital investment to generate power with the remaining bagasse, However today, eleven state electricity boards in the sugar cane growing regions pay almost 2.25 Rs. per kWh and have entered into a 13 year contract for decentralised power from the sugar mills. The cane industry estimates that burning all of the bagasse in the 460 Indian sugar factories will add 3,000 megawatts of generation, equivalent to adding 5,000 megawatts of new central generation and 5,000 megawatts of new T&D wires. Full recycling of all of the bagasse will produce 5 per cent of Indian power, reducing costs, emissions and greenhouse gases.

Total Installed Capacity of Power Generation from Various Non-Conventional Energy Sources

Source/Technologies	*Units**	*Cumulative Achievements***	*India's Position in the World*
Power Generation			
Wind Power	MW	1,870	Fifth
Small Hydro Power (up to 25 MW)	MW	1,519.28	Tenth
Biomass-based Power	MW	484	Fourth
Biomass Gasifiers	MW	53.17	First
Solar Photovoltaics (Grid connected)	MW	2.50	-
Energy from Urban and Industrial Wastes	MWe	25.75	-
Total		**3,954.70**	-

Notes : *- MW: Mega Watt.
**- As per the latest figures available.

Source: Ministry of Non-Conventional Energy Sources, Government of India *http://www.mnes.nic.in*. Accessed on March 15, 2005.

Conclusion

DDG can helps in meeting dispersed demand efficiently through penetration of safe, proven, and low-cost technologies for local conditions. However certain steps are still required for the programme to take-off. The first is the need of a sustained research and development programme which would aim at customising these technologies based on local requirements and help in bringing down their costs. At the same time policies relating to explicit pricing of power from these sites needs to be made clearer and at the same time awareness of the benefits of DDG need to be highlighted. Scaling up still remains a major challenge, the country has not been able to replicate globally successful models.

Annexure A-5.10

Noida Power Company Ltd's (NPCL) Project of Reconfiguring its Distribution Network Metering and Demand Side Management—A Typical Case Study[66]

Summary Abstract

The Noida Power Company Limited (NPCL) project involved upgradation of the distribution infrastructure, undertaking metering of unmetered consumers and demand side management (DSM) in Greater Noida to achieve significant energy savings and reduction in greenhouse gas (GHG) emissions. ICICI Bank provided financial assistance of Rs. 29.0 million to meet a part of the cost of the project of Rs. 58.0 million through USAID's ECO Programme.

Energy audit studies had estimated an energy savings potential on account of losses of Rs 0.6 million kWh per year. Studies also estimated savings in terms of CO_2 emissions of 600 tonnes per year, both of which have been achieved. The project has been successfully completed on 30.09.2004 and the company now proposes to replicate this project to other areas within its jurisdiction, to be financed out internal accruals/other sources.

Situation Prevailing Earlier and Major Issues

NPCL belongs to the R.P. Goenka group and is a power utility. The utility distributes power in Greater Noida in the state of Uttar Pradesh near Delhi. Greater Noida is one of the fastest growing industrial areas and therefore has a steady gowth in demand for power. The source of revenue for NPCL is from sale of power to industrial, commercial, domestic and agricultural consumers. The company has a long term arrangement to buy power from the Uttar Pradesh Power Corporation Limited, whereas the Uttar Pradesh Regulatory Commission determines the cost of power. NPCL had been earlier sanctioned a rupee term loan of Rs. 100 million by ICICI for its capital expenditure. This loan is being repaid regularly.

Power transmission in India is typically associated with high distribution losses. The distribution losses of NPCL at 8.4 per cent were lower as compared to those of other large power utilities in the country. The utility proposed to further reduce these transmission and distribution losses, stop pilferage and increase the speed of commercialisation of sale of power to all its consumers. The company therefore decided to upgrade its distribution

66. Case study on NPCL by Product Technology team of ICICI Bank.

infrastructure, undertake metering of unmetered consumers and demand side management measures to achieve significant energy savings.

Elements of the Solution

The solution broadly included three main elements:

1. Reconfiguring the distribution network.
2. Metering.
3. Implementation of Demand Side Management (DSM).

Reconfiguring the Distribution Network: NCPL proposed the following to improve the distribution network so as to make load management efficient.

- Revamping of load management (by addition of HT transformers and feeders).
- Optimising distribution infrastructure (by additional HT transmission lines).
- Replacement of LT transmission by HT transmission.
- Reduction of line losses (by replacement of base conductors (LT) by insulated cables).

Metering: The company proposed to introduce metered supply to domestic consumers in rural areas and replace existing meters of high paying industrial and commercial consumers by tamper proof electronic meters. The company followed a two pronged strategy, to replace existing electromechanical type of meters with tamper proof electronic meters for high consuming customers and normal type for others. Also many households were unmetered and were paying a flat tariff. Therefore, the payment was not linked to the consumption. With the metering of these unmetered domestic households it was expected that NPCL would provide a guaranteed supply of uninterrupted quality power so that the benefits were perceived by consumers to opt for metered connections and pay commercial tariff. A total of 2696 meters were proposed to be installed for domestic consumers and an additional 50 meters for the energy efficient pump sets under this module.

Demand Side Management: The utility proposed to replace the entire existing pump sets used by farmers (about 50 nos) at its cost. The conventional pump sets used for agricultural operations of 5 HP rating equivalent to 3.75 kW would be replaced by 3 HP rating (equivalent to 2.25 kW) energy efficient pumps. Thus due to higher pumping capacity (water discharge rate is 19 litres/sec as against 15 litres/sec), the usage would reduce by 22 per cent. The final connection would be through a pole mounted 11 kV/415 kV transformer with the transformer rating sufficient to feed only the pump installed. The usage of energy efficient pumps was supposed to result in energy consumption savings of about 53 per cent. It was estimated that the pumps consuming 8,388 units of power annually would consume 3,948 units after implementation of DSM measures. The residual power would be available to the grid for sale to the new consumers or takes care of the growth in the demand from existing consumers. Therefore the average realisation from the use of distribution infrastructure would improve and also increase the asset turnover ratio. Alternatively, the power purchased from UPPCL would reduce to the extent of the savings and consequently reduce the power purchase cost. The company will thereby recover the capital cost incurred for replacing the pumps and at the same time increase revenue. Further, the supply would be metered and the HT supply would be near the pump site. It was expected that with the implementation of all the elements of this demonstration project, the overall reduction of losses (technical and commercial) in the module would be around 0.3 per cent resulting in a saving of about 0.6 million units.

The utility first implemented the aforesaid measures in two modules (Udyog Kendra and Surajpur area spanning almost 50 sq.km.) and then progressively rolled out to the remaining areas based on the experience of this demonstration.

Results Achieved

The utility installed 4170-metered domestic connections and 35-metered tubewell connections with energy-efficient pumps. A new 5 MVA 33/11 kV substation has been commissioned and 4-nos. of 11 kV feeders have been erected for domestic and agricultural consumers. The achieved power savings on account of reductions in technical and commercial losses were 1,728,000 kWh annually as against the estimated figure of 605,766 kWh. Savings in terms of CO_2 emissions were 1,700 tonnes per year as against estimated 600 tonnes per year (assuming that 1 MW of grid power (thermal power plant) generally generates 7,000 tonnes of CO_2 in a year and that quantum of savings on account of reduction in distribution losses and using the basis of 1 kg CO_2/kWh for calculating the GHG emissions.) The overall losses of NPCL in FY'05 continue to be 8 per cent, which is the lowest in India. Annual Saving due to assisted project was Rs. 20.2 million.

A brief comparison between the various realised *vis-à-vis* estimated progress parameters is tabulated in the following table.

Item	*Estimated*	*Actual*
No. of meters installed for domestic consumers (No.)	2696	4170
No. of EE pumpsets	50	35
5MVA 33/11 kV Substation	1	1
11 kV feeders (No.)	4	4
11 kV Lines (ckM)	36	34
LT lines with insulated wires	40	59
Unit consumed annually after implementation of DSM	3948	2763
Annual Saving on account of losses (kWh)	605766	1728000
Annual savings in terms of CO2 emissions (tonnes)	600	1700

Impact

NPCL's project is the first of its kind undertaken by utilities. This industry is characterised by high distribution losses and therefore based on the project's success the replication potential among other distribution companies is fairly high. The project not only promoted energy efficiency by upgrading the distribution infrastructure but also resulted in reduction in GHG emissions and reducing pilferage in addition to undertaking demand side management measures.

The perception of the farmers and residential property owners in rural areas regarding the impact of metering was that they will receive assured uninterrupted supply of power. This resulted in reduction in medical costs, better security, increase in rental incomes, improved lifestyles and an increase in small business opportunities. As a result of this project, farmers have confirmed an increase in rice yields due to the fact that they can now irrigate the crop three times as against once or at the most twice, prior to commissioning of this demonstration project. The awareness levels of the rural folk as regards the importance to conserve energy has gone up due to the work done by NGOs (through street plays etc.) who were hired by the utility. Besides the project has also promoted a cost-effective technology, which improves industry competitiveness.

Annexure A-5.11

Financing of Rural Roads

Rural Roads Status

About 300,000 Indian habitations have no links to the outside world. Till date, out of 39,623 km of targeted rural roads only 35 per cent i.e. 10,748 km have been built. Rural roads, particularly rural feeder roads are considered basic to the whole process of rural development. Farm-to-market roads promote commercialisation of agriculture, raise productive capacity and increase social mobility. For an effective farming system where a farmer can make a round trip to a market centre, agriculture extension services, farm production and proper credit investment, feeder roads are crucial.

To date out of 39,623 km of targeted rural roads only 35 per cent i.e. 10748 km have been built. More than 0.2 million villages are unconnected and out of the 67 million habitations 40 per cent have no link to the outside world. GoI is committed to providing accessibility to the remaining 40 per cent of villages. The commitment, if fully realised, would involve upgrading/ construction of about 1,100,000 km of rural roads at a cost of about Rs. 1,100 billion. The current estimated value of the existing rural road network, based on the value of construction work, is about Rs. 2,400 billion. The maintenance of the existing rural road network requires about Rs 50 billion per annum, out of which only 20-30 per cent is available.

It is estimated by an independent study[67] that for every Rs. 1 million invested in rural roads, 165 people would be lifted out of poverty. Many villages still rely on earth tracks that are unsuitable for motorised traffic due to poor riding quality, and which become practically impassable during the rainy season because of missing bridges and culverts. Much of the network is underdeveloped, of low standard and poor quality, structurally weak, poorly maintained, and extremely deteriorated. The lack of roads means that an estimated 20-30 per cent of the agricultural, horticultural and forest produce gets wasted because of inability to transport the produce to marketing and processing centres. Financing rural roads through Diesel cess has been one of the good initiatives. However it is constrained by the pace of availability of funds for accelerated development.

---

67. Kumar, Ashok, Zhi Liu, Piers Vickers (2002).

Possible Approaches in Funding and Rural Roads Construction

Using Mandi Cess

Madhya Pradesh (MP) has made significant strides in the roads development under the Pradhan Mantri Gram Sadak Yojana (PMGSY) scheme. In addition to its share of PMGSY, which hovers around 9 per cent of total PMGSY fund, MP is leveraging its *mandi* cess receivables from the State Mandi Board for borrowing from the banks and using the money raised for accelerated rural roads development. The state government has started levying a 1 per cent extra cess on foodgrains and other agricultural products traded in *mandis* of which 0.85 per cent is being spent on roads. In this manner, the MP Government has been able to generate Rs. 1 billion additional funds every year. This additional source of revenue is being leveraged to borrow funds from banks for undertaking high cost projects and undertake road development in a systematic and planned fashion rather than in an *ad hoc* manner. The MP example has proved, how simple innovations can effect big changes and can be easily replaced in the other states. Similarly leveraging on the *mandi* cess receivables could be employed as a strategy for construction of rural roads and also for modernisation and upgradation of state *mandis*.[68] An effort in this direction has also been done by Punjab through the Punjab Rural Development Board. Similarly, Uttar Pradesh has established a road fund by diversion of the marginal revenue increase from rise in sales tax on transport fuels. Funds are applied to the entire state network, including maintenance of rural roads. Warana dairy is another organisation that volunteered to build rural roads along the milk route taking funding assistance from Government of India under road development scheme.

Bundling of Assets and Services

The challenge in most of these projects with large positive externalities is that it is difficult to find a way to get an entrepreneur to promote, and a bank to fund the project unless a way is found to identify revenue generating components and designing comfort levels and risk mitigation strategies for facilitating bank finance. A parallel could be drawn from the Bangalore-Mysore highway project wherein the private project promoter, in addition to construction of a road network, was given the rights to develop real estate component in the real vicinity. This created an incentive for the promoter to commit its funds to the project and also secure funding from banks on the

68. Since the rural roads are most likely to benefit agriculture in the first instance and perhaps lead to increase in the amount of cess that *mandis* receive this may also be viewed as a long-term investment by the *Mandi* in its own interest.

basis of increase in the market value of area because of construction of roads. Similar models could be attempted in the rural domain. In fact, one such idea of constructing rural roads is being contemplated by an MFI Vivekananda Sewa Mandir Sishu Udyan (VSSU), based in 24 South Parganas, West Bengal. The village road with an estimated cost of Rs. 7.5 million would be built through a special infrastructure. SPV (Special Purpose Vehicle) which could involve multiple partners like VSSU, land owners around the road who will gain from the price rise. The model on similar lines with Bangalore-Mysore highway project intends to develop commercial properties in the vicinity of road and also charge for access to the road, which would be connecting village to the market. Such innovations especially in the rural context can go a long way in bridging the urban rural divide and enhance the economic status of the rural population.

Community Participation in Rural Roads

In many countries, the costs of local access roads are shared between the government and benefiting local communities. For instance private road cooperatives manage about 70 per cent of the road network in Sweden, with subsidies ranging from 40 to 80 per cent from the government. In China, the model is such that the government provides material, equipment, and technical assistance, while local communities provide voluntary labour for road construction. In Finland, 78 per cent of the road network is privately owned and managed through road cooperatives, which receive funding support from central government, municipalities, and cooperative members. In Lesotho, the government provides limited financial assistance and training in labour-based work methods to villagers who wish to construct rural roads and paths on a voluntary basis. In India, in Uttaranchal State and parts of Punjab, paths, tracks, and footbridges are being constructed on a cost-sharing basis with local communities located in remote and inaccessible areas (under the Integrated Watershed Management Project). These pilots must be scaled up such that there is increased stakeholders participation in construction of rural infrastructure.

Prioritisation of Roads Construction

The funds for rural roads construction from government funds have basically being driven by political considerations rather than any socioeconomic criterion leading to uneconomic utilisation of funds and unbalanced growth. A strategic options study could be done in all the states for preparing a master plan for rural road network. The master plan must identify priority projects in each state/district and funds under the Rural

Infrastructure Development Fund of NABARD which could be made available to finance only the identified projects. The study could prioritise creation of such a network on the basis of desirability, social benefits, economic value etc. This would ensure planned and economic flow of funds rather than projects driven by vested interests.

Annexure A-5.12

Agricultural Extension Services

There are some basic issues in agricultural extension:

1. It is very manpower intensive. For effective national coverage one will need approximately 100,000 people to be employed.
2. Farmers are already reasonably well informed and do not require guidance unlike what is generally believed. They require input for specific pest problems, soil deficiency solutions or if there is a change proposed in cropping pattern.
3. Today each state has an elaborate agricultural extension network which has fallen into various stages of disuse. There is also substantial physical infrastructure on the ground which is well spread out. Also all Agricultural Universities have an extension wing.
4. All agricultural input companies run a parallel extension network. Their focus is on their own products but also serve as advisors on cropping needs—as estimated 50,000 people would already be involved in this.
5. For extension services to be effective they need to be very location specific, factoring not only climatic and soil conditions but also farmer practices.
6. For all commercial crops there are consultants who offer advisory services at a price to farmers, for example in crops such as grapes, apples, tea, pomegranate, and tomatoes. These consultancy services are provided by a variety of trained individuals.

Given this reality, any routine approaches to this service may not serve a purpose and potentially completely different approaches may need to be developed.

- One approach would involve the identification of new initiatives and focus crops. For example use of drip irrigation in cotton in Rajasthan or switch to citrus fruits in Punjab or growing of medicinal plants in MP or increasing tomato yield in Karnataka from 10Ts/acre to 30 Ts/

acre through deep ploughing, etc. There are a number of such possibilities which could cover the entire country with the possible exceptions of the wheat and rice belts of North India and rice growing areas of coastal Andhra Pradesh.

- Setting up of technology demonstration farms at suitable locations using state-of-the-art techniques the world has to offer is another approach. Farmers, in order to be convinced would need a demonstration of its operational and commercial viability. Bring farmers and show them how it works. This can make a substantial difference.
- In terms of public extension infrastructure, *mandis* should be interlinked for dissemination of prices and market information and KVKs should be modified to better cater to needs of the rural poor by installation of modern Information and Communication Technology (ICT)[69] facilities and instilling the personnel with an attitude to serve more effectively.
- PPP in agriculture extension[70] could be utilised to derive better results. In an example of PPP in extension, the government extension officials including scientists from the Punjab Agriculture University (PAU) have undertaken joint extension activities with Pepsi officials to promote introduction and commercialisation of the new tomato varieties in the state. This strategy was found to be complementary with the public agency offering its network and reach and the private agency offering its technology edge for the betterment of the farmers.
- Commodity based group approaches in extension have been found to be effective in quite a number of cases. For instance, Kerala initiated the group approach to extension in rice farming in 1989, which was subsequently extended to other crops. This approach involved formation

69. The widespread availability and convergence of information and communication technologies (ICTs)—computers, digital networks, telecommunication, television etc in India in recent years have led to unprecedented capacity for dissemination of knowledge and information to the rural population. The village knowledge centres initiated by the M.S. Swaminathan Research Foundation (MSSRF) in Puducherry aims at building a model for the use of ICTs in meeting the knowledge and information requirement of rural families. Value addition to the raw information, use of local language (Tamil) and multi-media (to facilitate illiterate user participation) and participation of local people from the beginning are the noteworthy features of the project.

70. Punjab Agro-Foodgrains Corporation (PAFC), a wholly owned subsidiary of the Punjab Agro Industries Corporation, has entered into agreement with private extension services providers such as Rallis and Mahindra Shubh Labh Services for contract farming in Punjab. These companies provide professional extension services to farmers, charging a nominal fee from farmers as well as PAFC.

of commodity groups to improve productivity and reduce cost of cultivation through collective purchase of inputs and services. Extension efforts and delivery of subsidised inputs were routed through these farmers groups. Similarly, in Andhra Pradesh, farmer clubs have been formed at each village primarily to facilitate group extension. These clubs are involved in propagating developmental schemes and facilitating transfer of agricultural technology among farmers in the village.

Given the increasing importance of horticulture in the agricultural GDP and vast possibilities of value addition in horticulture, we feel that horticulture, would require special focus including a few of the suggested interventions below:

- Setting up of institutions to carry out ongoing Educational and Training programmes on EurepGap/CODEX ALIMENTARIUS, HACCP and other certification processes. These are increasingly being demanded by all importers worldwide and compliance will ensure access to the most developed markets, with consequent better price realisations and may also help us beat competition from some African/Caribbean/Latin American countries. Market discussions have revealed that while discipline is a prerequisite, compliance is not difficult and with some sustained encouragement can become widespread.
- Setting up of multiple testing and certification agencies who can carry out this certification on an ongoing basis. These need to be geographically dispersed and available locally to farmers to ensure widespread utilisation of their services. They also need to be recognised by, and accredited to international bodies.
- Systematic and sustained brand promotion activities for promoting Indian Agricultural produce like mangoes, grapes and bananas as successfully done by New Zealand for KIWI Fruit and as also being undertaken by South Africa.
- Strong encouragement to Organic cultivation and certification of produce. In India we are at an advantage since many areas have always used only organic cultivation methodologies and this gives us an edge over even domestic EU production, since they have integrated schemes for export promotion activities related to agricultural produce, instead of the current multiplicity through APEDA, NHB/NHM, Ministry of Agriculture, Ministry of Food Processing, Tea Board, Coffee Board, etc. as is the case in India.

References

Akula, Vikram (2006). An article in *Economic Times,* March 20. CEO of SKS Micro finance.

Ananth, Bindu, Soju Annie George (2003). "Scaling Up of Micro Financial Services: An Overview of Challenges and Opportunities", *Working Paper Series, icicisocialinitiatives.org,* August.

Balakrishnan, R. (2006). An article in *Business Line.* April 7. Executive Director, NABARD.

Basu, Priya (2006). An article in *Economic Times,* March 20. World Bank.

Beck,Thorsten, Asli Demirguc-Kunt and Maria Soledad Martinez Peria (2005). "Reaching Out: Access to and Use of Banking Services across Countries", *Policy Research Working Paper Series* No. 3754. September. World Bank.

Breckenridge, Keith (2002). *Biometric Government in the New South Africa.*

Firpo, Janine (2005). *Banking the Unbanked: Technology's Role in Delivering Accessible Financial Services to the Poor.* Australia: The Foundation for Development Corporation. *http://www.fdc.org.au/100462.php*

Foster, Andrew and Mark Rosenzweig (2005). *Inequality and the Sustainability of Agricultural Productivity Growth: Groundwater and the Green Revolution in Rural India,* June.

Government of India (2005). *Economic Survey 2004-05.* New Delhi: Ministry of Finance.

Hollinger, Frank (2004). *Financing Agricultural Term Investments.* Food and Agriculture Organization of the United Nations (FAO) and Deutsche Gesellschaft für Technische Zusammenarbeit (GTZ). January.

Jones, Stephen (2006). *Infrastructure Challenges in East and South Asia,* March.

Panthary, Rajiv (2005). *Enhancing Investment Credit in Agriculture,* CFMR, March.

Prahalad, C.K. and Allen Hammond (2002). *What Works: Serving The Poor, Profitably A Private Sector Strategy For Global Digital Opportunity.* Washington DC: World Resources Institute.

Rajan, Raghuram and Luigi Zingales (2003). *Saving Capitalism from the Capitalists.* New York: Crown Business.

Reserve Bank of India (n.d.). *RBI Statistics.* Mumbai.

————. (n.d.). *RBI Banking Act.* Mumbai.

Ruchismita, Rupalee. *Catalytic Funding to Scale Micro Finance in India.*

Skees, Jerry, Peter Hazell and Mario Miranda (1999). *New Approaches to Public/Private Crop Yield Insurance.* World Bank Publication.

Sinha, Sanjay (2000). *The Role of Central Banks in Micro Finance in Asia and the Pacific.* Asian Development Bank.

Whelan, Steve. *Building Financial Systems for the Poor.* With contributions from CGAP Staff and Exchange, LLC, *CGAP.*

Winters, L.A. (2000). *Trade Liberalisation and Poverty.* Brighton: University of Sussex.

Young, Robin. "Credit Bureaus in Latin America". Senior Development Specialist, Development Alternatives Inc.

http://www.rbi.org.in.

http://www.nabard.org.

http://www.indiabudget.nic.in.

http://www.sadguru.org.

http://www.teriin.org/.

6

Environmental Degradation and its Correctives in the Agriculture Sector

S.S. JOHL

Environmental degradation today is a serious challenge to the life forms on the planet earth. It is adversely affecting not only the individuals and human societies in various ways and in different degrees, but is also influencing the changes that are detrimental to the health and growth of all forms of life. The effect is cumulative in its nature and is in an acceleration mode now. Of course, the climate of the earth has never been stable during the history of evolution and the ecosystems and species have evolved within the climatic history (Green *et al.*, 2003). The change in the modern era, however, has exceeded anything experienced in the past ten thousand years. This accelerated change is threatening a high level erosion of species, which is expected to be between 100 and 1000 times greater than the earlier ones (Pimms *et al.*, 1995).

Some of the areas and regions of the world are in a virtual whirlpool of fast deteriorating living conditions and there is no place free from the impact of environmental degradation. Climate has changed worldwide over the last century. The average temperature of the earth has risen by 0.6° C since 1900. The last decade was the warmest decade globally and 1998 was the warmest year since 1861 (since when temperature had been recorded with adequate global coverage). Because of this warming, snow cover is decreasing, glaciers are receding, rainfall patterns are changing and extreme weather events have become more frequent. There have been more heat waves and heavy rainfalls. There have been fewer frosts. As the oceans have warmed, sea levels have risen by 10 to 20 centimetres. Even the remote areas away from densely populated industrial centres are not any more insulated from this debilitating impact. Ozone hole, climate changes, global warming, enhanced influence of La Nina and El Nino factors, receding glaciers and changes in precipitation patterns, water and air pollution and soil degradation should be, therefore, of vital concern to the human race at this juncture. Since these negative developments are affecting all the life forms all over the world, it is not a matter of concern for a few societies or individuals only. The whole of the human race in every part of this world has to wake up to the ground realities of this fast deteriorating situation.

Over the past two decades, an enhanced level of awareness has come about these perceptible changes that have occurred in the patterns of typhoons, hurricanes, precipitation intensities and their spatial as well as temporal distribution. Yet, in spite of tremendous technological refinements that have been introduced in climate forecasting models, annual or seasonal rainfall patterns still carry a high degree of error in their predictability. Localised, intensive and short duration rainfalls in some places or areas and scant, delayed, unevenly distributed, late arrival and early withdrawal of rains in others have become a matter of serious concern. These unpredictable abnormalities and frequent aberrations bring disasters, loss of life and property. Droughts entailing long duration sufferings, uncertainty in food and fibre production threatening food security in many areas, regions and countries of the world are assuming serious proportions.

Glaciers that are the primary source of clean water for irrigation and life systems and provide stability to the climate pattern, are receding at an alarming rate. For instance, Himalayan glaciers have receded by more than one kilometre over the last 100 years. The sight of the main streams flowing full to their brims with crystal-clear water in summer is an eyesore to the one who knows that the water flows from the excessive melting of glaciers in the feeding area. In the long run, which is not a very long run, this is going to affect the climate change in turn in an interactive manner and will adversely affect the availability of water.

Climate change is rapidly becoming a significant threat to bio-diversity. This change may lead to major geographical shifts in natural vegetation zones leading to changes in the distribution of characteristic species of these zones. The climate change, thus, adds to the pressure that has already begun by several other routes to affect biodiversity in modern times. Some recent studies have reported a shift in species distribution of plants and animals ranging from grasses to trees and mollusks to mammals. However, for most species, effective migration or adaptation in relatively shorter time frame is not possible and the time span is often not enough to withstand the impact of environmental change. Thus, a lot many species may not be able to reach places where the climate is suitable for them. Consequently, many plant and animal species may not survive the climate change. It is estimated that a loss up to one-third of the known populations of some of the land plants and animals could occur (Thomas *et al.*, 2004)

A high degree of spatial variability in climate change will lead to different species within the same community responding differently and will impact the existing community structure. For instance, the variable thermal response of species of marine algae to change in sea temperatures and differences in degrees of change in summer and winter will lead to species-specific responses (Hiscock *et al.*, 2004)

Species have to cope with the changing conditions and are likely to face competition from new species spreading into their environment. Native species often struggle to compete with invasive species that may be better adapted to the new conditions. Invasive species can also bring in diseases that the native species may be poorly equipped to resist. The survival of the native species may depend on their ability to move into new areas as rapidly as their preferred habitats shift geographically. This may particularly put many arctic species in difficulties because their typical habitats may ultimately vanish altogether (Chapin *et al.*, 2003)

As stated earlier climate change is also expected to increase the frequency of extreme climatic events. In some regions heavy rains, floods and hurricanes may occur more often, while other areas may suffer droughts and desertification. As the pack ice that covers much of the Arctic Ocean is melting and is shrinking in mountain ranges such as the Andes and the Himalayas, global warming is accelerating. A warming of 5° C can eliminate 20 per cent of the coastal wetlands by the year 2080 (IPPC report, 2002). If glaciers and ice caps continue to melt at the present rate, the sea level will gradually rise, coastal flooding will become more frequent and certain low-lying coastal regions and small island states may become permanently submerged. An indication of global warming is available in Siberia. Forests here are beginning to spread across the Tundras as the summers have become warmer and growing season has lengthened. The annual growing season in Finland has lengthened by several days over the last thirty years.

The widespread melting of permafrost could mean that more fresh water enters the North Atlantic *via* the rivers that flow into the Arctic Ocean. If in the process, the salinity of the North Atlantic falls below a certain level, the Gulf Stream could slow, stop or even change its course. Such a change could bring about a potentially disastrous cooling in the climate of North Europe instead of warming. Thus, there are several uncertainties. Enhanced CO_2 concentration and subsequent acidification of ocean waters are likely to affect the process of calcification by which key marine species including corals will be affected adversely. Our understanding of the impact of ocean acidification and its interaction with climate change is currently very poor and it is difficult to predict how the marine system will respond to the combination of these drivers of change (The Royal Society, 2005)

Due to the fast increasing population, especially in the developing countries and least developed countries, demand for food and fibre and other necessities and amenities of life is increasing fast. In many countries, food security is at a critical stage and is being threatened by non-availability of food and often lack of access to food. As a consequence, the production of food, fibre, industrial goods and services is being increased through intensive cultivation and chemicals based production systems. This is leading to over exploitation of scarce natural resources in different countries, especially the cultivated and arable land and water. Ever enhancing level of production of industrial goods and services is considered to be the major source of environmental degradation through the emission of greenhouse gasses (GHG), especially the carbon dioxide, methane and nitrous oxide. Efforts are afoot and systems are in place such as the Kyoto Protocol,

European Union Emission Trading Scheme (EU ETS), the United Kingdom's ETS, Chicago Climate Exchange (CCX) in USA , Regional Greenhouse Gas Initiative (RGGI) in North- Eastern United States, New South Wales carbon market (NSW) in Australia for the sale and purchase of carbon credits in order to put a check on the emission of Greenhouse Gases. Quite a few Corporates, especially the power companies and private players, brokers and agents are operating in the spot and forward markets for trading in carbon credits. Under the Cap-and-Trade regime, European Union Allowances (EUAs) have been allocated in First Phase in order to control CO_2 emissions from various enterprises. In the phase II, the caps are going to be at much lower level of emissions. Market in carbon trading has developed quite fast. Carbon Credit Markets operate like share markets and stock exchanges in respect of spot purchases and future hedging. The value of the global carbon market was more than US$ 10 billion in 2005 and expected to be between US$ 25 to 30 billion in 2006. Average price of the 79 million tonnes of carbon credit traded in the 1st quarter of 2006 is reported to be US$ 11.45 per t CO_2.(Capoor and Ambrosi, 2006). In view of the stricter regimes expected to be imposed in the industrially developed countries in respect of carbon emission, the market in carbon trading is expected to be quite flourishing in future. However, improvements in production technology and cleaner fuel substitutions that will reduce or minimise the carbon emission might have a depressing effect on the carbon trading market, especially in the future trading. Therefore, it is difficult to project the trends of this market as yet. It is, however, encouraging to note that the financial market is linking up itself with the carbon trading market, with the banks showing interest in investments in Clean Development Mechanism (CDM). Advances are being offered for Certified Emission Reductions (CERs). Recently the World Bank has entered into two agreements with Chinese Companies to buy carbon credit (emission reduction credits) at a rate of Euros 6 per tonne of Carbon dioxide (t CO_2e) for seven years.

However, these efforts so far have remained focused primarily on industrial emissions. Due attention has not been paid to the agriculture sector on this aspect as yet. Concerted effort on increasing agricultural production and food security is putting a tremendous strain on environmental elements. Ever increasing use of fertilisers, pesticides and other chemicals are polluting the environment to a level of deep concern throughout the world. For instance in the United Kingdom, the Royal Commission on Environment has reported that every year, farmers spray some 30,000 tonnes of pesticides over Britain's broad acres. Over a million people are put at risk by this spray, drifting into their homes from the fields. The rest of the population consumes the poisons in their food. Recent official measurements found traces of 80 different pesticides in the edible agricultural products ranging from apples to butter, bread, chocolates to chicken nuggets. Fifty of these pesticides have been identified by the international authorities, including the World Health Organisation, as acute poisons, suspected causes of cancer and likely hormone disrupters believed to have weird 'gender-bender' effects on both humans and wildlife. Arable crops are sprayed on average five times before being harvested. Potatoes are astonishingly sprayed 13 times. Fruits are doused even more frequently—13 applications on average, with some apples receiving a mind-blowing 18 doses.

After examining medical studies and actually going to see people who claimed to have been affected by drifting spray, the commission concluded that the victims were 'genuinely ill' and that there was a 'plausible link' between pesticide exposure and disease. The Royal Commission cited official studies that suggested that such exposure could cause Parkinson's Disease, and expressed particular concern that it might lead to cancer and disabling 'multi-system disorders' like chronic fatigue syndrome.

Most of the intensively cultivated irrigated areas of the world are suffering from technology fatigue that is leading to declining factor productivity. In order to maintain the same level of output, more and more intensive use of chemicals (fertilisers and pesticides) is being resorted to. For instance, take the case of Punjab province in India. The state is only 1.5 per cent of the geographical area of the country, but contributes between 40 to 49 per cent of rice and 50 to over 70 per cent of wheat to the central foodgrain stocks of the country (Department. of Agriculture, Punjab). It has amounted to a contribution of over 20 million tonnes of foodgrain annually for more than three and a half decades. More important, more than 90 per cent of the interstate movement of foodgrain has been of the grains from Punjab. One can well imagine what would have been the fate of the country on food front and food security, if this much of annual supply of foodgrain had not been contributed by this tiny-big state. Punjab genuinely takes pride in this achievement, but seldom realises the unduly very heavy social cost the state is paying for it, in monetary as well as physical terms. Also, it is a question of sustainability in the physical sense which can be viewed in terms of utilisation of the most scarce resources(s) and productivity of the resource-use along with negative externalities on agroecology and environment at large. In case of resource use, the main question mark is on the utilisation of underground water. The water balance in the state is getting seriously disturbed through excessive withdrawal of underground water. Over the last decade, 75 to 80 per cent of the water requirements of crops in state have been met through tubewells. Consequently, the water table is receding at a rate of over 70 centimetres per year (PAU estimates). Today, hand pumps in the central Punjab districts have become antique items. About 30 per cent of the centrifugal pumps have gone dysfunctional and have been replaced with submersible pumps. Depending upon the depth of the water table and size of the pump, a submersible pump costs between Rs. 50,000 to Rs. 80,000 in the central Punjab. More important, submersible pumps dry out the centrifugal pumps located in their vicinity, affecting the farmers around, specially the small farmers, adversely. The small farmers around do not have the resources to replace their pumps with a submersibles. It is estimated that if the conditions remain as they are, at the present rate of withdrawal of water from the aquifer, in the next about 10 years, there will be no areas in the central Punjab with a water table less than 25 metres deep and all the pump sets will have to be replaced with submersibles. At the present rate of withdrawal of underground water, the situation is, therefore unsustainable. The water, which is the most scarce production resource in the state, is *de facto,* being mined because of the withdrawal exceeding the recharge.

This situation has developed primarily because with the construction of Bhakhra dam, free flow of water and floods in the river basin that lies in the central Punjab, have been controlled, canals have been lined and whatever excess water flows from the dam to the areas below has been canalised through constructing earthen banks (*Dhusi Bandhs*) of the river. Thus, water has been excessively diverted from the river basin and crop production has to depend for about 80 per cent of its irrigation requirements on the underground water. Thus, the situation is not only unsustainable, but more so it poses serious environmental challenges. There is a danger of under ground brackish water from the South-western districts invading into the central districts, rendering the underground aquifer brackish in these areas also.

Power is another scarce resource with the state. Lifting of underground water accounts for more than 95 per cent of the power consumption in the farm sector. The agriculture sector consumed 25.418 billion units of electricity costing Rs.7628.1 crores net to the state over the last four years and the state had to buy electricity from outside costing Rs.7310.98 crores. This year the state will be purchasing electricity from outside worth over Rs 3300 crores and subsidy to agriculture is going to exceed Rs 2100 crores, because the power supply to the farm sector is now free. This situation is also not sustainable in the state which is not very comfortable on financial resources. More important is the fact that free supply leads to overuse and misuse of both power as well as water which are the two most scarce resources in the state and the state cannot afford that on a sustainable basis.

In respect of the adverse impact of growing paddy in June to August on the ecology of the state, it leads to the disquietening levels of soil, water and air pollution. During the months of June to middle of September, with temperatures ranging around 40°C, relative humidity above 95 per cent and scheduled as well as unscheduled long and extensive cuts in electricity supply, environment of the state becomes totally unlivable. Also in the months of October-November, in spite of the government ban, the farmers burn paddy stubbles that pollute the environment extensively, which creates serious breathing problems for the people. It has happened twice that in the end of October the smoke emerging out of burning paddy stubbles got trapped under the clouds in the absence of blowing winds. Fortunately, the rain and winds cleared it. Had it continued for a couple of hours more, there could have occurred serious casualties.

For the state of Punjab, and for that matter Haryana, Western UP, and many other states of the country two main issues need to be tackled with urgency. First issue is that of depleting water resources and the second is environmental degradation. Both of these issues are closely related ones, particularly in the context of growing of paddy, which is a very high water consuming crop. Growing of paddy leads to excessive withdrawal of under ground water resulting in imbalance in the sense of withdrawal of water exceeding its recharge. For instance, the Central Board on underground water has reported that in central districts of Punjab the underground water being withdrawn as a per cent of recharge exceeds almost everywhere. For instance, this percentage is 350 in Jalandhar East block, 317 in Nakodar, 217 in Jalandhar West, 205 in Moga I, 187 in Moga II, 180 in Ahmadgarh, 169 in Sangrur and the lowest is Mahal Kalan at 119. Thus, almost no where in central districts the water balance is positive. This situation is unsustainable.

The second issue of environmental degradation is not only in terms of high temperature, high humidity, soil and water pollution, more importantly it is in terms of the emission of Greenhouse Gasses (GHG), primarily Carbon dioxide, Methane and Nitrous oxide, that are emitted into the environment from the paddy fields. Paddy growing in standing water is in fact a most unsuitable crop for Punjab and other such areas. Yet, it is becoming difficult to remove this crop from the cropping patterns because of (1) lack of more remunerative or even equally remunerative alternative crops that have lower level or even same level of production risks and price uncertainty compared with paddy crop. Perishability, production risks and lack of effective market clearance are the main constraints to replacing the rice crop. Further, free water and electric power, prompt market clearance, often with relaxed quality specifications, are the factors that keep the farmer from shifting the area from under rice. Right pricing of the irrigation water and power and equally efficient market clearance for alternative crops can easily tilt the balance against paddy crop; (2) Food security of the country is another serious concern. The wheat crop is not that much of a problem in respect of water consumption in the state. It is therefore essential that technology must be developed such that ponding of paddy fields is avoided that would lead to reduction or even elimination of emission of Green House Gases and check degradation of soils, reduce water consumption and put a stop to degradation of environment

On the issue of greenhouse gases, rice plant has intercellular spaces that conducts these gases to be emitted into the atmosphere. The anaerobic bacteria, under the anaerobic conditions created around the rhyzosphere of the plant by the constantly standing water, produce these gases. The plant also absorbs and conducts oxygen from the atmosphere to the root zone for the anaerobic bacteria that work on organic matter under standing water. It is estimated that rice crop growing in standing water over a period of ninety days produces more than 0.45 tonnes of methane, which is emitted into the air. Accounting for all green house gases, one hectare of rice crop over its growing period emits equivalent of about 20 tonnes of Carbon dioxide. If this emission, through avoiding the ponding of water in the rice field, is checked and certified, this can earn carbon credits ($etCO_2$) which can be traded in the carbon markets of the world. One hectare of rice, if replaced with other crops or even rice that is grown without standing water has the potential of earning carbon credits worth more than Rs.10,000 in three months of its growing period. If rice can be cultivated under aerobic conditions, this can revolutionise rice cultivation without impairing the food security of the country and having a solitary positive effect on the environment and reduction in demand for irrigation water.

Agricultural technologists of the Department of Agriculture, Punjab have developed one such technique of rice cultivation under aerobic conditions, which has been authenticated through average of 12 experiments conducted by the Punjab Agricultural University (PAU). This technique saves water by about 40 per cent, increases yield by about 6 to 8 per cent, improves the quality due to drier micro-climate, and improves the soil quality. The technique is catching up with the farmers, but very slowly and hesitantly. PAU is expected to approve of this technique from the next season. Once the PAU formally approves and recommends this technique, this can revolutionise rice cultivation in the irrigated areas of the state. The technique will help not only Punjab, but also other areas of the country and even the world where rice is grown in ponded fields through artificial irrigation. If farmers can be encouraged through some incentives out of the money earned from carbon credits through project mode in the carbon futures market, this system can pick up very fast. It is estimated that Punjab can earn something like Rs.20,000 crores in 10 years through these carbon credits if all the rice area can be brought under aerobic conditions. At least One-half of this money can be transferred to the farmers.

The technique is very simple. The land is prepared as is done for any other crop like wheat or maize. Ridges and furrows are drawn two feet apart with a ridger. Water is applied in the furrows (water should not flow over the bunds). Paddy nursery is transplanted four inches above the bottom of the furrow on both sides of the ridges with plant to plant distance of six inches. Water is kept standing in the furrows for five to six days. Then water is applied once a week. If there is rain, irrigation may not be required. Under such aerobic conditions, the emission of green house gases is reduced to almost nil. Yet, this carbon credit earning technique needs to be certified through accredited agencies after authenticated research results that may be brought out by the Punjab Agricultural University or any other research institute of the National Agricultural Research System (NARS). Some slides depicting the technique are available in the appendices.

On the issue of use of chemicals (fertilisers and pesticides), use of bio-fertilisers and bio-pesticides and organic farming are the options. Productivity and production might get a setback for a couple of years, but the experience shows that soon productivity picks up. For instance, Cuba presents a workable model on this aspect, where booming requirements of protective foods are being met through organoponicos on small plots of land allotted to individual farmers. Cuba is filled with more than 7,000 urban allotments or 'organoponicos', which fill perhaps as many as 81,000 acres. They have been established on tiny plots of land in the centre of tower-block estates or between the crumbling colonial homes that fill Havana. More than 200 gardens in Havana supply its citizens with more than 90 per cent of their fruit and vegetable.

Such farms barely existed in the late 1980s. Back then, Cuba's economy was extraordinarily reliant on subsidies from its political elder brother, the Soviet Union. It's agriculture was designed with one aim in mind—namely to produce as much sugar as possible, which the Soviets bought at more than five times the market price, in addition to purchasing 95 per cent of its citrus crop and 73 per cent of its nickel. In exchange, the Soviets provided Cuba with 63 per cent of its food imports and 90 per cent of its petrol. Such a relationship made Cuba extraordinarily vulnerable.

With the collapse of the Soviet Union, such subsidies halted almost overnight. Suddenly, the future looked bleak. By necessity, this meant a back-to-basics approach; with no Soviet oil for tractors or fertilisers, it turned to oxen and natural compost and the production of natural pesticides and beneficial insects. It is estimated that more than 200 locally based centres specialising in biopesticides annually produce 200 tonnes of verticillium to control whitefly, and 800 tonnes of beaveria sprays to control beetles. Cut banana stems baited with honey to attract ants are placed in sweet potato fields, which have led to control of sweet potato weevil. There are 170 vermi-compost centres, the annual production of which has grown to 9,300 tonnes (Andrew Buncombe, The Independent, UK)

Crop rotations, green manuring, intercropping and soil conservation have all been incorporated into polyculture farming (Report by Jules Pretty). Remarkably, this organic revolution has worked. The proof of this is that annual calorie intake per head in Cuba now stands at about 2,600 a day. UNFAO estimates that the percentage of the population considered undernourished fell from 8 per cent in 1990-92 to about 3 per cent in 2000-02. Cuba's infant mortality rate is lower than that of the US, while at 77 years, the life expectancy is the same.

Thus, alternatives to the use of chemicals (fertilisers and pesticides) exist and can be innovatively developed to avoid the impending environmental disaster. Crop patterns can be changed such that productivity of most scarce resources (land and water) improves and farm incomes are enhanced without negative externalities of environmental degradation and threat to food security. The Universities and research institutes of NARS have a challenge before them in this respect, which can be met with a vision and grit.

References

Chapin, F.S. E.S. Zavalets, V.T. Eviner, Rosamond L. Naylor, P.M. Vitousek, O.E. Sala, H.L. Reynolds, D.U. Hooper, M. Mack and E.S. Diaz (2003). "Consequences of the Changing Biodiversity", *Nature,* Vol. 405: 234-42.

Capoor, Karan and Philippe Ambrosi (2006). *State and Trends of Carbon Market 2006.* Washington DC: The World Bank and International Emission Trading Association.

Green R.E., M. Harley, L. Miles, J. Scharlemann, A. Watkinson and O. Watts (2003). *Global Climate Change and Biodiversity.* Norwich, UK: University of East Anglia.

Hiscock K., A. Southward, I. Tittley *et al.* (2004). "Effects of Changing Temperature on Benthic Marine Life in Britain and Ireland, Aquatic Conservation", *Marine and Freshwater Ecosystems,* Vol. 14: 333-62.

IPPC (2002). "Climate Change and Biodiversity", *IPPC Technical Paper* V.

Pimm, S.L. and R. Askins (1995). "The Future of Biodiversity", *Science,* Vol. 269: 347-50.

Thomas C.D. *et al.* (2004). "Extinction Risk from Climate Change", *Nature,* Vol. 427 (8): 145-48.

7

India's Irrigation Economy

In the Throes of a Transition

TUSHAAR SHAH

Introduction

Stagnating agriculture has emerged, during recent years, as a speed breaker in India's otherwise splendid and enviable growth story. The failure of rapid economic growth to bring about poverty reduction in commensurate manner is also another major concern linked with stagnant agriculture. It has been widely thought that the slow down in public investment in agriculture, mainly irrigation development, is the main culprit behind the deceleration in agricultural growth. Government of India's Accelerated Irrigation Benefits Programme (AIBP) was conceived of as a response to the plea for increased public investment in irrigation. In recent budgets, the Union Finance Minister has been laying great stress on completing the 'last mile irrigation projects' to step up the pace of irrigation development. Despite these initiatives, the area irrigated by public irrigation systems in India has remained stagnant for nearly a decade. In this paper, I want to argue that irrigation in India is in the throes of a major transition. The irrigation business model that India has followed since the early decades of the 19th century has rapidly changed, and public policies based on colonial model of irrigation development are no longer in sync with new developments in Indian agriculture. Neither the goals of India's irrigation policy, nor our irrigation development strategy, jives with the reality of our irrigation economy today.

Irrigation statistics compiled by the Government of India (GoI) underestimate the scale of India's irrigation economy which is booming like never before. Official estimates of the net irrigated area in India based on land use surveys is 57 M ha and the gross irrigated area is around 90 M ha. Other sources, however, suggest that there is great deal more irrigation going on in India. The most striking have been new estimates of global irrigated area published recently by the International Water Management Institute (IWMI). Based on the analysis of high resolution satellite imagary backed by extensive ground-truthing work, IWMI's estimate suggests that in 2004, India had 99 M ha of net irrigated area and 132 M ha of gross irrigated area. Both these estimates are over 50 per cent higher than the official estimates. In fact, IWMI's estimates of irrigated area of today are nearest to what the government of India would like to achieve by 2020. Incredible as these new estimates may sound, recent rounds of national sample survey also suggests that India's irrigation economy may be considerably larger than reflected in the official estimates.

The Groundwater Revolution

At the heart of the transformation that India's irrigation economy has been undergoing is the wresting, by millions of small farmers, of the initiative for irrigation development from the hands of the State. Under the model of irrigation development that India followed since the 1830's, the State has been the architect, entrepreneur, engineer and manager of irrigation systems. 'Command area' and 'duty' were the *mantra* of irrigation planning and management. The Government was the provider of irrigation and the farmer a passive recipient. In this model of unbalanced irrigation development, command areas were created near hydraulically opportune sites where reservoirs or weirs could be built and downstream areas could be 'commanded' by gravity flow. Farmers in the rest of the country were left to fend for themselves. Post-Independence, India followed much the same strategy for irrigation development that created pockets of prosperous command areas, leaving other parts to rainfed farming.

By 1970, the population pressure on farm lands in many parts of India had become so inexorable that farmers everywhere felt compelled to work their small farm holdings twice, or even thrice every year. Population pressure on farm lands then flagged off India's tube well revolution. India—especially, in the western and north-western parts— had a centuries old tradition of irrigating with wells.

Even in 1900, India had some 4 M ha under groundwater irrigation. At the time of independence, the areas irrigated by groundwater and surface water were evenly balanced. However, it was hardly expected by anybody that India would witness massive spread of tube well irrigation in the surface water-abundant Ganga-Brahmaputra basin or hardrock peninsular India. Such a pattern of irrigation development appeared wholly inconsistent with the country's hydrogeology.

At the onset of the 20th century, R.C. Dutt articulated the prevailing thinking about how irrigation should develop in different parts of India:

> Every province in India has its distinct irrigation requirements. In the alluvial basins of the Ganges and the Indus the most suitable irrigation works are canals from these rivers; while away from the rivers, wells are the most suitable. In Bengal with its copious rainfall, shallow ponds are the most suitable works and these were numerous in the olden times, sometimes of very large dimensions. In Madras and Southern India, where the soil is undulating and the underlying rock retains the water, the most suitable irrigation works are reservoirs made by putting up large embankments and thus impounding the water descending from hill slopes. Such were the old reservoirs of Madras. (Dutt, 1989: Vol. II, p.119, footnote 1).

This thinking was endorsed 70 years later by the second Irrigation Commission.[1] For millennia, irrigation in India had remained largely faithful to this dictum. Adaptive, minimalist, unobtrusive irrigation in India of 1800 was a reflection of this hydrogeologic make up of the subcontinental terrain. Constructive imperialism pioneered by Arthur Cotton in the south and Proby Cautley in the north took liberties with this ideal scheme. However, come the 1970s, and this age-old wisdom lay in tatters as a new era of 'atomistic irrigation' unfolded and engulfed South Asia with small-pump irrigation spreading everywhere like wildfire—in canal commands and outside, in arid, semi-arid and

---

1. "The character of [irrigation] works was largely conditioned by the physiographical features of the area in which they were located. In the arid and semi-arid plains of North India, perennial rivers like the Indus and the Ganga made it relatively easy to divert flood flows through inundation channels. In the peninsula, where the rainfall is scanty, the practice of trapping storm water in large tanks for domestic and agricultural purposes was widespread. In areas where a high groundwater table permitted lift irrigation, wells were common." (GoI, 1972: 61).

humid areas, upstream 'and' downstream of river basins, in excellent alluvial aquifers as well as in poor, hard rock peninsular aquifers with limited storage potential. If the era of 'constructive imperialism' began tinkering with the hydrology of river basins, the recent era of atomistic irrigation with small wells and tube wells went about reconfiguring it totally.

The rise of groundwater irrigation also transformed the organisation of irrigation at the local level. In pre-Colonial India, co-operation at the community level was the dominant irrigation institution. Under colonial rule, collaboration between the State and the engineering profession was at the centre stage of centralised, bureaucratic irrigation development and management. In this new era of atomistic irrigation, the State as well as science became onlookers in a ballgame whose rules and logic they did not understand, much less dictate. In an incipient atomistic irrigation economy of the 1980's and later, neither the State nor the community was the entrepreneur, builder, or the manager of irrigation; it was the multitude of small-holders—Marx's 'millions of disconnected production units'—each with his tiny, captive irrigation system, ostensibly unconnected with the rest. Until now, crops had to wait for water to be released and flow through a network of canals before getting irrigated; now, water was scavenged on-demand and applied just-in-time when crops needed it most.

Between 1960 and 1985, India invested in irrigation projects many times more capital in real terms than the British had invested during the entire 110 year period between 1830 and 1940. Yet, even according to the GoI's figures, over 60 per cent of irrigated areas are today served by groundwater. Other indicators suggest that even this may be a serious underestimate. Remote sensing data as well as national sample survey suggest that as much as 75 per cent-80 per cent of India's irrigated area today is served by groundwater wells. Until 1960, Indian farmers owned just a few tens of thousands of mechanical pumps using diesel or electricity to pump water; today India has over 20 million modern water extraction structures. Every fourth cultivator household has a tube well; and two of the remaining three use purchased irrigation service supplied by tube well owners (Shah, forthcoming).

Socioeconomic Impacts of the Groundwater Boom

Shallow tube wells have done to Indian irrigation what PCs have done to computing globally; they have democratised irrigation. They took irrigation away from command areas to the nook and corner of the country. Among several things, the booming pump irrigation economy has: (a) offered 'some' irrigation access to an overwhelming majority, rather than concentrating 'all' irrigation benefits on small privileged groups in command areas; (b) thereby, helped soften growing farmer unrest in the region's vast dry land areas, which would have otherwise destabilised social and political structures; (c) has come to account for over 60 per cent of irrigated areas, and 80 per cent of irrigated farm output and resultant incomes; (c) drought-proofed the region's agriculture against at least one monsoon failure and made large-scale famines, history; (e) improved farm wages and increased demand for farm labour year-round; (f) demonstrated a strong pro-poor, inclusive bias in irrigated agriculture; (g) supported a new drive towards intensive diversification to high value products such as milk, fruit and vegetables, especially in dry land areas in a scale-neutral format. These impacts have benefited—directly and indirectly, to lesser or greater extent—around half a billion rural people in South Asia. One cannot say that the South Asian peasant is much better off in 2000 compared to 1975; but one can confidently say that, other things being the same, he would have been immensely worse off but for the pump irrigation boom.

Thanks to its myriad and widespread benefits, pump irrigation revolution, aided by irrigation service markets, has been amongst the most powerful rural poverty alleviation phenomena without which the region would arguably have been in the throes of massive social and political instability. The pump irrigation boom in India since 1975 has created more irrigation in 30 years than public investments in canal irrigation did in 170. Pump irrigation has also brought about greater spatial equality in irrigation; it is spread all over the country unlike canal projects which have created concentrated pockets of agrarian prosperity in canal commands. Vibrant local, informal markets for pump irrigation service have helped the 20 odd million Water Extraction Mechanisms (WEM) owners to reach irrigation benefits to another 40-60 million small holder families, covering a vast majority of the farming community with access to supplemental irrigation. Especially in north-western India, the rise of groundwater irrigation on private initiative has reduced water logging, which otherwise would have required massive public investment in drainage and salinity management. The pump irrigation economy has been the driving force behind national growth in food and agricultural economies, for example, transforming West Bengal (and Bangladesh) as the region's rice bowls. Pump irrigation farmers apply less water per hectare, achieve higher ratio of evapo-transpiration to consumptive fraction, and obtain higher yields/ha compared to flow irrigators. Across rural economic classes, the distribution of pump ownership is more equal than landholdings. In dry land areas, supplemental pump irrigation has had a dramatic impact of stabilising rainfed yields and promoted agrarian diversification. The impact of a widespread drought on agricultural and food production today is much more muted compared to the 1960s and before. Pump irrigation boom has been instrumental in all but banishing starvation deaths in the subcontinent. In effect, it has activated a subsurface reservoir on a subcontinental scale—that always existed but remained largely unused—but which now captures and stores over 250-270 km^3 of water in a normal year, creating on a massive scale space, time and form utility in agricultural water use, the object of any reservoir.

Sustaining the Groundwater Boom

Nothing is an unmixed blessing; and this is true about South Asia's pump irrigation revolution since the 1970s which has been a prominent target of doomsday prophecies about an impending socioecological disaster (see, e.g., Seckler *et al.*, 1999; Postel, 1999; Vaidyanathan, 1996). There is much truth in this concern; however, tube well irrigation has generated substantial socio-ecological dividends as well. In flood prone eastern India, it has helped mitigate the rapacity of floods and water logging by reducing 'rejected recharge' by creating more storage in the aquifers. In the Indus basin too, tube well irrigation has reduced water logging and salinisation, a task which would have taken hundreds of million dollars of investments in drainage.

Groundwater horror stories of India are, however, becoming increasingly frightening in arid alluvial and hard-rock aquifers. In some coastal plains along with arid alluvial plains facing overdraft, the central resource governance challenge is coping with salinisation and depletion which, in a chronic form are already visible in some parts, may seal the fate of agriculture, and of human settlement itself. Then, in hard rock areas of peninsular India, where tube well irrigation expansion is way out of proportion to the limited storage offered by aquifers, resource depletion is a serious issue in itself but has also aided growing concentration of fluoride and other salts in groundwater which is the main source of drinking water supply for rural as well as urban populations. Problems of geogenic contamination of groundwater—such as with arsenic in eastern Ganga basin and fluoride in much western and peninsular India are large and serious. The causal role of pump irrigation in mobilising fluoride and other salts in groundwater is clearer than in arsenic contamination whose chemistry is still tenuous and disputed.

The Real Water Management Challenge

Although Indian irrigation planning by governments and international agencies is still steeped in harnessing rivers and developing surface water, the real challenge facing the country is managing its vast, informal groundwater irrigation economy. The role of the State as the sole provider of irrigation is passé, as farmers have taken the irrigation development initiative in their own hands. What the State needs to do is implement a strategy that will help sustain this informal irrigation economy. Key challenges of groundwater management are set out in Table 7.1.

Since the 1970's, at a rather low cost to the public exchequer, Indian farmers have opened up a vast reservoir—in the form of aquifers— that we always had but for millennia, only sparingly used. Around 1950, India hardly used 15-20 billion cubic metres of groundwater; now, Indian farmers withdraw over 200 billion cubic meters of water from aquifers every year; and during every year of good monsoon, this reservoir gets replenished, without virtually any management effort invested by the government in it.

Table 7.1

Groundwater Management Challenges Facing India

Hydro-geological Settings		Socioeconomic and Management Challenges: Resource Depletion	Optimising Conjunctive Use	Secondary Salinisation	Natural Groundwater Quality Concerns
A. Major Alluvial Plains	A.1. Arid	••	••	•••	•
	A.2. Humid	•	•••		••
B. Coastal Plains		••	•	•••	•
C Inter-Montane Valleys		•	••	•	•
D. Hard-rock Areas		•••	•	•	•••

Note: The number of dots suggest the scale and severity of a challenge.

No reservoir anywhere in the world can keep delivering without proper management. The more intensively a reservoir is used, the more intensively it needs to be managed. Yet, India's groundwater aquifers—the country's largest reservoir—are hardly managed, if at all. India's irrigation officialdom do not even recognise aquifer management as a part of their responsibility. Indeed, one can assert that rural development programmes in India—that support watershed development, tank improvement, rainwater harvesting, etc—do more to sustain India's groundwater irrigation economy than the irrigation bureaucracy does. The growing concern about groundwater depletion, falling water tables and salinisation are a result of this lack of management of our biggest and most precious reservoir. In an average year, India receives 4,000 cubic KM of rainfall precipitation. Against this, farmers use only 200 cubic KM of groundwater, barely 5 per cent of our total water resources. All we need today to make the country's groundwater economically and environmentally sustainable is to ensure that 5 per cent of our total water availability is recharged into groundwater aquifers. True, there is the big question of spatial variability. Punjab, Haryana and Rajasthan use a lot of groundwater but have little rainfall precipitation. But many of these regions have large volumes of canal water being spread on them; the first charge on this water needs to be for 'managed' groundwater recharge rather than flow irrigation. If a tenth of the Himalayan water presently available in the Indian side of Indo-Gangetic basin were used for recharging aquifers in a managed manner, north-western India should never face the groundwater stress it is experiencing now.

In sum, irrigation planners in India need to rewrite the country's mission in the water sector. In his *Seeing Like the State*, James C. Scott (1998) analyses how the official conception of forests in many colonised countries like India during the 19th century was shaped by the German foresters' obsession with the idea of revenue yield as the central objective of managing forests. This obsession encouraged single-minded conversion of natural forests into monoculture timber plantations. Scott argued that, long after colonialists withdrew, forest management for revenue yield stayed as the defining logic of local forest bureaucracies, themselves the product of the idea. Strikingly similar has been the evolutionary trajectory of official irrigation thinking in South Asia. Like revenue yield of forests, the 'mantra' of irrigation planning during the colonial era were 'command' and 'duty' in flow irrigation systems. Myriad other ways that India's small-holders have now been figuring out to mobilise, store, scavange, apply water to relieve moisture stress of plants were largely outside the purview of the mainstream irrigation thinking and practice.

To be effective in different circumstances, our irrigation planning needs to chuck this "path-dependence" (North, 1990), a phrase institutionalists use to describe the property of an institution to keep self-reinforcing itself, even at the risk of inviting irrelevance. We need to wake up to this new reality of agricultural water use in India. In this new reality, managing the vast underground reservoir that South Asia's farmers have created for free is the overarching priority to thrive in an anarchy that the state has neither the power nor wherewithal to tame.

References

Dutt, R. (1989). *The Economic History of India*, Volume II. New Delhi: Government of India, Ministry of Information and Broadcasting.

Government of India. (1972). *Report of the Irrigation Commission*. New Delhi: Ministry of Irrigation and Power.

North, Douglass C., (1990) *Institutions, Institutional Change, and Economic Performance*. New York: Cambridge University Press.

Postel, S. (1999). *Pillar of Sand: Can the Irrigation Miracle Last?*. New York: W.W. Norton & Company. xvi, 313p. (Worldwatch Book)

Scott, James C. (1998). *Seeing Like a State: How Certain Schemes to Improve the Human Condition Have Failed*. Yale ISPS Series and Yale Agrarian Studies. New Haven, Conn. and London: Yale University Press.

Seckler, D., R. Barker and U. Amarasinghe (1999). "Water Scarcity in the Twenty-First Century", *Water Resources Development* 15(1-2): 29-42.

Shah,Tushaar (forthcoming). *Taming the Anarchy: Governing South Asia's Irrigation Economy.*

Vaidyanathan. A. (1996). "Depletion of Groundwater: Some Issues", *Indian Journal of Agricultural Economics* 51(1 & 2), January-June

8

Towards a Competitive Manufacturing Sector

RAJIV KUMAR and ABHIJIT SEN GUPTA

Introduction

The Indian economy grew at an impressive growth rate of over 8.5 per cent during 2004-05 to 2006-07, primarily on the back of robust growth in the manufacturing and services sector. The manufacturing sector has witnessed remarkable growth rates of over 9 per cent during the last three years reaching up to as high as 12.3 per cent during 2006-07. This is significantly higher than the average annual growth of 5.7 per cent during the previous five years. A sustained double digit growth of the manufacturing sector is essential for achieving the desired GDP growth of 8 to 9 per cent and more importantly to generate much needed employment.

In this context, the objective of this study is to analyse the growth potential and competitiveness of the Indian manufacturing sector. Section 2 of the paper evaluates the performance of the manufacturing sector over time and makes a cross country comparison. In Section 3, we identify the factors that have contributed to marked divergence in regional development of this sector. Section 4 looks at both the organised and unorganised sectors and examines the factors that have resulted in the marked dualism between these two sectors. Section 5 analyses the employment generation potential of the manufacturing sector, while Section 6 looks at its export performance. Section 7 identifies the challenges facing the Indian manufacturing sector to make the transition to mass manufacturing, and discusses possible means to address these challenges or constraints. Finally, Section 8 summarises the main conclusions of the paper.

Aggregate Manufacturing Scenario

The Indian manufacturing sector experienced a strong resurgence in the last three years. It witnessed an average annual growth rate of around 10.13 per cent in 2004-2007, compared to 5.7 per cent during the preceding five years. Buoyed by this impressive growth in the manufacturing sector, the Indian economy grew at an average annual rate of 8.6 per cent in 2004-2007 compared to just 5.4 per cent during 2000-2004.

Given, India's stage of development, manufacturing would be considered to be the engine of development. However, this is apparently not happening as the growth has been primarily driven by services. In fact, Kochhar *et al.* (2006) point out that the change in the share of manufacturing in GDP in India between 1980 and 2000 has been 2.5 percentage points lower than the average country at the same stage of development, while the change in service share was 10 percentage points higher than average.

Over time, it can be seen (Figure 8.1) that the share of value added by the manufacturing sector in India's GDP has been stagnant. From 1965 to 2004 the decline in agriculture's share was nearly matched by the increase in service's share. However, the share of industry increased from 21 per cent to 27 per cent but the increase in the manufacturing sector's share was only from 14 per cent to just over 16 per cent, over a period of 40 years. Surprisingly, the share of the manufacturing sector has declined since 1995 when it peaked at just over 18 per cent. It declined to 15 per cent in 1999, before settling around 16 per cent in recent years. The contribution of the other components of industry, namely, mining, construction, electricity, water and gas, has increased steadily from 6 per cent to 11 per cent.

A cross-country comparison shows that contribution to GDP by the manufacturing sector in India is much lower compared to other developing countries. While in China, the manufacturing sector accounts for nearly 35 per cent of the GDP, in South Korea, Malaysia and Indonesia, the share of the manufacturing sector is around 30 per cent. Even in Latin American economies like Argentina and Brazil, the manufacturing sector contributes around 24 per cent to GDP. It is important to examine the reasons that have constrained the growth of

Figure 8.1

Change in Sector Shares (1965-2004)

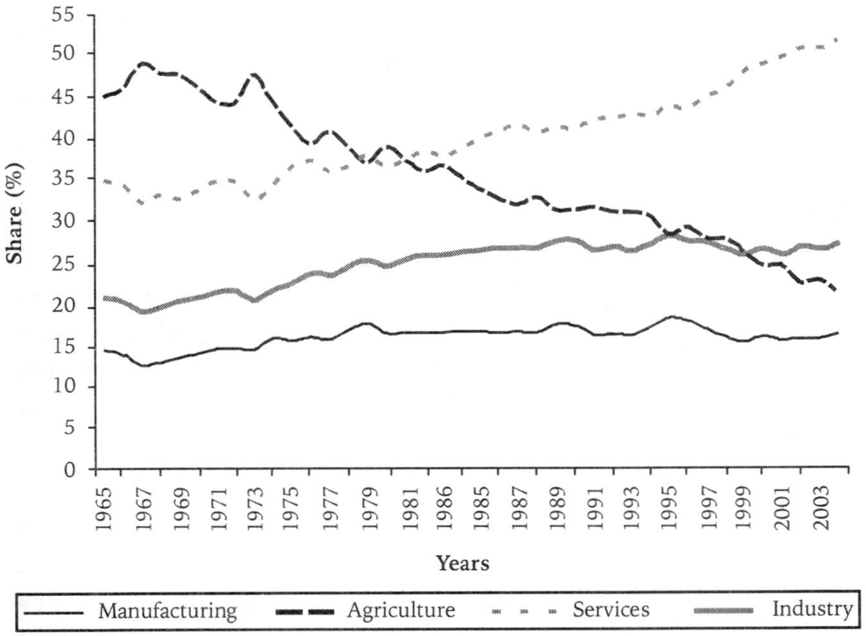

Source: World Development Indicators 2006.

the manufacturing sector in India and resulted in a stagnation of its share in GDP.

Manufacturing sector growth has been cyclical with downswings being notably shorter than upswings. Figure 8.2 plots the quarter to quarter growth rate of the manufacturing sector from the first quarter of 1982-83 to the first quarter of 2006-07.

The sector witnessed strongest growth during the 1980s when the annual rates of growth for manufacturing, registered manufacturing and unregistered manufacturing were 7.0, 8.1 and 5.8 per cent respectively. The reorientation of industrial and trade policies in the mid-1970s was reinforced in the 1980s with the introduction of major policy reforms. Nagraj (1990) and Ahluwalia (1991) have provided several explanations for improved growth performance in the 1980s.

Figure 8.2

Performance of the Manufacturing Sector

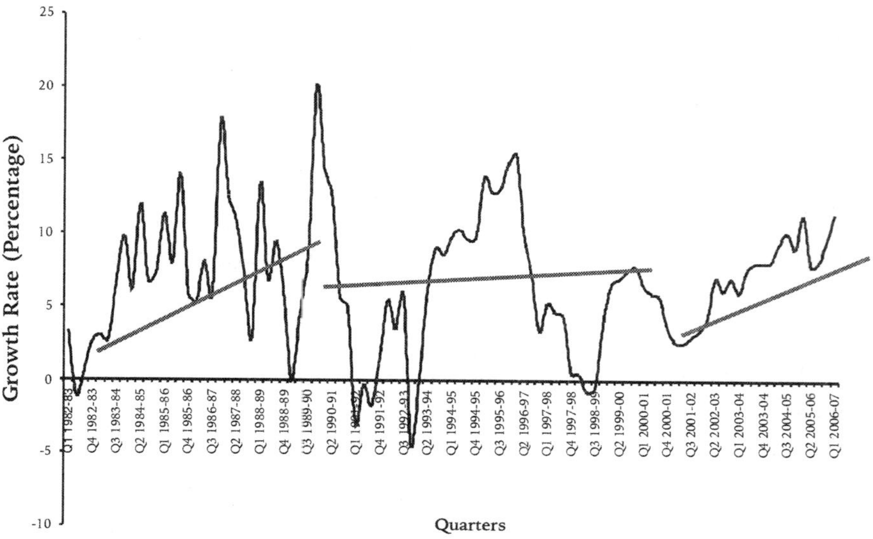

Source: Central Statistical Organisation.

These range from increase in infrastructure investment and better management of these sectors, growth of per capita income to widespread reforms in industrial and trade policies. The policy reforms and infrastructure investment resulted in significant improvements in total factor productivity.[1]

The 1980s also witnessed significant relaxation of industrial controls. In 1985, 25 industries were delicensed and the number had reached 31 by 1990. The limit on requirement of an industrial licence

1. The industrial and trade reforms undertaken during the 1980s had a positive impact on the performance of the manufacturing sector. Access to imported capital goods was vastly increased by the reform of the Open General Licensing (OGL) and canalised import schemes. The OGL list identified items that could be imported without a licence from the Ministry of Commerce and was steadily expanded over this decade. Intermediate inputs were also placed on this list and their numbers steadily improved over the decade. This was accompanied by a strong decline in the share of canalised imports. As a result, the share of imports that were neither canalised nor subject to licensing increased from 5 per cent in 1980-81 to 30 per cent in 1987-88. Consequently, firms could import machinery or raw material at cheaper costs, which contributed significantly to the productivity.

was raised from Rs. 3.5 crores to Rs. 50 crores in backward areas and Rs. 15 crores elsewhere. In many industries, broad banding was introduced, which allowed firms to switch production between similar items, and expand capacity by 25 per cent without applying for a licence. The asset limit, over which firms were subject to Monopolies and Restrictive Trade Practices (MRTP) Act regulations was raised from Rs. 20 crores to Rs. 100 crores. This freed half of the 180 large business houses from restrictions on growth in established product lines. For several industries, the requirement of MRTP clearances was completely waived off. Price controls on cement and aluminium were abolished. This eliminated the prevailing black market and the resulting expanded production led to substantial reduction in prices.

Finally, this period also witnessed introduction of several export incentives, which reduced the foreign exchange constraints faced by the firms and allowed them to import machinery and raw material. Replenishment (REP) licences were given to exporters to import goods on the restricted list and these were made freely tradeable in the market. Kelkar and Kumar (1990) argue that as a result of these reforms, the manufacturing sector at the end of the 1980s looked significantly different from the end of the 1970s.

The reform process was more aggressively pursued during the 1990s. There was a change from a 'positive list', where only items on the Open General License (OGL) did not require a licence for import, to a 'negative list', where an item could be imported unless it was explicitly on the restricted list. The New Industrial Policy (NIP) of 1991, removed investment licensing and entry restrictions on MRTP firms, reduced public sector monopoly and abolished industrial licensing for all firms, except those specified on health, safety, security and environmental grounds. In the area of foreign investment, the Reserve Bank of India was empowered to approve equity investment up to 51 per cent in almost all industries except those subject to public sector monopoly and industrial licensing. There was also some reduction in the number of products reserved for the small sector.

Import licensing was abolished on almost all intermediate and capital goods. However, restrictions on consumer goods imports continued to remain in place. Tariff rates on several products were raised in the 1980s to convert quota rents into tariff revenue. Since 1991 these tariff rates have been lowered by compressing the top tariff rate and rationalising the tariff structure. The rupee was devalued by 22 per cent in 1991 to reflect its correct value and as a result, Indian exports have become more competitive in global markets.

To analyse the impact of trade and industry reforms on the manufacturing sector performance, we look at the performance of some of the sectors that underwent significant liberalisation during the 1980s and 1990s. We identify products at the three digit level, where the effective rate of protection was significantly reduced compared to 1980-85 and automatic approval of foreign direct investment up to 51 per cent was allowed under the NIP 1991. Das (2002) shows that during 1985-90, compared to the period 1980-85, effective rate of protection fell significantly in fabricated structural metals (26.56 per cent), electrical industrial machinery (22.71 per cent), motor cycle and parts (21.74 per cent) and iron and steel (13.41 per cent). In these products automatic approval of FDI was also allowed up to 51 per cent. On the other hand cotton textiles witnessed an increase in the effective rate of protection of about 14.22 per cent. It was also one of the sectors where automatic approval of FDI was not allowed.

Figure 8.3 shows that sectors which witnessed a substantial decline in the effective rates of protection and got access to FDI, performed relatively better compared to sectors where the rate of protection was increased. Sectors which were opened up to foreign markets and competition like fabricated structural metals, electrical industrial machinery, motor cycle and parts and iron and steel experienced average annual growth rates of 5.21 per cent, 7.45 per cent, 15.76 per cent and 7.06 per cent respectively. On the other hand, cotton textiles, a closely protected sector, grew at a meagre 1.44 per cent during 1980-1981 to 1997-98. Thus, liberalisation had a positive impact on sectoral growth rate by giving them access to better technology and ensuring more efficient use of resources.

However, manufacturing growth witnessed a slowdown beginning from 1998. Several reasons have been attributed for the slowdown. Export growth fell during this period due to erosion of India's competitiveness on account of steep depreciation of the East Asian

Figure 8.3

Performance of Selected Sectors during the 1980s and 1990s

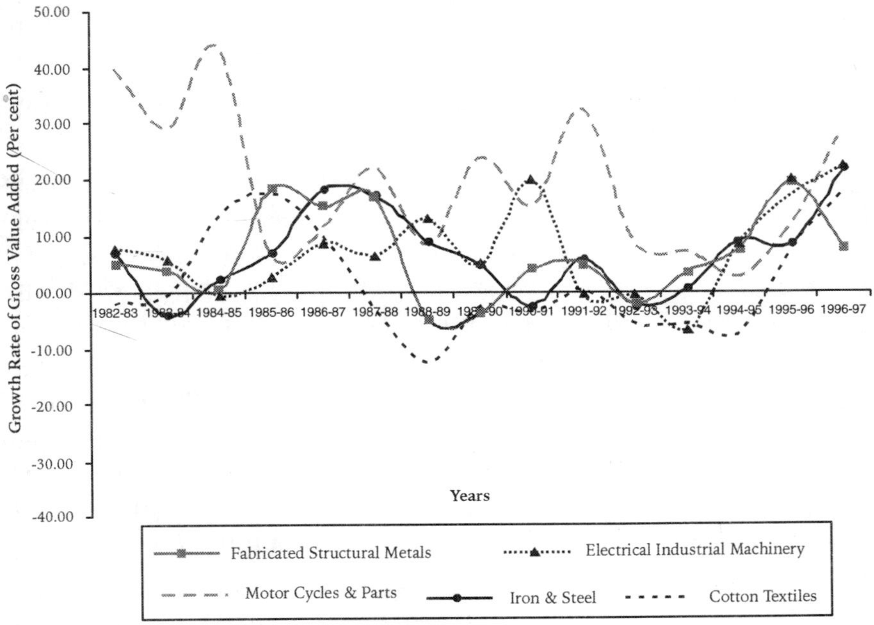

Source: Central Statistical Organisation

currencies. Moreover, rural demand declined due to low agricultural output and slow take off of some key infrastructure projects. Desai (2001) argued that the credit squeeze in 1996 and high interest rates stifled manufacturing growth. Nagraj (2003) contends that the slowdown could be attributed to low agriculture growth and reduction in public investment. After a brief turnaround in 1999-2000, the manufacturing growth again slowed down in 2000-01. The main reasons for deceleration were low domestic and external demand, high real interest rates and infrastructure bottlenecks.

The growth rate in the manufacturing sector has picked up strongly since the last quarter of 2001-02. Since then the manufacturing sector has witnessed the longest ever upswing since the 1990s. From the last quarter of 2001-02, the manufacturing sector witnessed an impressive average growth rate of over 8.4 per cent. Some of the previously existing deficiencies were rectified in this period and more significantly, capital became cheaper since 2001, which facilitated restructuring of the existing infrastructure. This resulted in a marked improvement in transport connectivity. Moreover, the last few years also witnessed an impressive export performance.

In fact the manufacturing sector has performed significantly better than several of the core infrastructure sectors (Figure 8.4). Comparing the manufacturing sector with other core sectors, namely, coal, cement, steel, electricity and crude petroleum, we find that the manufacturing sector has grown faster than electricity, coal and crude petroleum, while steel and cement sectors have grown faster than the manufacturing sector. The slow growing sectors, namely, electricity, coal and crude petroleum are primarily owned by the public sector. On the other hand in manufacturing, cement and steel, the private sector has a dominant presence. Thus we find that the ownership of the sectors is related to the performance of the sectors, with privately owned sectors performing better than publicly owned ones. This divergent performance of manufacturing and core or intermediate sectors could impose binding constraints on future growth.

The sub-sector composition of manufacturing output has hardly changed between 1980-81 to 2003-04. Food beverages and tobacco, which constitute the largest component, has maintained its share at 16 per cent of manufacturing output. The share of basic and fabricated metal stood at 15 per cent in 1980-81. It went up marginally to 17 per cent in the early 1990s but was back at the original level in 2003-04. Chemicals and related products also maintained their share at 14 per cent over this period. Sectors whose share increased were coke, petroleum and nuclear fuel, whose share rose from 8 per cent in 1980-1981 to over 14 per cent in 2003-04, and motor vehicles, which had a share of 6 per cent in 2003-04. Textile has been the biggest loser with its share declining from 15 to 8 per cent during the same period (Figure 8.5).

The Indian manufacturing sector is typified by an extremely skewed employment structure. Tybout (2000) points out that such an employment structure is common to several developing countries but the situation in India is rather extreme. As is evident from Figure 8.6, in India, an exceptionally large number of workers are engaged in the

Figure 8.4

Comparison of the Manufacturing Sector with Core Industries

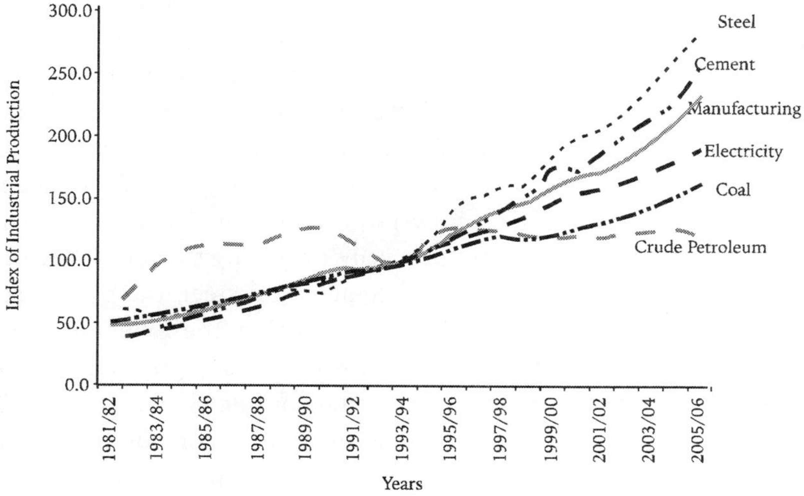

Source: Central Statistical Organisation

smallest size group of 6-9 workers.[2] At the other extreme there is a fairly high proportion of large establishments that employ more than 500 workers. Consequently, as pointed out by Mazumdar (1998), the manufacturing sector in India is characterised by 'missing middle' that is, a very small proportion of the workers being employed in medium scale establishments, employing between 50 and 500 workers. This skewed structure has implications for both efficiency as well as equity.

Apart from the existence of such a skewed structure, what is more worrying in the Indian context is that such a structure has remained in place over the last 16 years. While in 1984-85, 37 per cent of the manufacturing workforce were engaged in establishments employing 6-9 workers, the number increased to around 45 per cent in 2000-01 after declining briefly in the mid-1990s. At the other end of the

2. These are workers engaged in Directory Manufacturing Establishment (DME) which employs more than six workers but less than nine.

Figure 8.5

Change in Composition of the Manufacturing Output (1980-81 to 2003-04)

1980-81

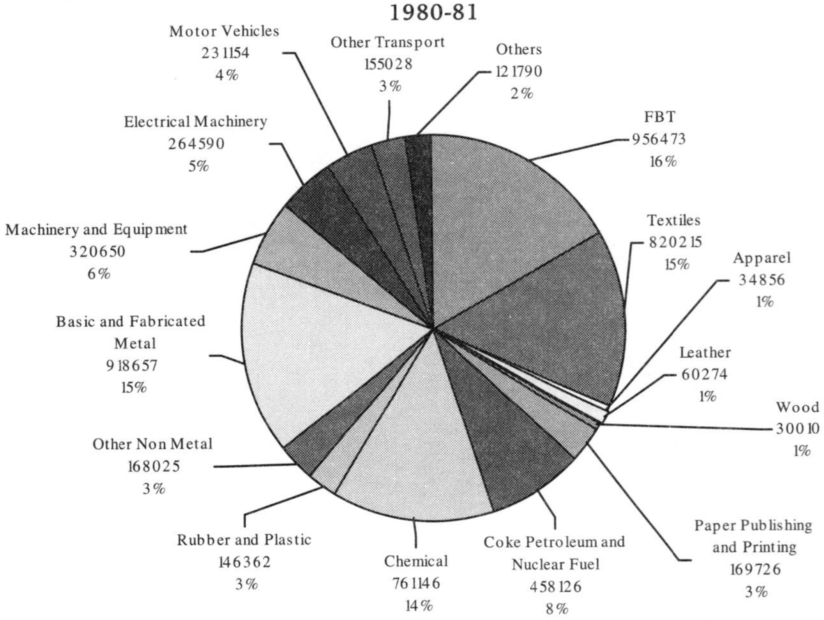

1990-91

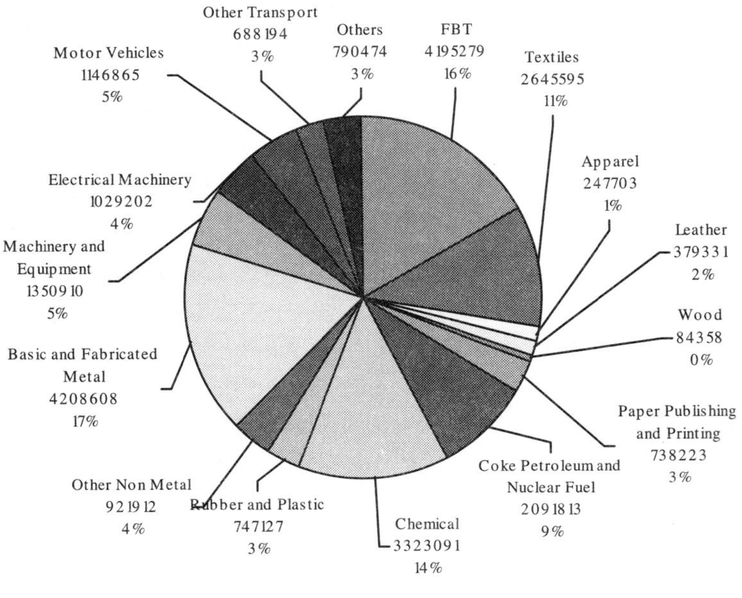

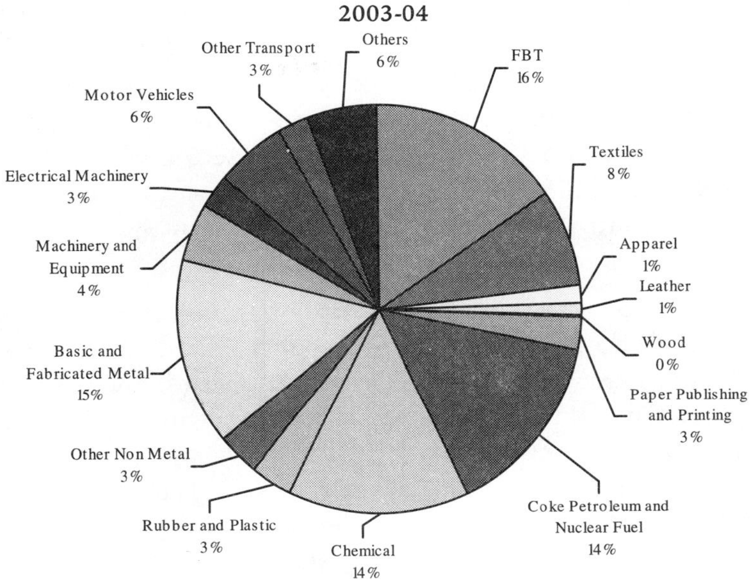

Source: *Annual Survey of India*, Various Issues

Figure 8.6

Distribution of Enterprises on the Basis of Employment

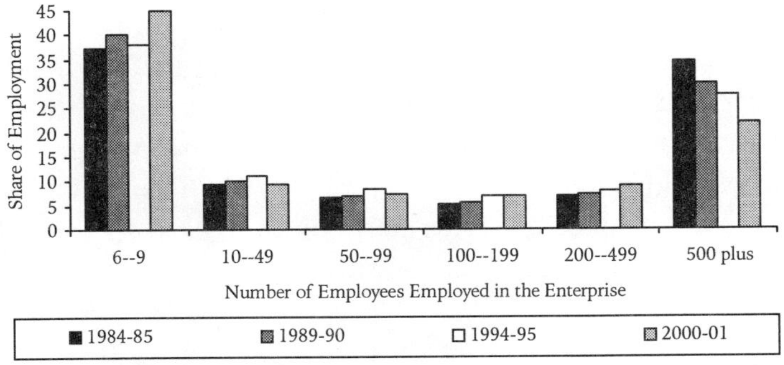

Source: National Sample Survey Organisation and *Annual Survey of Industries*, Various Reports

spectrum, the share of establishments employing more than 500 workers decreased from 34 per cent to 22 per cent during the same period. Thus at one end we have establishments that are characterised by extremely low levels of productivity, while at the other end there are large firms that are able to compete globally. As a result of this skewed structure, the share of establishments employing between 50 and 500 workers have remained more or less constant during this period. In 1984-85 such firms employed around 19 per cent of the manufacturing workforce, while in 2000-01 their share increased only marginally to 23.5 per cent. Thus, there is a dearth of middle sized firms which are often the main employment generators in the manufacturing sector, while producing reasonably high quality goods. In other rapidly growing Asian economies like China, South Korea, Hong Kong and Taiwan the employment structure is far more evenly distributed.

This dualistic structure of Indian manufacturing is a consequence primarily of two sets of government policies, namely, small scale industry (SSI) promotion and labour market policies. The SSI policies are characterised by fiscal incentives, subsidised credit, input subsidies and above all the reservation of a large number of sectors exclusively for SSI units. This policy regime has effectively encouraged small units to remain small. By remaining small they achieved higher profitability, and apparently in a range of industries the policy incentives outweighed the returns that could be achieved by larger size and economies of scale. This incentive to remain small has been greatly reinforced by the plethora of labour market policies that in effect sharply raise labour costs above a fairly low threshold. The strongest disincentive against scaling upwards arises from the uncertainty created by the combination of labour policies and non-transparent set of complex government processes. These have resulted in a very high rate of attrition and an unsupportive investment environment. The rewards for breaking these barriers against size are very large. But only a very few could achieve the breakthrough. This nexus of two long-standing 'pro-socialist' policies perhaps best explain the missing middle or the dualistic structure of the Indian manufacturing sector.

Regional Disparities

The manufacturing sector has not developed uniformly across India. Some states have achieved a high level of industrialisation, where as others are lagging far behind. Moreover, there is also a significant difference between the share of states in total manufacturing output and its share in the number of workers (Figure 8.7).[3]

3. These shares have been calculated using the data provided by *Annual Survey of Industries* and hence are an indication of the organised sector only.

Figure 8.7

State-wise Decomposition of Output and Workforce, 2003-04

Output

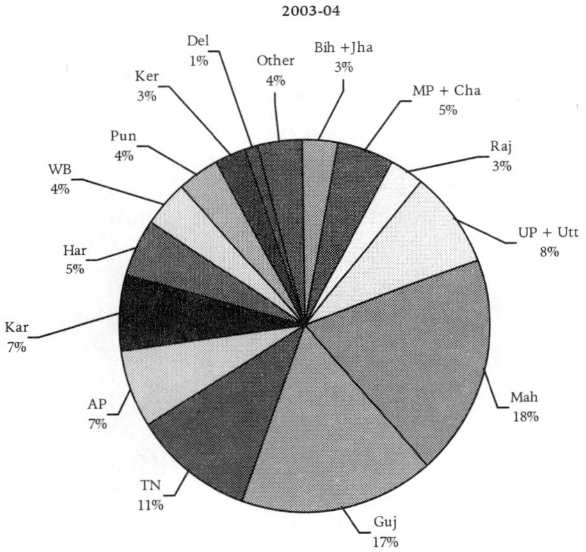

Workers

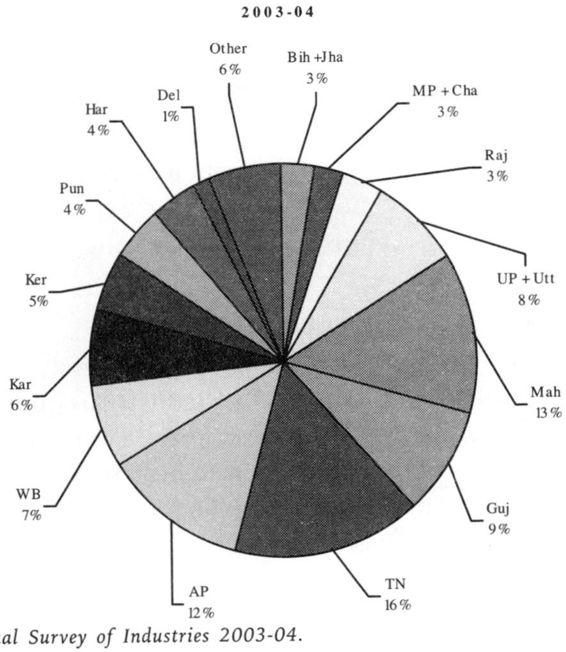

Source: *Annual Survey of Industries 2003-04.*

Maharashtra, which is the leading contributor to manufacturing output at 18 per cent, accounts for only 13 per cent of the workforce. Similarly, Gujarat employs only 9 per cent of the workforce but produces 17 per cent of the manufacturing output. On the other hand states like Tamil Nadu, Andhra Pradesh and West Bengal together employ as much as 35 per cent of the manufacturing workforce but contribute only 22 per cent of the output.

In Maharashtra, four industry divisions produced more than 50 per cent of the manufacturing output. These were (i) chemical and chemical products (15.67 per cent), (ii) coke, refined petroleum products and nuclear fuel (14.09 per cent), (iii) food and beverages (11.66 per cent) and (iv) basic metals (10.39 per cent). In Gujarat, these four sectors accounted for nearly 75 per cent of the manufacturing output. The shares of these sectors were 27.31 per cent, 33.00 per cent, 8.45 per cent and 6.22 per cent. According to Burange (1999), barring food and beverages, all the other above sectors are classified as capital intensive industries. This explains how Maharashtra and Gujarat have been able to contribute more to the manufacturing output than their employment share. Figure 8.8 looks at the state-wise decomposition of output at three different points 1970-71, 1990-91 and 2003-04 and shows that the states' shares have not remained constant over this period of time. Maharashtra and Gujarat have been the front runner over this entire period.

The more robust growth of manufacturing in Maharashtra and Gujarat is a consequence of pro-active and supportive policy regimes.[4] On the other hand several states' shares have declined dramatically like West Bengal, whose share declined from 13 per cent in 1970-71 to 4 per cent in 2003-04. Thus, West Bengal seems to have experienced a severe de-industrialisation during this period. Lahiri and Yi (2006) find that productivity differences—attributable to both total factor productivity and human capital—account for 75 per cent of the difference between manufacturing sector performance in Maharashtra and West Bengal. The other major difference is likely to be due to

4. Both Maharashtra and Gujarat have provided several fiscal incentives to promote the growth of the manufacturing sector. They have also emphasised on setting up of Industrial parks, upgradation of infrastructure, R&D, enhancing exports, etc. with a view to increase the output of the manufacturing sector.

Figure 8.8

State-wise Decomposition of Manufacturing Output

1970-71

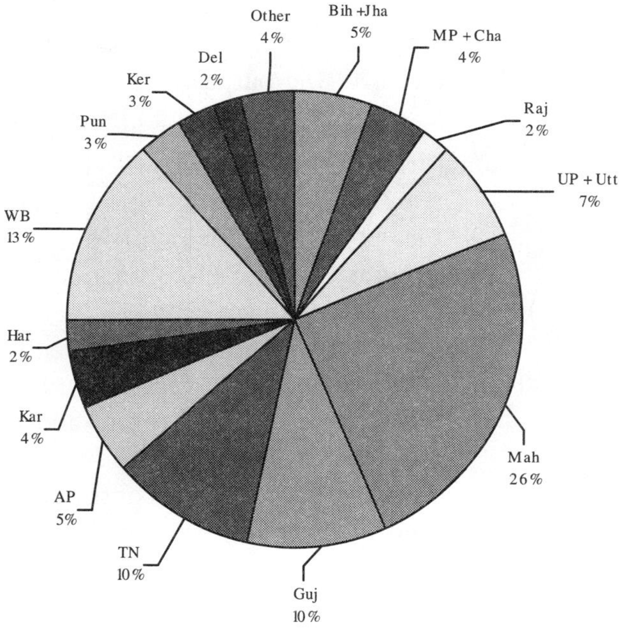

1990-91

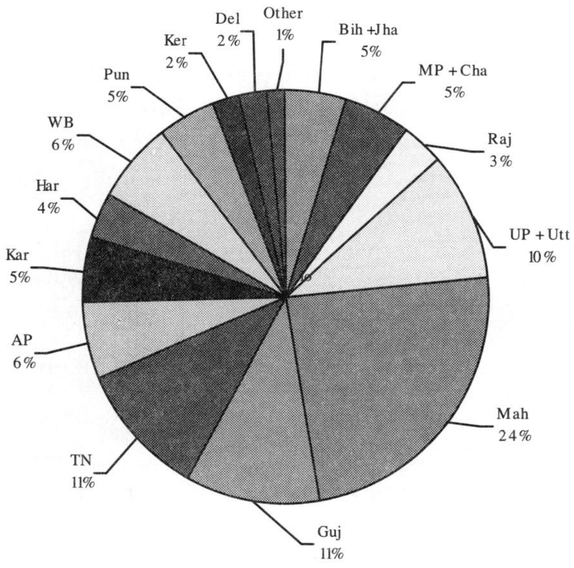

2003-04

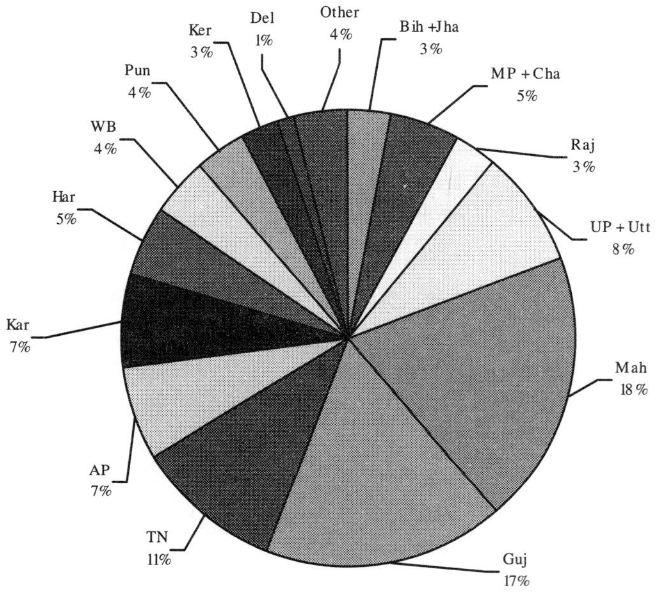

Source: Annual Survey of Industries, Various Issues

labour market problems in West Bengal. During the last three decades West Bengal has witnessed a significant rise in the bargaining power of trade unions. This induced more aggressive trade union demands for higher wages and more labour friendly work rules. According to the Labour Bureau, in 2005, out of the total loss of 23.27 million man-days in the country, West Bengal alone accounted for 13.99 million man-days or 60.15 per cent.

Others, which have witnessed a decline in their shares, are the BIMARU (Bihar, Madhya Pradesh, Rajasthan and Uttar Pradesh) states. In 1990-91, these states accounted for more than 23 per cent of the manufactured output. However, in 2003-04, their contribution fell to 19 per cent. The decline in their share seems to be due to the poor condition of infrastructure. Manufacturing is heavily dependent on several key infrastructures like power, telecom, ports, roads, railways, urban infrastructure, finance, etc. Mitra *et al.* (2002) construct a composite infrastructure indicator using principal component analysis.

The variables that go into the construction of the indicator include electricity availability, density of road and rail networks, number of vehicles, development of postal system, school enrolment rate, infant mortality rate and financial depth of the states. Figure 8.9 looks at the relationship between this infrastructure indicator and performance of the manufacturing sector and shows that there are strong disparities across states, with Maharashtra, Gujarat, Punjab and Tamil Nadu being best equipped in terms of infrastructure. Barring Punjab, these are also the states in which the manufacturing sector contributes significantly to the states' GDP. Figures 8.10 and 8.11 show the relationship between manufacturing share and state of power availability and the state of the roads. It is clear that states with better availability of infrastructure have seen a higher growth of manufacturing. Similarly, Figure 8.12 shows that states with greater supply of skills have attracted more industrial investment.

Figure 8.9

Significance of Infrastructure for the Manufacturing Sector

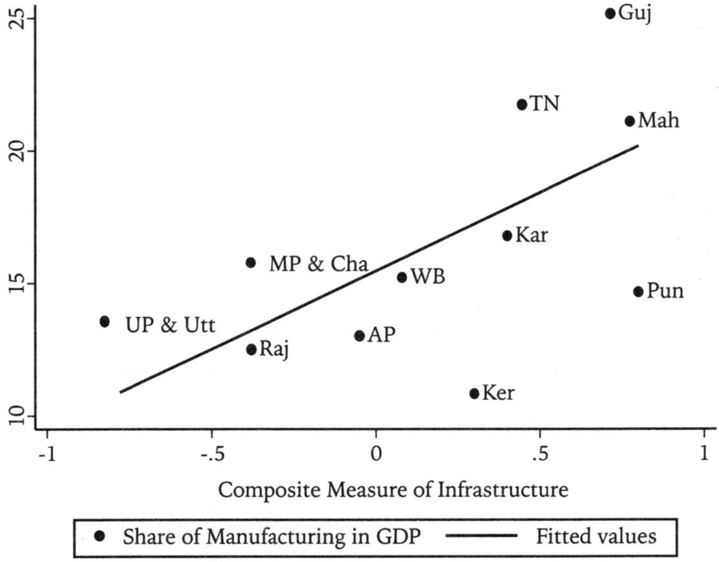

Source: Mitra *et al.* (2002) and *State Domestic Product*, CSO, Various Issues.

Figure 8.10

Significance of Power for the Manufacturing Sector

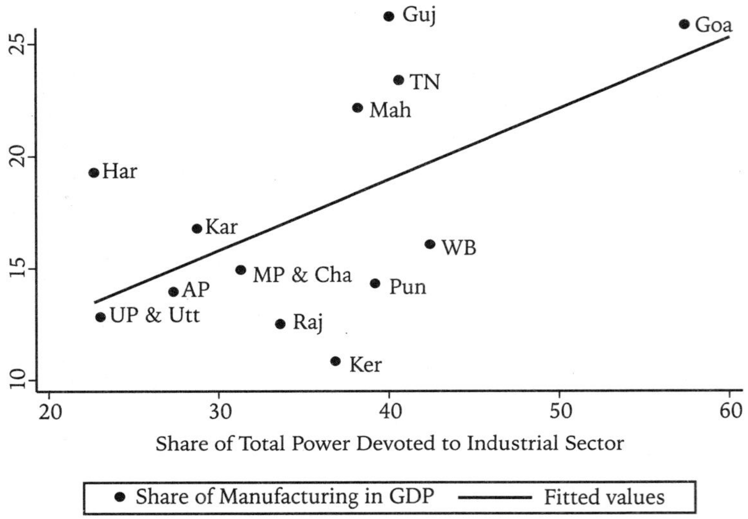

Source: *Statistical Abstract of India* and *State Domestic Product*, CSO, Various Issues.

Figure 8.11

Significance of Roads for the Manufacturing Sector

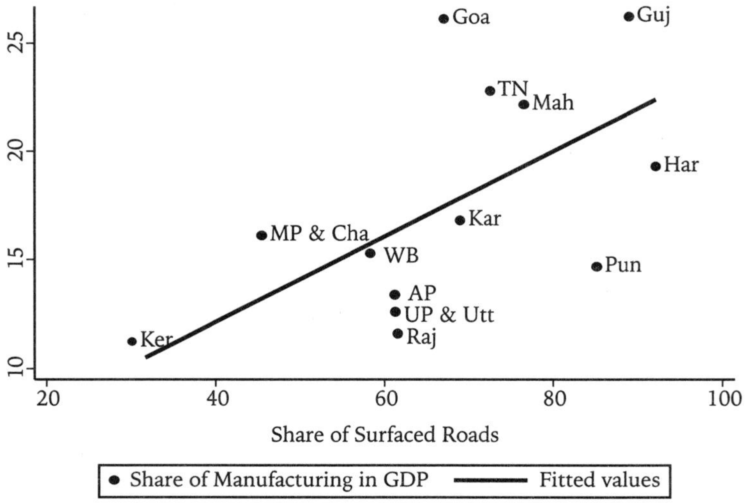

Source: *Statistical Abstract of India* and *State Domestic Product*, CSO, Various Issues.

Figure 8.12

Significance of Higher Education for the Manufacturing Sector

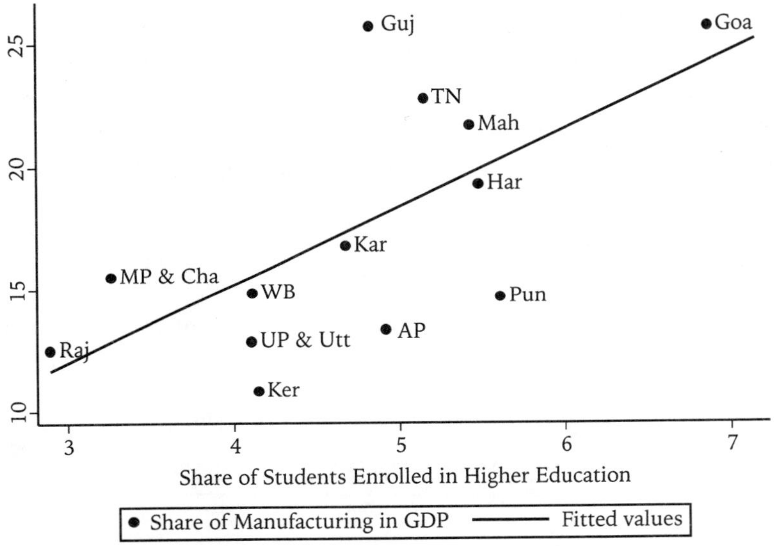

Source: *Statistical Abstract of India* and *State Domestic Product*, CSO, Various Issues

The nature of the existing labour market also plays a significant role in attracting entrepreneurs into a state and thereby influences the share of the manufacturing sector in the states' GDP. To capture the variation in inter-state labour laws we start with Besley and Burgess (2004) coding of state amendments to the Industrial Dispute Act (IDA).[5] We change the signs of the numbers in Besley and Burgess (2004) so that a higher number implies more flexible labour conditions. However, an often pointed out problem with this coding is that Maharashtra and Gujarat, two of India's most industrialised states, are characterised as having inflexible labour markets, as they passed pro-employee amendments to IDA. It is highly questionable that businesses would consider setting up manufacturing firms in these states if they found the labour market to be quite rigid.

---

5. Besley and Burgess (2004) consider state level amendments to IDA. They code the amendments as 1, -1 or 0 depending on whether these amendments were pro-employee, anti-employee or neutral. The scores are then accumulated over the years. The numbers range from 4 for West Bengal to -2 for Andhra Pradesh and Tamil Nadu.

To overcome this problem we supplement the data in Besley and Burgess (2004) with World Bank (2003), which looks at a firm level survey of managers. According to World Bank (2003), Maharashtra and Gujarat are categorised as having 'Best Investment Climate.' We quantify the responses of the managers in this study and then take a weighted average of this measure and the measure used in Besley and Burgess (2004) to arrive at a composite measure of labour market rigidity.[6] The index goes from -2 to 2.5 and a higher number indicates greater labour market flexibility. In Figure 8.13, we look at the relationship between labour market rigidity and share of manufacturing in GDP.

It is evident that states which have greater labour market flexibility like Goa, Gujarat, Tamil Nadu and Maharashtra are the ones where the

Figure 8.13

Significance of Labour Market Flexibility for Manufacturing Sector

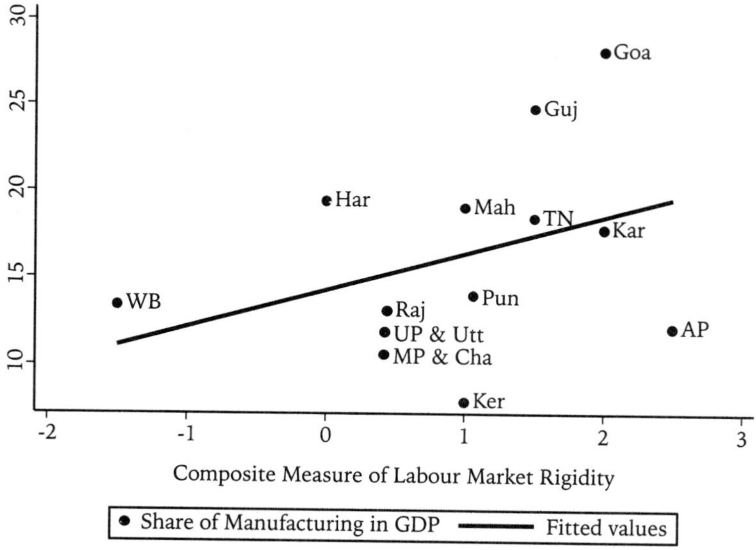

Source: Authors' Calculations and *State Domestic Product*, CSO, Various Issues.

6. World Bank (2003) categorises the investment climate as poor, medium, good and best. We quantified these responses by assigning 1 to poor, 2 to medium, 3 to good and 4 to best.

Figure 8.14

Significance of Financial Depth for the Manufacturing Sector

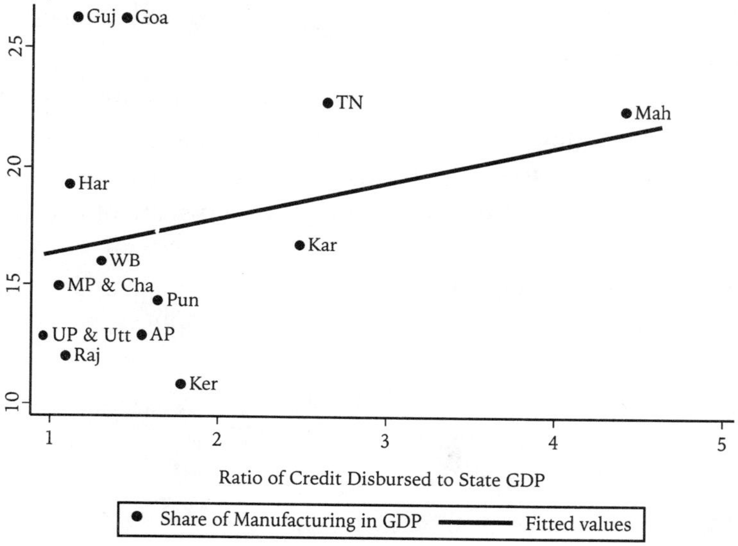

Source: Reserve Bank of India and *State Domestic Product*, CSO, Various Issues.

manufacturing sector is accounting for 20 per cent of the GDP or more. Rigid labour laws are a big deterrent for setting up new enterprises and the entrepreneurs, wary of the fact that they will be unable to offload workers, do not hire them in the first place.

The performance of the manufacturing sector is also affected by the ease of access to finance. Burgess and Pande (2005) investigate the effect of rural branch expansion of banks across 16 Indian states and conclude that states with more rapid branch expansion into unbanked areas witnessed greater increase of per capita output in the unregistered manufacturing sector. While the above paper focuses on the financial density, we look at the impact of financial depth on the performance of the manufacturing sector. We measure financial depth with the ratio of credit disbursed to GDP. We find that states where this ratio is high are the ones where the manufacturing sector plays an important role. States like Maharashtra and Tamil Nadu, which exhibit relatively good financial depth, are the ones with a strong manufacturing sector. On the other hand, in Gujarat and Goa, the manufacturing sector is strong despite a lower degree of financial depth. Finally, states like Uttar Pradesh (including Uttarakhand), Rajasthan and Madhya Pradesh (including Chhattisgarh) are characterised by extremely low financial depth and consequently a weak manufacturing sector.

These results have strong policy implications for state governments. It is clear that states like Goa, Gujarat, Maharashtra and Tamil Nadu, which have undertaken substantial infrastructural reforms, and have relatively high financial depth in some cases, boast of a manufacturing sector, whose contribution to GDP is in excess of 20 per cent. Moreover, these are also states that have undertaken steps to ensure greater labour market flexibility and as a result have attracted both domestic and foreign investors.

Unorganised and Organised Manufacturing Sector

The Indian manufacturing sector is broadly divided into two segments, organised and unorganised. The organised sector includes all units that are registered under the Factory Act 1948, 2 m(i) and 2 m(ii). Other units fall under unorganised manufacturing. Table 8.1 below compares some of the key characteristics of the two sectors in 2000-01.

Looking at the total number of units in column (i) and (ii) of Table 8.1, we find that more than 99 per cent of all manufacturing units fall in the unorganised sector. The organised sector accounts for only 0.72 per cent of the enterprises. An industry-wise break up shows that out of the 23 industry divisions, in only 7 divisions, the organised sector's share is greater than 10 per cent. Major industry divisions among these include office accounting and computing machinery (57.69 per cent), radio television and communication equipment and apparatus (15.71 per cent), basic metals (15.38 per cent) etc. Similarly, column (iii) and (iv) show that more than 86 per cent of the manufacturing workforce finds employment in the unorganised sector. Industry divisions where more than 80 per cent of the workers are working in the unorganised sector include recycling (98.39 per cent), furniture (97.13 per cent), wearing apparel, dressing and dyeing of fur (94 per

Table 8.1

Shares of Unorganised and Organised Sector (2000-01)

(in per cent)

	Units		Workers		Fixed Capital		Outstanding Loan		Wages		Output		Gross Value Added	
	(i) Unorg	(ii) Org	(iii) Unorg	(iv) Org	(v) Unorg	(vi) Org	(vii) Unorg	(viii) Org	(ix) Unorg	(x) Org	(xi) Unorg	(xii) Org	(xiii) Unorg	(xiv) Org
Food Products and Beverages	99.21	0.79	87.03	12.97	37.74	62.26	5.62	94.38	22.55	77.45	22.98	77.02	35.15	64.85
Tobacco	99.87	0.13	88.24	11.76	58.04	41.96	8.68	91.32	14.24	85.76	26.00	74.00	37.76	62.24
Textiles	99.44	0.56	84.95	15.05	23.07	76.93	3.71	96.29	31.47	68.53	20.25	79.75	35.53	64.47
Wearing Apparel; Dressing and Dyeing of Fur	99.88	0.12	94.18	5.82	82.42	17.58	17.33	82.67	60.15	39.85	44.77	55.23	67.69	32.31
Leather and Leather Products	98.76	1.24	77.71	22.29	43.66	56.34	4.46	95.54	33.33	66.67	22.59	77.41	37.73	62.27
Wood and Wood Products	99.88	0.12	99.29	0.71	90.53	9.47	40.03	59.97	82.93	17.07	83.75	16.25	92.55	7.45
Paper and Paper Products	96.40	3.60	64.32	35.68	9.40	90.60	2.04	97.96	14.80	85.20	11.72	88.28	15.35	84.65
Publishing, Printing and Reproduction of Recorded Media	97.75	2.25	86.64	13.36	56.45	43.55	21.03	78.97	37.45	62.55	30.13	69.87	35.93	64.07
Coke, Refined Petroleum Products and Nuclear Fuel	89.09	10.91	31.88	68.12	0.48	99.52	0.06	99.94	1.32	98.68	0.49	99.51	0.81	99.19
Chemical and Chemical Products	95.51	4.49	51.10	48.90	2.31	97.69	1.58	98.42	4.83	95.17	2.94	97.06	2.12	97.88
Rubber and Plastic Products	93.48	6.52	64.01	35.99	17.39	82.61	6.41	93.59	24.43	75.57	13.03	86.97	15.54	84.46
Non-metallic Products	98.58	1.42	89.78	10.22	15.19	84.81	3.05	96.95	45.42	54.58	27.18	72.82	33.54	66.46
Basic Metals	84.62	15.38	23.91	76.09	1.54	98.46	0.99	99.01	3.13	96.87	3.03	96.97	2.57	97.43
Fabricated Metals	98.76	1.24	87.87	12.13	56.88	43.12	10.63	89.37	39.36	60.64	34.24	65.76	45.41	54.59
Machinery and Equipments	94.66	5.34	63.91	36.09	25.82	74.18	4.86	95.14	14.49	85.51	10.76	89.24	14.00	86.00

Contd. ...

...Contd. ...

	Units		*Workers*		*Fixed Capital*		*Outstanding Loan*		*Wages*		*Output*		*Gross Value Added*	
	(i) *Unorg*	*(ii)* *Org*	*(iii)* *Unorg*	*(iv)* *Org*	*(v)* *Unorg*	*(vi)* *Org*	*(vii)* *Unorg*	*(viii)* *Org*	*(ix)* *Unorg*	*(x)* *Org*	*(xi)* *Unorg*	*(xii)* *Org*	*(xiii)* *Unorg*	*(xiv)* *Org*
Office, Accounting and Computing Machinery	42.31	57.69	7.84	92.16	1.78	98.22	0.14	99.86	0.96	99.04	1.06	98.94	0.89	99.11
Electrical Machinery and	94.04	5.96	61.46	38.54	12.65	87.35	4.68	95.32	15.60	84.40	49.60	50.40	13.28	86.72
Radio, Television and Communication Equipment and Apparatus	84.29	15.71	36.21	63.79	6.76	93.24	0.60	99.40	6.93	93.07	2.08	97.92	4.23	95.77
Medical, Precision and Optical Instruments, Watches and Clocks	89.66	10.34	42.85	57.15	13.66	86.34	2.40	97.60	8.63	91.37	6.09	93.91	8.02	91.98
Motor Vehicles, Trailers and Semi-trailers	88.80	11.20	36.47	63.53	6.01	93.99	0.49	99.51	7.03	92.97	2.87	97.13	4.63	95.37
Other Transport and Equipment	88.76	11.24	31.78	68.22	9.47	90.53	1.22	98.78	6.55	93.45	3.70	96.30	5.77	94.23
Furniture	99.83	0.17	97.13	2.87	86.10	13.90	26.07	73.93	73.54	26.46	45.26	54.74	66.86	33.14
Recycling	99.92	0.08	98.39	1.61	99.14	0.86	55.53	44.47	88.24	11.76	89.30	10.70	97.25	2.75
All	**99.28**	**0.72**	**86.15**	**13.85**	**20.56**	**79.44**	**3.34**	**96.66**	**24.23**	**75.77**	**17.76**	**82.24**	**24.43**	**75.57**

Source: Authors' calculations using *Annual Survey of Industries 2000-01* and *NSSO Report of the 56th Round.*

cent), non metallic products (89.78 per cent), tobacco (88.24 per cent), etc. Thus we find that, both in terms of number of enterprises and the number of workers, the Indian manufacturing sector is heavily dominated by the unorganised sector. However, in spite of this overwhelming majority in units and workers, the unorganised sector's contribution to both output and value added is extremely small. Column (xiii) and (xiv) indicate that the unorganised sector accounts for less than one-fourth of gross value added compared to the organised sector. If we look at the total output produced in column (xi) and (xii), the numbers are even more distorted. Here the unorganised sector's share falls to well below 20 per cent. Thus, it can be clearly seen that there exists a big discrepancy in the share of the unorganised sector in number of units and workers and its share in gross value added and total output.

The large divergence between share in total population of enterprises and share in value added is almost fully explained by the much higher capital intensity of the organised sector enterprises. This can be seen both in the share of fixed capital and in the share of outstanding loans. The unorganised sector gets slightly more than 20 per cent of the total fixed capital.[7] Overall fixed capital per worker in the unorganised sector is Rs. 0.27 lakh, while fixed capital per unit is Rs. 0.60 lakh. On the other hand, for the organised sector these numbers are Rs. 6.67 lakhs and Rs. 321.09 lakhs. Thus the unorganised sector has been forced to work with a fraction of fixed capital available to the organised sector.

The picture for 'Outstanding Loans' is even more skewed. Of the total outstanding loan, the unorganised sector gets a miniscule 3.34 per cent. In the organised sector, outstanding loan per unit and outstanding loan per worker turns out to be Rs. 202.26 lakh and Rs. 4.20 lakh respectively. In comparison, for the unorganised sector these are Rs. 0.05 lakhs and Rs. 0.02 lakhs. Thus the outstanding loan per unit in the unorganised sector is 1/4000th of the organised

7. According to the NSS 56th Round "Fixed Capital" has been defined as "current market value of the fixed assets." As such both the price and age factors have been incorporated as reflected in the perspective of the owner. On the other hand according to the ASI, "Fixed Capital" is defined as "depreciated value of the fixed assets owned by the factory as on the closing day of the accounting year." Thus the comparisons made in the paper are subject to definitional limitation.

sector. Similarly, the outstanding loan per worker in the unorganised sector is 1/180th of the organised sector. All these features further reinforce the dualistic nature of the Indian manufacturing sector.

As Table 8.2 shows the real cost of labour i.e. nominal wages adjusted for productivity appear to be similar across organised and unorganised sectors. However, there are significant differences across different industry divisions.

Employment Generation

According to the seventh quinquennial survey on Employment and Unemployment carried out in the NSS 61st round (July 2004-05), 42 per cent of the population of the country was usually employed. The survey also estimates a workforce of 40.825 crores.

Looking at Table 8.3, we find that there have been notable changes in the employment patterns during the latest round, compared to the last round. The late 1990s was a period of a very low growth rate. The overall employment growth rate was only 1.07 per cent. The decline in overall growth rate was primarily due to near stagnation of employment in agriculture. However, the most recent data indicates a strong recovery. Both agriculture and industry experienced a strong employment growth rate of above 4.5 per cent during 1999-2000 to 2004-05. Within the manufacturing sector, employment grew at a slightly lower rate of 3.21 per cent. This was the highest growth rate since the mid-1980s. Surprisingly, the service sector witnessed the slowest growth rate of less than 2 per cent during the latest period.

A decomposition of the employment growth rate between the organised and unorganised sector shows that employment has grown faster in the unorganised sector. Within the unorganised sector, industry divisions such as machinery and equipment, basic metals and textiles and leather have recorded impressive employment growth compared to the organised sector. On the other hand, in sectors like other manufacturing (including wood) and chemicals and chemical products employment grew at a faster rate in the organised sector.

According to the Tenth Plan, employment elasticity in the manufacturing sector declined from 0.59 in 1983-88 to 0.33 in 1993-2000. The decline has been particularly significant in the organised and

Table 8.2

Wages and Gross Value Added in Organised and Unorganised Sector (2000-01)

	Wage per Worker (Rs. lakh)		Gross Value Added per Worker (Rs. lakh)		Labour Cost (Wages per Gross Value Added)		
	(i)	(ii)	(iii)	(iv)	(v)	(vi)	(vii)
	Unorg	*Org*	*Unorg*	*Org*	*Unorg*	*Org*	*Ratio*
Food Products and Beverages	0.022	0.515	0.155	1.923	0.144	0.268	1.862
Tobacco	0.004	0.196	0.070	0.865	0.062	0.227	3.653
Textiles	0.045	0.557	0.140	1.432	0.325	0.389	1.200
Wearing Apparel; Dressing and Dyeing of Fur	0.038	0.409	0.167	1.288	0.229	0.318	1.388
Leather and Leather Products	0.062	0.434	0.237	1.363	0.263	0.319	1.212
Wood and Wood Products	0.013	0.372	0.106	1.189	0.122	0.313	2.557
Paper and Paper Products	0.073	0.758	0.208	2.066	0.351	0.367	1.043
Publishing, Printing and Reproduction of Recorded Media	0.116	1.261	0.339	3.920	0.343	0.322	0.937
Coke, Refined Petroleum Products and Nuclear Fuel	0.078	2.714	0.242	13.792	0.322	0.197	0.612
Chemical and Chemical Products	0.058	1.203	0.163	7.854	0.359	0.153	0.427
Rubber and Plastic Products	0.131	0.723	0.390	3.766	0.337	0.192	0.569
Non-metallic Products	0.058	0.617	0.161	2.797	0.364	0.220	0.606
Basic Metals	0.137	1.328	0.462	5.505	0.296	0.241	0.816

Contd. ...

...Contd. ...

	Wage per Worker (Rs. lakh)		*Gross Value Added per Worker (Rs. lakh)*		*Labour Cost (Wages per Gross Value Added)*		
	(i)	*(ii)*	*(iii)*	*(iv)*	*(v)*	*(vi)*	*(vii)*
	Unorg	*Org*	*Unorg*	*Org*	*Unorg*	*Org*	*Ratio*
Fabricated Metals	0.075	0.839	0.241	2.099	0.312	0.399	1.281
Machinery and Equipments	0.131	1.373	0.372	4.044	0.354	0.340	0.960
Office, Accounting and Computing Machinery	0.209	1.843	0.469	4.440	0.446	0.415	0.931
Electrical Machinery and	0.165	1.424	0.408	4.252	0.404	0.335	0.829
Radio, Television and Communication Equipment and Apparatus	0.179	1.362	0.403	5.184	0.443	0.263	0.594
Medical, Precision and Optical Instruments, Watches and Clocks	0.155	1.230	0.463	3.979	0.335	0.309	0.924
Motor Vehicles, Trailers and Semi-trailers	0.187	1.420	0.434	5.136	0.431	0.276	0.642
Other Transport and Equipment	0.154	1.021	0.472	3.585	0.326	0.285	0.875
Furniture	0.059	0.721	0.222	3.718	0.267	0.194	0.726
Recycling	0.055	0.449	0.223	0.386	0.247	1.163	4.712
All	**0.041**	**0.793**	**0.162**	**3.124**	**0.251**	**0.254**	1.011

Source: Authors' calculations using *Annual Survey of Industries 2000-01* and *NSSO Report of the 56th Round.*

Table 8.3

Sectoral Employment Growth (Current Daily Status Basis)

Sectors	*Employment (Million)*				*Annual Growth (Per cent)*			
	1987-88	*1993-94*	*1999-00*	*2004-05*	*1983 to 1987-88*	*1987-88 to 1993-94*	*1993-94 to 1999-00*	*1999-00 to 2004-05*
Agriculture	163.82	190.72	190.94	238.82	1.77	2.57	0.02	4.58
Industry[a]	47.85	50.99	59.15	73.89	5.61	0.73	2.84	4.55
Manufacturing	32.53	35.00	40.79	47.76	3.64	1.23	2.58	3.21
Services	60.72	75.11	86.65	95.53	4.05	3.61	2.41	1.97
All Sectors	272.39	315.84	336.75	408.25	2.90	2.50	1.07	3.93

Note: a. Industry also includes Construction.

Source: Authors' calculations using reports of different NSSO rounds.

mechanised segments, which has contributed very little to employment generation. Kumar *et al.* (2007) looks at the change in labour intensity in the organised manufacturing sector and finds that there has been a significant decrease in labour intensity across most product groups in the organised manufacturing sector.[8] Figure 8.15 highlights the change in labour intensity in these products from 1990-91 to 2003-04.

Export Performance

Manufactured products have always formed a major part of merchandise exports. However, its share has varied a lot over time. From being just over 50 per cent in 1970, the share of manufacturing products rose steadily to almost 80 per cent in 1999. Over the next few years there has been a decline in the share of manufactured products in total merchandise exports with the share coming down to 72 per cent in 2004 and further to 67 per cent in 2007. This should be a policy concern as this may reflect that the Indian manufacturing sector may well be loosing its competitiveness in global markets.

In a recent article, Kumar and Palit (2007) point out that the latest export figures point unambiguously to a slowdown in India's

8. The decrease has been more prominent in highly labour intensive goods. In 1990-91, the top five labour intensive products were (i) tobacco, (ii) luggage, handbags, and the like, saddlery and harness, (iii) apparel except for wearing apparel, (iv) saw milling and planning of wood and (v) macaroni, noodles, conscious and similar farinaceous products and other food products n.e.c.

Table 8.4

Employment Growth in Manufacturing Sector

(per cent)

Major Industrial Groups	*Unorganised*	*Organised*
Food, Beverages and Tobacco	0.9	0.96
Textiles and Leather	3.05	1.21
Paper and Products	1.69	0.1
Chemicals and Products	0.87	2.02
Non-metallic Mineral Products	0.65	0.82
Basic Metals	3.9	-0.91
Metal Products	2.89	2.05
Machinery and Equipment	4.1	0.82
Transport Equipment	1.44	0.02
Other Manufacturing (Including Wood)	1.29	3.88

Note: * Period covered for Unorganised Manufacturing is 1989-90 to 2000-01.
** Period covered for Organised Manufacturing is 1990-91 to 2003-04

Source: ICRIER, 2008.

Figure 8.15

Labour Intensity in Top Five Labour Intensive Products

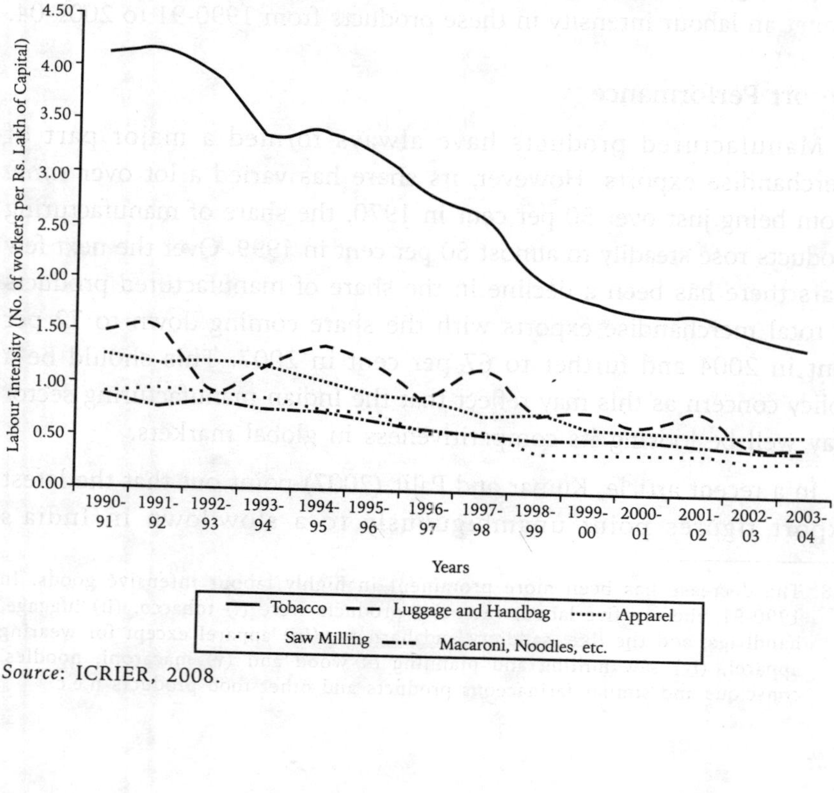

Source: ICRIER, 2008.

merchandise exports. During the first seven months of 2006-07, the growth rate of merchandise exports was 8 per cent lower than the corresponding period of 2005-06. The picture becomes significantly grimmer once we look at the exports growth net of petroleum exports. The latter have grown by 85 per cent during April-October 2006-07 compared to the same period in 2005-06. There is a strong deceleration in manufactured goods exports, which have dropped to 18.3 per cent in 2005-06 from 25 per cent in 2004-05 and further to 14.3 per cent in the first seven months of 2006-07, being less than half of 30.1 per cent in the same months of 2005-06.

Within manufacturing, gems and jewellery, a major foreign exchange earner for India, is likely to suffer an absolute decline in growth for the first time in 2001-02 if the current trend continues. Textile, textile products, and handicrafts are other key industries showing signs of export deceleration. The growth in chemical exports in 2006-07 is almost half of what it was in 2005-06. The silver lining is provided by engineering goods whose exports growth at 37.9 per cent is the fastest among manufacturing. However, even this sector witnessed a marginal decline in its growth rates compared to last year.

Figure 8.16

Share of Manufacturing Exports to India's Total Merchandise Exports

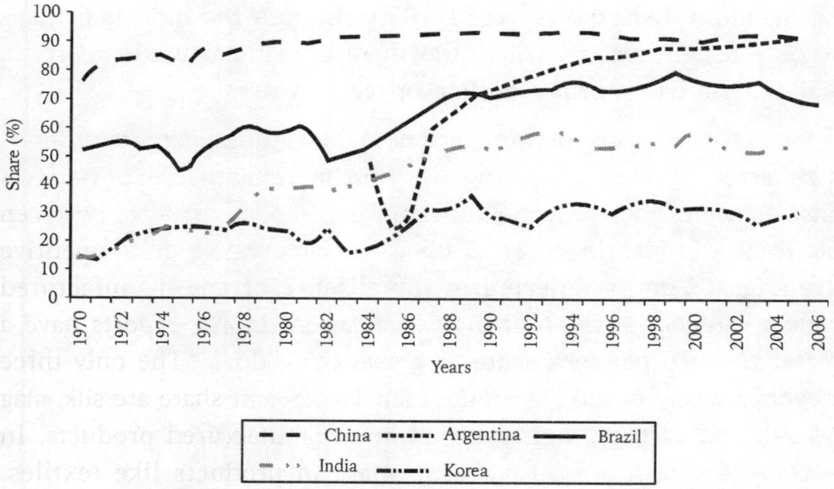

Source: *World Development Indicators 2006.*

Table 8.5

Volume of Manufactured Exports (2005)

USD billion

	Argentina	*Brazil*	*China*	***India***	*Indonesia*	*South Korea*	*Malaysia*
Iron and steel	1.61	9.07	19.28	**5.30**	0.94	14.35	1.84
Chemicals	3.40	7.29	35.77	**11.08**	4.49	27.75	7.62
Pharmaceuticals	0.40	0.51	3.78	**2.81**	0.11	0.51	0.14
Machinery and transport equipment	4.30	30.47	352.23	**10.21**	13.60	173.49	76.54
Office and telecom equipment	0.08	3.71	225.96	**0.99**	6.74	82.99	60.09
Electronic data processing and office equipment	0.02	0.48	110.70	**0.45**	2.94	17.76	22.92
Telecommunications equipment	0.05	3.06	94.86	**0.29**	3.07	37.75	13.41
Integrated circuits and electronic components	0.00	0.17	20.41	**0.24**	0.74	27.49	23.76
Automotive products	3.05	11.97	9.96	**2.59**	1.27	37.75	0.73
Textiles	0.21	1.33	41.05	**7.85**	3.45	10.39	1.36
Clothing	0.10	0.35	74.16	**8.29**	5.11	2.58	2.48
Manufactures	12.28	61.57	700.34	**69.75**	40.17	258.20	104.86

Source: *Statistical Database*, World Trade Organization.

Figure 8.16 and Table 8.5 compare the performance of India's manufactured exports with East Asian and Latin American economies. Our manufactured exports were 1/10th of China's and India is perhaps the only Asian economy where the share of manufactured exports in total exports has shown a decline in recent years.

This relatively poor performance of manufacturing exports in India, as reflected by their declining share in merchandise exports, is a consequence of four principal factors. First, the country has not been able to clearly identify or build upon its comparative or competitive advantages. This is reflected in the absence of any manufactured product category at the four digit level where Indian exports have a greater than 10 per cent share in global trade flows. The only three categories where we do have more than 10 per cent share are silk, slag and ash and carpets, which are all non manufactured products. In contrast, China has a 10 per cent share in products like textiles, garments, footwear, machinery and transport equipment, and office and

Table 8.6

Share of Major Manufactured Exports of India in World Exports

Share (per cent)

HS Code	*Product*	*2000*	*2004*
50	Silk	11.3	11.1
26	Ores, slag and ash	1.9	10.7
57	Carpets and other textile floor coverings	7.5	10.7
71	Pearls, precious stones, metals, coins, etc.	6.5	7.4
63	Other made textile articles, sets, worn clothing etc.	6.3	7.0
52	Cotton	6.6	4.9
42	Articles of leather, animal gut, harness, travel goods	4.1	3.5
53	Vegetable textile fibres nes, paper yarn, woven fabric	4.5	3.5
25	Salt, sulphur, earth, stone, plaster, lime and cement	2.7	3.3
67	Bird skin, feathers, artificial flowers, human hair	1.7	3.0
62	Articles of apparel, accessories, not knit or crochet	3.6	2.9
68	Stone, plaster, cement, asbestos, mica, etc. articles	1.9	2.7
41	Raw hides and skins (other than fur skins) and leather	1.8	2.4
55	Man-made staple fibres	2.0	2.4
61	Articles of apparel, accessories, knit or crochet	2.1	2.3
46	Manufactures of plaiting material, basketwork, etc.	0.1	2.0
29	Organic chemicals	1.2	1.7
64	Footwear, gaiters and the like, parts thereof	1.4	1.7
32	Tanning, dyeing extracts, tannins, derivatives, pigments, etc.	1.5	1.6
58	Special woven or tufted fabric, lace, tapestry, etc	2.4	1.4
72	Iron and steel	0.9	1.3
28	Inorganic chemicals, precious metal compound, isotopes	0.6	1.0
73	Articles of iron or steel	1.2	1.0
83	Miscellaneous articles of base metal	0.5	1.0

Source: *Economic Survey 2005-06*.

telecom equipment. As Table 8.6 reveals, in 24 product categories Indian exports have a more than 1 per cent share in global trade volumes. The interesting part, however, is that out of these motley group, four achieved this only in 2004 and was lower than 1 per cent in 2000. The major weakness of India's export performance has been to have 'scatter shot' rather than a focused approach that would sustain and build the country's competitive advantage.

In recent years there have been several manufacturing products like scientific instruments, whose exports have increased substantially.

However, India has been unable to sustain these increases. There are several products in whose exports India can hope to claim a significant share in the near future. These include, electronic and electrical items, processed food items, electro medical appliances, among others. The government must allow the market to select winners but then focus all its efforts to ensure that these winners become leaders in global markets. This would require a change in the existing strategy practice of fixing aggregate targets, over which it has no control, to fixing 'market share targets' for a small group of established winners. This could be accompanied with a clear plan of action to achieve these targets.

The second main reason for the weak performance has been that India's manufactured exports have languished in the 'low value added' categories and are often 'concentrated' in 'sunset' segments. The latter feature was noted as early as 1982 by Martin Wolf (1982) who points out that India's export purchasing power in the early 1980s was far behind that of petroleum exporters as well fast growing manufactured goods' exporters.

Looking at the overall composition of exports in Figure 8.17, it can be clearly seen that there has been a significant change in the composition of Indian manufacturing exports during the last 20 years.[9] In 1987-88, textiles and textile products constituted the bulk of Indian exports accounting for more than one-third of total exports. By 2005-2006, its share had come down to less than one-fourth. Similarly, the share of leathers and manufactures also declined from 12 per cent to 4 per cent during this period. Gems and jewellery, which has always been an important component of Indian exports, also experienced a small decline in its share. On the other hand, engineering goods, which accounted for only 14 per cent of manufactured exports in 1987-88, more than doubled its share to 29 per cent by 2005-06. Chemicals and related products also doubled its share from 10 per cent to 20 per cent during this period.

A further decomposition of the major industry divisions show that majority of the products that are being exported are low value

9. Due to change in commodity classification by DGCI&S, data before 1987-88 will not be strictly comparable to the latest data.

Figure 8.17

Change in Composition of Manufactured Exports

1987-88

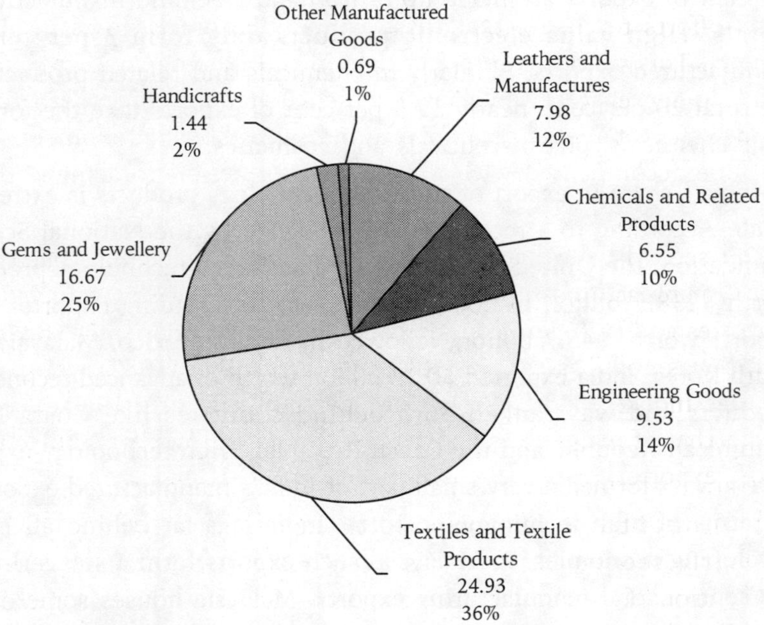

2005-06

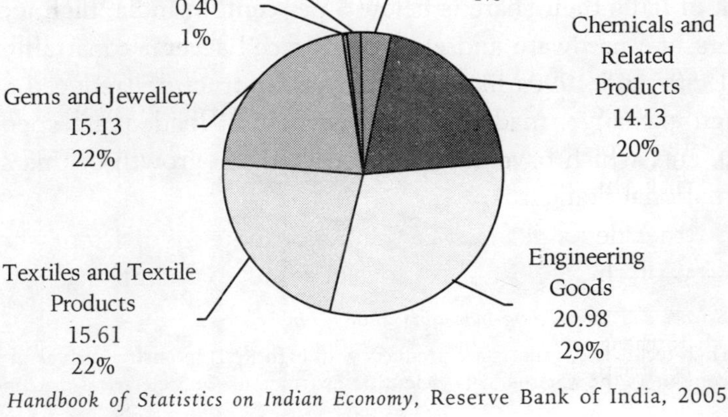

Source: *Handbook of Statistics on Indian Economy*, Reserve Bank of India, 2005-06.

products. The concentration of exports in low value categories is the third factor that explains the relatively weak performance of Indian manufactured exports. A product-wise break up of the largest segment, engineering goods, shows that out of the total 29 per cent, nearly 11 per cent of exports are made up of iron and steel and manufacture of metals. High value electronic products only form 3 per cent of manufactured exports. Similarly in chemicals and related products, of the total 20 per cent, nearly 12.5 per cent of exports take the form of basic chemicals, pharmaceuticals and cosmetics.

India's share in export of advanced technology products is extremely small. According to a recent report published by the National Science Foundation, the United States imported advanced technology products worth $238.5 billion in 2004.[10] China was the leading exporter with exports worth, $45.7 billion, followed by Japan, Mexico, Malaysia and South Korea. India exported $0.32 billion worth of advanced technology products and was ranked 36th behind countries like Costa Rica, Dominican Republic and the Czech Republic. High technology exports have always formed a very small part of India's manufactured exports.[11] In terms of high technology exports, India lags far behind all major developing economies. In Malaysia, such exports form a staggering 55 per cent of total manufacturing exports. Malaysia houses some of the world's leading exporters of semiconductors, air conditioners and consumer electronics. Malaysia has developed several Free Trade Zones and Industrial Parks to support the manufacturing sector.

In countries like China and South Korea, high technology exports are around 30 per cent of total manufactured exports. On the other hand, in India their share is below 5 per cent. In India, high technology sectors like hardware and electronics faced several constraints during the 1980s and 1990s like distorted tariff structure, reduced access to foreign exchange, inadequate infrastructure, inadequate spending on R&D, etc., which have severely restricted the growth of this sector to international standards.

---

10. *Science and Engineering Indicators 2006*.

11. High-technology exports are products with high R&D intensity, such as in aerospace, computers, pharmaceuticals, scientific instruments, and electrical machinery.

Figure 8.18

Export of Technology Intensive Goods and Services

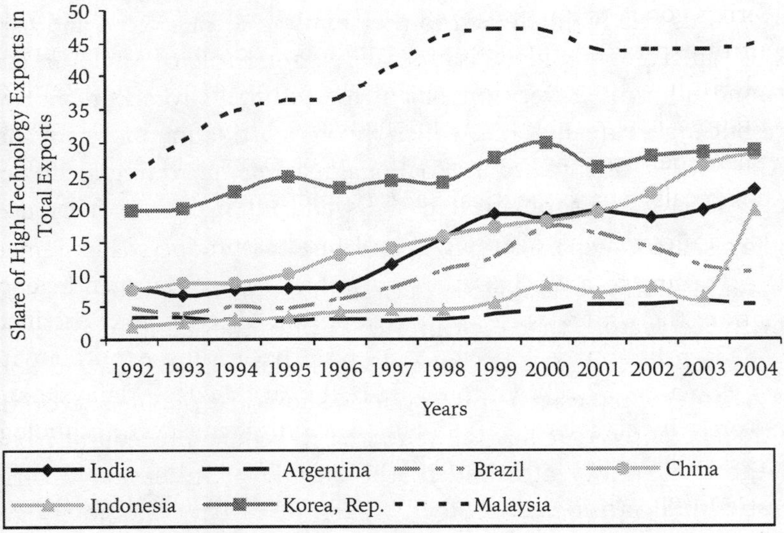

Source: *World Development Indicators 2006*.

However, India has done relatively better if we look at the combined exports of technology intensive goods and services. Figure 8.18 shows that India's share of technology intensive exports in overall exports has been around 20 per cent during the last few years. This is higher than Latin American economies like Argentina and Brazil as well as some Asian economies like Indonesia, but lower than other Asian economies like China, South Korea and Malaysia. In China and South Korea such exports account for more than 28 per cent of overall exports. In the late 1990s, India's share was greater than China owing to the boom in export of IT-enabled services. However, since then China has overtaken India primarily due to a rise in export of technology intensive goods.

The fourth factor affecting Indian manufactured exports is the relatively poor inflow of foreign direct investment (FDI) especially in export oriented industries. Total FDI flows until March 2006 was only $38.90 billion, which improved to $50.10 billion by January 2007. However, of this amount, less than 10 per cent have gone towards export-oriented units. The majority of the investment continues to be destined for domestic market production. FDI for exports has significant advantages in terms of their marketing tie-ups, buy back arrangements, product knowledge etc. Lall (2000) points out that export success is highly linked to the ability to attract more and better FDI. Given increasing globalisation and a larger role of MNCs in trade and innovation, it is very important for countries to secure not just more but higher quality FDI, which involves attracting more advanced MNC activities, oriented to international markets, providing technology, using and creating sophisticated skills and taking the host economy into dynamic systems of international production.

India needs to review more carefully its policies towards FDI and identify the factors that continue to thwart these inflows into the export oriented sectors *a la* China, Malaysia and other East and South East Asian economies. The SEZ policies should be pursued vigorously and transparently as it has the potential to reduce procedural hassles and the uncertainty attached to the supply of necessary utilities, infrastructural facilities and other inputs. SEZs have the potential to change the scenario for manufactured exports from India.

Transition to Mass Manufacturing: Prospects and Issues

It is a well known fact that India is the largest user of WTO compatible provisions for anti-dumping suits, most of which are directed against Chinese manufactured imports. This reflects both the non-transparent nature of price discrimination by Chinese exporters as also the revealed competitive weakness of Indian firms even in their domestic markets. One of the key drivers of the competitive strengths of the Chinese firms is the significant cost advantages that accrue from economies of scale now enjoyed by them. These have come about by the successful transition to mass manufacturing by Chinese firms helped in great measure by their foreign joint venture partners that have brought in FDI and export orders.

India today faces the key question—whether it should in effect vacate the large manufacturing spaces to China, given their strong competitive strengths and concentrate its resources in building a lead in the services sector and small niche of complex technology and design intensive manufacturing products. In our understanding, India cannot afford to move away from the entire light engineering and simple manufacturing, simply because if it does so, it will be unable to generate the required number of employment opportunities for the growing working population, including workers moving out of agriculture. The key question, however is, whether or not the Indian manufacturing firms can also make the transition to mass manufacturing.

Comparing the scale of operations in India's manufacturing sector with other countries, we can see that the sheer size of China dwarfs all other developing countries. The value added by the manufacturing sector in India is less than 15 per cent or 1/8th that of China. Even smaller countries (in terms of GDP and population) like South Korea and Brazil have larger manufacturing sectors than India.

The picture is even more dismal if we look at the per capita value added across different countries. India ranks well below most of the major developing nations. Its per capita value added is one-fifth of China and one-fifteenth of Malaysia. Looking at the absolute scale of some key manufactured products in Table 8.7 we again find that China is way ahead of all other countries. The manufacturing sector in China has evolved tremendously in terms of capabilities to mass manufacturing products at low costs. India, on the other hand, is well behind and clearly not in the same league, as most of its emerging economy competitors.

Table 8.7

Cross-country Comparison of Production of Some Key Products

	Personal Computers (Million)	*Motor Vehicles ('000s)*	*Steel (MMT)*	*Telephone Mainlines (Million)*
Argentina	3.70	319.75	5.39	8.7
Brazil	19.35	2528.30	31.62	42.38
China	52.99	5707.69	352.54	312.44
India	13.03	1626.76	38.08	43.96
Indonesia	3.02	494.55	—	9.99
South Korea	26.20	3699.35	47.77	26.05
Malaysia	4.90	—	—	4.45

Note: Figures for Personal Computers and Telephone Mainlines are for 2004, while figures for Motor Vehicles and Steel are for 2005.

Source: Word Development Indicators, International Organization of Motor Vehicle Manufacturers and International Iron and Steel Institute.

Figure 8.19

Cross-country Comparison of the Manufacturing Sector (2004)

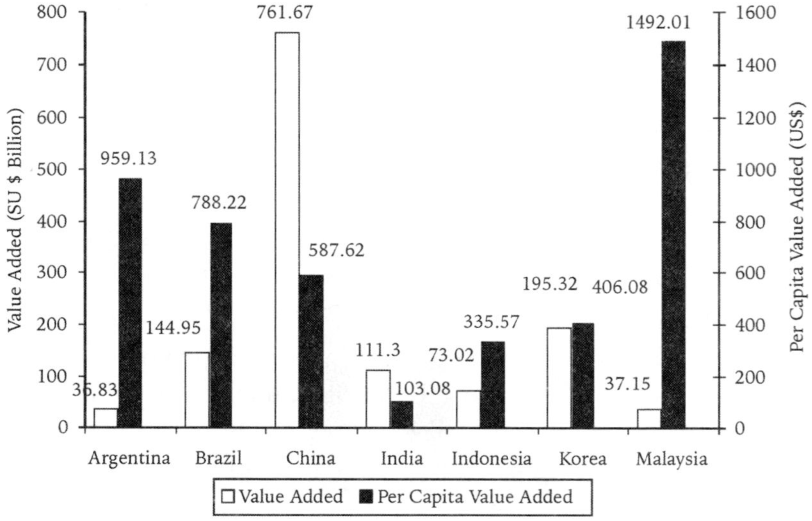

Source: *World Development Indicators 2006*.

The significantly larger scale of manufacturing in some of India's major competitors is expectedly reflected in the size of the manufacturing sector workforce. From Figure 8.20 it can be seen that India ranks next only to China in terms of the size of the workforce. This implies that in countries like South Korea and Malaysia, even with a fraction of India's labour force, the manufacturing sector has contributed significantly more in terms of value added showing a far higher value added per worker. This points again to the dualistic structure of India's manufacturing sector. India's transition to mass manufacturing can be achieved only if the problem of the 'missing middle' or the dualistic structure of its manufacturing can be effectively addressed.

There could be other reasons for this relatively poor performance of the manufacturing sector.[12] Poor quality and irregular supply of infrastructure and intermediate services such as power, roads, ports,

12. NMCC (2006) provides an excellent overview of the major challenges facing Indian manufacturing and provides several key recommendations as to how they can be dealt with.

Figure 8.20

Cross-country Comparison of Workers in the Manufacturing Sector (2004)

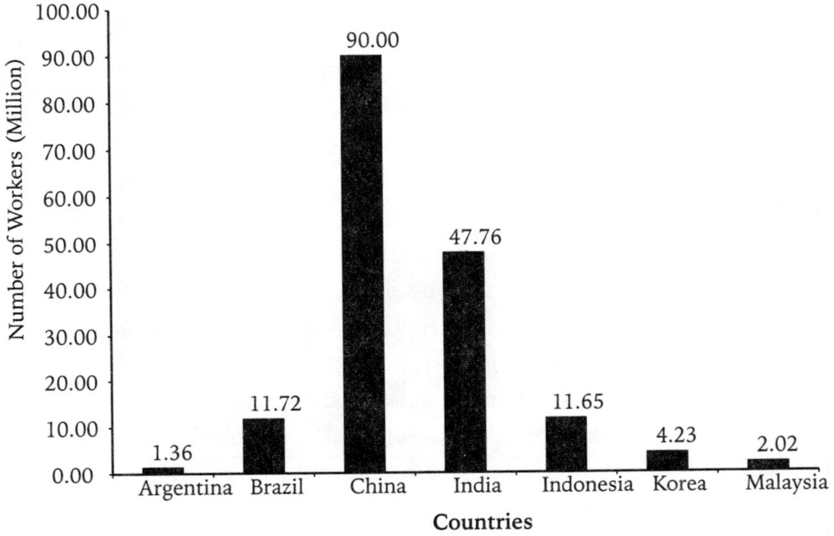

Source: ADB Database.

airports, etc., that are predominantly in the public sector, act as a major constraint for the transition to mass-manufacturing.

Typically, there are two possible routes to achieve mass manufacturing. The first one is to expand manufactured exports far more vigorously and increase our shares in major global markets. This would bring about a transformation of our export structure, which as Table 8.6 showed had very few products in which India enjoys any significant share in world exports. To be able to successfully achieve a far higher share in global markets and generate mass employment in export oriented industries, one of the routes would be to emulate China in attracting much greater volume of FDI. Even though in recent years India has replaced the United States as the second most attractive destination for FDI in manufacturing, actual volume of FDI inflow continues to be substantially lower than China.[13] In 2006, India

13. ATKEARNY (2005).

received a net $11.12 billion in foreign direct investment (FDI), less than a fifth of China's $63 billion.

The second route is to develop a manufacturing sector that can cater to the domestic demand and at the same time increase the size of the domestic market. However, here it must be understood that despite the recent surge in growth rates, India is still a largely poor country. According to the recent NSSO survey report, the number of people below the poverty line is in the range of 220 to 230 million. With a per capita GDP of $3,700 in PPP terms, the overall purchasing power of the country is quite low. This low purchasing power of the country as a whole makes it mandatory for the manufacturing sector to produce goods that are affordable and still of high quality. The only way this is possible is by investing heavily in R&D and achieving far greater product innovation that satisfies the specific requirements of the Indian market. This would be a critical part of the process for "producing for the bottom of the pyramid" as articulated by Prof. C.S. Prahlad. Moreover, in global markets, product life cycles are getting shorter and product innovation is emerging as a key determinant of competitiveness. This implies that retaining their shares in both domestic and foreign markets and especially to rely on expanding domestic demand to support the transition to mass manufacturing, Indian firms will have to strengthen their R&D and technological capabilities.

Looking at the share of R&D spending in GDP in Table 8.8, it can be seen that India is one of the smallest spenders on R&D among developing countries. Moreover, in India the bulk of the R&D spending is cornered by defence related organisations like DRDO, ISRO and the Department of Atomic Energy. As a result, R&D spending on manufacturing is woefully short of global standards. Similarly, India is also facing an acute shortage of researchers. India has one of the lowest number of researchers among major developing countries. There are only 120 researchers for every million people. This is 1/5th of China and 1/25th of South Korea. The last column of Table 8.8 shows that India is also the smallest importer of foreign technology. In China, the amount spent on royalties and license fees as a percentage of GDP was three times that of India, while in South Korea it was more than 11 times.

Table 8.8

Cross-country Comparison of Research and Development (2005)

	Spending on R&D as a Percentage of GDP[a]	*Number of Researchers per Million People*[b]	*Amount Spent on Royalties and Licence Fees as a Percentage of GDP*[c]
Argentina	0.42	715	0.23
Brazil	1.03	324	0.19
China	1.30	633	0.14
India	0.77	120	0.05
Indonesia	0.2	413	
South Korea	2.5	2970	0.57
Malaysia	0.70	294	

Note: a. Research and development is defined as current and capital expenditures (including overhead) on creative, systematic activity intended to increase the stock of knowledge. Included are fundamental and applied research and experimental development work leading to new devices, products or processes

b. People trained to work in any field of science who are engaged in professional research and development (R&D) activity. Most such jobs require the completion of tertiary education.

c. Royalties and licence fees cover the exchange of payments and receipts between residents and non-residents for the authorised use of intangible, non-produced, non-financial assets and propriety rights and with the use, through licensing agreements, of produced originals or prototypes.

Source: *Human Development Report 2005* and *IMF Balance of Payment Statistics 2006*.

In 2005, India's total domestic spending on R&D rose an estimated 9.7 per cent to $4.9 billion, or 0.77 per cent of GDP. China, on the other hand, is spending more than 1.3 per cent of its GDP, equivalent to $29.4 billion, on R&D. China plans to increase its R&D investment to 2 per cent of GDP by 2010 and 2.5 per cent by 2020. The relatively low spending on R&D is seriously hampering India's potential to export Advanced Technology Products (ATP). As stated earlier, in 2004, the United States imported around $238 billion worth of ATPs. While countries like China, Malaysia, South Korea and Taiwan were the main sources of these imports, India was ranked 36th, and accounted for only $0.32 billion of such imports into the United States.[14]

14. *Science and Engineering Indicators 2006.*

Table 8.9

Cross-country Comparison of Resident Patent Filed (2004)

	Patent Filings per Million Population	*Patent Filings per $ Billion GDP*	*Patent Filings per $ Million R&D Expenditures*
Argentina	28.41	2.32	0.56
Brazil	21.16	2.81	0.29
China	50.75	9.37	0.71
India	6.65	2.3	0.22
South Korea	2188.96	116.19	4.4
USA	645.44	17.7	0.68

Source: World Intellectual Property Organization.

As can be seen from Table 8.9, India's relative weakness in R&D is also reflected in the number of patents India has obtained in recent years. Measuring across three yardsticks, that is, patents filed per million population, patents filed per billion GDP and patents filed per million R&D expenditure, India's performance has been rather weak.

In India, the government is still expected to be the predominant R&D player. Even in 2005, 70 per cent of the total spending on R&D was carried out by Central and State governments, with public sector industries accounting for another 5 per cent. Private sector industries contributed only 20 per cent of the total R&D spending with universities and other higher education contributing less than 5 per cent. For achieving higher market share and accelerating the growth in domestic markets it is imperative that the private sector and universities step up their spending on R&D and strengthen their collaboration for commercialising their R&D. In any case the R&D effort has to be greatly strengthened if Indian manufacturing is to become competitive.

Given the rather weak and public sector dominated R&D capacity, the private sector manufacturing firms may have to rely on more technological advances from their joint venture partners for product innovation, both for domestic and foreign markets. Greater attention to R&D and more openness to FDI may both be crucial for achieving the transition to mass manufacturing.

Apart from low levels of R&D and FDI, some other major issues to be addressed for achieving greater competitiveness are i) presence of entry barriers, ii) labour market rigidities, iii) procedural constraints, iv) exit barriers, v) emerging skill constraints, and vi) infrastructure. We discuss some of these in greater detail in the following paragraphs.

(i) Entry Barriers: A major impediment faced by new entrants relates to procedures associated with starting a business in India. There are 11 procedures involved in starting a business, beginning from presenting the name of the company for approval to the registrar of companies (ROC) to registering for employees' provident fund and medical insurance. As shown in Table 8.10, while these procedures are necessary and must be put in place, the time required to cover these procedures can be reduced. While in India, it takes 35 days to start a business, it only takes 5 days in the United States and 6 days in Singapore. Moreover, the World Bank's *Doing Business in South Asia* also lists high start-up costs as a major impediment to starting a business in India.

(ii) Labour Market Rigidities: Compared to other developed as well as some developing countries like China, South Korea, Malaysia, etc., companies find it relatively difficult to hire workers. India is even more rigid when it comes to firing workers. Table 8.10 shows that among the major developed and developing countries, India scores extremely high on difficulty of firing index. Only Egypt, Venezuela and Peru score higher on this index.

The single most important labour law is arguably the Industrial Disputes Act of 1947. This law almost makes it impossible for firms to fire workers. An amendment to this act in the mid-1980s requires that any firm employing more than 100 workers needs to get permission from the state government before retrenching workers. Such laws leave absolutely no room for free contracting and hiring of contract workers that may be required seasonally to meet additional demand. The net effect of the prevailing labour market regime is to convert labour into a fixed cost and one that also results in significant transaction costs and source of uncertainty. This results from the prevailing statutory provisions that give almost complete and unquestioned authority to the government in matters relating to labours' working and employment conditions. The net result is deterrence to labour intensive and large scale investment and a binding constraint on SMEs trying to achieve greater scale.

There is a need for a law that allows employers greater flexibility in hiring labour in line with the specific requirements. Some workers may sign a contract for a high wage but one that requires them to quit at short notice; others may seek the opposite. This would allow firms to employ different kinds of labour depending on the volatility of the market they operate in. Hiring and firing of workers is not the only or even the most important issue in the current circumstances of skill scarcity and high attrition rates but there is an urgent need to improve the existing labour dispute resolution system. As of October 2005 there were as many as 1,61,117 cases pending in the various labour courts in India

(iii) Procedural Constraints: Entrepreneurs also face a significant delay in registering property in India. According to Table 8.10, in India it takes 62 days to register a property compared to 32 days in China, 11 days in South Korea and 12 days in the United States. Moreover, entrepreneurs have to go through significantly more procedures to enforce contracts in India, which leads to substantial delays. Apart from having to go through more procedures in India, entrepreneurs also find that the average time on each procedure in India is far higher than other countries. For example, in India it takes an average of 25.36 days to complete one procedure to enforce a contract compared to 9.42 days in China and 7.93 days in South Korea. Again, this is primarily due to the stifling culture of red tape and needs to be curbed.

(iv) Exit Barriers: Apart from stringent entry barriers, entrepreneurs also have to deal with very complex and dysfunctional exit barriers. It normally takes 10 years for a firm to close its business in India, compared to 2.4 in China and 1.5 in South Korea (Table 8.10). This has significantly impeded the entry of new players into Indian manufacturing. Again, a careful review of the existing procedures is needed and redundant procedures weeded out.

Table 8.10

Doing Business across Countries

Country	*Starting a Business*		*Dealing with Licences*		*Employing Workers*		*Registering Property*		*Enforcing Contracts*		*Closing a Business*	
	Procedures (number)	*Time (days)*	*Procedures (number)*	*Time (days)*	*Difficulty of Hiring Index*	*Difficulty of Firing Index*	*Procedures (number)*	*Time (days)*	*Procedures (number)*	*Time (days)*	*Time (years)*	*Recovery rate (cents on the dollar)*
Argentina	15	32	23	288	44	20	5	44	33	520	2.8	36.2
Bangladesh	8	37	13	185	11	40	8	425	50	1,442	4	24.9
Brazil	17	152	19	460	67	0	14	47	42	616	4	12.1
China	13	35	29	367	11	40	3	32	31	292	2.4	31.5
Hong Kong	5	11	22	160	0	0	5	54	16	211	1.1	78.9
India	11	35	20	270	33	70	6	62	56	1,420	10	13
Indonesia	12	97	19	224	61	50	7	42	34	570	5.5	11.8
South Korea	12	22	14	52	11	30	7	11	29	230	1.5	81.8
Malaysia	9	30	25	281	0	10	5	144	31	450	2.3	38.7
Mexico	8	27	12	142	33	40	5	74	37	415	1.8	63.2
Pakistan	11	24	12	218	78	30	6	50	55	880	2.8	39.9
Singapore	6	6	11	129	0	0	3	9	29	120	0.8	91.3
Taiwan, China	8	48	32	206	78	30	3	5	28	510	0.8	89.5
Thailand	8	33	9	127	33	0	2	2	26	425	2.7	42.6
United Kingdom	6	18	19	115	11	10	2	21	19	229	1	85.2
United States	5	5	18	69	0	0	4	12	17	300	1.5	77

Notes: The Difficulty to Hiring/Firing Index goes from 0 to 100.

Source: *Doing Business in 2006* (World Bank and International Finance Corporation).

(v) Emerging Skill Constraints: The competitiveness of Indian manufacturing is heavily dependent on the availability of a low-cost skilled workforce. In recent years several industries are experiencing an increasing shortage of skilled workers. To meet this demand, there is a need to undertake significant reforms in the education sector. The policy focus so far has been on raising literacy levels and improving access to primary education through schemes like *Sarva Shiksha Abhiyan* on the one hand and establishing some top world class institutes like IITs, IIMs, etc. There is a case of the 'missing middle' in the education sector also, which refers to the relatively weak vocational and technical education sector. The number of vocational schools and courses are only a tenth of that in China and a massive resource infusion is needed to address this issue.

(vi) Infrastructure: It is now widely recognised and commented upon that the manufacturing sector suffers from a severe infrastructure deficit. A range of estimates for resources required to address the deficit is available with some studies suggesting a requirement of $350 billion over the next five years. Given the constrained fiscal space, these resources cannot come only from public investment. Hence the strong emphasis given in recent years to promoting public-private partnership and for creating necessary regulatory framework for facilitating private investments needs to be encouraged further. The target for India should be to raise the investment in infrastructure from its current level of about 3 per cent to 9 per cent of GDP as has been achieved by China.

Some progress has been made, notably in the telecom sector where reforms were initiated in the mid-1990s. The supply response has been tremendous with teledensity increasing from 0.8 per cent in 1994 to nearly 13 per cent at the end of 2006. The telecom sector has attracted around $16.61 billion in foreign investment since 1991.

The Electricity Act of 2003 has provided the statutory basis for reforming the sector. Some states have implemented the provisions of the Act but others have not. Some major issues like transmission and distribution losses, continued loss making by State Electricity Boards and extensive subsidy to some consumer groups like the farmers are yet to be addressed. There has been an unfortunate regression in the sector from 1994 when all the states had agreed to charge a minimum tariff even for electricity supplied to farmers.

The Electricity Commissions, created under the 2003 Act in every state and in the Centre, have been asked to rationalise tariff to progressively reflect cost of supply and institute anti-theft provisions. To ensure a competitive manufacturing sector it should not be burdened with subsidising power to other sectors and should also be allowed 'open access' to power supply. This would imply that the units can directly source their electricity from any generator located anywhere in the country. These would introduce competition and propel states to perform better.

The development of the Golden Quadrilateral (GQ) and East-West (EW) and North-South (NS) corridor projects are steps in the right direction and must be given the highest priority. Special attention must be paid to development of high speed roads and railway links connecting the hinterland to ports. The 1995 Amendment to the National Highways Act of 1956 allows private investment in road development, maintenance and operation and this is beginning to show results with significant private sector participation in the national highways sector.

Two other areas, however, need special and urgent attention. First, the urban infrastructure, especially in Tier I and Tier II cities and towns has deteriorated under the presence of rural to urban migration and sheer lack of investment by municipal authorities. Secondly, the project design and implementation capacity in both the Central and State governments has to be augmented. This would include means to remove inter-ministerial bottlenecks that presently create great uncertainties and risks in the execution of infrastructure projects.

(vii) Foreign Direct Investment: The Chinese experience shows that FDI can play a major role in transition to mass manufacturing.

FDI not only brings capital into the country but also advanced technology, know-how, managerial expertise, global marketing networks and best-practise systems of corporate governance. Thus there are considerable spillover effects that work through supply chains and spin-offs, which will facilitate the transition to mass manufacturing.

In India, there has been considerable liberalisation of FDI-related policies since 1991. However, the flow of FDI has not been very encouraging. From August 1991 to March 2000, cumulative FDI in India was only $16.48 billion at an average of $1.83 billion per year. Though FDI flows have picked up in the recent past, even for the period 2000-2006, FDI inflows averaged a mere $5.5 billion per year. It is only in 2006-07 that FDI inflows have picked up substantially. In the first 10 months of the fiscal year around $16.44 billion of FDI had come into India.

As per the extant policy, FDI up to 100 per cent is allowed, under the automatic route, in most sectors/activities. FDI under the automatic route does not require prior approval either by the Government of India or the Reserve Bank of India (RBI). However, some irritants do remain, which have impeded the flow of FDI into the country to an extent. For example, Press Note No. 18 (1998 series) points out that automatic route for FDI would not be available to those who have or had previous joint ventures in the same or allied field in India. Investors belonging to this category will have to go through the FIPB/PAB approval route and they have to provide requisite justification and proof that the new venture will not jeopardise the current interests of their existing or former joint venture partners.

These issues related to FDI need to be addressed urgently for India to undertake a successful transition to mass manufacturing. Thus, while it is important that Indian indigenous manufacturers themselves upscale to mass production levels, FDI can also play a very important role in the transition.

Conclusion

This paper tried to undertake a broad evaluation of the Indian manufacturing sector. During the last few years the manufacturing sector has witnessed impressive growth, which has helped the GDP to post historically high growth rates. Currently, the manufacturing sector is witnessing its longest period of upswing since the 1980s but there is a clear divergence between the performances of sectors that are primarily privately owned, namely, manufacturing, steel and cement and sectors that are primarily in the public sector like coal, electricity and crude petroleum. A state-wise analysis reveals wide differentials in the performance across states with Tamil Nadu and Gujarat having significantly increased their share in manufacturing output while West Bengal and 'BIMARU' states have been the biggest losers. Better quality of infrastructure and skill availability expectedly emerge as two key determinants of the growth of manufacturing sector across states.

The paper finds that the unorganised sector is overwhelmingly dominant in terms of number of enterprises and its share in total manufacturing sector workforce. However, the sector is only a marginal contributor to value added. Thus, the unorganised sector is characterised by extremely low value added per worker. The paper argues that this problem of the dualistic structure of the Indian manufacturing sector and the 'missing middle' is a direct consequence of public policy. This needs to be rectified.

The manufacturing sector, especially organised manufacturing, has failed to generate adequate employment. The primary reason for this is widespread automation and decline in labour intensity, principally in response to the prevailing policy regime, in both organised and unorganised sectors. Evaluating the export performance, the paper finds that although there have been significant changes in the composition of exports in the last 20 years; India is still a very small player at the global level, especially in knowledge intensive and advanced technology products. The surprising and the disappointing feature has been the decline in the share of manufactured exports in total exports in recent years.

Finally, the paper explores India's prospects for successfully making the transition to mass manufacturing and emerging as a hub for manufacturing exports. The main challenges in doing so are the low level of R&D and scarcity of skilled personnel in India. Other impediments to the realisation of this transition, essential for generating the required employment opportunities, are inadequate infrastructure, entry and exit barriers and low volumes of foreign direct investment.

Sustaining a rapid growth of manufacturing and achieving the transition to mass manufacturing requires another major push to the reform agenda. In the absence of these reforms, the manufacturing sector will continue to retain its dualistic structure and be unable to address the apparent trade-off between growth and equity that can be best addressed by massive expansion in manufacturing sector employment.

References

Ahluwalia, I.J. (1991). *Productivity and Growth in Indian Manufacturing.* New Delhi: Oxford University Press.

ATKEARNY (2005). *Foreign Direct Investment Confidence Index.* Global Business Policy Council.

Besley, T. and R. Burgess (2004). "Can Labour Regulation Hinder Economic Performance? Evidence from India," *Quarterly Journal of Economics,* Vol. 119(1).

Burange, L. (1999). "Industrial Growth and Structure: Manufacturing Sector in Maharashtra." *Economic and Political Weekly,* February 27, pp.M39–M48.

Burgess, R. and R. Pande (2005). "Do Rural Banks Matter? Evidence from the Indian Social Banking Experiment," *American Economic Review,* Vol. 95(3).

Das, D.K. (2002). "Trade Liberalisation and Industrial Productivity: An Assessment of Developing Country Experiences", *ICRIER Working Paper* No. 77.

Desai, A. (2001). "A Decade of Reforms," *Economic and Political Weekly,* Vol. 49 December 15.

Government of India (2006). *Towards Faster and More Inclusive Growth: An Approach to the 11th Five Year Plan.* Planning Commission.

ICRIER (2008). "Labour Intensity and Employment Potential of Indian Manufacturing", Submitted to National Manufacturing Competitive Council, Government of India.

Kelkar, V.L. and R. Kumar (1990). "Industrial Growth in the Eighties: Emerging Policy Issues," *Economic and Political Weekly,* January 27, pp.209-222.

Kochhar, K., K. Kumar, R. Rajan, A. Subramanian and I. Tokatlidis (2006). "India's Pattern of Development: What Happened, What Follows?" *IMF Working Paper* 06/22.

Kumar, R. and A. Palit (2007). "Has the Fuel Run Out of Indian Exports," *Business Standard,* February 26.

Lall, S. (2000). "The Technological Structure and Performance of Developing Country Manufactured Exports, 1985-1998," Queen Elizabeth House, University of Oxford, *Working Paper* No. 44.

Lahiri, A. and K-M.Yi (2006). "A Tale of Two States: Maharashtra and West Bengal," Federal Reserve Bank of Philadelphia, *Working Paper* 06-16.

Mazumdar, D. (1998). "Size-Structure of Manufacturing Establishments and the Productivity Differentials between Large and Small Firms: A Comparative Study of Asian Economies," *CIS Working Paper* No. 7, University of Toronto.

Mitra, A., A. Varoudakis and M-A Véganzonès Varoudakis (2002). "Productivity and Technical Efficiency in Indian States' Manufacturing: The Role of Infrastructure" *Economic Development and Cultural Change*, Vol. 50: 395-426.

NMCC (2006). *The National Strategy for Manufacturing*. The National Manufacturing Competitiveness Council.

Nagraj, R. (1990). "Industrial Growth: Further Evidence and Towards an Explanation and Issues," *Economic and Political Weekly*, Vol. 25(41), October 13.

———. (2003). "Industrial Policy and Performance: Which Way Now?" *Economic and Political Weekly*, August 30-September 5, Vol. 38(35).

Tybout, J.R. (2000). "Manufacturing Firms in Developing Countries: How Well Do They Do and Why?" *Journal of Economic Literature*, Vol. XXXVIII: 11-44

Wolf, M. (1982). "India's Exports". World Bank and Oxford University Press.

World Bank (2003). "Improving the Investment Climate in India,". Washington DC: World Bank.

The authors would like to thank Deb Kusum Das, Bibek Debroy, Badri Narayanan, Deepika Wadhwa and conference participants at ICRIER's Silver Jubilee Conference on *India and the Global Economy* and NCAER-NBER Neemrana Conference for their very helpful comments. They would also like to thank Karan Singh and Gaurav Tripathi for excellent research assistance.

9

Making Indian Manufacturing Competitive

BIBEK DEBROY

The Background

The etymology of the word "manufacture" isn't certain. But it seems to have a link with the Latin *manu factum*, meaning 'made by hand.' Irrespective of ingredients of technology, capital (plant and machinery), entrepreneurship, and perhaps even land, entering as inputs or factors into production processes, labour remains a core input. And there is no denying that India possesses, or should possess, a comparative advantage in labour. As with every other developing country, that has always been the case. Labour is relatively more abundant than capital. In a completely integrated and globalised world, national boundaries should make no difference. But that ideal never happens. Even if cross-border movements of technology and capital are relatively free, there will be restrictions on cross-border movements of labour. Integration of labour markets will only happen in niches, in selected segments. Therefore, India should be in a position to exploit its cost advantage in labour, and in natural resources, to push manufacturing growth. Nor should one forget India's strengths in science and technology and in education. These reinforce the labour cost advantage.

To this traditional labour cost advantage has been added, what is called the demographic dividend. Stated simply, this means that populations in developed countries are aging, whereas in developing countries, the working age population is increasing. Perhaps the most spectacular of extrapolations is the Goldman Sachs BRIC (Brazil, Russia, India, China) report.[1] This makes the point that in the period

1. Wilson, Dominic and Roopa Purushothaman (2003). "Dreaming with BRICs: The Path to 2050," *Global Economics Paper* No. 99, Goldman Sachs. October 01. There have been two subsequent follow-up BRIC reports also.

leading up to 2050, India alone, among the BRIC countries, is unlikely to face a labour constraint. A labour shortage in developed countries means scope for immigration or for outsourcing manufacturing activities. Except for niches and small segments, the former is never likely to be quantitatively significant. After all, even WTO mandated agreements visualise cross-border movements of skilled personnel alone, that too, for temporary periods. In contrast, outsourcing and offshoring of manufacturing activities is likely to be much more significant. There are estimates that offshoring of manufacturing activities to low cost countries can be significant and that India can reap part of this dividend.[2] Outsourcing to India has happened and has even figured in election debates in developed countries. But that has been for services. In the 1970s, 1980s and even the 1990s, India missed opportunities in offshoring of manufacturing. There is no reason why that should happen in the next two decades also.

The 10th Five Year Plan (2002-2007) projects an annual average real GDP growth of 8 per cent. The National Common Minimum Programme (NCMP) of the government targets 7 to 8 per cent growth over the next decade. While an average of 8 per cent during the 10th Five Year Plan may now be impossible[3], there is no denying that a trend rate of 8 per cent plus over the next decade and more is feasible. Other countries in the world have exhibited such high rates of growth, even approaching and crossing 9 per cent. In 2003-04, in constant prices, the primary sector[4] accounted for 24.4 per cent of GDP, the secondary sector[5] accounted for 24.6 per cent and the tertiary sector accounted for 51 per cent. There is often euphoria about tertiary sector growth. However, in the history of economic development, no country has developed riding on service sector growth alone. The

---

2. CII-McKinsey (2004). *Made in India—The Next Big Manufacturing Export Story.* October.
3. The *Draft Approach Paper to the 11th Five Year Plan (2007-12)* states the following. "The average growth rate in the last four years of 10th Plan period (2003-04 to 2006-07) is likely to be a little over 8 per cent, making the growth rate for the entire 10th Plan period 7.2 per cent. This is below the 10th Plan target of 8 per cent, but it is the highest growth rate achieved in any plan period."
4. With mining and quarrying (2.3 per cent) also included in the primary sector, together with agriculture, forestry, logging and fishing. However, mining and quarrying can also be included under industry.
5. Manufacturing, construction, electricity, gas and water supply.

transition has been from the primary to the secondary and thereafter to the tertiary. That apart, such sectoral growth rates are not independent of one another. Tertiary sector growth requires secondary sector growth and in India's growth experience, the two have always gone together, the 1990s representing a slight aberration from the trend. The *Draft Approach Paper to the 11th Plan* states, "Although growth in the manufacturing sector has accelerated compared to the 9th Plan it is unlikely to exceed 8 per cent in the 10th Plan. This is unacceptably low. If we want our GDP to grow at 9 per cent, we have to target a 12 per cent growth rate for this sector.[6] Our remarkable success in IT enabled services has prompted some observers to conclude that China has a comparative advantage in manufacturing and India in services. It has thus been suggested that we should concentrate on growth of high value services. This approach is simplistic. India's performance in IT enabled and other high end services is clearly a source of strength that must be built upon. However, India cannot afford to neglect manufacturing." Sectoral compositions of GDP are not constant. They change over time. However, with the present sectoral compositions, what sectoral growth rates can ensure 9 per cent real GDP growth? The secondary sector (including mining and quarrying) needs to grow at 11 per cent-plus, which means manufacturing needs to grow at 12 per cent-plus, the target assumed in the 11th Plan, since other elements of the secondary sector (mining and quarrying, manufacturing, electricity, gas and water supply and construction) will grow relatively slowly.[7]

Nor should one forget the employment angle. A quote from the NCMP is pertinent. "The UPA government will set up a National Manufacturing Competitiveness Council to provide a continuing forum for policy dialogue to energise and sustain the growth of manufacturing industry like food processing, textiles and garments, engineering, consumer goods, pharmaceuticals, capital goods, leather, and IT hardware. Household and artisanal manufacturing will be given greater technological, investment and marketing support. In the past few years, the most employment-intensive segment of small-scale

6. The industry target is 11.5 per cent.

7. As a weight in the index of industrial production, manufacturing contributes 79.36 per cent to the secondary sector.

industry (SSI) has suffered extensively. A major promotional package for the SSI sector will be announced soon. It will be freed from the Inspector *Raj* and given full credit, technological and marketing support. Infrastructure upgradation in major industrial clusters will receive urgent attention." While this quote directly mentions employment only in the context of the SSI sector, employment is an area of concern for the UPA government, within the NCMP framework and outside it. What is worrying is that the annual average growth in employment has slowed. While the average annual growth rate in employment was 2.89 per cent between 1983 and 1987-88 and 2.50 per cent between 1987-1988 and 1993-94, it was 1.07 per cent between 1993-94 and 1999-2000. This slowing down is largely because in the 1990s agriculture failed to create jobs. However, it is not pure agriculture's business to create jobs. The history of development is one of pulling people out of agriculture, into non-farm activities, into manufacturing and into services, not retaining them there. In that sense, India has witnessed a failed industrial revolution. If 10 million new jobs have to be created a year, manufacturing also has a role to play.

Between 1993-94 and 1999-2000, manufacturing hasn't done that well in creating jobs either. The average annual employment growth in manufacturing during this period was 2.58 per cent, compared to 3.64 per cent between 1982 to 1987-88. Between 1993-94 and 1999-2000, the overall employment elasticity was 0.16. But at 0.33, it was higher for manufacturing, although the progressive decline in the employment elasticity of manufacturing should cause concern. For instance, this elasticity was 0.59 between 1983 and 1987-88, declining to 0.33 between 1993-94 and 1999-2000. This employment elasticity translates into jobs in the following way. Employment in manufacturing was 40.79 million in 1999-2000. If manufacturing grows at 9 per cent, with an employment elasticity of 0.33, 1.2 million jobs are created in manufacturing a year. But if the employment elasticity is 0.59, as it was between 1983 and 1987-88, with 9 per cent manufacturing growth, 2.2 million jobs are created a year. And if manufacturing growth increases to 12 per cent, with an elasticity of 0.59, 2.9 million jobs are created a year in manufacturing. There is a target of creating 10 million jobs a year. However, this is for the entire economy and not all of this 10 million is expected to be created in manufacturing. But manufacturing can make its contribution. This is also the right place to mention interstate differences. Most of the demographic dividend, in terms of new entrants into the labour force, is going to occur in central parts of India, leading eastwards. In an era of industrial licensing, manufacturing capacities could be set up in geographical areas where labour forces existed. But industrial licensing is not only impossible now, it is also undesirable. Nor will employment growth primarily happen through the public sector, and it must not be forgotten that many sick public sector units (PSUs) are precisely in these geographical regions and they will eventually be closed down. If one is to avoid tensions over a few jobs in the Railways, private sector job creation, including in manufacturing, must compensate. What should be of concern is the declining employment elasticity of manufacturing in the 1990s, compared to say, the 1980s. While labour market rigidities may be partly responsible, these haven't worsened in the 1990s. The answer therefore probably lies in restructuring consequent to competition, leading to shedding of surplus jobs, and even a sectoral change in manufacturing sectors that have shown relatively higher rates of growth in the 1990s.

This is also the right place to mention the organised *versus* unorganised sector dichotomy. In 2000, the total work force is estimated to be 397.88 million. Of this, 28.15 million, or 7.07 per cent is in the organised sector[8]. The unorganised sector accounts for employment of 369.73 million, or 92.93 per cent. There are indeed three different definitions of organised/unorganised, although they do overlap. First, there is the labour law kind of definition, the Factories Act of 1948 being the obvious example, although this only applies to 'factories'. Registration is required if a factory employs 20 or more people and doesn't use power or if it employs 10 or more people and uses power. Registration is equated with organised and everything else is unorganised. Second, there is a definition of SSI, in terms of threshold levels of investment in plant and machinery. SSI is often equated with unorganised manufacturing. Third, there is a threshold level of turnover below which, excise doesn't have to be paid. Excise exemption constitutes yet another definition of unorganised. However,

8. *Economic Survey 2004-05* has an organised sector figure of 27 million in 2003, with a breakup of 18.6 million in the public sector and 8.4 million in the private sector.

whichever definition of unorganised/organised one uses, the organised sector accounts for less than 8 per cent of the work force. For instance, the 369.73 million work force figure is for 1999-2000. In 2002, the work force is 397 million. And only 27.2 million is employed in the organised sector, constituting 6.9 per cent. 93.1 per cent or 369.6 million are employed in the unorganised sector. Of the total employment of 27.2 million in the organised sector, 18.8 million (69 per cent) is in the public sector. Public sector employment has stagnated in the 1990s. The private sector accounts for 8.4 million employment (31 per cent) in the organised sector. This has increased a bit in the 1990s, but only from 7.6 million in 1990 to 8.4 million in 2002. These figures are of course for total private sector employment. Private sector employment in organised sector manufacturing is 4.9 million in 2002, compared to total manufacturing employment of 40.79 million.[9] Public sector employment in organised sector manufacturing is 1.4 million in 2002. Total employment in organised sector manufacturing is thus 6.3 million, 15.4 per cent of total manufacturing employment. This organised/total ratio may be higher for manufacturing than for overall employment, but is still fairly low. With reforms, the dichotomy between the organised and unorganised sectors should break down. The organised sector is under the purview of labour laws, which are certainly rigid. Liberalisation will involve making labour market provisions in the organised sector more flexible. However, it should also be noted that the unorganised sector is completely outside the purview of most labour laws, and this includes social security. Liberalisation will also involve extending protection to labour in the unorganised sector. This is indeed the thrust of the recommendations of the Second National Commission on Labour, which submitted a report in 2002.

One should now move on to the definition of manufacturing and quality of data. The basic classification of all economic activities is the UN system's International Standard Industrial Classification (ISIC).[10]

9. These figures keep changing. *Economic Survey 2004-05* has a figure of 4.7 million as private sector organised employment in manufacturing in 2003, a slight decline compared to 2002.

10. Revision 3.1. This is not identical with the North American Industrial Classification System (NAICS) used in the CII-McKinsey study, although difference surface at levels of disaggregation are far beyond the 2-digit level.

At the 2-digit level, these are also the classifications followed by the CSO (Central Statistical Organisation). Section D constitutes manufacturing in the industrial classification and the 2-digit codes and descriptions (common to both ISIC and CSO) are given in the table below. This then constitutes the definition of manufacturing, both for cross-country comparisons and for Indian data. What should be noted is that some of these categories are sometimes not included in data on manufacturing. Examples are codes 22, 36 and 37.

ISIC 2-Digit Code	*ISIC Description*
15	Manufacture of food products and beverages
16	Manufacture of tobacco products
17	Manufacture of textiles
18	Manufacture of wearing apparel; dressing and dyeing of fur
19	Tanning and dressing of leather; manufacture of luggage, handbags, saddlery, harness and footwear
20	Manufacture of wood and of products of wood and cork, except furniture; manufacture of articles of straw and plaiting materials
21	Manufacture of paper and paper products
22	Publishing, printing and reproduction of recorded media
23	Manufacture of coke, refined petroleum products and nuclear fuel
24	Manufacture of chemicals and chemical products
25	Manufacture of rubber and plastics products
26	Manufacture of other non-metallic mineral products
27	Manufacture of basic metals
28	Manufacture of fabricated metal products, except machinery and equipment
29	Manufacture of machinery and equipment n.e.c.
30	Manufacture of office, accounting and computing machinery
31	Manufacture of electrical machinery and apparatus n.e.c.
32	Manufacture of radio, television and communication equipment and apparatus
33	Manufacture of medical, precision and optical instruments, watches and clocks
34	Manufacture of motor vehicles, trailers and semi-trailers
35	Manufacture of other transport equipment
36	Manufacture of furniture; manufacturing n.e.c.
37	Recycling

The boundaries of manufacturing and other sectors often tend to get blurred. Beyond such problems, there are serious issues with CSO's data collection exercises. "The entire manufacturing activities are classified into two broad sectors, *viz.*, manufacturing—'registered' and 'unregistered.' The registered manufacturing sector covers all factories covered under sections 2m (i) and 2m (ii) of the Indian Factories Act (IFA), 1948 which respectively refers to the factories employing 10 or more workers and using power or those employing 20 or more workers but not using power on any day of the preceding 12 months and *bidi* and cigar establishments registered under the Bidi and Cigar Workers (Condition of Employment) Act, 1966 and employing 10 or more workers using power or 20 or more workers and not using power."[11] Indeed, factories where a manufacturing process is not carried on are excluded. "The 'manufacturing process' is defined as any process for (i) making, altering, repairing, finishing, packing, oiling, washing, cleaning, breaking up, demolishing or otherwise treating or adapting any article or substance with a view to its use, sale, transport, delivery or disposal; (ii) pumping oil, water, sewage or any substance; (iii) generating, transforming or transmitting power; (iv) composing types for printing, printing by letter press, lithography, photogravure or other similar process or book binding; (v) constructing, reconstructing, repairing, refitting, finishing or breaking up of ships or vessels; (vi) preserving or storing any article in cold storage. Factories registered under the IFA but not engaged in manufacturing activities are excluded."

There is thus a dichotomy between registered manufacturing and unregistered manufacturing. For registered manufacturing, data are collected annually through the Annual Survey of Industries (ASI). This is part survey (sample) and part census. Unregistered manufacturing, which also includes own account enterprises, is covered much less frequently, typically, once every five years. In 2001, there was a fairly serious critique of the entire Indian statistical system.[12] Although the criticisms were greater for other sectors of the economy, manufacturing data were also criticised—in all the four components of ASI, unregistered manufacturing, SSI and the index of industrial production (IIP). For instance, other than time lags and sampling and non-sampling errors, the ASI includes units that shouldn't be included (they have closed down) and excludes units that should be included.

11. CSO (1989). *NAS—Sources and Methods.*

12. *Report of the National Statistical Commission*, August 2001.

Different databases of unregistered (census or survey) manufacturing vary widely, perhaps understandably, because differing concepts and definitions are used. This is compounded by lack of adequate data on SSI and unorganised traditional industries (village and small industries). Finally, other than the problem that the index of industrial production (IIP) represents only 80 per cent of manufacturing, there are problems associated with low response rates, small samples, unsatisfactory weights and non-representation of the unorganised sector. As a generalisation, manufacturing data are, therefore, somewhat satisfactory for registered manufacturing and extremely unsatisfactory for everything else.

As was mentioned indirectly earlier, traditional models of development involve a transition from the primary sector to the secondary sector and subsequently, a transition to the tertiary sector. Indeed, many other developing countries have much higher shares of manufacturing in GDP, as compared to India. This is evident from the data in the table, the source being the World Bank[13] and the year being 2003. China's share of 44.5 per cent may be a striking outlier. And the fact that other South Asian countries have shares similar to India's is neither here nor there. There is an obvious correlation with emphasis on import substituting industrialisation. 44.5 per cent may be spectacular. But there is no reason why manufacturing's share in Indian GDP should not be 30 per cent. Notwithstanding the euphoria about services, the expected decline of agriculture's contribution should be mirrored by an increase in manufacturing's share. It isn't the case that manufacturing's share in Indian GDP hasn't increased. But the increase has been very slow. The 15.8 per cent figure in the table is from World Bank sources and is for the year 2003. Central Statistical Organisation (CSO) sources show a share of 16.85 per cent in 2001-02 and 17.22 per cent in 2002-03. The share used to be 13.82 per cent in 1980-81. It increased gradually to 17.68 per cent in 1997-1998, before declining and then reviving again.

---

13. *http://web.worldbank.org/WBSITE/EXTERNAL/COUNTRIES/0,,pagePK:180619~theSitePK:136917,00.html*

Share of the Manufacturing Sector in GDP (Per Cent)	
India	15.8[14]
Argentina	23.9
Brazil	11.4[15]
Chile	15.8[16]
Mexico	18.1
South Africa	18.9
China	44.5
Indonesia	25.0
South Korea	23.7
The Philippines	22.9
Thailand	34.2
Malaysia	31.1
Pakistan	16.2
Sri Lanka	15.5
Bangladesh	15.8

What does it mean to say that manufacturing's share of GDP should be 30 per cent? At one level, one is arguing that historically, manufacturing could have done better and compared to other countries, there is no reason why the share today should not have been 30 per cent, as compared to 8 per cent. This is a valid point to make. But at another level, one is arguing that there should be a game plan to take manufacturing's share to 30 per cent. This is more questionable, more so if it is articulated in terms of manufacturing's share, as opposed to industry's share. Manufacturing's share is a function not only of manufacturing growth, but also of growths in the other sectors. For instance, there is no reason why service sector growth should slow down from the historical trend. Indeed, in the next twenty years, the service sector share in GDP should inch up towards 60 per cent. Nor is there any particular reason why non-manufacturing industrial growth should slow down. And non-manufacturing industry will continue to account for at least 10 per cent of GDP. While agriculture's share in GDP ought to progressively

14. India's share was 16.3 per cent in 1983.

15. Brazil's share was 33.2 per cent in 1983.

16. Chile's share was 21.2 per cent in 1983.

decline, no reasonable projection will assume an agricultural contribution of less than 10 per cent in the next 20 years. That leaves a manufacturing contribution to GDP of 20 per cent and no more. Anything more than a 20 or 25 per cent contribution of manufacturing to GDP is extremely implausible. As the historical trend shows, it has taken more than 20 years to increase the manufacturing share by five percentage points to around 18 per cent. Another five percentage points will take another 20 plus years, in a business-as-usual kind of scenario. In a non business-as-usual kind of scenario, the transition will at best be accelerated. If the target is expressed as manufacturing's share in GDP, and the timeframe is the next 10 years, one should at best hope for something like a 23 per cent share in 2015. Not 30 per cent.[17] Targets are better articulated in terms of manufacturing's growth alone, independent of growth rates in non-manufacturing sectors.

Competitiveness Constraints

What are the constraints in pushing up manufacturing growth still further? The constraints themselves suggest the solutions. Some of the constraints are generic in the sense that they cut across all manufacturing sectors. The others are more specific and pertain to specific sectors. In this paper, we only concentrate on the generic problems.

At a very broad level, some indications of competitiveness can be obtained from *World Competitiveness Reports*. More accurately, there are two such reports—*Global Competitiveness Report (GCR)*, published by World Economic Forum[18] and the *World Competitiveness Yearbook (WCY)*, published by the International Institute for Management Development (IMD).[19] The bifurcation of one initial report into two highlights problems associated with defining competitiveness. While neither report is about manufacturing competitiveness alone, manufacturing does form an integral part of the rankings. Consider WEF's *GCR* first. This has a growth competitiveness index (GCI),

17. The CII-McKinsey aspiration is 18-21 per cent share of GDP by 2015.

18. Since 1979.

19. Since 1989.

which captures an economy's capacity to grow in the future. Using a splicing of hard data and subjective perceptions, GCI builds on three pillars of macroeconomic environment, public institutions and technology. There are thus three indices for each of these heads and the three individual indices are aggregated to derive the overall GCI. Quite often, reports about GCI are based on India's relative rank over the years. For instance, India's rank was 45th in 1996 and 55th in 2004. These ranks are however misleading because the number of countries ranked has changed down the years. The values of GCI are a better indication of movements than ranks. On the three pillars of macroeconomic environment, public institutions and technology, India obtains a 63rd rank on the technology index, a 52nd rank on the macroeconomic environment index and a 53rd rank on the public institutions index. In addition to the macro and medium-term focus of GCI, *GCR* also has a shorter term and micro business competitiveness index (BCI). India shows quite a sharp improvement on this, the rank having improved from 37th in 2000 to 30th in 2004. To quote from the 2004 version, "Another low-income country with large improvements is India, up 8 ranks, showing the benefits of increased company sophistication and strengthened clusters."

This is not the place to debate *GCR vis-à-vis WCY*, or even GCI *vis-à-vis* BCI. What is pertinent for our purposes is that companies compete. Countries or economies don't compete. However, government policies provide the environment within which companies compete. These macro policies feed into *GCR*'s GCI through the three intermediary indices of a macroeconomic environment index, a public institutions index and a technology index. And if one scrutinises the heads that go into GCI, one finds eight heads—openness of the economy to international trade and finance, role of the government budget and regulation, development of financial markets, quality of infrastructure, quality of technology, quality of business management, labour market flexibility and quality of judicial and political institutions. However, these macro policies need to be supplemented with other micro variables captured in BCI through two indices of company operations and strategy and quality of the national business environment. To keep the record complete, one should mention that India performs far better on IMD's *WCY*, the Indian rank having jumped from 50th (out of 60 countries ranked) in 2003 to 34th in 2004. *WCY* also has a ranking of regions and Maharashtra's rank has jumped from 44th in 2003 to 38th in 2004.

While one can complain about variables included (or excluded) and the methodology used in *GCR* or *WCY*, there ought not to be any great debate about the heads that aid or constrain manufacturing competitiveness. As was mentioned earlier, in this paper, we only concentrate on generic heads. There are indeed sector-specific problems, but we will ignore those. A list of these major heads now follows.

Import Duties

This import duty head has several different strands. First, there is an argument that import duties need to be reduced. This argument is usually advanced when items imported are raw materials and intermediates and not finished goods. The Kelkar Task Force[20] recommended a four-tier import duty (that is, for manufactured goods) structure in 2006-07—5 per cent for basic raw materials (coal, ores and concentrates, xylenes), 8 per cent for intermediate goods (capital goods, basic chemicals, metals), 10 per cent for finished goods other than consumer durables and 20 per cent for consumer durables. Some comments are in order about these recommendations. During the Uruguay Round (1986-94), some of India's manufactured goods were exempt from binding commitments. Consumer goods and non-ferrous metals are examples. The Doha Development Agenda started in 2001 and was certain to have import duty reduction commitments. When there are no bindings, the GATT/WTO system is unclear about the base on which reduction commitments will apply. The base could have been applied rates. Hence, there was a reluctance to unilaterally reduce duties on consumer goods and this was reflected in the Kelkar Task Force's recommendations. But since those recommendations were submitted, there has been a framework agreement in Geneva on 1st August 2004 and this states that, in the absence of bindings, the base will be twice the applied MFN (most favoured nation) rate in 2001. Although there

20. Ministry of Finance and Company Affairs (2002). *Report of the Task Force on Indirect Taxes*. December.

are some exemptions for developing countries, this agreement also provides for zero duties on sectoral basis. There are two arguments that follow. First, while there are arguments for reducing import duties on raw materials and intermediates, there is resistance to reducing duties on finished goods, spliced with fears about an appreciating rupee. Within the WTO system, is there any possibility of import duties higher than 5 per cent on raw materials and intermediates and 10 per cent on finished goods, perhaps 10 years down the line? The answer is probably no. Add to that a plethora of FTAs (free trade agreements) outside the WTO system, which invariably involve manufactured products, with eventual zero duties. Second, and this is a policy question, should one even attempt to have a tiered structure of import duties? When developed countries have such tiered structures, developing countries like India invariably argue that this discourages value addition in developing countries. More importantly, it becomes impossible to decide what is a raw material and what is an intermediate. Consequently, as long as variations across sectors continue, trade facilitation will never improve and customs formalities will never have low transaction costs. Stated differently, the policy problem is the following. Should we standardise or should we attempt to differentiate? And as long as we resist reduction of general import duties, the FTA problem will remain. What do we do about rules of origin and value addition requirements? As long as these issues remain, customs formalities will never be eased.

Second, this is the right place to mention customs formalities, highlighted also by the Kelkar Task Force. For example, there are issues like use of EDI (electronic data interchange) and online filing of declarations, self-assessment of Bills of Entry, filing of complete Import General Manifests before arrival of the cargo, establishment of Trade Facilitation Committees, deadlines for processing of documents, payment of customs duties through cheques and licensing and registration systems for Custom House Agents.

Third, there is a level playing field kind of argument that goes beyond mere protectionism. At one level, this is about non-imposition or non-enforcement of standards on imported products, or even about testing and certification requirements. There are also arguments about systemic problems in imposing safeguard or anti-dumping duties. But there is also a different kind of duty argument. While the basic customs duty may be zero, imported products should face duties equivalent to domestic indirect taxes paid by domestic manufacturers. The countervailing duty (CVD) is meant to be precisely this, but is presently only equal to central excise. That ignores State-level sales tax and other local levies. The 2005-06 budget has a provision for an additional CVD of 4 per cent, but that is presently restricted to IT products. Unfortunately, this reform gets linked with reform of the domestic indirect tax system.

Domestic Indirect Taxes

Domestic indirect taxes are often singled out as a major reason why Indian manufacturing is uncompetitive. For instance, the CII-McKinsey report argues that total taxes on manufactured goods are 25 to 30 per cent of the retail price in India, compared to 15 per cent in China and indirect taxes contribute 50 per cent to the difference in retail prices between India and China. That the Indian indirect tax structure is cost-cascading and non-transparent is known. It also imposes significant transaction cum compliance costs on business. But conceptually, one must be clear about the argument that is being advanced. Why do high duties *per se* render Indian manufacturing uncompetitive? And where? They shouldn't render Indian manufacturing uncompetitive in export markets, because domestic indirect taxes are supposed to be waived or reimbursed. The argument should then be that these waivers and reimbursements don't work satisfactorily. Nor should high domestic duties render manufacturing uncompetitive in the domestic market, because through the CVD route, importers are also supposed to pay these duties. The argument then becomes that the CVD system doesn't work satisfactorily. The argument about high domestic indirect taxes should, therefore, be more indirect. High compliance costs impact productivity by pre-empting management time. There is bribery and corruption associated with both excise and sales tax. Lower duties would have boosted the domestic market and permitted synergy (exploitation of economies of scale, attracting FDI) between domestic and export markets.

Reforming indirect taxes is also contingent on reforming direct taxes. In 2004-05, total tax revenue is 10.2 per cent of GDP, if one includes Central taxes alone.[21] If one includes State and local level levies, the figure is more like 15 per cent. Given expenditure commitments and demands on the government, this ratio probably needs to be 3 per cent more as a share of GDP. The Kelkar Task Force on implementation of the FRBM (Fiscal Responsibility and Budget Management) Act also argues that fiscal consolidation will primarily have to occur *via* the revenue route rather than the expenditure contraction route.[22] Central tax revenue as a share of GDP has stagnated at around 10 per cent (sometimes even 9 per cent) of GDP since 1990-91. Kelkar's FRBM projections visualise an increase to 12.96 per cent in 2008-09, provided that tax reforms take place. The stagnation in the tax revenue share in the 1990s however masks an increase in the direct tax contribution from 1.9 per cent of GDP in 1990-91 to 4.5 per cent in 2004-05, neutralised by a decline in the indirect tax contribution from 7.9 per cent of GDP in 1990-91 to 5.7 per cent in 2004-05. This is primarily because of a drop in the customs share, but the share of excise has also declined. On welfare grounds, it is valid to argue that taxation through the direct route is preferable to indirect taxation. However, in a developing country like India, notwithstanding direct tax reform, this argument cannot be pushed too far. Indeed, the Kelkar Report's projections have a 6.46 per cent share of direct taxes in GDP in 2008-09 and an indirect tax share of 6.46 per cent also. The simple point is that the indirect tax contribution to GDP must also increase. The argument for reducing multiplicity and increasing transparency should not be confused with a drop in this share.

The broad shape of indirect tax reform is clear. There should be a combined goods and service tax (GST), with service sector taxation integrated into the VAT framework instead of being a tax on turnover. This will be accompanied by a withdrawal of all other taxes like central excise, central sales tax, octroi, State-level sales tax, entry tax, stamp duties, transportation taxes and so on. The complete VAT is a long way off. But three points are pertinent. First, when there is a

21. *Economic Survey 2004-05.*

22. *Implementation of the Fiscal Responsibility and Budget Management Act, 2003, Report of the Task Force*, July 2004.

complete VAT, what is likely to be a VAT rate that is revenue neutral? The State VAT proposed has two basic rates of 4 per cent and 12.5 per cent, with an attempt to push several items to the 4 per cent category. 12.5 per cent is not a revenue neutral rate. A revenue neutral rate, with Central and State VAT both included, is likely to be more like 20 per cent. Indeed, the Kelkar standard rate is 12 per cent for Central VAT and 8 per cent for State-level VAT. Consequently, a figure like the 15 per cent cited for China, is probably impossible. Second, even for something like 20 per cent to work, there has to be an end to discretion. Those who push for indirect tax reform should therefore simultaneously argue for standardisation and an end to discretionary treatment. Third, and this is an extension of the second argument, indirect tax reform will work only if all exemptions are terminated—product-specific exemptions, SSI exemptions, location-based exemptions. People often quote the CII-McKinsey report, which argues that indirect taxes in India are unnecessarily high. What they sometimes fail to quote is that this report also argues for removal of exemptions.

Export Incentives/Export Subsidies

There is a conceptual difference between export incentives and export subsidies. Export subsidies involve differential treatment to exports as compared to sales in the domestic market and are in general WTO-incompatible, although there are some exemptions for India. Export incentives are WTO-compatible, as they involve reimbursements (DEPB and duty drawback) or waivers (advance licences) for duties paid in exported products. Problems arise because of the present system of averaging across units in granting waivers. Legitimate export incentives thus become labeled as unwarranted export incentives and are exposed to countervailing duty impositions. This has already arisen in the case of DEPB, but is equally applicable to duty drawback also. In principle, implementation would be easier if one switched over completely to an advance license system. However, given that there are several small exporters, this might not be feasible. Nor should one forget that export procedures continue to be cumbersome because of procedures connected with export incentives/subsidies. If these are not availed of, procedures have become reasonably simple. Implementation of both DEPB and duty drawback will become simpler if there is a complete VAT system. In the absence of a complete VAT, the rates provide for some remission of domestic taxes other than excise and import duties, and because the system is non-transparent, the link becomes difficult to establish. Beyond this conceptual problem, there are also issues connected with procedures, such as delays in reimbursements.

FDI and Procedures

Foreign investments mean both foreign portfolio investments and foreign direct investments (FDI) and *Economic Survey 2004-05* emphasises FDI in its issues and priorities segment. In a classic sense, FDI has been regarded as desirable because it contributes towards bridging two gaps—the foreign exchange gap and the savings/investment gap. Neither of these is that relevant for India any more, certainly not the first. However, FDI brings better technology and management, access to marketing networks and offers competition, the latter helping Indian companies improve, quite apart from being good for consumers. This efficiency contribution of FDI is much more important. There was a slight problem with Indian FDI definitions, since these didn't conform to IMF guidelines. With the revised definition, FDI inflow figures are 3.40 billion US dollars in 2001, 3.45 billion in 2002 and 4.27 billion in 2004, there being a gap between approvals and inflows. However, in 2006, FDI inflows into India should approach 8 billion. This is still a far cry from China's 53.51 billion in 2003 and the target of annual FDI inflows of 10 billion a year. UNCTAD now has an FDI performance index ranking and an FDI potential index ranking. In 2001-03, India's FDI performance index ranking was 114th out of 140 countries.[23] In a large country like India, FDI as a share of GDP will never be very high. And barring certain sectors, FDI as a share of total investments will also not be very high. But there is no denying that India has under-performed.

Why has India under-performed? The reasons are obvious enough. First, FDI in manufacturing is now completely open, with Press Note No. 18 having been scrapped for new entrants, although there are some restrictions on mergers and acquisitions. Second, the bulk of

---

23. UNCTAD (2004). *World Investment Report 2004—The Shift Towards Services.*

cross-border FDI inflows are in the services sector and the services sector is still subject to equity caps, not everything having been placed on automatic approval. Third, policies in the infrastructure sector are often not in place. Fourth, there are procedural problems at all three levels of an enterprise's functioning—entry, functioning and exit, although foreign investors often tend to focus on the first. This is not purely a foreign investor issue. Courtesy national treatment, equally cumbersome procedures are also foisted on domestic investors. The expression transaction costs is sometimes used and such an expression also subsumes under it costs associated with inadequate infrastructure. We will talk about infrastructure later. For our purposes, transaction costs mean procedural costs alone. There is no real quantification of the extra cost disadvantage that Indian manufacturing faces because of transaction costs. There are some figures of around 20 per cent, but those include infrastructure costs also. However, a recent World Bank report benchmarks India's transaction costs with some other countries in the world.[24] One should remember that many, though not all, of these procedures are at the State government level. Land, labour, water, electricity, environment are examples. This also explains why conversion ratios (percentage of approvals converted to inflows) vary widely across States. Maharashtra, Delhi, Tamil Nadu, Karnataka, Gujarat account for the bulk of FDI approvals under the automatic route. Indeed, it is somewhat perverse that in 2006, FDI out of India is likely to exceed FDI into India, thus underlining the high costs of doing business in India.

Interest Rates

High interest rates and availability of credit are often cited as problems, as indeed they are. But one must be careful to separate out the price effect from a non-availability of credit problem. The prime lending rate (PLR) is around 10.25 per cent now, compared to a deposit rate of around 5.5 per cent. Household financial savings are 11.4 per cent of GDP. If combined Central and State-level deficits are in excess of 10 per cent of GDP, not to speak of artificially high

24. World Bank and IFC (2004). *Doing Business in 2005: Obstacles to Growth*. New York: Oxford University Press.

guaranteed rates of return on small savings, there will be upward pressures on interest rates. Whichever index one uses to measure inflation, annual inflation is around 6 per cent now. With a PLR of 10.25 per cent, this means a real rate of interest of 4.25 per cent. In a capital scarce country, real interest rates will never be as low as global interest rates, although this is qualified by the harmonisation that has taken place between global and domestic interest rates. Some parts of the Indian corporate sector are now allowed to borrow globally, though not all. Why are real interest rates still so high? Other than deficits and small savings, one needs to highlight the interest spreads of banks. This masks inefficiencies in the banking system. But it also incorporates elements of priority-sector lending (at pre-determined interest rates) and significant non-performing assets (NPAs). On the latter, it is necessary to recognise that competition means free entry as well as exit. And there is a tendency to prevent exit, notwithstanding the Securitisation and Reconstruction of Financial Assets and Enforcement of Security Interest (SARFAESI) Act. This locks up capital in unproductive sectors and units. There are also special problems with exit in the SSI sector.

Beyond the cost of credit issue, there are problems with availability of capital, not just bank finance, but also through the stock market, and this includes venture capital. As a general proposition, too much capital flows to relatively larger units. There are collateral problems in the SSI sector. But there is also a mindset issue. Even if the risk premiums are not higher, and this need not always be the case, the administrative costs of delivering credit to the SSI sector will be higher. *Ipso facto*, interest rates will be higher, regardless of the euphoria about microfinance and micro credit. The argument that credit to the SSI sector will have to be at a few percentage points below PLR then seems to be counter-productive.

Infrastructure

Infrastructure means several different things and there can be no quarrel with the proposition that inadequate infrastructure renders Indian manufacturing uncompetitive. *Economic Survey 2004-05* lists power, telecom, posts, roads, ports (airports and seaports), civil aviation, railways, urban infrastructure and legal infrastructure as infrastructure. As a generalisation, the infrastructure area where there have been visible improvements is telecom, with roads perhaps following as a somewhat distant second. The contours of unbundling, user charges and regulatory agencies are known. The issue is simply one of getting infrastructure reforms implemented and some areas of physical infrastructure are State subjects. From the manufacturing perspective, perhaps the most important infrastructure areas are power, ports and railways, followed by roads. The issues are twofold. First, given scarce government resources, where are these best deployed? Second, again given scarce government resources, what is the scope for private sector involvement? The *Draft Approach Paper to the 11th Plan* states, "A major constraint in achieving faster growth in manufacturing that needs immediate attention, is the inadequacy of our physical infrastructure. Our roads, railways, ports, airports, communication and above all electric power supply, are not comparable to the standards prevalent in our competitor countries. This gap must be filled within the next 5-10 years if our enterprises are to compete effectively. In the increasingly open trading environment that we face today, our producers must compete aggressively not just to win export markets, but also to retain domestic markets against competition from imports. Indian industry recognises this and no longer expects to survive because of protection. But they do expect a level playing field in terms of quality infrastructure. Development of infrastructure must therefore be accorded high priority in the 11th Plan."

Labour Laws

Labour law reform is usually equated with Chapter V-B of the Industrial Disputes Act (IDA), but the issues are more complicated. Subject to the caveat that labour is on the concurrent list of the Constitution, there are 45 Central Acts and 16 associated rules that deal directly with labour. There are others that indirectly deal with labour, like *the Boilers Act (1923), the Collection of Statistics Act (1953), the Dangerous Machines (Regulations) Act (1983)* and the *Emigration Act (1983)*. There is thus an issue of unification and harmonisation, the lack of which contributes to the inspector *raj*. Consider also the time span of the legislation, from the *Fatal Accidents Act of 1855* to the *Public*

Liability Insurance Act of 1991. Over a period of time, concepts and definitions have changed. So has the case law, contributing to further confusion. For example, there is lack of unanimity about definitions of wages, workman, employee, factory, industry and child labour. Reforming labour law has many dimensions and issues like reducing State intervention in industrial relations are identified with an exit policy for labour and are therefore controversial. But unification and harmonisation is an issue on which there should be no lack of consensus.

From unification and harmonisation, we now move on to reductions in State intervention, in areas other than industrial relations. *The Factories Act* is a good example of unnecessary government stipulations, sometimes through resultant rules and this includes provisions on over-time. *The Shops and Establishments Act* of 1954 is yet another example. It is no one's case that welfare provisions should not exist. But are welfare provisions enacted in 1948 or 1954 still relevant? Assuming that they are, is the present government-mandated system with a regime of inspectors the best way to achieve the objective?[25] Each labour legislation has a separate inspector and visits of inspectors are not synchronised across all labour enactments. Barring *the Payment of Wages Act*, where a maximum period of three years is stipulated, no other labour statute prescribes a maximum period for which records and registers must be maintained. Compliance is thus impossible and visits of inspectors result in bribery and rent-seeking. This system is not distributionally neutral as it tends to hurt the small-scale sector much more than it hurts large-scale industry. That apart, returns under various labour laws are not standardised and inspectors insist on maintenance of manual records and registers. There can be a common format for computerisation of required records. There should be a single inspector for a given area. Some inspections for site and building and site plans or testing equipment can be farmed out to recognised private agencies. With the

25. A recent FICCI survey (*Inspector Raj and Administrative Reforms Required for Indian Manufacturing*) mentions an average of 37 annual inspections, with 67 inspections in some cases. In decreasing order of importance, these inspections concern the environment, labour, sales tax, excise, provident fund, electricity, ESI and industrial safety and health.

opening up of insurance, some social security provisions can be farmed out. For example, *the Employees' State Insurance (ESI) Act* hasn't worked at all well.

We now move on to industrial relations. The three statutes that impinge on industrial relations are *the Contract Labour (Regulation and Abolition) Act, the Trade Unions Act and the Industrial Disputes Act. The Contract Labour (Regulation and Abolition) Act* was never meant to prohibit contract labour. Section 10 provided the appropriate Government the discretion of prohibiting contract labour in selected areas. In fact, in the title of the act, regulation comes before abolition. Contract labour allows flexibility and permits outsourcing. However, a few court judgements have affected this flexibility. There is an argument doing the rounds that *the Contract Labour (Regulation and Abolition) Act* should be scrapped. This is probably facile. If the 1970 statute is scrapped, decisions on abolition of contract labour will revert from the government to industrial tribunals. To take *the Factories Act* as an example, industrial tribunals are likely to conclude that since canteens are mandated under Section 46 of *the Factories Act*, no contract labour can be employed in canteens. It seems to be a better idea to retain the 1970 act and tighten up Section 10 so that ambiguity about continuance of contract labour and absorption following abolition is removed.

Next one should mention *the Trade Unions Act*. As a minor point, child labour is not prohibited in India. It is only prohibited in hazardous processes. Yet, under Section 21 of *the Trade Unions Act*, those under fifteen are not allowed to be members of trade unions and under Section 21-A of *the Trade Unions Act*, those under eighteen are prevented from becoming office bearers. But more important are provisions of *the Trade Unions Act* that lead to multiplicity. Under Section 4 of *the Trade Unions Act*, any seven people can form and register a trade union and these seven people need not even be workers. There is no cap on office bearers being from outside either. Nor is there any test for representativeness of a trade union, through secret ballots or otherwise. The multiplicity problem impinges on collective bargaining because an agreement with one union is not necessarily binding on others. This is partly due to Section 18(1) of *the Industrial Disputes Act*, which states, "A settlement arrived at by agreement between the employer and workman otherwise than in the course of conciliation proceeding shall be binding on the parties to the agreement." It is not mandatory on others. Maharashtra and Gujarat are the only States where there are laws requiring recognition of trade unions by employers for purposes of collective bargaining. Following recommendations of the Second Labour Commission, the government has introduced amendments to *the Trade Unions Act*. The number of persons required for registration of a trade union will change from seven to 10 per cent of the labour force. Not more than one-third of office bearers (subject to a maximum of five) can be outsiders. And the holding of annual elections and auditing of accounts will be mandatory.

Next one moves on to *the Industrial Disputes Act (IDA)* and the following is a list of sections where there are problems—Section 9-A, Section 11, Section 11-A, Section 17-B, Sections 22/23 and Chapter V-B/Sections 25-K, 25-L, 25-M, 25-N and 25-0. The argument about Chapter V-B of IDA is indeed a valid one. Labour markets become artificially rigid, employers adopt artificially high capital intensity and circumvent the legislation. An employer-employee relationship ought to be in the nature of a personal contract, with an optional provision of resorting to the government in case of exploitation. However, the provisions of *the Industrial Disputes Act* make recourse to the government and thus to Labour Commissioners, mandatory. Given the other provisions of labour legislation, the requirement of governmental permission can be dispensed with, without adversely affecting the interests of labour. Unless this rigidity in labour markets is removed, higher growth will not necessarily translate into greater employment. What is involved is not primarily an exit policy for labour. The statute makes it impossible for companies to exit. Competition cannot function without free exit. Everyone who is against reforming labour markets criticises the government for trying to introduce hire and fire. Everyone who is in favour of reforming labour markets criticises the government for not introducing hire and fire. The recently published *Economic Freedom of the World 2004* is an example. Scores are out of 10 and the higher, the better. India gets an overall score of 6.3. But for flexibility in hiring and firing, the Indian score is 2.0.[26] The point is that this is probably largely perceptional rather than real. And more importantly, while a consensus on Chapter V-B is being rustled up, why not amend the other sections of IDA and implement the other labour law reforms? One should also mention the Second National Commission on Labour, which submitted a report in 2002, the first National Labour Commission having been set up in 1929. If implemented, these recommendations will harmonise labour laws under five heads of industrial relations, wages, social security, safety and welfare and working conditions. While flexibility will improve in the organised labour market, there will simultaneously be better social security provisions in the unorganised one. Implementation of the latter of course remains a problem.

Before concluding this section on labour, one must also mention development of skills, in the absence of which, the demographic dividend will also fail to materialise. No one denies that skill development is important. The issue is, who will deliver these skills? The public sector driven initiative, through *the Apprentices Act* and ITIs (Industrial Training Institutes) has failed to deliver. The 500 ITIs, promised in the 2004-05 budget, or other forms of vocational training, must be through public-private partnerships, if not outright private sector provisioning, with training authorities de-linked from certifying ones.

The Private Sector

The onus for everything mentioned above has implicitly been on the government. But that is only part of the answer. Access to technology, larger investments that drive exploitation of economies of scale and scope, accessing market information and so on are in the private domain, although there is often a tendency to expect the government to provide or subsidise these efforts. But given fiscal and other limitations, there are constraints on what the government can effectively do. And some services, like some areas of physical infrastructure (water treatment is an instance), marketing information or skills development, are not even global public goods. One is not

26. This is the Fraser Institute's economic freedom index, not the ones brought out by Freedom House or Heritage Foundation (in collaboration with Wall Street Journal).

even certain that they are local public goods. They are probably collective private goods. In other words, once policy-induced entry barriers are removed, it is up to the private sector to deliver these services collectively, with appropriate user charges imposed.

The revival of Indian manufacturing shows that Indian manufacturing companies can compete. It is a matter of getting the facilitating environment right, through the reforms that have been mentioned.

10

Returning Competition to the Factory Floor

Building Manufacturing Capabilities

PANKAJ CHANDRA

Introduction

Gains in Indian manufacturing in the last few years have been quite significant. Manufacturing growth has averaged around 7 per cent over the last several years (though the year-on-year growth in January 2007 was about 11 per cent) but the challenge before industry and government now is to ensure that the sector grows at about twice that rate so that its contribution to national GDP grows from about 19 per cent to at over 30 per cent. Globally, while China continues to lead the pack with its high volume production, Indian manufacturing may be ready to script one of the most interesting stories in global manufacturing through rationalisation of industrial policies and aggressive manufacturing strategies at the firm level.

The changing infrastructure in the country (albeit slowly) and the lowering of trade barriers is starting to give enterprises their due place in the economy. Their roles in the growth of the economy are quite well understood and their limitations in the country are well recognised. In this paper, we argue that what is missing from the policy and strategy discussions is an understanding of the activities of the shop floor. Competitiveness is built on the manufacturing shop floor and unless this shop floor becomes the focus of attention, policy efforts will be skirting the main issues. Whether it is the airport or a bus station or managing the Kumbha Mela or the operations of the *dabbawallas* or a large road building project or even a manufacturing plant, two key systemic issues define the productivity of an operating environment—the 'infrastructure' (which in turn defines the capacity of the system) and the 'operational system.' With liberalisation has come a strong argument towards building adequate capacities in the country—whether it is in power or roads or ports or the logistics system. The 'operational system,' however, has been ignored—perhaps, its role is less understood by the policy makers in the country. It is the 'operational system' that defines how well does an 'infrastructure' gets used and consequently the productivity of the operating environment. So the arrival and departure schedules or the sequencing of the boarding gates at the airport or the queuing of the buses or the route planning at Kumbha or the deployment of a road roller across different competing road stretches or reduction of setup times on machines in a plant constitute elements of the operational system. The more effective an operating system, the higher would be the value delivered by an infrastructure. The country is seeing an unprecedented investment in infrastructure capacity both within plants and outside. Policy discussion needs to incorporate an understanding of the accompanying operational system if this investment is to generate commensurate economic returns and not turn into a liability. It is this issue that we would like to focus on in this paper—how to bring the focus of manufacturing policy discussion back to issues that are relevant on the shop floor—the location where competitiveness is built.

The challenge before Indian manufacturing is twofold—develop capabilities for both large volume-low variety or mass manufacturing as well as low volume-high variety or flexible manufacturing (perhaps by different firms or by different plants within the same firm) and development and implementation of new technology to enhance productivity. The second issue first. The need is to, either, introduce new products through innovative process technology or improve on the cost, quality and delivery of existing products through improvements in product, process and practice technology. This requires investment in innovation on the shop floor by developing a strong technology driven view of the firm. The first issue concerning 'scale' is even simpler. For a manufacturing environment as diverse as in India, both large volume and low volume manufacturers will need to exist. Some in industry and the government believe that India should be producing high value add, low volume products thereby presenting a limited view of Indian abilities and reflecting a weak understanding of strategic policy making in manufacturing. Large volume operations are necessary to remain competitive in most growing sectors like semiconductors, electronics, textiles, auto-components etc. where firms compete on cost and the time required to recover investment is increasingly becoming short. And if, as a country, we desire to eradicate poverty through industrial development and by providing wide-spread employment opportunities then growth in these and many such sectors will be crucial. The reason why this distinction on scale is necessary at the policy level is because large volume-low variety and low volume-high variety manufacturing require different capabilities, different technologies, different managerial practices and different parameters of competition. Any possible policy intervention will require a clear understanding of these differences before its execution can be made effective.

Challenge and Promise of Large Volume Operations

In this section we will present the rationale for promoting large volume operations in India and present a few illustrations on how such an operation can be configured and the benefits that it can provide. First the promise—large volume operations have the potential of deploying scale that will address the employment question favourably while creating a supply chain that will help integrate emerging technology with low cost manpower in India. The economics of large volume or mass production is based on a very high utilisation of capacity and resources as opposed to a low volume-high variety production environment where capacity utilisation needs to be kept lower in order to provide the flexibility to meet the requirement of variety and variability in orders. When interest rates are high (as is the situation in India), manufacturers benefit by turning their working capital quickly. Mass manufacturing facilitates this practice. Moreover, a cost based advantage through large volumes provides a high quality producer (and manufacturing quality does indeed comes 'free') a significant advantage in global markets especially when every country is trying to pitch their hat in the global market. Process innovations (where Indians have developed some useful abilities) and incremental improvements on shop floors help maintain cost, quality and lead time advantages in this environment. The challenge is to provide policy support to run large volume operations seamlessly, to prompt adoption of a strategy based on systems and methods, to help develop precision skills that are useful in repetitive operations, and to facilitate deployment of dedicated technology at short lead times. This challenge in India today is by no means trivial. Nevertheless, such shop floors do exist in India and need to grow even more.

Nokia's new factory in Sriperumbudur produces, at a single location, more than 1 million mobile handsets each month and deploys 1200 operators for this production. Achieving production of this size has required deployment of very specialised automated equipment, transport of raw material including semiconductor devices from various parts of the world, development of assembly and testing skills in people to perform repetitive tasks at high precision, and development of managerial systems that deliver productivity and quality in this high throughput environment. It might be appreciated that such a manufacturing environment requires regular and stable power supply (the penalty for unstable power is quite high), availability of skilled workforce, technology upgradation at frequent intervals and facilities to move material rapidly across boundaries. As the volume of production grows, so will the extent of movement of goods either to the ports for export or to the rest of the country. Changes in logistics infrastructure have to accompany this growth in manufacturing. The impact is far reaching—the logistics providers of Nokia are already acquiring other smaller players in the Nokia supply chain to make this movement seamless for the manufacturer. Similar to the growth of mobile phones, the growth of wall clocks in India is no less spectacular. Ajanta Clocks' factory in Morbi in Gujarat produces 25,000 units of quartz clocks and time pieces at a single location each day (with a peak production record of 40,000 pieces per day). It employs 5000 operators in the factory. A few years ago, in the face of very stiff competition from Chinese products in India, Ajanta set up a plant in China. It allowed them to learn about large volume operations and how to manage a tight supply chain as firms operate on wafer thin margins in these operations. It has helped Ajanta become the largest clock manufacturer in the world.

While the above examples illustrate the success of scale at a single plant, there are other models of achieving large volumes. We present here two distinctive models in that direction—AMUL in India and DAISO in Japan. AMUL, the famous dairy network in Gujarat has established a large scale network of milk and milk products production and distribution based on the foundation of a large number of small cooperative enterprises. The AMUL network comprises three independent organisational layers—the marketing federation (i.e., GCMMF), 12 unions or production plants (including the one in Anand called AMUL Dairy), and about 12000 Village Societies (or milk collection centres) comprising 2.5 million milk farmers. Daily milk collection in the network is about 6.3 million litres per day and the sales turnover of GCMMF was Rs 3776 crores (2005-2006). The scale in this network is made up of small volume contributions from a large number of farmers and village societies. DAISO is one of the largest 100 Yen retail stores in Japan. It sells products like wicker baskets, candle stands, wrapping paper, curios, cutlery, stationery, spectacles, food items, cosmetics, books, CDs etc—each priced at 100 Yen. Non-Daiso stores sell these products at a price higher than 100 Yen. DAISO has 2400 retail stores and is opening about 30 stores each month. It has 380 stores outside Japan. Its sales turnover was US$ 3bn in 2006 and was the 10th fastest growing company in global retail. Variety is crucial for DAISO (about 70,000 items per outlet) hence turning the stock daily is most important. The issue here is one of global procurement and achieving a scale in purchase such that with quantity discounts a more expensive product starts to cost less than 100 Yen! It is also obvious that such volume cannot be sold in a single neighbourhood store, hence the need to establish a large number of stores. Such a large volume operation requires distribution effectiveness and reach to match high sales efficiency.

Large volume operations have already taken roots in India. The only question is whether we are going to execute it efficiently. One key challenge of large volume operations is whether it will receive the necessary policy attention that will facilitate production, transportation and distribution of a large volume of goods. Some of the issues like physical infrastructure, credit at favourable interest rates, taxes (i.e., high throughput and quick turnaround manufacturing cannot afford to have tax refunds tied up for long periods as it happens now; while working with tiny margins, the timing of fund flow is extremely crucial) IT requirements to track flows etc. are well understood. However, the role of some other manufacturing related parameters are less well understood especially in terms of implications of policy on these issues. In the next section, we discuss some of these other parameters and argue for a change in the frame through which policy looks at promoting Indian manufacturing especially in the context of large volume operations.

Changing the Frame

There is a need to change the frame through which manufacturing policy is looked at in India in order to build capabilities in plants and operations. Five key issues need to be understood and addressed in this respect. These are: lead time, skills, scale, strategy and tools of production. This section draws from Chandra (2007); Chandra and Sastry (1998, 2004).

Lead Time

Most operational costs can be subsumed in the measure of lead time. It's the amount of time taken to deliver a good to a customer (internal or external). Lead times are directly related to many parameters of competition, e.g., quality (poor quality leads to higher rejects or rework or work stoppages thereby leading to higher lead times), working capital deployed (higher inventory or poor product mix leads to higher lead times) etc. By focusing on lead times, firms are able to control many other parameters that affect productivity. Short lead times ensure reduced turn around time for project implementation, faster turnaround of capital, and resources (including power, credit, technology, etc.) are tied up for a shorter period of time. All of these enhance the productivity of the operating environment. For example, a slow unloading of baggage (due to poor operational planning and poor scheduling of accompanying resources) from an airplane leads to under utilisation of bottleneck resources like baggage conveyor (especially at peak hours) and unloading crew (leading to wastage of resources), delays passengers. It leads to customer dissatisfaction and opportunity loss for them. In addition, it might delay other flights that might be next in the queue to use the same unloading conveyor, and may delay the departure of these waiting flights which in turn may trigger similar losses at other networked airports. Penalties due to long lead times are very high in today's competitive environment. It can range from loss of customers to bankruptcies.

Table 10.1 exhibits the story of a mid-size textile supply chain based on primary data collected from a small sample of firms in India. It may be noted that these are average figures and are representative of only the sampled firms and not of the entire sector. The data in the table explain why lead time is very crucial in defining the competitiveness of firms. The first column gives a list of processes representing a textile and apparel supply chain. The second column gives the processing time in days for converting a batch of raw material. For instance, if a given batch of cotton is processed in a ginning plant, it will take 12 days (assuming that the machines are available as this batch arrives). Similarly, if the same batch of ginned cotton is converted into yarn, the processing time will be 8 days. If this same batch of yarn is woven, then the processing time alone is 23 days; the same quantum of woven cloth gets processed in 11 days while the same batch of processed cloth will need at least 15 days to convert it into garments. On the other hand, the last column of the table gives the delivery lead times in days—it is the average amount of time that the batch actually takes in the sampled supply chain. So, the batch sent for ginning actually takes about 25 days when it should be taking only 12 days. The difference of 13 days is the amount of time that the batch spends waiting. Waiting on the shop floor could be for a variety of reasons—waiting due to poor scheduling, waiting for machines to get operational from breakdown, waiting due to non-availability of manpower, waiting for non-availability of utilities like power, steam, water etc., waiting for missing tools, waiting for rework to get completed, waiting due to non-availability of auxiliary raw material, waiting due to non-availability of inspectors etc. One can appreciate that congestion on highways or delays at customs or late running of goods train, all have the net effect of increased waiting, increased lead times and under-utilisation of resources. It may be seen that in the case presented above, the average total lead time of an order to be delivered overseas (i.e., sum of the lead times in the last column) is more than the fashion season (i.e, the fashion season is about four months when the delivery lead time is more than six months). It is obvious that this supply chain will not be able to serve its customer and will lose the customer for sure. Long lead times make Indian supply chains less competitive.

Table 10.1

An Illustrative Textile Supply Chain

Process	*Manufacturing Cycle T ime (in days)*	*Delivery Lead Time (in days)*
Ginning and Pressing	12	25
Spinning	8	38
Weaving	23	40
Processing	11	21
Garmenting	15	49
Customs	–	10
Transport (Overseas)	–	35

The following anecdotal evidence of the new drivers of manufacturing competitiveness is illustrative. Flextronics, one of the world's largest electronics component producer, was in discussion with Malaysian customs officials to see how they could further reduce a consignment clearance time at customs from 30 minutes to 15 minutes. The same in Sri Lanka for its textile products is half a day while that in India can take anywhere from 3 days to 3 weeks. Semiconductor manufacturers ship out their production batches within 24 hours of production to various locations globally in order to feed the consumer and industrial electronics plants all over the world, just-in-time. The need is to reduce cycle times and production and service delivery times significantly 'everywhere' in the supply chain else we as a country will never be able to get into high value added manufacturing like electronics. Incidentally, most of the countries in SE Asia like Taiwan, Korea, China, Malaysia, Singapore, Thailand etc. have moved into industrial development through a strong electronics sector!

Skills

Chandra (2007) has argued that skilled manpower is the operating bottleneck that stands between Indian manufacturing and its aspiration to become a dominant competitor globally. Lets take the textile and apparel sector. The government and the industry have set an export target of US$50bn by the year 2010. Based on current investments in plant and equipment, it is projected that Indian textile and apparel industry will invest at least Rs 1400 bn by the year 2010. The manpower requirement to run these additional plants and equipments is illustrative of the skills crisis facing the sector—the Textile sector will require about 70,000 supervisors and 1.05 mn operators while the Apparel sector will need to hire about 112,000 supervisors and 2.8 mn operators. The total skilled manpower being trained in these sectors annually does not exceed 3000, of which there is a large exodus of trained engineers to the IT sector. It may be noted that most apparel training courses are of duration between 6-9 months; consequently, the skills imparted are quite limited. This is not to mention the lack of auxiliary service skills required in these new plants or old plants with new equipment like mechanical, electrical, instrumentation, chemical, design, etc.

Skill formation in India poses a very peculiar dilemma. While the country has one of the highest percentage of 18-28 year old young men and women, their unemployment rates are high and all of this while the industry is suffocating due to non-availability of skilled manpower. Government policy has created a foundation of vocational education which is weak technically (due to non-availability of quality technical instructors), is bureaucratic as it is run by government departments, has outdated equipment as it does not have resources to upgrade the equipment, and imparts skills that are not much in demand. There are three other features of this regime that need mention. One, the number of trainees admitted to these programmes are so small that they are merely a drop in this ocean of requirement. Two, Indian bureaucrats have created rule bound systems in these institutions that only require clerks to run them and not thinking individuals with higher learning (this is true in almost all institutions of higher education in India as well). Institutions flourish when those within understand the need of the society and their students and then use their discretion to craft unique strategies for their stakeholders and they do this continuously. As a result, most of these institutions are pools of mediocrity and bureaucracy and rarely do they inspire a young trainee to excel. They also do not attract brighter students. As a result, most of these institutions force young minds into becoming non-creative, non-curious members of the work force. Three, the industry faces the music both ways—it is dammed if it hires these poorly skilled people and it is damned if it does not. Yet, it consistently refuses to participate seriously in the training of their young apprentices. Many see their job as one of producing goods and not of training the workforce. But the opposite is exactly what good firms all over the world do whether it's the fabled *Berufsschulen* (the two or three year vocational education) or the *Berufsfachschulen* (the intermediate technical schools) in Germany that educate more than 2 mn students each year or the technical education programmes of firms like Toyota or the Vocational Training Schools run by apparel firms in Sri Lanka. The Sri Lankan example is instructive. The apparel firms faced acute shortage of trained manpower in rural areas where they were located. Many of them established training schools to prepare industrial workers for their own apparel factories. Soon the enrollment grew and these schools became stand-alone operations from where other firms in the region also started to source their manpower requirements. Among other factors, this has been a key contributor to the growth of large volume production of apparel in Sri Lanka as skilled workers are crucial to execute the volume strategy.

Scale

The issue of scale of manufacturing operation is very central in assigning a role to manufacturing either as a key contributor to the growth of the Indian economy or one with missed opportunity. A comparison with China is in order here. Lets start with one of the key industrial sectors in India—the textile and apparel sector. Except for spinning, all other sub-sectors suffer from the problem of scale. Indian firms are typically smaller than their Chinese or Thai counterparts and there are fewer large firms in India. Some of the Chinese large firms have 1.5 times higher spinning capacity, 1.25 times denim (and 2 times gray fabric) capacity and about 6 times more revenue in garment than their counterparts in India thereby affecting the cost structure as well as ability to attract customers with large orders. Indian firms tend to add capacity once the order has been won rather than ahead of the demand (perhaps because they do not understand global scale trends or they are more risk averse or the credit is so expensive in India that it dissuades addition of capacity). Customers go where they see both capacity and capabilities. The Chinese manufacturing strategy is to have capacity lead demand. Hakkai Creates, an SME from Niigata in Japan, is the world's leading manufacturer of hinges for mobile phones as well as a producer of precision moulds for making plastic parts. When its key customer, SONY, moved its play station manufacturing to China, it asked Hakkai to move its manufacturing as well if it was to retain its status as supplier to SONY. The dilemma before this SME was what would happen if it sets up a new plant in China, the play station does not succeed and they have to close the plant—would they be able to manage this transition? Instead of setting up a plant in China, Hakkai found a ready made plant with most of the equipment in place and a manpower contractor willing to provide ready to use operators. It took Hakkai less than three months to start production in China in this plant. Sure enough, a year or so down the road the play station performed poorly and SONY decided to stop its production in China. Hakkai was able to wind up its manufacturing and move it to Thailand in a short span of time. In the meanwhile, the company that had rented the plant to Hakkai did precious business out of its spare capacity.

Scale needs to be understood as the supply chain scale and not always as a single plant's scale (Chandra, 2006). There is perhaps a need to think through new organisational forms that networks SMEs to deliver scale. The Technology Advanced Metropolitan Area or TAMA is a cluster of small firms that are located in the adjoining areas of Saitama, Tokyo and Kanagawa prefectures in Japan. The key agency that coordinates the activities of these firms is the TAMA Association which was set up by MITI in 1996. TAMA firms (i.e., those located in this cluster) employ 4 million workers and shipped goods worth US$ 214 bn in 1998 which was twice the shipment value of all the firms in the Silicon Valley. The total value added per worker was US$116,447 for TAMA firms as compared to US$110,184 for all Japanese firms and US$94,970 for all US firms. On many counts, TAMA firms are found to outperform other Japanese firms. The key to this performance lies in the structure of TAMA—it comprises about 300 'product developing' SMEs (firms that produce/assemble an end product), about 16000 'product processing' SMEs (firms that perform specialised process for the product developing SMEs and innovate on their processes, e.g., cold drawing, to deliver an advantage to product developing firms), about 15 R&D units of large enterprises, and about 34 Universities and Colleges with science, engineering, and management departments (that provide the manpower and perform specialised R&D and testing for these firms). All of the firms are R&D oriented and the TAMA Association coordinates the entire network. This is an example of how by creating linkages between firms, networks can achieve a scale of a large firm even when all or most members of the network are themselves small. We have found two other networks that have a similar structure—the Wenzhou network in the Zhejiang province of China whose success is linked to creating markets for components as opposed to finished goods alone and where the local municipalities have followed the policy of 'one village, one product' to achieve scale in output from a village (consisting of a large number of tiny enterprises), and focusing of specialised inputs; the other example is the Rajkot cluster (which can be referred to as 'God's own engineering land') where a large number of product processing SMEs operate in a highly outsourced environment with several local coordinators. Few firms, however, are innovating on the processes (partly due to non availability of technical manpower).

There is also the need for emergence of specialist firms that will consolidate orders, book capacities, manage warehouses and logistics of order delivery especially in network operations.

Strategy

Large capacity typically goes with standardised products. For the size of the Indian economy, it will have to have bigger firms producing standard products in large volumes as well as small and mid size firms producing large variety in small to mid size batches. Managerial strategy for large volume operations is distinctively different from low volume operations. The low volume, high variety strategy requires better design skills, ability to bid accurately, and a focus on flexible capacity to manage the inherent variability in business. Large volume operations, on the other hand, require focused managerial skills of coordinating high throughput lines with a quick delivery pass through of products. Is it possible that Indian managers have perhaps not developed the managerial strategy required to create focused factories with disciplined workers to run high throughput lines?

The role of the domestic market in creating scale needs to be explored as well. It is when the domestic market is used to complement the manufacturing demand of external markets, that volume grows. Unless domestic markets become integrated with international markets, the scale advantages to Indian manufacturers will not only elude them but will also provide opportunity to producers outside India to win over the large domestic market.

One more element of strategy that needs to be looked into relates to linkages between small and large firms to create both economies of scale and scope—small firms focusing on technology development and large firms performing product assembly and establishing focused factories. The former are quite adept and flexible in playing that role. Globally, SMEs are very hi-tech and there is no restriction on the nature and extent of deployment of technology in their plants. This allows them to innovate and develop new products and processes. Unfortunately, in India small firms are forced to remain low tech as they lose many tax and other benefits once their investment in plant and equipment rises beyond Rs three crores—an amount which is very restrictive when it comes to technology investments.

Tools of Production

Tools of production in Indian manufacturing are often very outdated and inept for precision tasks. Many a times shop floors do not have appropriate tools to perform their task thereby affecting the quality and productivity on the shop floor. For example, most small producers in the machine shops of Taiwan operate CNC machines while those in India will use *addas* or manual lathes that require enormous operator effort, have short life and are not capable of producing precision products. This prevents the small producers from playing up their strengths of a low volume, high variety, value producer. Similarly, use of a pneumatic wrench controls the torque better and renders an application (e.g., wheel fitting in an automotive vehicle) more safe and conforming to precise specifications. Use of manual wrench, in this case, could lead to inappropriate application of torque which may lead to unsafe usage of a machine and decreases operator productivity. In the long run, this increases the cost of operations. Mass manufacturing is about high first pass yields, low wastage, high process quality, low breakdowns and quick repairs, pull production and just-in-time material delivery—inappropriate tools will adversely affect all of these and make mass production more elusive for Indian manufacturing.

New Policy Imperatives

The policy debate on manufacturing must refocus to include the above mentioned issues. It can be clearly seen that an agenda to build competitiveness must include issues other than just infrastructure or taxation or credit. In this section we draw policy implications of the above discussion.

Broadly, there are five areas that need policy attention. First, increasing operational productivity must become the most crucial objective of any policy intervention. Emphasis must move away from tax based benefits to supporting enhancement of productivity in firms. Tax holidays, free power, free water etc. are inefficient methods of encouraging firms to set up enterprise in a region. Many States in the country have been chasing this weak methodology. More than a decade ago, Silvassa provided many such benefits and saw the establishment of a flourishing industrial base. Then came Baddi in Himachal Pradesh and firms started to move. In the second round of this geographical tournament, new locations emerged—Jammu in J&K and now Dehradun in Uttarakhand—both providing tax holidays—and firms have started to move from these other locations to the new favourites. Silvassa is fast becoming a ghost town. In the current framework, how long will firms stay in Uttarakhand is dependent on what subsidies do other States provide and not on any long term capability that a firm develops. Governments should realise that today its very easy to move plant and equipment from one location to another. Such policies also lead to adverse selection of entrepreneurs. What retains firms is an environment that helps them build sustainable capabilities. Institutions that provide highly skilled manpower, good highways and management of borders that will reduce stoppages on the way, quick turnaround time at ports and short waiting times, no stoppage of work by inspectors, easy and cheap credit for investment in productivity enhancing technology etc. will go long ways in retaining good firms and will encourage them to invest in plant and equipment. Similarly, higher productivity must be rewarded. One of the conditions, for instance, for receiving the Technology Upgradation Fund (offered by the Ministry of Textiles) must be a verifiable commitment to enhancement of productivity, achieving tough quality targets etc.

Second, it must recognise that firms build capabilities and it can facilitate this process. Research shows that large volume operations will require investments in modern tools of production, higher inter-firm linkages and support for establishing high throughput manufacturing lines. Government policy, all over the world, has provided incentives to promote certain technologies—CNG based public transport technologies in Delhi and Ahmedabad are good examples. The fabled role of MITI in helping Japanese firms develop technologies that were superior to those coming from the US and Europe in several sectors in a focused manner has been very well documented. The Bureau of Industrial Standards must play an active role of informing Indian industry of new standards in the tools of production. And industry associations must move away from their lobbying role to a role where they are disseminating information on technology and tools of production as this helps firms build long-term capabilities.

Expensive credit has been a bane of technological investment in Indian manufacturing. The worst affected are the SMEs who have to borrow at the rate of 14.0-14.5 per cent making their production costs very high. Government policy will have to appreciate the impact of its action on various constituents of the manufacturing community. But there is something that manufacturers can also do. Small producers must come together to form a large consortium firm that in turn can borrow competitively on the markets and seek overseas investments. Small firms in the same sector have a higher likelihood of creating a large marketing company with a common umbrella brand that can make technology and capacity related investments in the smaller member firms. Small firms retain their flexibility while their joint firm overcomes the market failures that they face in credit, marketing, technology and capability building. Details on this strategy are described in Chandra (2006).

Third, policy needs to urgently focus on the quality and quantity of technical manpower available in India. Vocational education that is removed from a close interaction with the user industry will wilt in the long run. It also requires a strong involvement of industry and the sooner it realises it, the better will become the state of availability of manpower. There is a need to create large capacities for training including on-line self study facilities and certification mechanisms. Perhaps, a fraction of the education cess that the government collects from each organisation could go into an escrow fund that can be withdrawn for funding training of operators at these vocational training institutions or even within the firms. Vocational education policy has to be implemented in a partnership mode and neither the government nor the industry can shy away from their joint responsibility. Real wages of technically trained workforce in production and R&D has to increase in order to attract better people to the manufacturing sector. In addition, vocational education programmes have to provide opportunity for upward mobility via evening classes and rigorous certification examinations so that a young person joining as an operator can also aspire to become an engineer with appropriate effort.

Fourth, new organisational forms can provide scale and they need to be supported. Here the role of small enterprises needs to be re-thought. Small enterprises are better suited to perform flexible, technology driven, high variety-low volume operations. However, due to market uncertainties, they desire to become ancillary units of large assemblers with adverse economics *vis-à-vis* a large competitor. Over time, they lose their technological edge and versatility and rarely survive technological or product changes in customer firms. Young technical entrepreneurs need to be supported through a government programme to set up R&D based and R&D driven niche firms. Most small firms should be encouraged to become 'product processing' firms as opposed to becoming 'product producing' firms. It is here that small firms are most innovative and any investment in such firms will yield satisfactory returns. Producing products (as opposed to processing products) and selling in the market requires diversified resources and product marketing infrastructure which most small firms do not have.

Policies that facilitate outsourcing or joint order completion will go long ways in tying up small manufacturers together to build scale. Cluster related programmes must be stepped up. Strategies like 'one village, one product' in China and now being widely implemented in Thailand are good models for building scale through integration of a large number of small producers. They also facilitate funneling of resources to build capabilities in a focused manner and lead to ease of logistics in the movement of goods. This is an ideal strategy to convert rural areas into production centers. If today goods flow from New Delhi to New York due to cheap manufacturing at the former then why should goods not flow from New Delhi to New Bongaigaon? Should it not be the reverse?

And fifth, in order for Indian firms to become part of the global supply chain, we will need to attract world class producers of goods and machinery to set up manufacturing and R&D facilities in India. India suffers from low FDI in manufacturing especially by world-class producers. It is necessary for these firms to operate from India for the rest of the eco-system to learn about world class technology and managerial practices. Globally, some of the best producers are the industrial goods manufacturers and not necessarily the consumer goods producers (of which we have a surfeit in India). Industrial policy makers must selectively invite, with accompanying support, such world-class producers to set up manufacturing facilities in India. It will also have the effect of enhancing the value of 'made in India.' Same for machinery manufacturing and R&D firms. India needs better quality tools of production. If 'Juki' had a world class manufacturing facility in Bangalore then the garment firms there and in India can rest assured of the availability of the latest technology at the earliest. In addition they could also modify machines to suit the needs of local firms. These are sources of competitive advantage that Indian firms are deprived of. Industry associations and the government must create a permanent exhibition of machinery across sectors where global firms may exhibit their latest technology. Cheap equipment and process R&D are essential for establishment of a wide spread large scale production environment in India. And this requires policy support for the machinery sector in India.

Unless the policy debate becomes more informed of the economics, technology and management of manufacturing, it will continue to be hijacked by demagogues and soothsayers whose prescriptions are too self-serving or broad, or magical to come true. Manufacturing capabilities are built by assiduously working towards making shop floors more responsive to customer requirements. Its time that policy makers and policy commentators understood this reality and took note of its implications. Only then will their actions help Indian manufacturing to become competitive and grow.

References

Chandra, P. (2006). "Networks of Small Producers for Technological Innovations: Some Models", *Working Paper* No. 2006-03-02. Ahmedabad: IIM.

———. (2007). "The Textile and Apparel Industry", in Kaushik Basu (ed.) *The Oxford Companion to Economics in India*. New Delhi: Oxford University Press. pp.525-529.

Chandra, P. and T. Sastry (1998). "Competitiveness of Indian Manufacturing: Findings of the 1997 Manufacturing Futures Survey", *Vikalpa*, Vol. 23(3): 25-36.

———. (2004). "Competitiveness of Indian Manufacturing: Findings of the 2001 National Manufacturing Survey", *Technology, Operations and Management* (Forthcoming).

11

Convertibility Now? No, Thanks

VIJAY JOSHI

Should India's external payments regime be dismantled? In particular, should the rupee be made fully convertible? This burning issue of contemporary Indian economic debate is addressed below. The paper begins with some relevant theory. It then proceeds to examine in broad terms the performance of India's existing payments regime after its installation in 1993, followed by an analysis of possible future regimes. I argue that the ability to separate monetary and exchange rate policy, which the present regime provides, is an important policy freedom that it would be unwise to surrender at this stage in the country's development. The conclusion of the paper is that the present regime should be retained in its essentials for a near-term horizon of, say, five years or somewhat longer.

Terminology and Concepts

The economics of exchange rate arrangements is a minefield of confusion and ambiguity. I begin, therefore, by defining some terms and concepts.

In this paper the term 'exchange rate' is used to denote the 'nominal' exchange rate. When I want to refer to the 'real' exchange rate I do so explicitly. I use the term 'fixed' exchange rate to mean an exchange rate that is 'irrevocably' fixed, i.e. a super-hard peg such as a currency board. By an 'intermediate' exchange rate, I mean any arrangement, other than a fixed exchange rate, in which the authorities have an exchange rate target. The target does not have to be fixed or explicit. It could be informal, unannounced or moveable. Thus the 'intermediate' category covers not only the whole gamut of adjustable pegs, exchange rate bands and target zones, crawling pegs and crawling bands but also 'managed floating', if the float is tightly managed to attain an informal target level, band or path of the exchange rate. An exchange rate is 'floating' if the authorities do not pursue an exchange rate target, formal or informal. This obviously includes a clean float. It also includes 'managed floating' if the 'management' does not involve an attempt to target the exchange rate, formally or informally (e.g. if it is purely of a 'leaning against the wind' variety). The exchange rate and capital control arrangements, taken together, constitute the 'external payments regime' or simply the 'payments regime'. Note finally that I use the terms 'capital account convertibility' and 'convertibility' interchangeably.[1]

The Impossible Trinity

In any open economy, policymakers are confronted with a trilemma, sometimes referred to as the Impossible Trinity, to which they must perforce respond. The standard formulation of the Impossible Trinity says that it is impossible to achieve the following three desirable goals simultaneously: exchange rate stability, capital market integration and monetary autonomy. Any pair of the above goals can be achieved by choosing a suitable external payments regime but requires abandoning the third goal. Specifically:

(i) Exchange rate stability and capital market integration can be combined by adopting a fixed exchange rate but requires giving up monetary autonomy. The authorities lose the power to vary the home interest rate independently of the foreign interest rate.

(ii) Monetary autonomy and capital market integration can be combined by floating the exchange rate but requires giving up exchange rate stability. The authorities have freedom to choose the home interest rate but they must in consequence accept any level of exchange rate that the market dictates.

(iii) Exchange rate stability can be combined with monetary autonomy but requires giving up capital market integration. In the presence of capital controls, the interest rate-exchange rate link is broken.

---

1. Current account convertibility is not at issue. India adopted it in 1994.

Two arguments could be advanced to show that the Impossible Trinity does not, in practice, impose a stringent constraint. Firstly, it is a theorem only if capital market integration is understood to mean perfect capital mobility. Capital account convertibility (hereafter CAC), meaning absence of 'policy' barriers to capital flows, is consistent with imperfect capital mobility because there can be 'natural' barriers to mobility, for example due to risk, that make domestic and foreign assets imperfect substitutes. This creates some scope for sterilised intervention, which enables policymakers to decouple monetary and exchange rate policy, even if the latter consits of a fixed or targeted exchange rate. But sterilised intervention can be costly. Moreover, even high (though less than perfect) capital mobility can result in capital flows that are large enough to make sterilised intervention very difficult if not impossible.[2]

Secondly, it could be argued that, strictly speaking, the Impossible Trinity has nothing to say about intermediate arrangements between fixed and floating exchange rates. Why should a country not enjoy 'partial' exchange rate stability and 'partial' monetary autonomy, consistently with CAC? But such a compromise would only be feasible in a less developed country that is not closely connected to the world capital market and consequently is insulated from capital flows. This is manifestly not the case in 'emerging markets', of which India is one. If such a country were to operate an intermediate exchange rate arrangement with CAC, it would run up against a difficult choice. Which policy should rule the roost: exchange rate policy or monetary policy? If it targeted a particular level or path of the interest rate, say for stabilisation purposes, it would have to let the exchange rate go. If it targeted a particular level or path of the exchange rate, say to maintain trade competitiveness, it would lose control of interest rate policy, because money supply changes induced by capital flows would be too large to be feasibly offset by sterilisation.

In sum, the Impossible Trinity, appropriately interpreted, does set a constraint that policymakers must respect. Exchange rate targeting, monetary autonomy and CAC constitute a triad that is, for all practical purposes, impossible to achieve in combination.

---

2. Note that China and India, which have employed the sterilisation technique on a large scale, have both had capital controls. 'Impossible' should be understood to mean technically unfeasible and/or unduly expensive.

India's External Payments Regime 1993-2006[3]

A convenient starting point for an analytical review of India's external payments regime is March 1993 when, as part of the economic reform process, the government inaugurated what was officially called a 'market determined exchange rate.' This appellation is a misnomer. The rupee exchange rate is not 'market determined' in the sense of a clean float. It is heavily managed so as to keep the real effective exchange rate fairly stable, until now in an informal band of about +/– 5 per cent around the 1993-94 level (see Table 11.1). India's external payments regime in fact consists of an intermediate exchange rate arrangement buttressed by capital controls.[4]

Table 11.1

India: Nominal and Real Exchange Rate

(Base: 2004/5=100)

	Re/$	*NEER*	*REER*
1993-94	31.4	144.4	98.6
1994-95	31.4	138.9	104.3
1995-96	33.5	127.7	99.8
1996-97	35.5	125.2	99.6
1997-98	37.2	126.8	102.9
1998-99	42.1	111.7	94.7
1999-00	43.3	111.2	96.2
2000-01	45.7	111.6	101.3
2001-02	45.7	109.6	101.2
2002-03	48.4	102.7	96.1
2003-04	46.0	100.7	97.5
2004-05	44.9	100.0	100.0
2005-06	44.3	103.1	105.2
2006-07 (Qtr 1)	46.3	98.9	101.2

Note: Re/$ = Bilateral exchange rate, Rupees per U.S. Dollar;
NEER = Nominal effective exchange rate;
REER = Real effective exchange rate.

Source: *Reserve Bank of India Bulletin*.

3. For a more comprehensive analysis, see Joshi (2003) and Joshi and Sanyal (2004).
4. India's intermediate arrangement does not take the form of a formal target or band. It could be described as a 'discretionary crawl' or a 'tightly managed float'.

The rationale of such a regime follows straightforwardly from the discussion in the preceding section: it enables policymakers to deploy monetary policy and exchange rate policy as 'separate' instruments to achieve internal and external balance. Capital controls are an essential component of the regime. Without them, the separation could not be sustained.

India's capital controls are not comprehensive. They are fairly light for foreign direct and portfolio equity investment but very restrictive for debt-creating inflows, particularly of the short-term variety. All permitted inflows are freely repatriable. Capital outflows by residents are in general tightly controlled. A crucial aspect of the system is controls on banks. This is important because bank borrowing has been strongly associated with crises. Banks' foreign asset and liability positions are monitored and subject to set limits. Offshore trading of the rupee is not permitted (though a thin offshore market does exist). There are restrictions on domestic currency lending to non-residents, so opportunities for short-selling the currency are very circumscribed. The swap and forward markets are also controlled since these markets could be used to speculate against the rupee by circumventing the restrictions on short-selling. Thus, the overall policy thrust has been to limit forward trading to hedging current account transactions. Of course, there is a price to pay: the forward market lacks adequate liquidity and depth.

The above paragraph is an accurate summary description of India's capital controls from 1993-1999. In the current decade, the controls have been moderately liberalised (see below), but without any radical change in the system.

Regime Performance in the 1990s

India's external payments regime performed well in the 1990s and enabled the country to manage a capital-inflow surge from 1993-1995, avoid contagion from the East Asian and other currency crises, and offset an industrial slowdown towards the end of the decade.[5] These

5. Lal, Bery and Pant (2003) argued that the Indian exchange rate policy in the 1990s was seriously defective and resulted in excessive reserve accumulation, which reduced growth by up to 2.7 per cent per year. Their conclusion was based on the fallacious and preposterous argument that absorbing $x million of reserves could have increased domestic investment by a multiple of $x million. See Joshi and Sanyal (2004) and Joshi (2006).

disturbances were handled by a mixture of monetary policy (including sterilised and unsterilised intervention) and moderate exchange rate changes, a tightrope walk that would not have been possible without the shelter of capital controls.

A comparison of India and the East Asian countries in 1996 (i.e. just before the East-Asian crisis of 1997) is highly instructive and indicates why India escaped crisis and contagion during that crisis. It is clear that in most respects, India's 'fundamentals' (fiscal balance, inflation, current account balance, non-performing assets, debt-exports ratio and debt-service ratio) were worse or no better than in the crisis-countries.[6] Exchange rate policy too was not a distinguishing feature. All these countries had an intermediate exchange rate though the precise mechanism—band, crawl or crawling band—varied. India's exchange rate was no more volatile than the exchange rates of the crisis-countries, so the incentive for unhedged borrowing too was very similar.[7] The critical difference between India and the crisis countries is that India managed to keep short-term debt under control, in relation to total debt and foreign exchange reserves. Thus, India avoided the crisis by avoiding an unstable debt structure—an outcome that was the direct result of controls on debt-creating short-term inflows or 'hot money'.

Regime Performance 2000-2006

The current decade has been characterised by a dramatic improvement in the balance of payments. This led to substantial reserve accumulation since the Reserve Bank intervened in the foreign exchange market to buy dollars. The stock of reserves rose from $38 billion in March 2000 to $151 billion in March 2006 (Table 11.2).

Table 11.3 throws light on the sources of balance of payments strength, though the point-to-point comparison masks some fluctuations. The largest contribution to reserve accumulation has come from invisibles, particularly exports of software services and

---

6. See Joshi (2003) and Joshi and Sanyal (2004).

7. India's exchange rate policy was however better in one respect. When the dollar began to appreciate in 1995, the Indian authorities allowed the rupee to depreciate against the dollar. So, unlike the crisis-countries, India's real effective exchange rate did not appreciate much in 1996.

Table 11.2

India's Balance of Payments

	2000-01	*2001-02*	*2002-03*	*2003-04*	*2004-05*	*2005-06*	*2006-07*
Current Account (% GDP)	-0.8	0.2	0.8	1.4	-0.7	-1.3	-2.0
Capital Account (% GDP)	1.9	2.2	2.3	3.6	4.4	3.0	4.0
Foreign Exchange Reserves ($ billion) (months of imports)	42.3 (8.6)	54 (11.3)	75.4 (13.8)	112.9 (17.0)	141.0 (15.0)	151.0 (12.0)	160.0 (10.0)

Source: Reserve Bank data. The figures for 2006-07 are the author's estimates, based on data for the first six months.

inward remittances. The surpluses on invisible account led to growing current account surpluses until 2003-04. This is because the trade deficit was fairly steady, reflecting below-trend growth. But in the following three years, there was a strong recovery, the trade deficit rose sharply and the current account moved modestly into deficit.

Table 11.3

India: Sources of Increase in Reserves (2000/1-2005/6)

Share of Total Change (%)

Current Account	4.9		
Trade Balance		-129.4	
Invisibles		134.3	
Software Exports		51.5	153.8
Remittances		103.3	
Other		-20.5	
Capital Account	95.1		
FDI		19.1	
Portfolio Investment		36.0	
Miscellaneous Capital Inflows*		40.6	76.6
Commercial Loans (M&LT)		4.1	
Foreign Aid		-4.7	
Increase in reserves	100		

**Note*: Miscellaneous Capital Inflows = Banking Capital + Other Capital + Short-term Capital + Errors and Omissions.

Source: Author's calculations, using RBI's published balance of payments data.

Apart from invisibles, the main contributor to balance-of-payments strength has been the capital account. But neither foreign direct investment nor medium and long term borrowing have been significant until very recently. The main drivers of the capital account surplus have been portfolio equity investment and what I call 'miscellaneous capital inflows', the latter comprising in the Reserve Bank's terminology, banking flows, short-term capital inflows, other capital inflows, and errors and omissions.

The payments regime has maintained continuity with the past. The exchange rate arrangement continues to be an intermediate exchange rate, which takes the form of a tightly managed float. As before, the exchange rate has been managed to keep the real effective exchange rate in a narrow range despite large changes in the exchange rates of major currencies. Capital controls have been selectively liberalised; even so, the new system falls well short of capital account convertibility.[8]

Within this regime, policy was conducted flexibly. The main policy decision was to resist or moderate exchange rate appreciation despite rising current and capital account surpluses for three years at the start of the decade (see Tables 11.1 and 11.2). The authorities took the view that the current surpluses were mainly a cyclical phenomenon, reflecting a growth slowdown during those years. They therefore waited for the cycle to turn, while undertaking some expansionary policies. Interest rates were lowered and fiscal consolidation was put on "pause." Excessive monetary expansion that might have resulted from balance of payments surpluses was blocked by sterilisation on a significant scale, as shown in Table 11.4. The third column of this Table shows the extent of sterilisation. It can be seen that in the first five years of the decade, more than half the reserve accumulation was sterilised. Note that interest rates in India were higher than interest rates in the advanced

---

8. Resident banks have been allowed to borrow from abroad subject to individual ceilings. There has also been some capital outflow liberalisation. Outward foreign direct investment by Indian companies, portfolio investment abroad by domestic mutual funds, overseas money market investments by banks, and transfer of wealth abroad by residents and non-residents have been permitted subject to ceilings. Despite these changes, the new arrangements fall far short of CAC. Debt-creating short-term inflows, as well as bank flows, inward and outward, continue to be severely restricted. The implication is that although capital mobility has to be factored into macroeconomic policy to a greater extent, it is still possible to combine exchange rate targeting with monetary autonomy.

countries throughout the period. Capital controls were important in preventing massive arbitrage inflows into India, which would have made it unfeasible to pursue the above policy package.

Table 11.4

India: Sources of Reserve Money Growth

(Rupees Billion)

Year	*ΔRM*	*ΔNFA*	*ΔNDA*
2000-01	227	313	-86
2001-02	347	668	-321
2002-03	309	942	-633
2003-04	673	1262	-588
2004-05	525	1284	-759
2005-06	839	602	237

Note: Notation: Δ = increase; RM = Reserve Money; NFA = Net foreign exchange assets of RBI; NDA = Net domestic assets of RBI.

Source: *Reserve Bank of India Bulletin*

The Future

There has been a lot of discussion in India recently about whether or not to dismantle the external payments regime. This debate has been prompted by the continuing strength of capital inflows, the comfortable level of reserves, the dynamism of the economy, and lobbying from elements in the financial sector keen to establish a global presence.

The wisdom of abandoning the present regime can only be judged by considering relevant alternatives. Four alternatives are sequentially considered below: (i) fix the exchange rate and make the capital account fully convertible; (ii) float the exchange rate and make the capital account fully convertible; (iii) retain the present intermediate exchange rate arrangement but make the capital account fully convertible;[9] (iv) retain the present external payments regime *viz.* intermediate exchange rate along with capital controls.

9. Of course under this third option, one could consider different types of intermediate regime. I assume that if an intermediate regime is to be retained, the present version is to be preferred as it gives more flexibility and discretion compared with other alternatives, such as crawling pegs and bands.

Fixed Exchange Rate plus Convertibility

I shall spend little time on this option as it is so obviously unsuitable to India's circumstances. Firstly, India is a low-inflation country with a fairly conservative financial tradition. Unlike some Latin American countries, it does not need the exchange rate as a nominal anchor. Secondly, the country is subject to plenty of asymmetric cyclical and structural shocks relative to potential peg-countries such as the US. It would be very costly to respond to adverse negative shocks without exchange rate adjustment, i.e. by demand management alone. The latter might suffice if India had downwardly flexible money wages and prices, but that is not the case.[10] Favourable positive shocks, such as a surge in capital inflows, would also be problematic. The adjustment would have to involve a real exchange rate appreciation via domestic inflation, clearly not an acceptable option. Thirdly, India needs flexible monetary policy for macroeconomic stabilisation because the flexibility of fiscal policy for that purpose faces significant constraints. But a flexible monetary policy is incompatible with adopting this regime.

Floating Exchange Rate plus Convertibility

The second alternative is to float the exchange rate and make the capital account fully convertible. It could be argued that this would be the simplest way to absorb the strong net capital inflows that India is currently experiencing. The exchange rate would appreciate and automatically create a current account deficit (and hence an excess of domestic investment over domestic saving) equal to the net capital inflow, a better way of using foreign resources than tying them up unproductively in foreign exchange reserves.[11] As the Impossible Trinity makes clear, in this regime policymakers would have monetary autonomy. Monetary policy could be geared to domestic macro objectives and the balance of payments would look after itself.

---

10. The inflexibility of money wages and prices means that exchange rate changes are necessary for real adjustment. But India does have flexible real wages and prices; so exchange rate changes are also effective in promoting real adjustment.

11. Note that a rise in the investment/saving gap is compatible with a rise in investment or a fall in savings. So there is no guarantee that investment would rise much or even at all.

The case outlined above sounds plausible but is, in my judgement, unacceptable for two reasons. The first objection is that the current balance-of-payments strength may be temporary. It should be noted in this context that India is now targeting 8 per cent plus growth; given the associated import requirements, it would be very surprising if the current account deficit came in at less than 2 per cent of GDP, despite the expected buoyancy of invisibles. As regards the capital account, large net FDI inflows, though expected, are not yet a reality. Most of the contribution to the capital account surplus in the last five years has been from inflows of portfolio equity and miscellaneous capital, the former not particularly stable, the latter unstable (see Table 7.3). Adoption of a floating exchange rate and CAC could lead in the current 'feel good' environment to a further rapid increase in the unstable variety of capital inflows, a substantial rupee appreciation, and consequent resource reallocation away from the tradable sector. If the inflows then slow down or stop, there would have to be a costly reversal.[12] Export markets, once lost, are not easy to recapture. In other words, if the inflows are temporary, the costs of adjustment may outweigh the benefits of a temporary increase in absorption.

There is a second, more important, objection, which applies even if it is assumed that the balance of payments has durably strengthened. This is that loss of control over the exchange rate would be undesirable at the present stage of India's development in which it is important to maintain a 'competitive', i.e. mildly undervalued, exchange rate. A significant nominal and real exchange rate appreciation would adversely affect export growth and consequently growth of employment and output.

This heterodox point needs some elaboration. Historically, super-fast growth has been based on harnessing a labour surplus to produce labour-intensive manufactured goods for the world market. This was true of Japan in the 1950s and of several countries in East Asia, especially China, since then. The reason is that exporting to the world market at approximately constant terms of trade enables an economy to realise the advantages of 'unlimited supplies of labour.' (In contrast,

12. It is too readily assumed, in the present euphoria, that there will be no adverse shocks. What, for example, would be the consequence if there is a disorderly adjustment of the US current account deficit?

a labour-surplus closed economy cannot stave off diminishing returns to capital accumulation, since the internal terms of trade turn against the modern sector.) Labour-intensive export growth also helps in three other ways: (a) it boosts the incentive to save and invest; (b) it leads to rising employment and therefore to poverty redressal, 'without' having to rely on 'trickle-down'; (c) it creates 'learning externalities' that arise from having to compete on the world market. If rapid export growth is important for the above reasons, it makes sense to err on the side of undervaluation of the real exchange rate, which enables a country's exports to grow faster than world exports for a considerable period.

This argument should not be read as implying that large undervaluation is desirable. While undervaluation increases the incentive to invest by creating export demand, it also reduces the total resources available for investment by improving the current account (and thus reducing the inflow of foreign savings). Beyond a point, this unfavourable effect would dominate. Excessive undervaluation must therefore be avoided. But this does not overturn the presumption that moderate undervaluation relative to a market determined level of the exchange rate would be desirable.[13]

The application of this argument to the Indian situation is manifest. India needs to maintain an 8 per cent growth rate, and if possible increase it further. It is also vitally important that growth be labour-demanding. India's recent employment record has been dismal. In the organised sector, employment has barely changed since 1991. Total employment (organised plus unorganised) has been growing, but at a slower rate than the growth rate of the labour force. The expected 'demographic bonus' will thus create a severe employment problem unless there is growing demand for unskilled labour. It is clear that exports of labour-intensive manufactured goods will have to make a major contribution in this regard. A durable export boom, in turn, will need to be supported by a competitive exchange rate.[14]

13. The theory underlying this view has been spelled out by Williamson (2003). The empirical connection between undervaluation and growth has been shown by Bhalla (2007). See also Joshi and Sanyal (2004).

14. Needless to say, rapid export growth in labour-intensive manufactures will also require infrastructure improvements and labour market reform.

Intermediate Exchange Rate plus Convertibility

This option consists of retaining India's present exchange rate arrangements but moving rapidly to full convertibility on capital account. The supposed rationale of this regime is that it would enable policymakers to enjoy the benefits of exchange rate targeting, monetary autonomy and CAC simultaneously.

But this regime faces two serious problems. The first was discussed in Section II. For an emerging country like India that is integrated with the world capital market, the regime would not be viable. An attempt to make it stick would be defeated by large capital flows driven by interest arbitrage.

The second serious (and associated) problem is the vulnerability of this regime to currency and banking crises. This is because an exchange rate target for the authorities also provides a target for speculators to shoot at. Modern theory has confirmed the intuition that speculative attacks can take place even if the fundamentals are sound (or not manifestly unsound). Crises can be 'self-fulfilling' because a speculative attack can succeed by raising the political and economic cost to the authorities of maintaining the exchange rate at the target level, even if the fundamentals are in good order. Another reason for crisis-vulnerability is that exchange rate targeting can lull economic agents into complacency about exchange risk. This can encourage unhedged foreign currency borrowing and lead to an unstable debt structure that vastly increases the potential damage of a speculative attack.

The above argument is confirmed by the experience of the last 15 years, which shows that all intermediate exchange rate arrangements (not simply old-style adjustable pegs) are crisis-vulnerable in the presence of CAC. Currency crises have occurred in the ERM countries (1992), Mexico (1994), Thailand, South Korea, Malaysia, Indonesia (1997, 1998), Russia (1998), Brazil (1999), Argentina (2001) and Turkey (2001). Notably, four of these countries (Mexico, Indonesia, Russia and Turkey) had crawling bands. One could insist that all these crises were rooted in fundamentals and would not have occurred, if only fiscal and financial policies had been sound enough. But this line of thinking no longer carries conviction.

The upshot is that intermediate exchange rate arrangements can be safely managed only by retaining some capital controls on 'hot money'. To put it another way, partial exchange rate targeting and partial monetary autonomy are possible but only by having partial capital mobility.

Intermediate Exchange Rate plus Capital Controls

All the three regimes discussed above are thus seriously problematic. This naturally leads to the thought that the least bad regime is the one that India presently has, *viz.* an intermediate exchange rate *plus* capital controls. Of course capital controls impose costs but these may be outweighed by the other benefits of the regime.[15]

The costs of capital controls are they reduce the scope for desirable intertemporal trade and risk diversification. Arguably, they also reduce the discipline on policymakers.[16] But the costs of capital controls can be reduced by limiting their scope. Capital controls need not and should not have a wide sweep. Foreign direct investment brings large benefits and is generally stable and 'bolted down'. Foreign portfolio equity investment is also beneficial and reasonably stable, since changes in stock market prices provide a natural corrective to large inflows and outflows. The unstable elements are predominantly debt and credit flows, especially bank loans, in particular those that are short-term and have to be rolled over frequently. It is to these volatile flows that capital controls should ideally be directed.[17] India's capital controls closely match such a template.

The advantage of focussed capital controls on hot money is that they permit most of the beneficial capital movements, while significantly reducing the crisis-vulnerability of intermediate regimes. In addition, they give macroeconomic policy an extra degree of freedom by enabling policymakers to exercise some control over the interest rate and the exchange rate simultaneously. In the current Indian context, this is a huge benefit, because monetary autonomy and

15. The costs and benefits of capital controls are discussed by Bhagwati (1998) and Cooper (1999).

16. Experience indicates, however, that the 'discipline' imposed by capital markets can be highly capricious.

17. Empirical evidence confirms the difference in the stability of different varieties of capital flow. See Prasad *et al.* (2003).

exchange rate targeting are both essential ingredients of Indian macroeconomic policy. The case for monetary autonomy follows directly from the need to vary the interest rate in order to stabilise economic fluctuations. The case for exchange rate targeting is, as already explained, that the level of the exchange rate is a matter of legitimate policy concern at the country's present stage of development.[18] In recent years, the Reserve Bank has followed an active monetary policy. In the early years of the present decade, it lowered interest rates in response to a slowdown in growth. Since 2004, it has raised them to combat inflationary pressures. It is notable that in both phases, there has been an international interest rate differential in India's favour. If the country had embraced a floating exchange rate and CAC, capital inflows would have appreciated the exchange rate significantly. This would have run counter to the needs of macroeconomic stabilisation from 2000-2004. Moreover, it would have damaged the competitiveness of both visible and invisible exports (including exports of software exports) throughout the period. In sum, focussed capital controls have enabled the Indian authorities to respond to balance-of-payments strength by a moderate and controlled appreciation (not the uncontrolled appreciation of a floating rate) while simultaneously pursuing an interest rate policy geared to internal balance and low inflation.

Another relevant question concerning this regime is whether focussed capital controls are feasible. Market fundamentalists say 'No' on the ground that the market would always find a way round them. But this view is belied by the experience of some highly successful emerging countries, notably Chile, China, Malaysia, Singapore, Taiwan and, of course, India. Capital controls may be porous but that is not necessarily a sign of failure if they can prevent large and sudden movements of hot money.[19] Of course, a precondition of their

---

18. As already emphasised, exchange rate targeting does not imply that policymakers have to embrace a fixed exchange rate target. The target can be varied in discretionary fashion. What it does imply is the ability to choose an exchange rate level different from that which would prevail in the presence of discretionary monetary policy combined with CAC.

19. Note that proponents of CAC in India often hold both of the following two contradictory positions *viz.*, (a) capital controls have deleterious effects; and (b) capital controls are ineffective.

effectiveness is a minimum level of administrative competence and honesty and avoidance of gross macroeconomic irresponsibility.[20] India passes these tests.

How much Reserve Accumulation?

I have suggested above that it would be desirable to continue for the time being the policy of keeping the rupee mildly undervalued in the context of an 'intermediate exchange rate plus capital controls' regime. It follows, notwithstanding the controls, that there will from time to time be strong upward market pressure on the exchange rate, which the authorities would have to counter by sterilised intervention.

Sterilisation involves costs, economic and quasi-fiscal, which have to be compared with the insurance benefits of reserve accumulation.[21] There is in practice no 'scientific' way to determine the optimum size of the reserve stock. Old benchmarks such as 'reserves should equal three months imports' have been rendered irrelevant in a world of high capital mobility. A modern consensus view is that reserves should equal the stock of short-term capital (the Greenspan-Guidotti rule). But following this rule could be quite costly if the return on reserves is less than the cost of short-term foreign borrowing, which is often the case. If so, an argument in favour of controls on short-term capital inflows is that they lessen the need for costly reserve accumulation.

India's reserve position is currently comfortable by all standard criteria. In March 2006, India's reserves were $151 billion, approximately equal to: 12 months merchandise imports; 20 per cent of GDP; 70 per cent of gross external liabilities; 120 per cent of external debt; 117 per cent of reserve money; and ten times short-term external debt. Policy should fix some manifestly safe ratio that reserves should satisfy, say "10 months' imports or five times short-term debt, whichever is higher." Foreign exchange inflows that would raise reserves above this level should be absorbed by a mix of policies, rather than added to reserves.

---

20. These conditions are no harder to meet than the ability to run the prudential and supervisory systems which are agreed to be prerequisites of a stable financial system.
21. This issue is discussed in some depth in Joshi and Sanyal (2004), which also gives rough estimates of economic and quasi-fiscal costs.

A policy package to absorb inflows could consist of monetary and fiscal policies, import liberalisation and exchange rate appreciation. The judicious policy-mix cannot be laid down in advance. I incline to the view that in India's specific circumstances, the package should be tilted in favour of fiscal consolidation and import liberalisation and against real exchange rate appreciation through nominal appreciation or inflation.[22]

Concluding Remarks

Of course, India should not continue with the present external payments regime indefinitely. In the long run, India's integration into the world economy and its position as a future global economic power are not compatible with the presence of capital controls. Convertibility will, in due course, become a necessary complement to inward and outward foreign direct and portfolio investment, deep risk markets in foreign exchange, and an efficient and internationally competitive financial sector, which can realise India's potential comparative advantage in financial services. But it does not follow from this that there should be a rapid move to CAC. The issue is one of timing and sequencing.

Two basic reasons underlie the wisdom of a slow approach to CAC. Firstly, CAC has a tendency to make the economy crisis-vulnerable, whatever the exchange regime.[23] Crisis-vulnerability can be reduced by making sure that some prerequisites are achieved before a move to CAC. In this regard, India still has some way to go. The combined fiscal deficit of the Centre and States is too high (Table 11.5). So is government debt, especially if we include contingent liabilities. Though the most recent trends in the fiscal deficit are encouraging, it is not yet certain they will last.[24] With CAC, the government would borrow in an integrated world market, so its cost of borrowing could

22. The composition of the optimum package is discussed in depth in Joshi and Sanyal (2004). Note that the tilt against appreciation is compatible with a moderate appreciation.

23. Large capital movements can create major recession or inflation if the exchange rate is fixed. They can move the exchange rate excessively, with attendant harmful effects, if the exchange rate floats.

24. The trends in the fiscal deficit are less encouraging if we include off-budget deficits, e.g. the reduction in the profits of government-owned oil companies.

rise sharply, especially if there were adverse shocks. This would make the dynamics of deficits and debt very tricky and increase the chances of capital flight. It would also not be sensible to have CAC before the domestic banking system has become more robust. In this regard, it is relevant that the incidence of non-performing assets in the banking system is still quite high.

Table 11.5

India: Major Macroeconomic Indicators

(% increase p.a. unless otherwise specified)

	GDP (overall)	*GDP (Industry)*	*Broad Money*	*Reserve Money*	*Wholesale Prices*	*Fiscal Balance (% GDP)*	*Govt Debt (% GDP)*
1993-94 1999/00	6.6	6.9	17.3	14.4	6.7	-9.4 (1990/1)	61.3 (1995/6)
2000/01	5.2	6.6	16.2	8.1	7.0	-9.5	70.8
2001/02	5.6	3.2	14.2	11.4	3.6	-9.9	76.4
2002/03	4.3	6.2	12.8	9.2	3.4	-9.6	81.0
2003/04	8.5	6.6	16.4	18.3	4.6	-8.5	81.6
2004/05	7.5	7.4	12.3	12.0	5.0	-8.4	82.5
2005/6	8.4	7.6	17.0	17.2	4.4	-7.5	80.0

Source: *Economic Survey*, Govt. of India.

Secondly, and this is the reason I have strongly emphasised in this paper, full convertibility is incompatible with the simultaneous pursuit of exchange rate targeting and monetary autonomy. Surrender of monetary autonomy that a fixed exchange rate implies would be undesirable as well as politically unacceptable in the Indian context. So full convertibility would have to be accompanied by a floating exchange rate. But in the prevailing circumstances, India would be ill-advised to lose control over exchange rate policy. A floating exchange rate may, for a considerable period, settle at a level that is quite unsuitable from the standpoint of employment and growth. The bottom line is that at the present stage of development, India's macroeconomic objectives require policy discretion with regard to the interest rate as well as the exchange rate. This is possible only with some focussed capital controls.

I conclude that India's present external payments regime will continue to be fit for purpose over a near-term horizon.[25] After another five to ten years of rapid growth of exports, national income and employment, as well as deeper economic reform, the need to target the exchange rate will fade and the country will be ready to adopt a floating exchange rate, convertibility, and inflation-targeting. The government should take steps to prepare for convertibility by strengthening the fiscal position and the financial system, and pursuing such gradual liberalisation of capital flows and the foreign exchange market as is compatible with the simultaneous exercise of exchange rate targeting and monetary autonomy. In the meanwhile, a rush to convertibility should be avoided since it could lead to loss of macroeconomic control and consequent disruption of the country's large and unfinished reform agenda.

References

Bhagwati, Jagdish (1998). "The Capital Myth: The Difference between Trade in Widgets and in Dollars", *Foreign Affairs*, Vol. 77(3): 7-12.

Bhalla, Surjit (2007). *Second Among Equals: The Middle Class Kingdoms of China and India.* (Forthcoming.) Peterson Institute of International Economics.

Cooper, Richard (1999). "Should Capital Controls be Banished?", *Brookings Papers on Economic Activity*, No.1: 89-125.

Joshi, Vijay (2003). "India and the Impossible Trinity", *The World Economy*, Vol. 26(4): 555-83.

Joshi, Vijay (2006). "Real Exchange Rate, Fiscal Deficits and Capital Flows: Refutation Again", *Economic and Political Weekly*, Vol. 41(5): 446-447.

Joshi, Vijay and Sanjeev Sanyal (2004). "Foreign Inflows and Macroeconomic Policy in India", in S. Bery, B. Bosworth and A. Panagariya (eds.), *India Policy Forum*, Vol. I: 135-188. NCAER and Brookings.

Lal, Deepak, Suman Bery and Devendra Pant (2003). "The Real Exchange Rate, Fiscal Deficits and Capital Flows: India 1981-2000", *Economic and Political Weekly*, Vol. 38(47): 4965-76.

Prasad, Eswar, Kenneth Rogoff, Shang-jin Wei, and Ayhan Kose (2003). "Effects of Financial Globalisation on Developing Countries: Some Empirical Evidence", *IMF Occasional Paper* 220. Washington: International Monetary Fund.

Reserve Bank of India (2006). *Report of the Committee on Fuller Capital Account Convertibility.*

Williamson, John (2003). "Exchange Rate Policy and Development", Paper presented to a conference of the *Initiative for Policy Dialogue.* Barcelona.

---

25. I thus agree with the broad thrust of the conclusions of the Tarapore Committee (Reserve Bank of India, 2006) which reported recently. The Committee did not, in my judgement, set out coherently the analytical basis of its recommendations.

12

Macroeconomic Policy

The Fiscal Dimension

SHANKAR ACHARYA

I have been asked to open this discussion of current macroeconomic policy issues in India with a few remarks on the fiscal dimension. Quite a few people in the audience probably expect me to give substantial weight to fiscal imbalances in explaining our overall macroeconomic performance, especially economic growth. I shall try not to disappoint!

As we bask in the glow of a fourth consecutive year of 8 per cent growth, we seem to have forgotten one of the perennial bugbears of the 1990s, the dreaded 'fiscal deficit'. Most economists accorded an important role to the high fiscal deficits of the late 1980s in causing the economic crisis of 1991. We spent much of the first half of the nineties decade striving, with partial success, to reduce the fiscal deficit. The second half was spent struggling, unsuccessfully, to contain the fiscal deficit from ballooning in the wake of the Fifth Pay Commission decisions. Several years of effort yielded the Fiscal Responsibility and Budget Management (FRBM) Act of 2003 (notified in 2004) at the central government level and many states have followed with similar laws (nudged along by some crucial conditionalities in the Twelfth Finance Commission's recommendations for debt relief). But today, 'the fiscal deficit' is a guaranteed conversation killer. Is that really justified? Have matters improved so much? Or has our dynamic economy matured beyond such mundane "accountant's concerns?"

Well, let's start with a few numbers. As Table 12.1 shows, there was a significant improvement in the consolidated (centre and states) fiscal deficit from an 8.9 per cent of GDP average in 1988-91 (it was an even higher 9.4 per cent in 1990-1991) down to 6.5 per cent in 1995-96. Then, as the Fifth Pay Commission decisions took hold and the tax revenue effort weakened, the overall deficit climbed back up to nearly 10 per cent of GDP by 2001-02. Subsequently, helped by fiscal responsibility laws and better revenue performance, the deficit has been brought down to 7.5 per cent of GDP in the two most recent years. So, in the last fifteen years, approximately spanning three five-year-plan periods, there has been a cycle in the fiscal deficit: down from a high level, then back up even higher and then down again.

It is interesting to note the inverse correlation between the fall-rise-fall of the fiscal deficit and the growth performance of the Indian economy during this period: strong growth of 6.7 per cent in the Eighth Plan (1992-1997) when the deficit was shrinking; some deceleration in the Ninth Plan (1997-2002) when the deficit was widening; and resurgent growth in the Tenth Plan (2002-2007) with the fiscal deficit again reducing. This inverse correlation is not wholly accidental. There may be some causality at work, operating through the usual transmission mechanisms of credit availability, real interest rates, savings and investment. (I don't wish to suggest that the variation in fiscal deficit levels is the 'sole' factor explaining changes in GDP growth outcomes; obviously, other factors were also at work).

The numbers do suggest that the reduction in the fiscal deficit in the first half of the 1990s helped to accommodate the upsurge in private corporate savings and investment of the period, just as the subsequent widening of the fiscal and revenue deficits in the latter half of the decade contributed to a significant drop in aggregate savings and investment, especially in public savings. The latest rebound in gross investment (to 30 per cent of GDP by 2004-05) has been greatly helped by the 4 percentage point positive swing in public savings, largely attributable to the substantial drop in public dissavings brought about by the large reduction in the consolidated revenue deficit (from 7 per cent in 2001-02 to 3.7 per cent in 2004-05).

To me, the lesson in these numbers is fairly clear: fiscal (and revenue) deficits matter. We forget this at our peril. It is also a trifle disquieting to note that, after the latest round of fiscal consolidation, our fiscal position is still somewhat weaker than it was a decade ago.

Today's (2005-06) fiscal deficit of 7.5 per cent of GDP is a little higher than the 6.5 in 1995-96. Actually, the gap is perhaps 0.6 per cent greater once we adjust upwards the fiscal deficit in 2005-06 by the Rs. 17,000 crores of oil bonds issued off-budget in 2005-06, as we should. (By the way, an 8 per cent fiscal deficit makes us one of the highest deficit countries in the world). Furthermore, the government debt to GDP ratio at 83 per cent in March 2006 is a good deal worse than the 63 per cent in March 1996. The vulnerability to increases in interest rates is obvious.

What's the fiscal outlook for the future? Mixed, at best. On the positive side are the recently enacted fiscal responsibility laws at the central and state levels. But we know from the central government's example in 2005-06 that such legislated trajectories can be 'paused' when the government finds the restraints too inconvenient. Nor does it help to have the Planning Commission and Left parties advocating further 'pauses' in the Eleventh Plan. The other positive feature of the fiscal outlook is the buoyancy in state government revenue associated with the switch to VAT systems of sales taxation in the last couple of years. This could yield further returns as organised retail trade gathers steam. So could the implementation of a well-designed system for national Goods and Services Tax (GST) as recommended by the Kelkar Task Force in 2004, which was announced for implementation in this year's budget speech. But the target date was put disappointingly distant (April 2010) and there are not many signs of serious preparatory work.

On the negative side, there are at least three major threats to fiscal consolidation in the medium term. First, the tax exemptions built into the Special Economic Zones scheme are unduly generous and could seriously erode the revenue base in the medium term. Second, the populist programmes (such as the national rural employment guarantee scheme) of the UPA government pose serious budgetary headaches for the future. Perhaps most important is the possible fall out from the Sixth Pay Commission, which is expected to present its report in late 2008. If it is similar to the consequences of the predecessor commission, then we are in for a very rough ride on the fiscal front.

The bottom line is that if we don't take the fiscal deficit seriously (as we don't seem to today), then it could easily widen and harm our future growth and development. It's done it before....it can do so again.

Table 12.1

Deficits, Savings and Investment
(% of GDP at Current Market Prices)

Year	1988-91 (Avg)	1995-96	2001-02	2004-05	2005-06 RE
1. Gross Fiscal Deficit (Consolidated)	8.9	6.5	9.9	7.5	7.5
2. Gross Primary Deficit (Consolidated)	4.8	1.6	3.7	1.4	1.6
3. Gross Revenue Deficit (Consolidated)	3.4	3.2	7.0	3.7	3.1
4. Gross Domestic Savings	22.1	25.1	23.6	29.1	NA
a) Household Sector	18.1	18.2	22.0	22.0	NA
b) Private Corporate	2.4	4.9	3.6	4.8	NA
c) Public Sector	1.6	2.0	-2.0	2.2	NA
(of which Govt.)	(-2.2)	(-2.0)	(-6.0)	(-2.7)	
5. Net Capital Inflow	2.9	1.8	-0.6	1.0	1.3
6. Gross Domestic Investment	25.0	26.9	23.0	30.1	NA

Average Growth Rate (%)

	Eighth Plan (1992-97)	Ninth Plan (1997-2002)	Tenth Plan (2002-07)
GDP	6.7	5.5	7.2*
GDP per capita	4.6	3.6	5.5*

Note: *– Assuming GDP growth in 2006-07 is 8 per cent as projected by RBI in October 2006.

Source: RBI, *Handbook of Statistics on the Indian Economy*, 2005-06 and CSO website.

13

Towards Globalisation of India's Financial Sector

JAIMINI BHAGWATI

Introduction

In the last 15 years, the Indian financial system has been incrementally deregulated and exposed to international financial markets along with the introduction of new instruments and products. Consequently, elements of the Indian financial sector e.g. spot equity and related exchange traded derivatives' markets are close to international standards. Global financial market conditions are favourable for India, characterised by low risk premiums along with the resurgence of flows to emerging markets after the East Asian meltdown in 1997. Despite some recent increases, medium to long-term interest rates remain below long-run averages. Swap spreads are at close to historic lows, reflecting improved fundamentals and also temporary factors including easy monetary conditions. Net capital flows (private and official) to emerging market countries have been in excess of $300 billion since 2004, up significantly from $200 billion during 2000-2002, and higher than the peak levels reached in 1997. This pick up in net capital flows over the past few years reflects strong gains in net private flows as well as declines in net official flows. Net private flows to emerging market economies (including debt and equity) have more than doubled since 2002 while net official flows (debt and aid) have declined marginally. In this environment, equity prices have risen significantly, particularly outside the US, with some markets looking richly valued; property prices have also risen but more diversely. These positive international conditions along with strong growth has made India an increasingly attractive destination for capital —resulting in more than $5 billion in foreign direct investment (FDI), $10 billion in foreign institutional investor (FII) and $6 billion in private equity flows in 2005-06. India enjoys a comfortable external position, with foreign exchange reserves now over $165 billion (more than ten times the level of short term debt). India's high foreign exchange reserves, stable real exchange rate and low inflationary pressures, insulate its financial sector from external shocks common to many developing countries.

On the down side, compared to Asian and other countries the depth of the Indian financial sector is relatively low. Intermediation costs in banking are high and the productivity of investments could be improved. Domestic interest rates are not adequately market determined, corporate bond markets are underdeveloped and the insurance, pensions sectors are lagging well behind international comparators. Most importantly, the financial sector's coverage of the informal sector needs to be widened. At the international level there are significant macro-imbalances. At the top of the list are the persistent US current account deficits, which have been funded by developing countries, including India, and by the petroleum exporting countries. A disorderly descent in housing prices in the US and resulting decrease in consumer confidence, combined with a rise in global interest rates could result in negative fallout for Indian growth.

One line of thinking is that the Indian economy is now robust enough to weather the risks stemming from global factors and India should integrate faster with international financial markets. That is, the opportunity costs of not moving faster are high since the international financial environment is benign and competition from foreign providers of financial services would hasten the development of the Indian financial sector with consequential benefits for savings and growth. On balance, the rate at which India's financial sector is exposed to global financial markets should be based on meeting the following objectives, namely how best to:

- increase competition and thereby enhance the efficiency of financial intermediation and promote overall savings;
- widen and deepen the reach of the formal financial sector;
- ensure that the country's savings are utilised most productively; and
- manage the risks stemming from disturbances in global markets to insulate the financial sector and the Indian economy.

The basic elements of any competitive market, which are equally relevant for an efficient Indian financial sector, are that:

- there should be an adequate number of buyers and sellers such that all market participants are price-takers;
- the primary market (for all issuance) should have a large number of participants;
- valuations in the secondary market should be transparent and liquid enough to allow easy exit; and
- the bid-ask spreads in the secondary markets should be narrow.

This paper divides the Indian financial sector into four sub-sectors, along the lines of regulatory control,[1] and examines the extent to which the criteria for competitive market conditions are met. Such a division of the financial sector is artificial since e.g. banking subsidiaries and affiliates provide services across all four areas. Another construct could be to examine the financial sector in terms of the end-uses of funds, namely bank deposits, equity and bonds. In many countries all forms of savings end up in one or the other of these investment destinations. In India, however, Government of India (GoI) and state government administered small savings schemes, pensions and provident funds are invested in 'special' securities. Interest and principal redemption payments on these special securities are invariably made on a pay-as-you-go basis out of annual budgets. Section II of this paper addresses systemic issues, which are common to all providers of financial sector services in India. The next four sections, from Sections III-VI, evaluate, in broad terms, the current state of development in the banking, capital markets, insurance and pensions sub-sectors. Any detailed examination of these sub-sectors is beyond the scope of this paper. Section VII presents conclusions and these are not intended to be comprehensive or definitive. This paper is aimed at setting out the principal 'issues' to facilitate discussion.

1. Banking—Reserve Bank of India (RBI); Capital Markets—Securities and Exchange Board of India (SEBI); Insurance—Insurance Regulatory Development Agency (IRDA); Pensions—Pension Funds Regulatory and Development Agency (PFRDA) and Employees Provident Fund Organisation (EPFO).

Systemic Issues: Opportunities and Risks

Depth of the Indian Financial Sector and Dominance of the Public Sector

Table 13.1 shows that India's financial depth, i.e. financial assets (equity, government and corporate debt, bank deposits and currency)[2] as a percentage of GDP, is lower than that of other Asian economies.

Table 13.1

Stock of Financial Assets as Per cent of GDP (2004)

Country	*Financial Assets*
India	160
Japan	420
Malaysia	400
South Korea	235
China	220

Source: McKinsey (2006). *Accelerating India's Growth through Financial Sector Reform*, May.

It is estimated that about two-thirds of private savings are mobilised by the financial sector. Out of these savings absorbed by the formal financial sector, about 70 per cent are pre-empted by government and public sector undertakings (PSUs) and the productivity of investments made by PSUs have been relatively low. However, this is not the only reason why large private investments are made in gold and the urban real estate sector. The reluctance to invest in financial assets, which are easier to track, is also related to widespread tax evasion. Hence, in addition to incentives of enhanced returns in a more efficient financial system there is a need for enforceable disincentives against private savings being directed to unproductive end-uses.

As of 2005, the private sector received about 43 per cent of total credit[3] while the remaining 57 per cent went to state owned

2. The growth in India's financial depth in recent years has not been faster than other Asian countries. Additionally, relative to other countries privately placed debt and postal savings deposits are not higher in India.
3. Gross bank credit to non-financial companies, corporate bonds and private placements, loans and investments from government to public sector undertakings.

institutions, agriculture and small businesses. The informal sector does not have adequate access to formal sources of financing. The volume of informal lending to retail businesses and the agriculture sector, which amounted to about US$ 85 billion in 2005, was a third of the total credit from formal sources.[4]

The dominance of government ownership and/or management is relatively high in the banking, insurance and pensions sub-sectors. In the capital markets segment, private sector participants are active in the equity and related derivatives markets but the debt market is mostly made up of government securities and private placements by state owned undertakings.

Capital Account Convertibility

It is often argued that a pre-condition for strengthening global linkages is greater capital account convertibility. India allows foreign firms, financial institutions, resident corporates and non-resident Indians a limited amount of capital convertibility in the context of inward and outward foreign direct investment (FDI) and portfolio investments. Resident Indian individuals are permitted a lower level of capital account convertibility and for non-resident foreigners there is practically no convertibility. The exchange rate continues to be managed and monetary policy independence is sought to be maintained by limiting capital account convertibility. Limitations on FDI have been relaxed over the years but sector specific ceilings e.g. in banks, insurance companies have been retained.

The RBI Committee set up to examine the next steps towards 'Fuller Capital Account Convertibility (FCAC)' submitted its report at the end of July, 2006. The report advocates a three phase relaxation of existing controls on movement of capital over the period 2006-2011, with reviews at the end of every 2 years. It also recommends a review of tax policies and treaties (e.g. the one with Mauritius) and expresses its reservations about specific micro-issues e.g. inflow of private equity capital and participatory notes in the equity market. Those who would proceed cautiously argue that central and state government fiscal deficits are still high (consolidated deficit is at 8.3 per cent of GDP) and important real sector reforms remain to be implemented.

4. On average, interest rates on informal loans are about 3 per cent higher than loans from formal sources. (Source: McKinsey Report, May 2006).

The Internal and External Price of the Indian Rupee (INR)

An important conditionality to improving financial sector efficiency is making the pricing of the INR as market determined as possible. Table 13.2 provides the break-up of outstanding GoI and state government domestic liabilities as of end March 2006. The total stock of internal liabilities amounted to 85.8 per cent (60.2 + 25.6) of GDP.

Table 13.2

A. Outstanding Internal Liabilities of Central Government

(INR Crores)

Year	*Internal Debt*	*Small Savings, Deposits, Provident Funds and Others Accounts*	*Reserve Funds and Deposits*	*Total Internal Liabilities*
2001-02	913061 (40.0)	308668 (13.5)	73133 (3.2)	1294862 (56.8)
2002-03	1020689 (41.7)	398774 (16.3)	80126 (3.3)	1499589 (61.2)
2003-04	1141706 (41.4)	456472 (16.5)	92376 (3.3)	1690554 (61.2)
2004-05	1275971 (40.91)	564584 (18.1)	92989 (3.0)	1933544 (61.9)
2005-06	1355943 (38.4)	669882 (19.0)	101170 (2.9)	2126995 (60.2)

Note: Figures in parentheses represent per cent of GDP.
Source: Budget Documents of Government of India; *RBI Annual Report 2005-06.*

B. Outstanding Liabilities of State Governments

Year	*Market loans + Loans from Banks and FIs (As % of GDP)*	*Total Outstanding Liabilities minus loans and advances from GoI(As % of GDP)*
2001-02	6.4	19.5
2002-03	7.5	22.4
2003-04	8.7	23.8
2004-05	8.9	25.4
2005-06	8.6	25.6

Source: RBI Annual Report 2005-06.

The stock of GoI and state governments' 'market' borrowings amounted to 47 per cent (38.4 + 8.6) of GDP as of end March, 2006. That is, approximately 38.8 per cent (85.8 – 47) of GDP was made up of small savings, pension and provident funds, reserve funds and deposits which carry administered interest rates, which are invariably higher than interest rates on comparable maturity government securities. If GoI securities are deemed to be free of default risk, domestic sovereign interest rates are the closest to market measure of the internal price of the INR. This high proportion of liabilities held at non-market interest rates distorts the domestic pricing of the INR. Further, banks, insurance companies and provident funds are compulsorily required to hold significant proportions of their assets in government securities.[5] Again, this adversely affects the market determination of domestic interest rates. While there are fiscal constraints in moving away abruptly from administered interest rates or easing the requirements for financial institutions to hold high levels of sovereign securities, GoI needs to wean itself away from these practices towards global norms.

The GoI yield curve needs to be arbitrage free for the domestic price of the INR to be market determined. As of now, short selling of GoI securities is permitted where dealers can hold their positions for up to five days. This limited short selling does not close out arbitrage opportunities. RBI needs to further relax its regulations for short-selling of GoI securities.

Public Debt Offices (PDOs) in the UK, Sweden, USA and a number of other countries issue government securities and manage the entire stock of internal and external debt. In India, RBI issues GoI debt and manages domestic debt while the Ministry of Finance manages external debt. This division of responsibilities in the management of GoI's liabilities is sub-optimal and the central bank should not be responsible for issuing government debt. A PDO is expected to be run by professional debt managers at an arm's length from the government concerned. The issuance of GoI debt by a PDO and management of all GoI debt (internal, external plus contingent liabilities) should lead to greater market content in the determination of sovereign interest rates.[6]

5. As of end 2004, more than 75 per cent of government securities were held by financial institutions that were required to hold them.

6. A 2001 Ministry of Finance (MoF) committee, the 2004 Kelkar committee on Restructuring of the Ministry of Finance, RBI's 2006 committee on Further Capital Account Convertibility (FCAC) Committee have recommended the setting up of a PDO.

There are restrictions on foreign participation in Indian debt markets. Specifically, there are ceilings on the amounts of government and corporate securities that Foreign Institutional Investors (FIIs) may hold.[7] These ceilings are probably based on a concern that foreign entities may take leveraged positions in GoI securities along the lines of participatory notes in the equity market. Another concern may be about the volume of inflows with concomitant sterilisation difficulties. And, the logic may be that if foreign hedge funds suddenly unwind their leveraged positions in dated securities there may be unpredictable consequences for domestic interest rates. A contrary point of view is that if foreign investors divest their holdings, domestic investors should pick up the debt securities and if they choose not to, interest rates were due for a correction. All things considered, it is time to allow unfettered foreign participation in Indian debt markets. It is the foreign investor who would be picking up the duration and exchange rate risks.

The external price of the INR is reflected in its exchange rate. RBI 'manages' the INR-US$ exchange rate and the rationale appears to be to retain export competitiveness and control over monetary policy. INR exchange rates are derived prices of INR interest rates, which reflect the domestic spot price of the INR. It is not useful to focus on pricing the derivative 'correctly' if the spot price is not adequately market determined. In short, for the present the emphasis could be on improving the market determination of sovereign interest rates.

Ownership of Indian Financial Institutions

Currently, there are sector specific ceilings on foreign ownership of Indian financial institutions e.g. foreign firms cannot increase their equity stake in banks above 5 per cent (till 2009) or hold more than 26 per cent of the stock of an insurance company. Consequently, the objective of promoting competition in the Indian financial sector has to be pursued by facilitating the entry of domestic private sector firms. The process of increasing competition through domestic private sector participation is likely to be slow and the spotlight could be on

7. As per RBI's Mid-term Review of Annual Policy for 2006-07, released on 31 October 2006, these ceilings have been revised upwards to US$ 3.2 billion for GoI securities and US$ 3 billion for corporate bonds from 31 March, 2007.

monitoring the growth in the number of market-makers and performance assessment against efficiency benchmarks.

Complexities of the Indian Legal System

A large number of Acts and Rules (subordinate legislation) are used by the Ministry of Finance (MoF) and the regulators to administer the Indian financial sector. In practice, there is considerable legal uncertainty about bankruptcy procedures and creditors rights in disputes with debtors.[8]

The lengthy and complicated legal processes in the Indian justice system are not unique to disputes involving financial sector firms. However, given the opportunity cost of business foregone concerted efforts are required to simplify laws and expedite their implementation.

Financial Sector Regulation

There is no universal model for financial sector regulation. Some developed countries such as the US have continued with multiple regulators. Others have set up a single regulator e.g. the Financial Services Authority in the UK, which is also responsible for banking sector regulation. Table 13.3 provides a cross-country comparison of financial sector regulators.

In India the issue of regulatory coordination has come up periodically, particularly when a so called 'scam' has occurred and there is a sense that greater interaction is needed among regulators. The MoF set up a High Level Coordination Committee on Financial Markets (HLCCFM) to post the banking and capital market irregularities in the early 1990s. The HLCCFM is headed by Governor,

---

8. The difficulties caused by overlapping and conflicting provisions in the law are illustrated by the following case. From 1996-2000, Diamond Wire Industries supplied products to Jay Engineering which subsequently became 'sick' and was referred to the Board for Industrial and Financial Reconstruction (BIFR). Diamond Industries moved the Industry Facilitation Council to recover its dues under the Interest on Delayed Payments to Small Scale and Ancillary Undertakings Act, 1993. Jay Engineering resisted by invoking the Sick Industrial Companies (Special Provisions) Act, 1985. Under the 1993 Act, Diamond Industries would have won the case while the 1985 Act favoured Jay Engineering's position. The Supreme Court ruled in favour of Jay Engineering, in September 2006, on the grounds that a later Act should prevail and the 1985 Act was deemed to be more recent since it was amended in 1994.

Table 13.3
Financial Sector Regulators

Country	*Regulators of Financial Services*
UK	Financial Service Authority (FSA)
Japan	Financial Service Agency (FSA)
Germany	The Federal Financial Supervisory Authority (BaFin)
India	Banking—RBI
	Capital Markets—SEBI
	Insurance—IRDA
	Pension—EPFO and PFRDA
China	Banking—China Banking Regulatory Commission (CBRC)[9]
	Capital Markets—State Council Securities Commission (SCSC)
	Insurance—The China Insurance Regulatory Commission (CIR)
USA	Banking—Federal Reserve Bank
	Capital Markets—Securities and Exchange Commission (SEC)
	Derivatives—Commodities and Futures Trading Commission (CFTC)

RBI and its members include the heads of SEBI, IRDA and Secretary DCA is an invitee. This is an effective body but since it meets once every few months it is not designed to provide real time coordination. The sub-committees of the HLCCFM need to work more closely. In terms of prioritisation, this issue—whether India should have one regulator for the financial sector as a whole could wait as the performance of single regulators in the UK, Japan and Germany is evaluated. However, within the banking, capital markets and pensions sub-sectors regulatory responsibilities need to be reallocated and this is covered in Sections III, IV and VI respectively.

Growth with Stability versus Higher Growth with Corresponding Risks

On average, Indian GDP (in real terms) has grown faster in the last 10 years than in earlier decades. It appears that growth may be around 8 per cent for 2006-07 and this level of growth may be maintained for the next few years. Under these circumstances, should India risk macroeconomic and financial instability by moving faster to integrate its financial sector with international markets? Some would argue that

9. CBRC was set up in April 2003 as an independent banking regulator and is separate from the central bank: People's Bank of China (PBOC).

the principal challenges for India are to keep its fiscal deficits in check, invest heavily in the infrastructure sector, improve public health facilities, provide qualitatively better primary and secondary education and improve productivity in agriculture. The logic is that if progress is achieved on these fronts, India would have the social stability it needs to continue to grow at 8 per cent or more. A contrary view is that 8 per cent growth is not sustainable without further real sector reforms and aggressive deregulation of the financial sector. Irrespective of these arguments, clearly there are huge opportunity costs in not improving financial sector efficiency faster.

Banking

The Indian banking sector has advanced on many fronts since RBI began incremental deregulation in 1991. For instance, on average, non-performing loans have declined to 5 per cent of loan assets with most banks compliant with Basel I capital adequacy norms. However, the banking system remains focussed on urban areas and is heavily public sector oriented with over 73 per cent of loan assets held by PSU banks. There are significant barriers to entry for new players although some high performing private banks have come up since deregulation began through dilution of public sector holdings as equity was offered to domestic and foreign private firms/individuals.

In March 2005, RBI announced a two phase roadmap for foreign banks in India, Phase I (March 2005—March 2009) and Phase II (April 2009 onwards). In the first phase, from March 2005 to March 2009, foreign banks wishing to establish a presence in India for the first time could either choose to operate through branches or set up a 100 per cent wholly-owned subsidiary. Foreign banks which have a presence in India cannot hold more than 5 per cent equity in a domestic private sector bank, except in private-sector banks that are identified by RBI for restructuring where foreign banks would be allowed to acquire a controlling stake of up to 74 per cent. In the second phase, from April 2009 onwards, RBI will consider removal of limitations on the operations of wholly-owned subsidiaries and treat them on par with domestic banks after reviewing the experience with Phase I.

It appears that RBI's plans for foreign banks to expand their operations in India would essentially take effect from 2009. Consequently, one way to increase competition in the interim period, is to widen the presence of domestic private banks either greenfield or through consolidation.[10] Further, major PSU banks could aim for international listings. This should be possible without reducing the public sector character of these banks. The process of international listing would motivate PSU banks to conform to international accounting standards and regulatory requirements.

The dominant market shares, in deposits and loans, of public *versus* private banks are shown in Table 13.4.

Table 13.4

Indian Banks—Market Shares

(in Per cent)

	Deposits		*Loans*	
	Mar. 2000	*Mar. 2005*	*Mar. 2000*	*Mar. 2005*
Public Sector	81.9	78.0	79.3	73.2
New Private	5.2	10.9	5.0	13.8
Old Private	7.4	6.4	7.6	6.2
Foreign	5.5	4.7	8.0	6.8

Source : RBI.

The cost of lending intermediation is high in India. For instance, the average spreads between bank lending and deposit rates in India are about 3 per cent higher than the average spreads in the USA, South Korea, Chile, Malaysia and Singapore.

Table 13.5 provides the volumes of commercial bank lending as a fraction of deposits in 2004. It can be seen that Indian banks lend a smaller proportion of their deposits than banks in China and other countries.

As can be seen from Table 13.6, penetration of banking products such as debit and credit cards has been relatively low in India even in comparison with other emerging economies. This is reflection of

10. In the last 10 years only two new private banks have opened, i.e. Yes Bank and Kotak Mahindra.

Table 13.5

Bank Lending as Percentage of Deposits (2004)

Country	*Lending as per cent of Deposits*
China	130
UK	114
Malaysia	101
USA	92
India	61

Source: RBI, EIU, McKinsey Global Institute.

dependence on cash as a medium for transactions which is inefficient and also non-transparent for tax purposes.

Table 13.6

Debit and Credit Card Penetration

Country	*(Per cent of Population)*
India	3
South Korea	174
Brazil	71
China	61
Thailand	54
Mexico	44

Source: *India Banking 2010*, McKinsey Global Institute Analysis.

There are inherent contradictions in the RBI's role as banking regulator and a provider of liquidity. Regulatory effectiveness and competition would be higher if RBI's regulatory function were to be assigned to an independent banking regulator. In April 2003, China separated the banking regulation function from its central bank (PBOC) and assigned it to the China Banking Regulatory Commission (CBRC).

NBFCs

A large number of Non-bank Financial Companies (NBFCs) had mushroomed towards the late 1990s. In 1998 these totaled about 30,000. It was clearly an untenable situation and the RBI has since laid down stricter norms for capitalisation and in the resulting shake-out many NBFCs have closed down. India is somewhat unique that many major private sector companies have set up multiple NBFCs. In the late 1990s there were examples of NBFCs, which were not able to repay small investors, prominent among which was the CR Bhansali conglomerate. It is possible that some NBFCs were set up for tax or regulatory arbitrage purposes and it is time to closely re-examine the working of NBFCs and limit them to permitted activities.

Capital Markets

Equity and Exchange Traded Derivatives' Markets and Mutual Funds

A number of significant reforms have been implemented in the spot equity and related exchange traded derivatives markets since the early 1990s. For instance, spot prices are mostly market determined, trading volumes in the derivatives markets exceed those in spot markets and market practices such as speed of settlement and dematerialisation are close to international best practices. This is primarily because the Bombay Stock Exchange has faced stiff competition from the National Stock Exchange (NSE).

Table 13.7 provides market capitalisation, value traded and the number of listed companies in six countries in 2005. Equity market capitalisation has increased substantially in India in 2006 while the US and UK markets have not grown at the same pace. Hence the gap has narrowed. The volumes traded in India and Germany are comparable and somewhat behind the US and the UK. The bid-ask spreads in the Indian spot markets and trading commissions are comparable with those in developed markets.

Table 13.8 provides the traded volumes of exchange traded and over-the counter (OTC) derivatives.[11] India is considerably behind the US and the major trading centres in London and Frankfurt. In contrast to the spot equity markets, bid-ask spreads and commissions in the OTC and exchange traded derivatives markets in India are higher than those in developed country markets.

11. Market participants in the exchange traded markets could be individuals or institutions while OTC players are predominantly institutions.

Table 13.7

Equity Market Capitalisation and Traded Values

(in Per cent)

Country	*Market Capitalisation*	*Value Traded*	*Listed DomesticCos.*
India	71	57	4763
USA	136	172	5143
Japan	104	109	3279
UK	139	189	2759
Germany	44	63	648
China	35	26	1387

Source: World Federation of Exchanges.

Table 13.8

OTC and Exchange Traded Derivatives[12]

Country/Region	*OTC Derivatives Markets Average Daily Turnover**[13]	*Exchange Traded Derivatives Markets Annual Turnover***
India (2005-06)	Not available	1[14]
USA (2004)	355	819
EU (2004)	1001	487

Note:* US$ billion; ** US$ trillion.

Source: Bank for International Settlements, *RBI Annual Report 2005-06*, National Stock Exchange (NSE).

On the negative side, there is considerable insider trading in the equity market because the proportion of equity held by corporate insiders is alarmingly high at almost 50 per cent. The volume available for investment to retail investors is only about 17 per cent and they account for almost 85 per cent of the trading. Compared to developed markets, trading continues to be concentrated in a few hundred stocks out of the over 4500 listed companies. Self regulation at the level of brokers and dealers has not progressed much. Additionally, unlike comparator countries domestic institutional investors e.g. pension funds and insurance companies are not significant enough in the equity markets.

---

12. All derivatives' markets including interest rate, currency, credit, equity and commodity.
13. Including forward exchange rate contracts, interest rate and currency swaps.
14. Includes stock index futures and options.

By international standards surveillance and successful prosecution of wrong-doing continues to be weak. The complex linkages between brokerages, banks, finance companies and domestic as well as overseas corporate bodies (OCBs) are difficult for SEBI to track without adequate staff with market and legal experience. Most infringements of securities laws in developed countries are settled out-of-court without admission of guilt. It is important for further progress to adapt some of these practices which have worked well in markets elsewhere.

Since 1993 when the SEBI Mutual Funds Regulations were put in place private sector mutual funds have grown sharply and particularly after the repeal of the Unit Trust of India (UTI) Act in 2003. For instance, as a fraction of total financial savings of the household sector, investments in private sector mutual funds (i.e. other than UTI) has jumped from 0.4 per cent in 2004-05 to 3.6 per cent in 2005-2006 (*RBI Annual Report 2005-06*).

However, it can be seen in Table 13.9, which provides a cross-country comparison of funds under management, that the Indian mutual fund industry is small compared to other countries.

Debt Markets

The debt market in India is mainly made up of government securities. The issuance volumes of GoI bonds, corporate debt and equity are shown in Table 13.10. It can be seen that corporate debt issuance is mainly confined to private placements and there has been a sharp increase in the last two years.

Over 80 per cent of the total volume of private placements in the last 10 years has been raised by PSUs and about 20 per cent of this issuance was by state level PSUs. Of the amounts mobilised by private corporates around 50 per cent has been for the financial sector. Of the public debt issues the overwhelming proportion was raised for the financial sector. That is, the private corporate sector has little access to the bond market. As for the municipal bond market this has not developed at all. Over the 10 year period 1995-96 till 2004-05 the total volume raised through municipal bonds was INR 851 crores.

Table 13.9

Mutual Fund Assets under Management

(US$ Billion end 2005)

Country	*Mutual Funds Assets*	*Per cent of GDP*
India	64	8
USA	8,905	71
France	1,363	65
Switzerland	117	32
UK	547	25
Netherlands	94	15
Germany	297	11
Japan	470	10

Source: IFSL estimates based on Watson Wyatt, Bridgewell, Merril Lynch, Swiss Re, Hennessee Group data.

Table 13.10

Issuance of Equity and Debt

Year	*Equity Issues Rs. Crores*	*GoI Securities Rs. Crores*	*Debt Issues*	
			Publicly Placed	*Privately Placed*
2004-05	28,200 (0.9)	1,06,501 (3.4)	4,094	55,408 (1.8)
2005-06	36,533 (1.0)	1,60,018 (4.5)	—	81,846 (2.3)
2006-07 (Apr.-Sep.)	8,205	BE 1,81,875	—	47,945

Note: Figures in parentheses are per cent of GDP

Source: *Prime Database; RBI Annual Report 2005-2006.*

It is clear from Table 13.11 that the Indian corporate bond market is relatively small.

The secondary market for Indian fixed income securities is made up overwhelmingly of central and state government debt. For example, in 2004-05 trading of corporate debt securities on the National Stock Exchange's wholesale debt segment amounted to slightly over 2 per cent while that of central government securities totalled over 90 per cent, that of treasury bills was about 8 per cent and trading in state government securities made up less than 1 per cent.

Table 13.11

Corporate Bond Markets (2004)

Country	*Per cent of GDP*
India	2
USA	145
Germany	116
UK	83
Malaysia	73
Thailand	22
South Africa	17
China	1

Source: McKinsey Global Institute.

In this context, introduction of credit derivatives and greater liquidity in the exchange traded interest rate derivatives markets should have a beneficial impact on the corporate bond market. Further, stamp duties are high and considerably different across states. Hence a rationalisation of stamp duties should also help.

Indian companies are, on average, less leveraged as compared to international companies. This has been partly forced on them because the corporate bond market is not developed. While the bigger companies have found ways around this problem, for new ventures lack of access to the bond market is a major barrier to entry. To the extent that firms have access to external commercial borrowings (ECBs) they do so. However, interest rate ceilings have been prescribed for ECBs, which makes it difficult for weaker credits to access this source of funding.

Private Equity

According to International Financial Services, London (IFSL), about US$ 135 billion of private equity was invested globally in 2005 which was 20 per cent higher than 2004. The private equity capital raised internationally during 2005 amounted to US$ 232 billion up 75 per cent from 2004. Of this amount, about US$ 6 billion found its way to India. North America's share of investments amounted to 40 per cent and Europe's share was 43 per cent and Asia-Pacific contributed about 11 per cent. Private equity is less liquid than listed equity and tends to be invested longer than portfolio capital. The difficulties in arriving at agreed exit valuations inhibit inflows of private equity into India. Consequently, mergers and acquisitions and other mechanisms which would facilitate exit should be allowed.

Asset Backed Securities

Table 13.12 shows that as of end 2005 the mortgage market in India was small compared to other countries.

Table 13.12

Mortgage Balances Outstanding

(Per cent of GDP)

Country	*Mortgage Balances*
India	3
USA	51
UK	54
South Korea	13
Thailand	9
Malaysia	23
Germany	48

Source: SEBI and International Financial Services London.

As the mortgage and consumer loan balances grow, the market for asset backed securities should develop gradually. The enabling legal framework has been provided with the passage of the Securitisation and Reconstruction of Financial Assets and Enforcement of Security Interest Act in 2002.

Interest Rate and Exchange Rate OTC and Exchange Traded Derivatives

The over-the-counter (OTC) derivatives market includes interest rate swaps and currency swaps. In India, the tenors for these OTC derivatives do not extend much beyond 10 years and the volumes are limited compared to international markets. That is, there is considerable scope for growth with attendant benefits for the hedging of interest rate and exchange rate risks.

Although exchange traded interest rate derivatives have been permitted since 2003, trading volumes are negligible. In contrast, exchange traded currency derivatives have not been allowed as yet. This is probably due to reservations about freeing up the management of the INR-US$ exchange rate. The risk management structure in terms of margining and other requirements are in place since these are currently used for individual stock/index futures and options. In any case, interest rate or currency futures can be derived if interest rate or currency swap curves are liquid and *vice versa*. That is, these markets are fungible and allowing OTC derivatives without permitting exchange traded derivatives is not meaningful.

Commodity Derivatives

The history of Indian commodity derivatives markets spans more than a hundred years. Currently, commodity derivatives are traded on stock exchanges,[15] which are regulated by the Forward Markets Commission (FMC). Although Indian trading volumes have increased dramatically in recent years, Table 13.13 shows that these are low compared to the USA and the EU.

Table 13.13

OTC and Exchange[16] Traded Commodity Derivatives

Country	*OTC Commodity Derivatives Trading (Average Daily Turnover 2004, US$ Billion)*	*Exchange Traded Commodity Derivatives (Annual Turnover 2005, US$ Trillion)*
India	—	0.33
USA	4.6	82
EU	13	49

Source: Forward Markets Commission (FMC), Bank for International Settlements, International Financial Services London (IFSL).

15. OTC commodity derivatives have not been initiated as yet in India.

16. In 2005, the top three commodity derivatives exchanges, in terms of turnover, were: New York Mercantile Exchange (Energy and metals); Dalian Commodity Exchange (China, agriculture); Chicago Board of Trade (agriculture, precious metals).

The FMC is administered by the Department of Civil Supplies in the Ministry of Agriculture. This allocation of responsibilities is anomalous. Irrespective of the nature of the underlying, whether it is the spot price of cotton, stock in a company, interest rate or exchange rate, derivatives markets are part of the securities markets in the capital markets sector. Regulatory efficiency would be enhanced if supervision and development of commodity derivatives were to be allocated to the same regulator as that for securities markets. In the USA, the Securities Exchange Commission (SEC) regulates the securities markets while exchange traded futures and options markets are regulated by the Commodity Futures Trading Commission (CFTC). OTC derivatives markets are regulated by the SEC, the Federal Reserve, CFTC or under general commercial laws depending on the parties involved. In the UK all regulatory control has been placed under one roof, namely the Financial Services Authority. While the broader issue of one regulator for the entire financial sector can wait, it is important for all activities in capital markets to be regulated by SEBI to block regulatory arbitrage across commodity and equity derivatives markets.

Corporate Governance

The Department of Company Affairs (DCA) in the GoI regulates corporates under the Companies Act. This is inconsistent with the current practice of statute based regulators for securities markets, banks, and insurance and pension firms. Indian firms are known to set up multiple finance companies, which have internecine holdings and are engaged in capital market and NBFC operations. Under such circumstances, there is lack of transparency regarding reporting of earnings, recognition of expenses, appointments of members of crucially important committees such as the Audit Committee. There are areas of regulatory overlap between the DCA and SEBI and in practice this diarchy or control does not work efficiently. Corporate governance would improve if the administration of the Companies Act were to be assigned to SEBI.

Insurance

Although the insurance industry dates back many decades, over 80 per cent of India's population is without any form of insurance cover.

Insurance companies were nationalised in the 1950s and an independent regulator was set up recently in 1999 following the passing of the Insurance Regulatory and Development Authority (IRDA) Act. The participation of foreign investors is limited to 26 per cent and life insurance companies must invest at least 50 per cent of their assets in government securities and another 15 per cent must be invested in the infrastructure and social sectors. From 1999 private insurance companies are being registered with IRDA and this should increase competition and improve coverage. Currently, however, the public sector is dominant.[17]

Tables 13.14 and 13.15 provide an international comparison of insurance penetration[18] and density.[19] Insurance penetration in India is comparable to China while it is lagging behind global averages and is considerably behind Japan and the UK. As regards insurance density, India is behind China and even more so compared to global averages.

Table 13.14

International Comparison of Insurance Penetration

Name	*2002*			*2003*			*2004*		
	Total	*Life*	*Non-life*	*Total*	*Life*	*Non-life*	*Total*	*Life*	*Non-life*
USA	9.58	4.6	4.98	9.61	4.25	5.15	9.17	4.12	5.05
UK	14.75	10.19	4.56	13.37	8.62	4.75	12.6	8.92	3.68
Germany	6.76	3.06	3.7	6.99	3.17	3.82	6.97	3.11	3.86
Japan	10.86	8.64	2.22	10.81	8.61	2.2	9.52	6.75	2.77
India	3.26	2.59	0.67	2.88	2.26	0.62	3.17	2.53	0.65
China	2.98	2.03	0.96	3.33	2.3	1.03	3.06	2.21	1.05
World	8.14	4.76	3.38	8.06	4.59	3.48	7.99	4.55	3.43

17. For instance, in 2004-05 among life insurers, the publicly owned Life Insurance Corporation's (LIC) market share of total premiums collected was 90 per cent plus and the balance 9 per cent plus was mobilised by the private sector. Among non-life insurers, in 2004-05 about 89 per cent of new policies were issued by the public sector and the balance was issued by the private sector.

18. Insurance Penetration: Measured as ratio of premium to GDP (in per cent).

19. Insurance Density: Measured as ratio of premium to total population (in per cent).

Table 13.15

International Comparison of Insurance Density

	2003			*2004*		
	Total	*Life*	*Non-life*	*Total*	*Life*	*Non-life*
USA	3637.7	1657.5	1980.2	3755.1	1692.5	2062.6
UK	4058.5	2617.1	1441.4	4508.4	3190.4	1318.0
Germany	2051.2	930.4	1120.8	2286.6	1021.3	1265.3
Japan	3770.9	3002.9	768	3874.8	3044	830.8
China	36.3	25.1	12.2	40.2	27.3	12.9
India	16.4	12.9	3.5	19.7	15.7	4.0
World	469.6	267.1	202.5	511.5	291.5	220.0

Source: IRDA *Annual Report-2005*; Swiss Re, *Sigma volumes*–8/2003, 3/2004 and 2/2005.

The insurance assets under management in India and other countries are shown in Table 13.16.

It is clear that the insurance segment of the Indian financial sector is relatively small and has immense growth potential which will impact positively on the bond and equity markets. Investment in long-term securities is central to the management of insurance assets, which is consistent with funding of the infrastructure sector. The current restrictions on tariff rates need to be lifted to enable insurance coverage to grow.

Table 13.16

Insurance Assets under Management
(US$ Billion end 2005)

Country	*Insurance Assets*	*Per cent of GDP*
India	22	3
USA	5,465	44
Japan	2,264	50
UK	1,907	87
France	1,527	72
Germany	1,370	49
The Netherlands,	385	61
Switzerland	337	91

Source: IRDA *Annual Report 2004-05*, IFSL estimates based on Watson Wyatt, Bridgewell, Merril Lynch, Swiss Re, Hennessee Group data.

Pensions

Out of an Indian workforce of 450 million[20] about 70 million in the organised sector have pension coverage. The remaining 84 per cent workers in the informal sector have negligible pension cover. GoI and state governments have provided the following schemes among other arrangements for the informal sector:

- Senior Citizens Savings Scheme
- National Old Age Pension Scheme (NOAPS)

Traditionally, central and state government employees, including defence, railways and post office personnel, plus workers in large public sector organisations are covered by defined benefits pension schemes. Pension payments for such schemes are made on a pay-as-you-go basis out of annual budgets. Starting from January 2004, new central government employees (except the armed forces) are covered under a defined contribution New Pension Scheme (NPS). Some state governments have decided to start defined contribution NPS type schemes. The NPS is to be regulated by a statute based Pension Fund Regulatory and Development Authority (PFRDA). The PFRDA Bill has not been approved by parliament as yet.

The Employees Provident Fund Organisation (EPFO) set up under an Act by this name administers[21] pension funds for private sector establishments which have more than 20 employees. Employers and employees make contributions[22] and the corpus of funds for the Employees Provident Fund plus Employees Pension Scheme (EPS) amounted to about INR 150,000 crores (approximately US$ 33 billion) in 2004. These funds, which are essentially placed with GoI and public sector fixed-term investments, earn administered rates of interest.

The 1968 Public Provident Fund (PPF) scheme provides for deposits from individuals and for tax purposes prescribes a ceiling for annual contributions. PPF deposits are maintained with PSU banks and these assets are mostly invested in government securities.

---

20. *Reforming India's Social Security System for the Twenty-first Century*. Mukul G. Asher and D. Vasudevan, Centre for Public Policy Paper Occasional.
21. EPFO is self regulated.
22. The wage ceiling to which mandatory contribution rates from employers, employees and government apply was INR 6,500 per month as of July 2005.

The pensions sub-sector is the least developed segment of the financial sector. This is primarily because this market is overwhelmingly dominated by government and regulatory control is fragmented. Table 13.17 shows the relatively small size of Indian pension assets.

Table 13.17

Pension Assets under Management (US$ billion end 2005)

Country	*Pension Assets*	*Per cent of GDP*
India	60*[23]	8
Switzerland	469	127
The Netherlands,	693	110
USA	12,119	97
Japan	3,419	75
UK	1,607	73
France	165	8
Germany	114	4

Note: * Estimate of total assets in schemes such as EPFO, EPS and PPF.

Source: IFSL estimates based on Watson Wyatt, Bridgewell, Merril Lynch, Swiss Re, Hennessee Group data.

Table 13.18 shows that pension funds in Japan, UK and USA are mostly invested in equity or bonds. The implication is that as the funded portion of the Indian pension sector grows in size and greater choice is available to pension account holders, Indian equity and bonds markets would get a boost.

Table 13.18

Asset Allocation of Pension Funds

Country	*Domestic Equity*	*International Equity*	*Domestic Bonds*	*International Bonds*	*Cash*	*Other*
Japan	29	16	26	11	11	7
UK	39	28	23	1	2	7
USA	47	13	33	1	1	5

Source: Global Development Finance–2005.

23. Data on contributions made under funded pension schemes is difficult to access.

Table 13.19 indicates that India's dependency ratio[24] was lower than the global average in 2005 and projected to remain so even as far out as 2050. Therefore, now is an appropriate time to start the transition from unfunded defined benefit pensions to funded pensions. The scope for growth in this sector is enormous with attendant high gains for the financial sector and the economy.

Table 13.19

Dependency Ratio
(Population Above 64 Years of Age Divided by the Population Between 14-64)

	2005	*2050*
World	11	25
G10	23	42
China	11	37
Latin America	9	29
India	8	22

Source: United Nations Population Division, *World Population Prospects-2004* revision.

Conclusions

As outlined in Sections II–VI, although there has been progressive deregulation accompanied by impressive gains there are systemic shortcomings in the Indian financial sector. One of the main deficiencies is the lack of adequate competition with negative consequences for intermediation efficiency and width of coverage. To summarise, the principal issues are:

- Only about two-thirds of private savings are mobilised by the financial sector. Incentives and disincentives are needed to attract a higher percentage of the savings into the formal financial sector.
- In 2005, about 40 per cent of commercial credit[25] went to PSUs. Productivity of investments should be given greater weightage in allocation of credit.

24. Population over 64 years of age divided by population from 14-64.
25. Gross bank credit to non-financial companies, corporate bonds plus private placements and loans and government investments in PSUs. Source: CSO, RBI, Public Enterprise Survey, McKinsey Global Institute.

- A gradualist approach to "Fuller Capital Account Convertibility" is in order. The risks stemming from potential demand for investments in foreign assets (including real-estate) are not quantifiable and may be unmanageable in times of domestic-international stress.
- Domestic interest rates are not adequately market determined i.e. there is need for further deregulation of interest rates.
- The banking sector has reformed considerably since the early 1990s but is excessively dominated by the public sector which receives 78 per cent of the deposits and makes about 73 per cent of the loans.
- Efficiency in the banking sector lags behind international comparators in terms of intermediation costs;
- Just two domestic private banks have entered this sector in the last 10 years.
- A coordinated effort is needed to hasten consolidation among and international listings of public sector banks and entry of new private sector banks.
- Indian equity and related exchange traded derivatives markets and to some extent the mutual fund industry compare well with international markets.
- The over the counter (OTC) interest rate and currency swap markets cannot grow without better market determination of domestic interest rates and further capital account convertibility (FCAC).
- The corporate debt market is miniscule and needs a series of reforms including stamp duty rationalisation, repos in corporate bonds, settlement and clearing of corporate bonds through the same clearing system as government securities, introduction of credit derivatives, lifting of limits for FII purchases of corporate bonds.
- Exchange traded interest rate derivatives should be encouraged since this will improve the market determination of domestic interest rates and help the corporate bond market to grow.

- Exchange traded currency derivatives can wait for next steps towards FCAC.
- Commodity derivatives markets should be regulated by SEBI.
- The Companies Act needs to be amended and SEBI strengthened to take over the regulatory responsibilities under this Act.
- The private equity market should be assiduously courted and exit valuation methodologies made transparent and predictable.
- The asset backed securities market will not develop without considerable preparatory work particularly on the legal issues involved. Hence, special efforts need to be directed to this end.
- In cross-country terms, the Indian insurance industry is small in depth and coverage and there is tremendous potential for growth. Premiums should be deregulated, the requirement to hold at least 50 per cent of assets in government securities should be gradually relaxed as also the ceiling of 26 per cent ceiling for foreign ownership.
- The pension sector is almost entirely in the public sector and covers only about 16 per cent of the work-force. Progress is hindered by a multiplicity of Acts, administered by several GoI Ministries, which have subdivided the sector. The pay-as-you-go government administered pension systems should be gradually replaced by defined contribution schemes in which pension assets are invested in securities, both debt and equity. The pension sector needs to be comprehensively reviewed, at a GoI wide level, in the light of the potential for it to help boost the equity and bond markets and thereby the entire financial sector.
- The complex web of legislation that applies to the financial sector needs to be simplified. Further, there are obvious anomalies in certain Acts e.g. those which provide for RBI representation on the boards of public sector banks such as the State Bank of India (SBI), and National Housing Bank (NHB).

The May McKinsey 2006 study makes the point that savings should be directed more to the corporate sector since this sector utilises funds more efficiently. It is to be expected that in India, where endemic poverty persists, this argument would not be won purely on the basis of efficiency. For instance, subsidies for the economically disadvantaged are not necessarily efficient from the point of view of growth. However, it cannot be anyone's case that policies, which are meant for economic inclusion, should be abandoned.

Taking a step back from the high-pitched arguments for and against faster progress towards globalisation of India's financial sector, it is likely that there may be greater agreement about the need to raise the level of domestic competition. Even as the financial sector inches towards closer integration with international financial markets, interim solutions have to be found to enhance efficiency e.g. easing of barriers to entry for domestically owned new private banks, insurance and pension companies. It may be easier to build consensus on not obstructing domestic private firms from increasing their market share as compared to allowing entry to global firms.

References

Abaid, Abdul, Nienke Oomes, and Kenichi Ueda (2004). "The Quality Effect: Does Financial Liberalisation Improve the Allocation of Capital?", International Monetary Fund *Working Paper* WP/04/112.

Agenor, P.R. (2001). "Benefits and Costs of International Financial Integration: Theory and Facts", World Bank *Working Paper*.

Aghion, P., P. Bachhetta and A. Banerjee (2003). *Financial Development and the Instability of Open Economies.*

Ayuso, J. and R. Bianco (1999). *Has Financial Market Integration Increased During the Nineties?.* Research Department, Banco de Espana.

Ahuja, Narinder L. (2006). "Commodity Derivatives Market in India: Development, Regulation and Future Prospects", *International Research Journal of Finance and Economics*, Issue 2.

Ayyagari, Meghana, Asli Demirguc-Kunt and Vojislav Maksimovic (2006). "How Important are Financing Constraints?", World Bank Policy Research *Working Paper* 3820.

Banerjee, Abhijit V., Shawn Cole, and Esther Duflo (2004). "Banking Reform in India", Massachusetts Institute of Technology, *Working Paper*.

Beck, Thorsten, Ross Levine, and Norman Loayza (2000). "Finance and the Sources of Growth", *Journal of Financial Economics*, Vol. 58(1-2): 261-300.

Bhattacharya, Himadri (2002). "Deregulation of Gold in India: A Case Study in Deregulation of a Gold Market", *World Gold Council Research Study* No. 27. London: Centre for Public Policy Studies.

Brouwer, G. (1999). *Financial Integration in East Asia*, Cambridge: Cambridge University Press.

Chakrabarty, Bidisha and Pankaj Jain (2005). "Understanding the Microstructure of Indian Markets", *NSE Final Paper* 128.

Corsetti, G., P. Pesenti and N. Roubini (1988). *What Caused the Asian Currency and Financial Crises? Part I: A Macroeconomic Review. Working Paper* No. 6833. National Bureau of Economic Research.

Demetriades, P. and K. Luintel (1997). "The Direct Costs of Financial Repression: Evidence from India", *Review of Economics and Statistics*, Vol. 79: 311-20.

Demirguc-Kunt, Ash, Luc Laeven and Ross Levine (2003). "Regulations, Market Structure, Institutions and the Cost of Financial Intermediation", *The World Bank Working Paper*.

Demirgue-Kunt, A. and E. Detragiache (1997). *The Determinants of Banking Crises: Evidence from Developed and Developing Countries.* IMF *Working Paper* 97/106.

Dornbusch, R. and T.C. Park (1994). "Financial Integration in a Second Best World: Are We Still Sure about Our Classical Prejudices?", *Policy Issue Series* 94-1, February. Korea Institute of Finance.

Feldstein, M. (1983). "Domestic Savings and International Capital Movements in the Long-run and the Short-run", *European Economic Review*, pp.139-151.

Fleming, J.M. (1962). "Domestic Financial Policies under Fixed and Floating Exchange Rates", *IMF Staff Papers*, Vol. 9(3): 369-379.

Government of India (1991 to 2003), *Economic Survey 2003 to 2005.*

International Monetary Fund (2005). *India: Selected Issues*. March.

———. (2005). *Global Financial Stability Report*, September.

(2005). "Investigating the Relationship between the Financial and Real Economy", Bank for International Settlements Papers No. 22. Monetary and Economic Department.

Jalan, B. (1999). "International Financial Architecture: Developing Countries Perspective", *Reserve Bank of India Monthly Bulletin,* October.

Kaminsky, G. and S. Schumkler (2002). "Short and Long-run Integration: Do Capital Controls Matter", *World Bank Discussion Paper.*

Kapila, Raj and Uma Kapila (eds.) (2004). *India's Banking and Financial Sector in the New Millennium,* Academic Foundation.

Kindleberger, C.P. (1984). *A Financial History of Western Europe.* London: George Allen and Unwin.

McKinsey (2006). *Accelerating India's Growth through Financial Sector Reform.* McKinsey Report. May.

Merton, Robert and Zvi Bodie (2004). "The Design of Financial Systems: Towards a Synthesis of Function and Structure", National Bureau of Economic Research *Working Papers.*

Mohan, Rakesh (2004). "Financial Sector Reforms in India: Policies and Performance Analysis", *RBI Bulletin.*

Mukul, G. Asher and D. Vasudevan (2006). *Reforming India's Social Security System for the Twenty-first Century.* Centre for Public Policy, IIM-Bangalore.

Mundell, R.A. (1963). "Capital Mobility and Stabilisation Policy under Fixed and Flexible Exchange Rates", *Canadian Journal of Economics,* Vol. 29: 475-485.

National Stock Exchange of India Limited (2005). *Indian Securities Market: A Review,* Vol. VIII. Mumbai, India.

Obstfeld, M. (1994). "Risk-taking, Global Diversification and Growth", *American Economic Review,* Vol. 84: 1310-29.

Rajaraman, I. (2004). "Fiscal Developments and Outlook in India", *Working Paper* 15. New Delhi: National Institute of Public Finance and Policy.

Reddy, Y.V. (2004). "Monetary and Financial Sector Reforms in India", in K. Basu (ed.). *India's Emerging Economy.* Cambridge: MIT Press.

Reserve Bank of India (2005-06), *Annual Report.*

Rodrik, D. (1998). Who Needs Capital Account Convertibility?. *Mimeo.* Harvard University.

Shah, Ajay (2005). "A Sustainable and Scalable Approach in Indian Pension Reform", GoI, Ministry of Finance *Working Paper.*

Shah, Ajay and Susan Thomas (2002). "The Evolution of the Securities Markets in India in the 1990s", *ICRIER Working Paper* 91.

Shaw, E.S. (1973). *Financial Deepening in Economic Development.* New York: Oxford University Press.

Singh, Charan (2005). "Financial sector reforms in India", Stanford Center for International Development *Working Paper* 241.

Volcker, P. (1991). "Financial Crises and the Macroeconomy", in M. Feldstein (ed.), *Risk of Economic Crises.* Chicago: University of Chicago Press.

Wolf, M. (2004). *Why Globalisation Works.* London: Yale University Press.

14

India's Role in the Global Economy

PRANAB MUKHERJEE

Many of us will recall the global excitement of the mid-1990s, when the technology boom was driving the global economy. The economic decline that followed—from the East Asian financial crisis to the downturn in technology stocks—had a greatly sobering effect on the global economy. Today, that sense of excitement is back, particularly for us in India. Yet, this time around the sense of exhilaration is different. That is because there has been a maturing of the global economy—there is a sense of steadiness and stability, but yet there is also dynamism in the global economy. The global economy is indeed well poised for growth. With this as the overall backdrop, the economic growth registered by India does not really come as a surprise.

For India, these are undeniably momentous times—as our brisk march forward into the 21st century depicts. As we stepped into the 21st century, the Indian economy registered a growth rate of about six per cent. In the more recent past it has been about eight per cent. Double-digit growth rate, which every economy aspires to achieve, is no longer in the sphere of conjecture in India; it is very much in the realm of possibility. There is cause for optimism on various accounts that are indicative of our general economic well-being—the Sensex has crossed the 13,000 mark, exports have crossed the US$100 billion mark and has been accompanied by a 25 per cent surge in exports, and there are rising foreign exchange reserves. It is not only government that is showing optimism on this account, the same is true of the economic pundits, national and international, as well as international economic investors. Forecasts by Goldman Sachs and Morgan Stanley are universally known and are only two of the several that have been made, which predict and project the promise of a significant growth scenario for India.

India's role in the global economy is defined by who we are. A nation of one billion people, where the principles of democracy form its core values, where free enterprise has free reign, where the rule of law is firmly rooted and an economy that has registered a sustained growth only matched by a few other countries.

In short, India's political stability together with reform in the economic sector, in particular the financial sector, has been the driver of India's economic development. But it would be remiss of me not to mention and acknowledge the commndable role of India's corporate sector—India's domestic entrepreneur who has proven his competitiveness in the international arena.

To understand India's role in the global economy, it is essential to have a sense of the state of the global economy. While the state of the global economy at the turn of the century did raise some concerns, global growth rates have been quite steady in the past four years or so, at over four per cent per annum. While large fiscal deficits continues to be an international phenomenon that raises concerns worldwide, there are also issues that are particular to a region or to a country that needs to be monitored carefully.

While geographic borders define nation states, economic borders are becoming increasingly seamless. The global economy is today a function of increasing crossfertilisation. An idea germinating in one country is incubated in another and finds application in a third. Real-time globalisation is in effect. The global economy is increasingly defined by freer and substantive movement of ideas and capital and this movement is facilitated by the technology revolution, in particular information technology.

For a developing country like India, as is true for many other developing countries, perhaps the greatest challenge is to deal with the phenomena of globalisation. How does a developing country derive the maximum benefits of globalisation, and yet insulate the economy from the risks that are quite inherent to globalisation? It is also necessary to be cautious that in this delicate process, there is no backlash against globalisation. In short, management of the process is a quintessential requirement. While the debate on the subject will continue, it is also a reality that India is inexorably engaged in this process of globalisation.

The role of India in the global economy is of no mean significance. In the ultimate analysis, this will only be enhanced as India's middle-class grows. Much has been said on the subject of India's middle class, and the growth of its purchasing power. The certainty of the potential that the growth of this sector of India's population presents is unquestionable.

It is essential for me to be able to define our objectives so that India can achieve its full potential. What is it that the government will have to do to ensure that our dreams of achieving growth rates that will propel us to those magic numbers that are being forecast?

First and foremost, the infrastructure deficit in the country will need to be addressed. For India to maintain its momentum of economic growth, it needs better infrastructure, including highways, ports and airports, railways and most of all urban infrastructure that meet world-class standards. There is an urgent need for aggressive investment to improve the country's infrastructure through higher levels of FDI. Here, public-private partnership can come together to play a critical role in the development of India's economy. The government is fully engaged in this process. And my Ministry will be engaged in this closely to explore new avenues to harness FDI for infrastructure into India.

Secondly, India's population potential is tremendous. We are a young country, with 50 per cent of the population below the age of 25 years. To ensure that young India is not disadvantaged by globalisation, education is of critical importance. Access to education is essential. While government has taken several measures through policy and legislative frameworks, there is need for all of us to work together for ensuring and enhancing quality education for all Indians.

Thirdly, it is a combination of the population and excellent education facilities that provides the distinctive human resource of India. India's competitive advantage has been on account of the highly skilled manpower that India has been able to produce. This has indeed been a matter of great pride. We must be able to harness the full potential by investing in R&D, and providing more opportunities for innovations and technology development. Greater participation of the private sector in this area can provide adequate impetus to this area is the necessity of our times.

Fourth, energy security is of vital importance for India's burgeoning economy. New and innovative methods of addressing the energy deficit in the global economy are a crucial need of the hour. While diversification of energy sources domestically will need to be accelerated on the one hand, diversification of energy sources internationally will also need to be intensified.

Fifth, greater global economic integration. India has for many years recognised the fact that its economic growth is closely linked to the economic progress of other countries. Measures have therefore been taken to strengthen the inter-linkages with other economies, institutionally. We have been very supportive of initiatives to strengthen SAFTA, BIMSTEC, and economic links with the ASEAN. This is in the neighbourhood of India. At the same time, efforts continue to strengthen linkages with our traditional partners in other countries in Europe, in Asia and in America. New initiatives in the Latin American continent and in Africa in recent times are also aimed at greater global integration.

Sixth, India has played a very significant role in the multilateral economic processes. We have worked closely with like-minded countries in the WTO, and in other economic fora so that the multilateral framework of economic cooperation can be harnessed for the benefit of India, and for other developing countries. Reform of the international financial architecture, *viz.* the multilateral economic institutions has also been an area of priority for us. Unfortunately, the international community has not been able to come together and develop a common approach to deal with issues that affect us all. India would need to continue to work with its partners to achieve its objectives in this important endeavour.

As I participate in this discussion and share with you my thoughts of India and the global economy, I am reminded of the importance of organisations such as ICRIER, which can play such a vital role in generating debate and discussion and in the opinion making on issues which are critical for taking the economic development of India forward.

It is imperative to turn the many challenges and constraints that face us into opportunities for investment and growth. India's renowned economists, so many of whom are represented in ICRIER and in this Conference, must dwell on the manner by which this can be done most effectively and quickly.